Michael Leah

STAR WARS

ROLEPLAYING GAME

BILL SLAVICSEK AND JD WIKER

THE DARK SIDE SOURCEBOOK

LUCAS BOOKS Wizards of the Coast d20 System

DESIGN
BILL SLAVICSEK AND JD WIKER

CREATURES AND ARCHETYPES DESIGN
CORY HERNDON

EDITING
BRIAN CAMPBELL AND MICHELE CARTER

MANAGING EDITOR
KIM MOHAN

STAR WARS RPG CREATIVE DIRECTOR
THOMAS M. REID

ART DIRECTOR
SEAN GLENN

GRAPHIC DESIGN
RICH ACHBERGER

LUCAS LICENSING EDITOR
BEN HARPER

LUCAS LICENSING ART EDITOR
IAIN MORRIS

TYPESETTING
ERIN DORRIES

COVER ART
JON FOSTER

INTERIOR ART
LEE BERMEJO, DAN BRERETON, TOMMY LEE EDWARDS, DOUG ALEXANDER GREGORY, ASHLEY WOOD, LUCASFILM LTD.

BUSINESS MANAGER
PETER KIM

PROJECT MANAGER
AMBER FULLERTON

PRODUCTION MANAGER
CHAS DELONG

Special thanks to Lucy Autrey Wilson and Howard Roffman of Lucas Licensing Ltd.; Jedi Master Lisa Stevens; Keeper of the Holocron Leland Y. Chee; all the authors and artists who have contributed to the expanded *Star Wars* universe and whose material we have drawn from; and George Lucas, just because.

Based on the *Star Wars Roleplaying Game* by Andy Collins, Bill Slavicsek, and JD Wiker, utilizing mechanics developed for the new DUNGEONS & DRAGONS® game by Jonathan Tweet, Monte Cook, Skip Williams, Richard Baker, and Peter Adkison.

U. S., CANADA
ASIA, PACIFIC, & LATIN AMERICA
Wizards of the Coast, Inc.
P.O. Box 707
Renton WA 98057-0707
Questions? 1-800-324-6496

EUROPEAN HEADQUARTERS
Wizards of the Coast, Belgium
P.B. 2031
2600 Berchem
Belgium
+32-70-23-32-77

www.wizards.com

www.starwars.com

CONTENTS

Introduction

The Force binds the galaxy together. It has a light side, full of promise and hope and life. It also has a dark side. This book explores the dark side of the Force, casting light into the shadows, revealing its secrets, and providing a wealth of new options for the *Star Wars Roleplaying Game.*

From the powerful warriors of the ancient Sith Empire to the visionary Darth Bane, from Darth Maul and Darth Vader to Emperor Palpatine himself, the dark side of the Force has seduced many with its siren call. Faster and easier, the dark side quickly leaps to aid a Force-user whenever the opportunity arises. The Force-user must choose to ignore the temptation—or embrace the power the dark side provides and step firmly onto the path of corruption.

This book illuminates that shadowy path, providing a map for playing the dark side from a variety of viewpoints. It starts with an overview of the dark side and a history of the predominant darksiders, the Sith. A section of new skills, feats, and dark side prestige classes follows, expanding the options available to those dabbling with dark powers as well as those who have given themselves fully to the dark side.

The chapter on Gamemastering contains advice, campaign ideas, and suggestions for introducing the dark side into your adventures. A section on dark side equipment follows, covering such diverse items as Sith swords and orbalisk armor.

No examination of the dark side would be complete without a detailed look at those who have walked the path of corruption. The next chapter provides game statistics and other information for such darksiders as Aurra Sing, Freedon Nadd, the Nightsisters of Dathomir, the Prophets of the Dark Side, the Shadow Academy, and the Sorcerers of Tund.

Dark side creatures and archetypes fill the next section of the book, covering Massassi and Dxun tomb beasts, as well as generic darksiders of various levels for the Gamemaster to use as allies and opponents in any *Star Wars* campaign. Finally, the book explores a number of ways to set up a dark side campaign, as well as a model for running adventures in the ancient time of the Sith Empire.

How to Use This Book

The Dark Side Sourcebook makes a great addition to your *Star Wars* library. It has a wealth of information for you to use, whether you're playing in a *Star Wars* campaign or running one as a Gamemaster. How you approach the contents of this book depends on the role you have in mind.

Star Wars fans can use this book as a reference tool for all aspects of the dark side. From the discussions

on the dark side of the Force and the stages of corruption to write-ups on all of the darksiders through the ages, there's plenty to interest fans.

For players in a *Star Wars* campaign, this book provides different methods for exploring the darker side of the Force. With your GM's permission, you can attempt to conquer the dark side by embracing it, in much the same way that Luke Skywalker tried in the *Dark Empire* comic book series. Or you can examine the moral consequences of using the dark side for the greater good—a struggle every Jedi Knight faces at some point in his or her career. Is any aspect of the Force truly good or evil, or is it simply a tool to be used to a character's best advantage? After you've perused this book, your character can fully explore these issues within the game.

For good or ill, the darksider is as much a part of the *Star Wars* tradition as the good and honorable Jedi Knight. For the player who wants to try something different, this book offers guidance for playing a character who has made the choice to follow the path of the dark side. But be careful! Taking this direction can be tricky, even potentially lethal to a campaign, especially if the other heroes in the campaign consider themselves to be of good intent. Don't tread the dark path lightly—at least have some idea of where you want your hero to end up. If the player and GM work together, the story possibilities for this option can be vast and rewarding.

For Gamemasters, *The Dark Side Sourcebook* contains an amazing collection of new options. Heroes can test themselves against the temptations of the dark side with new rules and prestige classes. Force-sensitive heroes can confront the dark side within themselves, measuring their resolve and strength of will. As the Gamemaster, you can define dark side opponents that will challenge and confound your heroes. You'll find a large selection of ready-to-use allies and opponents to drop into any gaming session. And the campaign and adventure hooks scattered throughout the book will help you develop your campaign in entirely new directions.

Doing good only means something if it can be contrasted against doing evil. In *The Dark Side Sourcebook*, evil has some exciting new options, new proponents, and some new temptations with which to seduce even the most noble Jedi Knights. A new path has opened before you—whether your hero follows it is up to you. However you decide to use this book, use it sparingly. No matter how tempting it might be to throw every creature and opponent into every adventure, too much of the dark side can easily overwhelm a campaign.

May the Force be with you—whichever path you choose.

Chapter One: The Dark Side

The dark side is one aspect of a mysterious energy field some call the Force. Aggression, fear, and anger fuel the dark side and are, in turn, fueled by it. The dark side offers great power to those who can hear its seductive call, but the price is high. To understand the dark side, we must first understand the Force.

The Force

One all-encompassing driving Force influences the destiny of the galaxy. An energy field generated by all living things, the Force surrounds and penetrates everything, binding the galaxy together. Universal balance—life and death, creation and destruction—is reflected in the Force, and thus is reflected from the Force back into the galaxy at large. The Force, for all the mystery and the power it provides, is as much a part of the natural order as suns and planets and life itself.

The Force has as many mysteries as it has aspects. It may be a nonsentient energy field, the sum of all creation. It may be an eternal entity, knowing and unknowable. It may be both of these and more; it may be something else entirely. The only certain truth is that the Force exists and is omnipresent, and that's enough for most who study its various influences. From the Living Force to the Unifying Force, this mysterious energy field consists of a multitude of properties. The light side and dark side are always present, constantly struggling for balance in the galaxy and within individual beings.

Indeed, certain beings are attuned to the Force. They can feel it flowing through them and can manipulate it to a greater or lesser degree. Most of these beings don't understand the ability, and few have direct control over it. Those with an acute sensitivity to the ebb and flow of the Force can study its patterns and draw upon its energy to enhance their natural abilities. Some can even manipulate the Force to gain almost supernatural powers, such as those demonstrated by the Jedi and the Sith.

The Dark Path

The natural order encompasses balance. Day and night, life and death, light and dark—each pair represents a different kind of balance. As a part of the natural order, the Force follows the same rules. The light side embodies peace, knowledge, and serenity. The dark side encompasses fear, anger, and aggression. Both sides exist simultaneously, but not always in balance. Sometimes the light side has predominance; at other times, the dark side dominates.

When the balance tips too far in either direction, conflict usually results.

And in conflict, the dark side flourishes.

Force-users of all light side traditions are warned from the very beginning of their training, in whatever terms they can comprehend, to beware the dark side. To give in to fear, to embrace anger, to relish aggression: These are the first steps on the dark path. The dark side dominates the destiny of any who follow it. It's easy to start down that path and exceedingly hard to step off it.

Fear leads to the dark side of the Force. When a person gives in to fear, he opens himself to anger. He directs anger at himself for being afraid and then unleashes it at the world around him as a way to mask his fear. The anger leads to hatred as the dark emotions grow more powerful and destructive. Hatred, full of hostility and animosity, sets the stage for suffering—the eventual destination of the dark path.

Any Force-sensitive being risks far more than suffering when delving into the dark side. More to the point, a Force-user who draws upon the dark side risks corruption and terrible loss in return for the shortcut to power that the dark path provides. Faster and easier, the dark side is quick to give of itself, but asks a terrible price in return. No matter how well a Force-user is trained, no matter how steeped in the techniques of the light, the temptation to draw on the fast and easy power of the dark side always exists.

And that's only the beginning of the danger.

Timeline: History of the Dark Side

The history of the Republic and the Empire that followed it marks the evolution of the galaxy's understanding of the Force. This overview of important historic events serves to demonstrate how the path of the dark side has paralleled the development of galactic society.

25,000 Years before the Battle of Yavin

Approximately 25,000 years before the first Death Star was destroyed through the efforts of a young Jedi-in-training named Luke Skywalker, sentients perfected the hyperdrive engine. With this technological wonder, the galaxy became a much smaller place. Travel that once took centuries could now be accomplished in a matter of weeks, days, or even hours. The hyperspace lanes allowed multiple star systems to form the Galactic Republic, a democratic union uniting a vast number of diverse species. The

Republic continues to grow as new worlds and star systems are added to the roster.

As explorers mapped the physical reality of the galaxy and the Republic's charter solidified, philosophers and academics from all parts of this union came together to study the mysterious energy field called the Force. Through study, meditation, communion, debate, and experimentation, the first coherent theories about the Force developed. Scholars documented living and unifying aspects of the Force and opened other, less defined attributes to theory and speculation. The part of the Force dedicated to knowledge and defense came to be considered the light side of the omnipresent energy field. The aggressive, jealous, covetous aspects of the Force were labeled aspects of the dark side.

The most dedicated students (and those strongest in the Force) formed the basis of the Jedi, and it wasn't long before they began to develop the techniques necessary to draw upon the Force and manipulate its energy. Through the Force, the Jedi learned to see faraway places without the need for scanners or macrobinoculars. They uncovered methods that allowed them to move objects with only the Force and their own strength of will. They learned to influence the thoughts of others, and to let the Force add speed and power to everything they did.

Time passed, and the Jedi developed into an order. The Jedi Knights set forth a code of conduct not only for using the Force, but also for living and interacting with the galaxy as a whole. They believed that their techniques should never be used for personal gain, only for knowledge and enlightenment. Academic pursuits gave way to a more active role in the galactic community, and the Jedi became the protectors of the Republic.

Even the best intentions sometimes go astray, and no one is immune to temptation. So it was that a few Jedi began to use the Force for their own gain. These individuals ignored the restrictions regarding the dark side and accepted the easy path to power that that aspect of the Force offered. Throughout the history of the Republic and the history of the Jedi, intertwined as they are, individuals arose who reveled in the power of the dark side. Dark and fallen Jedi, while few and far apart, always posed a danger to the Jedi Order and the galaxy at large. Differing traditions with other names and beliefs regarding the Force developed. Like the Jedi Order, these traditions were just as likely to have members dedicated to personal power—or outright evil.

The Jedi Knights stood fast, however, defending peace and freedom while protecting the Republic from those who would manipulate the Force for evil intent. Thanks to their efforts, the Republic grew and thrived.

Sometime during this ancient period, the first dark side uprising took place. The battle between the forces of light and darkness lasted more than a century. Eventually the dark side practitioners were driven into exile beyond the edge of known space. Far from the influence of Republic or Jedi Order, the Sith Empire was born.

The vanquished Dark Jedi found a primitive civilization called the Sith. This species welcomed them as gods, and the darksiders dominated them. With new resources and willing slaves at their command, the exiled Jedi forged the Sith Empire, beginning a golden age of evil thousands of light years from the farthest borders of the Republic. Each side forgot the other as millennia passed. The great schism that divided the early Jedi became a legend.

5,000 Years before the Battle of Yavin

The Republic enjoyed an unprecedented period of expansion five thousand years before the rise of Emperor Palpatine. Hyperspace routes were mapped. Dedicated explorers uncovered new regions of space at a dizzying pace. New alien species were encountered for the first time. Colonies appeared everywhere as the Republic's frontier stretched out farther and farther from the Core. Small conflicts arose throughout this period, but the Republic and the Jedi Knights worked hard to maintain peace and unify the galactic government.

Meanwhile, the Sith Empire had grown powerful. Its members had developed Sith sorcery and a variety of dark Force powers, but they had reached a crisis of their own. The great Dark Lord Marka Ragnos had died, and the resulting power vacuum threatened to ignite a civil war that would tear the Empire apart. As rival leaders Naga Sadow and Ludo Kressh struggled for the Dark Lord's crown, a pair of Republic hyperspace mappers arrived in Sith territory in their ship, *Starbreaker 12*. Each of the two rivals used the news of the Republic in his own way, but Naga Sadow emerged triumphant, proclaiming himself the Dark Lord of the Sith.

Following *Starbreaker 12* back to Republic space, Naga Sadow and his Sith forces ignited the Great Hyperspace War. The surprise attack turned into a storm of conflict that spread across the Republic. The Sith were relentless and unpredictable. The early tide of the war was definitely in their favor, but victories at Primus Goluud, Kirrek, and Coruscant eventually gave the Republic the upper hand.

After a long and bloody conflict, the Republic rallied its forces and repelled the invaders. Sadow and his battered ships retreated back to Sith space—and fled right into an ambush. Ludo Kressh and his loyalists had survived the earlier struggles, and they had waited to crush Sadow's returning fleet. Both sides were devastated in a wild, no-quarter-given battle. Then the pursuing Republic forces arrived, vanquishing the Sith threat in a decimating hail of blaster fire.

Naga Sadow escaped destruction, however. He went into hiding on the jungle moon of Yavin, where his loyal Massassi built great temples in his honor. Sadow used Sith technology and sorcery to place himself in suspended animation. Someday he would usher in a new Sith golden age, just as Dark Lord Marka Ragnos had foretold.

4,400 Years before the Battle of Yavin

Six centuries later, an ambitious Jedi Knight named Freedon Nadd set off for Yavin 4 to investigate rumors of dark powers on the jungle moon. After a brief struggle with the primitive Massassi guarding the area, Nadd discovered the focusing chamber of the primary temple. After awakening the spirit of Naga Sadow, he asked the Dark Lord to teach him his sorcerous ways. Sadow showed him the dark side of the Force and taught him skills the other Jedi Knights had not seen in centuries. With these new powers and weapons, Nadd left Yavin 4 and traveled to the primitive planet of Onderon.

Using Sith magic and the dark side, Nadd made himself the leader of Onderon. He was a tyrannical ruler, and eventually his subjects rebelled. For centuries, Nadd and his descendants worked to crush this rebellion, but to no avail. Even using the powers provided by Nadd's sarcophagus—a focus of dark side energy—his descendants could not put an end to the bloody civil war.

3,998 Years before the Battle of Yavin

Four centuries after the time of Freedon Nadd, the heirs to the Empress Teta system, Satal and Aleema Keto, dabbled in Sith magic and stole an ancient book of Sith secrets from a museum on Coruscant. Unable to translate the tome, the pair made their way to Onderon, where the spirit of Freedon Nadd arose to guide them. With Nadd's training and a wealth of Sith artifacts, Satal and Aleema returned to the Empress Teta system to find a way to restore the Sith Empire.

Meanwhile, a group of Jedi Knights imposed order on Onderon and sealed Freedon Nadd's sarcophagus in an armored tomb on the moon of Dxun.

3,997 Years before the Battle of Yavin

Using Sith knowledge and artifacts, Satal and Aleema marshaled their forces and took control of

the Empress Teta system from their relatives. The seven worlds revolted against the despots, giving the pair the chance to use their new dark powers to crush the opposition. As Republic forces and a team of Jedi Knights were dispatched to Empress Teta to put an end to the outbreak of violence, a young Jedi named Exar Kun went to find the tomb of Freedon Nadd.

Kun broke into the tomb and found the skeletal corpse of Nadd wrapped in menacing black armor. Nadd's spirit appeared before the young Jedi, revealing a cache of metal scrolls hidden beneath his remains. Kun took the scrolls and traveled to Korriban, the tomb world of the ancient Sith Empire. While exploring a spectacular crypt, Kun was trapped under a collapsed ceiling. Freedon Nadd's spirit appeared once more, promising to rescue the Jedi if he surrendered to the dark side. He did, and a blast of dark power swept away the rubble and repaired his damaged body.

Meanwhile, the battle at Empress Teta continued. On Ossus, Jedi met to discuss the implications of such strong tremors in the dark side. There, Satal and Aleema unleashed Sith war droids against the Jedi, killing the great Master Arca.

Exar Kun next traveled to Yavin 4, where he used his newfound Sith powers to destroy the spirit of Freedon Nadd. He then proclaimed himself the Dark Lord of the Sith. Later, he joined with another fallen Jedi, Ulic Qel-Droma. The two Sith Lords vowed to bring about the return of Sith glory.

3,996 Years before the Battle of Yavin

Exar Kun converted numerous weak-willed Jedi to the Sith as he traveled across the Republic as a prophet and dark teacher. Ulic Qel-Droma oversaw the strategic side of their plans and began the Sith War. Exar Kun sent his converts on missions to destroy their ex-masters. While only a few succeeded, the news of assassins striking at Jedi Masters spread fear through the Republic.

The bitter war continued until Ulic Qel-Droma killed his own brother, the Jedi Cay. With this horrific act, Ulic realized that the Sith War must end. He offered to help the Jedi, and soon the tide of battle turned. Exar Kun went back to Yavin 4 and used Sith sorcery to preserve his spirit inside the ancient pyramids. Kun survived, trapped for millennia in a prison of his own devising, but the Sith War was over.

3,986 Years before the Battle of Yavin

The disgraced Ulic Qel-Droma went into exile after the Sith War. Ten years later Vima, the daughter of

Jedi Nomi Sunrider, sought him out. She wanted Ulic to train her in the ways of the Force. He reluctantly agreed, teaching her to use her powers while providing instruction about honor and duty. Due to his own trials and tribulations, and thanks to his relationship with Vima Sunrider (who looked upon him as a father), Ulic found his way back to the light side. He found redemption and died as a Jedi Master.

2,000 Years before the Battle of Yavin

The Sith species disappeared into the shadows of history, and the glory of the Sith Empire was all but forgotten. The term Sith was used to describe a sect dedicated to the dark side of the Force. The teachings of the ancient Sith Lords continued to appear from time to time to threaten the Republic. About two millennia before the Galactic Civil War, a rogue Jedi Knight turned away from the Jedi Code and the Order to found a new Sith cult. As Exar Kun before him, this Dark Jedi attracted other Knights to his banner. The followers of this new Sith Lord grew in size and power over the next millennium, biding their time.

1,000 Years before the Battle of Yavin

The new Sith eventually declared war on the Republic. The battles were fierce, and the Jedi rose to oppose the Sith, but in the end the Sith fell to their own internal struggles. Unwilling to cooperate with each other or share power, Sith disciples destroyed each other.

Sith Lord Kaan survived this bloodbath and gathered twenty thousand devotees to establish an empire dedicated to rule by the strong. Kaan's Brotherhood of Darkness met Jedi Master Hoth's Army of Light on the planet Ruusan. Both sides were decimated over a series of seven battles, but eventually the Sith were destroyed.

Or so the Jedi believed.

One Sith Lord, Darth Bane, escaped the extermination. Bane selected one apprentice to keep Sith knowledge alive, but otherwise the Sith lived an existence of stealth and secrecy. The Sith went into hiding, following Lord Darth Bane's edict—there would never again be more than two Sith Lords at a time, a master and an apprentice. As the next thousand years unfolded, the Sith codified their teachings, meditated on the dark side, and planned in isolation ways to once again strike at their hated enemies, the Jedi.

32 Years before the Battle of Yavin

The Republic was slowly dying. Internal strife, greedy politicians, a sprawling territory, and a maddening set of checks and balances made the old government weak and ineffective. Stagnation set in, laziness and complacency became the rule, and corruption gained a foothold. As the government decayed, the Sith saw a new opportunity to gain power and glory.

During the blockade of Naboo by the Trade Federation, the surviving Sith finally revealed themselves to the galaxy. Lord Darth Sidious manipulated the greedy leaders of the Trade Federation, setting in motion events that would alter the leadership of the Republic Senate and open the door for the coming Empire.

While Darth Sidious worked in secret, his apprentice, Darth Maul, emerged from the shadows to confront a pair of Jedi Knights on Naboo. The Jedi lost Qui-Gon Jinn that day, but his apprentice Obi-Wan Kenobi was able to slay Darth Maul. Two factors were set in place to affect the galaxy for years to come: Anakin Skywalker, whom Qui-Gon believed to be the Chosen One of Jedi prophesy, was discovered and given to Obi-Wan for training; and Senator Palpatine of Naboo was elected the Chancellor of the Republic.

20 Years before the Battle of Yavin

Anakin Skywalker grew to manhood and became a powerful Jedi Knight under the tutelage of Obi-Wan Kenobi. As time passed, a series of threats to the Republic further weakened that ancient and sickly institution. The Clone Wars were the culmination of these threats, eventually sweeping the Republic into a terrible conflagration. Details of this dark time have been lost, but its repercussions affected the galaxy for decades to come: The Jedi Knights were wiped out, the Empire seized power, and Anakin Skywalker embraced the dark side, becoming Darth Vader.

With Darth Vader beside him, Emperor Palpatine unveiled his New Order to the galaxy. Strength would replace frailty. Order would replace chaos. Decisiveness would replace indecision. The public craved leadership, and Palpatine provided it.

The Empire was born.

The Rebellion and the Battle of Yavin

As years passed, the Empire became increasingly tyrannical. While life was more or less the same in the Core, the worlds and systems farther out were subjugated and exploited for the greater good of the Empire. The Emperor remade the galaxy according to his own desires. Nonhuman species were persecuted and enslaved. The Empire restricted communications and travel. The Imperial military expanded and grew powerful. All the while, various leaders in the Senate attempted to work against the Emperor using laws and debate. They found their laws easily repealed, and the more vocal opponents of the New Order were silenced.

A Rebellion against the New Order began. It was unorganized at first, but eventually the leaders who opposed the Emperor stepped forward to join the Rebellion. Separate groups became one group, agitated crowds became armies, and the Alliance to Restore the Republic came into being.

The first great victory of the Alliance occurred at Yavin, where Rebels led by Princess Leia Organa destroyed the Death Star battle station. The young man who fired the shot heard round the galaxy was none other than Luke Skywalker, heir to the Jedi legacy and son of Anakin Skywalker—now known as Darth Vader.

4 Years after the Battle of Yavin

After four long, hard-fought years, the Alliance made a final stand against the Empire at Endor. While the Alliance forces battled their way out of a trap set by Emperor Palpatine, a fully trained Luke Skywalker confronted Darth Vader and his master, Emperor Palpatine, aboard the second Death Star. Palpatine tempted young Skywalker with the powers of the dark side, hoping to turn him as he had turned his father. But when Skywalker refused to be tempted, the Emperor's own anger provided the seeds of his downfall.

The Emperor ordered Darth Vader to kill his son, and the two fought fiercely. Luke was able to defeat his father, but he refused to strike the killing blow. He tossed away his lightsaber even though the Emperor wasn't ready to admit defeat. Calling upon all his dark powers, the Emperor unleashed a fury of Force lightning at the young Jedi. He would have killed young Skywalker if not for the intervention of a wounded and dying Vader. Vader grabbed the Emperor and hurled him into the depths of the second Death Star, causing Vader to suffer further damage from a backlash of Force lightning.

Darth Vader died not as a Dark Lord, but as a Jedi Knight. He saved his son, destroyed the Emperor, and found redemption due to the efforts of Luke Skywalker. Without the Emperor to lead them, the Imperial forces were eventually routed by the Alliance.

The Empire was dead.

The New Republic was born.

And the galaxy emerged from the shroud of the dark side.

Balance was once again restored, just as the ancient Jedi prophecies had foretold.

Chapter Two: Playing the Dark Side

In a *Star Wars Roleplaying Game* campaign, characters controlled by players are heroes. We use the term "hero" to refer to the protagonist of a story, not necessarily a good person. Of course, most heroes in *Star Wars* tend to be working for the good guys. A few possess dubious ethics and morals, but generally they stand together to combat evil in all its forms.

The dark side, however, is a seductive lure. It tempts characters to stand on the side of evil and tyranny. Heroes may heed the dark side's call for the power it offers, the promises it makes, or simply the freedom it brings. In the end, all who walk the path of the dark side discover that it is a harsh master, one that cannot be trusted.

This chapter details how to create and play characters who are partially or fully in the grip of the dark side. It describes characters who give in to the dark side while still following their favored vocation or profession (as explained under Dark Side Templates), as well as characters who walk entirely new paths (as described under Dark Side Prestige Classes). Also included are new skills and feats to tempt the ambitious away from the light.

Keep in mind that any character can be evil, but to truly turn to the dark side, a character must possess the Force-Sensitive feat. Any character can gain Dark Side Points, but only a character who feels the flow of the Force, hears its call, and manipulates its energy—even just a little—can fully and completely embrace the dark side.

Dark Side Templates

Succumbing to the dark side turns Force-sensitive characters into sinister reflections of their former selves. As characters gain Dark Side Points, they fall farther and farther from the light side of the Force, eventually becoming pawns of the dark side.

The following rules describe how Dark Side Points affect Force-sensitive characters. The basic rules for Dark Side Points appear in the *Star Wars Roleplaying Game*, in Chapter 9: The Force.

Tainted Characters

When a character has performed enough dark deeds, or has called upon the dark side too many times, he is in danger of becoming lost to the dark side. The rewards are tempting enough to blind him to the drawbacks, but he still has time to atone for his misdeeds.

Creating a Tainted Character

"Tainted" is a template that is automatically added to any Force-sensitive character when he accumulates a number of Dark Side Points equal to half his Wisdom score or higher—but *not* if he is a dark side character (see below). The character continues to use all statistics and special abilities from his existing class, except as noted here.

Vitality: Same as the character.
Speed: Same as the character.
Defense: Same as the character.
Damage: Same as the character.
Special Qualities: Same as the character.
Saves: Same as the character.
Abilities: Same as the character.
Skills: A tainted character receives a +2 dark side bonus on any Force skill checks to use dark side Force powers, but suffers a –4 penalty on any Force skill checks for light side Force powers (such as Heal Another).
Feats: Same as the character.
Special: A tainted character can elect to decrease his total number of Dark Side Points by sacrificing Force Points specifically to do so. Each Force Point sacrificed in this manner reduces the character's Dark Side Points by 1. This act involves a period of meditation, reflection, and absolution on the part of the character. If the player and GM want, this period of contemplation can be worked into the campaign as part of an adventure, but it isn't necessary.

In addition, any act of dramatic heroism performed by the character—if completed without calling upon the dark side—reduces the character's total number of Dark Side Points by 1. When a dark side character uses dramatic heroism in this fashion, he does not gain a Force Point.

Dark Side Characters

As characters slip farther and farther into evil, the dark side takes a stronger hold. Once heroes cross over, they are effectively lost to the dark side. Only truly epic acts of heroism and atonement can bring them back from the darkness.

Creating a Dark Side Character

Each time a tainted character gains a Dark Side Point, she must make a Wisdom check (DC 10 + the number of Dark Side Points possessed). If the character fails

NON-FORCE-SENSITIVE CHARACTERS

Players and GMs should keep track of Dark Side Points for characters without the Force-Sensitive feat for two reasons. First, if one of these characters picks up the Force-Sensitive feat later, the Dark Side Points immediately apply. Past deeds count, after all. Second, even without the Force-Sensitive feat, the number of Dark Side Points a character possesses indicates just how evil that character has become. Even the most noble, good-hearted hero can rack up a Dark Side Point or two over the course of a few adventures, but the more Dark Side Points a character accumulates, the more that character reveals himself as an evil character.

When the character has a number of Dark Side Points equal to or greater than half his Wisdom score, he can definitely be considered a bad guy. He's more than willing to look out for himself first, rob an old Ithorian in the street, or kick a Jawa just because he can. When a character accumulates a number of Dark Side Points equal to or greater than his Wisdom score, that character is definitely Evil with a capital "E." When you see a Gamemaster character with a Wisdom score of 12 and a Dark Side Point total of 14, you'll know the character has been completely enthralled by the forces of darkness. ∴

this check, the "dark side" template automatically replaces the "tainted" template.

The "dark side" template is automatically added to any Force-Sensitive character with a number of Dark Side Points equal to or greater than her Wisdom score.

The character continues to use all statistics and special abilities from her existing class, except as noted here.

Vitality: Same as the character.
Speed: Same as the character.
Defense: Same as the character.
Damage: Same as the character.
Special Qualities: Same as the character.
Saves: Same as the character.
Abilities: Same as the character.
Skills: A dark side character receives a +4 dark side bonus on any Force skill checks for dark side Force powers, but suffers a –8 penalty on any Force skill checks made for light side Force powers.
Feats: Same as the character.
Special: Any Force Points spent by a dark side character automatically call upon the dark side of the Force.

A dark side character cannot lose Dark Side Points by atoning (see the *Star Wars Roleplaying Game*, Chapter 9: The Force). She may only turn away from the dark side by performing an act of dramatic heroism without calling on the dark side for assistance. Such an act should require extreme personal cost, be made in a selfless manner, and provide a significant benefit to the galactic balance. This act of dramatic heroism does not gain the character a Force Point. (Darth Vader performed such an act at the end of *Return of the Jedi* when he sacrificed his own life to save his son and destroy the Emperor. Kyp Durron performed a similar act of heroism by destroying the Sun Crusher, a prototype Death Star.)

If the GM accepts the act as being appropriately heroic, dramatic, and selfless, the character's Dark Side Point total is automatically reduced to one less than half the character's Wisdom score, rounded down. In addition, the dark side exacts a final toll by removing all of the character's remaining Force Points. Now, with no Force Points and a dangerous number of Dark Side Points remaining, the character must strive to follow the path of the light side and atone to remove any remaining Dark Side Points.

New Dark Side Skills

Characters who follow the path of the dark side have access to skills not normally available—at least without a price. The following section describes two types of dark side skills: general skills and Force-based skills. Details on how to acquire and use skills, and how to determine difficulty classes for skill checks, can be found in the *Star Wars Roleplaying Game*, Chapter 4: Skills.

Skill Descriptions

The following general skills are only available to tainted and dark side characters. (The GM may allow other characters to acquire these general skills, depending on the circumstances of the campaign.)

Knowledge (Sith Lore) (Int)
Trained Only
Knowledge skills represent a study of some body of lore—in this case, histories and legends of the ancient Sith. Like Knowledge (Jedi lore), Knowledge (Sith lore) enables a character to answer questions about Sith traditions and the powers of the Sith. See the Knowledge skill in Chapter 4 of the *Star Wars Roleplaying Game* for more information on Knowledge skill checks.

Read/Write Language (Sith) (None)
Trained Only
The Read/Write Language skill doesn't work like a standard skill. Full rules on the Read/Write Language skill can be found in the *Star Wars Roleplaying Game*, Chapter 4: Skills. Purchasing Read/Write Language for the Sith language enables a character to understand the ancient language of the Sith and create documents using the Sith language.

To be able to speak the Sith language, you must take the Speak Language (Sith) skill.

Retry: Not applicable. (There are no Read/Write Language checks to fail.)

Speak Language (Sith) (None)

Trained Only

The Speak Language skill doesn't work like a standard skill. Full rules on the Speak Language skill can be found in the *Star Wars Roleplaying Game*, Chapter 4: Skills. Purchasing the Speak Language skill for the Sith language enables a character to understand and speak the ancient language of the Sith.

To read and write the Sith language, you must take the Read/Write Language (Sith) skill.

Retry: Not applicable. (There are no Speak Language checks to fail.)

Force-Based Skills

With your Gamemaster's permission, your character can learn these Force-based skills as part of a dark side *Star Wars* campaign.

Alchemy (Int)

Dark Side; Trained Only; Requires the Force-Sensitive and Sith Sorcery feats

You are trained in the dark side's alchemical arts. You may use ancient Sith equipment, along with arcane formulae, to alter the molecular composition of living beings, creating mutants steeped in the dark side—and bound to your will. You can also reshape inanimate matter, making it sharper or stronger, as the ancient Sith frequently did with their weapons and

DC Alteration

DC	Alteration
15	Add claws (damage 1d6 + Str modifier) or fangs, user's choice (damage 1d4 + Str modifier)
15	Add horns; subject gains a gore attack (−2 to attack, damage 2d4 + Str modifier) in addition to its normal attacks
20	Grant darkvision (20 m)
20	−2 penalty on Will saves to resist your commands
20	Add +2 m to speed (maximum speed equals twice base speed)
20	Add +3 to Defense (treat as natural armor)*
25	Increase or decrease size by one category*
25	+1 Str/−1 Dex, Int, and Cha
25	+1 Str/−1 Int, Wis, and Cha
25	+1 Dex/−1 Str, Con, and Wis
25	+1 Dex/−1 Con, Int, and Cha
25	+1 Con/−1 Dex, Int, and Wis
25	+1 Con/−1 Dex, Wis, and Cha
25	+1 Int/−1 Str or −1 Con
25	+1 Wis/−1 Str or −1 Con
25	+1 Cha/−1 Int or −1 Wis

Each additional alteration increases the DC by 5.

armor. (See Chapter Four: Dark Side Equipment for details on using Alchemy with nonliving matter.)

Check: Altering the physical appearance of a living being (to a more horrific appearance) requires no skill check. All changes wrought by applications of dark side Alchemy result in horrific physical mutations. Any task that alters a fundamental aspect of the subject requires an Alchemy check. Note that altering multiple aspects requires multiple checks. Each check requires 1 minute, costs the user 5 vitality points, and gives the user 1 Dark Side Point.

Retry: Yes, but each attempt gives you another Dark Side Point. In addition, the subject may perish as a result of the mutation (see below).

Special: Using this skill requires thousands of credits worth of alchemical equipment and raw materials (in addition to a subject). The cost for using the skill on a particular subject is 10,000 credits; each additional use of the skill on that same subject consumes an additional 500 credits worth of raw material.

The metamorphosis is extremely physically taxing—perhaps even fatal. Each alteration deals 3d6 damage to the subject. The subject must attempt a Fortitude saving throw, with the same DC as the DC for the alteration. If the Fortitude save fails, the damage is applied against the subject's wound points (as with a critical hit).

Control Mind (Cha)

Dark Side; Trained Only; Requires the Force-Sensitive, Alter, and Force Mind feats

You can guide the actions of individuals who have strong connections to you, overriding their individual impulses and replacing them with your synchronized mental processes. This allows you to increase the efficiency of allies, subjects, or minions—not enemies, opponents, or unaligned bystanders. With a higher degree of ability, you can control more individuals at a much greater range. Note that this does not allow you to manipulate these beings like puppets; you only increase their efficiency.

Check: A Control Mind check (DC 20) allows you to coordinate the actions of one or more of your allies or minions. Each of these allies or minions gains a Force bonus on attack rolls and skill checks equal to one-fourth your Force-user level (rounded down, to a minimum of +1) for as long as you continue to spend vitality points. Initiating this skill requires a full-round action, costs 5 vitality points, and gives the user a Dark Side Point. Maintaining it requires a move action each round. The Force-user must also spend vitality points for each minute (that is, every 10 rounds) the power is used.

You can affect large numbers of allies, minions, or subjects with the same Control Mind check, provided they are not beyond your maximum range. However, the more people you wish to affect, the more vitality points you need to spend.

The targets of the Control Mind skill don't have to be willing; they just have to be allied to the user in some fashion. This usually takes the form of subjects (such as those who acknowledge the Emperor as their leader) or minions (the willing lackeys of any dark side Force-user). This power is considered a dark side skill because of its intrusive nature and the energy it steals from those subjected to it.

Number of Targets	Vitality Point Cost/Minute
1–10	1
11–100	5
101–1,000	10
1,001–10,000	15

Special: The maximum range for this ability is based on your mastery of the Force. With the Force Mind feat, you can affect any allies on the same planet. If you have the Knight Mind feat as well, you can affect any allies in the same star system. If you also have the Master Mind feat, you can affect any allies within the same sector. (A system consists of a star and its related planets. A sector consists of several associated stars and their planets, such as the Elrood sector or the Anoat sector.)

Using this power creates tremendous physical and psychic stresses in your allies. When you cease spending vitality points to maintain this skill, all the affected allies are considered exhausted. (This reduces their base speed by half and confers an effective penalty of –6 to both Strength and Dexterity.)

Vitality Point Cost: 5 to initiate, then the cost varies to maintain; see above.

Drain Energy (Con)

Dark Side; Requires the Force-Sensitive and Alter feats

You can draw energy out of power packs, energy cells, and similar power sources, allowing it to harmlessly dissipate. This effectively renders electronics and powered weaponry useless until the power pack is replaced. It also shuts down items using other power sources (such as energy from generators).

Check: Your Drain Energy check sets the DC for the target's Will saving throw. (Remember that unattended items receive no save. Items grasped or worn by a character receive a save just as if the character were making the saving throw. Treat droids as unattended items for purposes of this skill.)

On a successful save, the targeted item is unaffected; on a failed save, the item's power pack,

energy cell, or other energy source is drained, and the item becomes useless until it is recharged.

Result	Will Saving Throw DC
15 or less	10
16–25	15
26+	20

The vitality point cost depends on the item being drained:

Power Source	Examples	VP Cost
Simple device	Datapad, holorecorder, droid caller	2
Power pack	Blaster, ion gun	4
Energy cell	Lightsaber, force pike, vibro weapons	8
Portable generator	E-Web repeating blaster, droid	12

Power generators larger than a portable generator, such as a standard or fusion generator (as found in power droids, vehicles, and ships) are too large to be drained by this ability.

Drain Energy is a full-round action. It can affect a single target up to 10 meters away from the Force-user. Because this ability uses dark side energies to siphon energy, using this ability grants a Dark Side Point.

Vitality Point Cost: Special; see above.

Drain Knowledge (Int)

Dark Side; Trained Only; Requires the Force-Sensitive and Sense feats
You can drain specific memories, relating to a single subject, from a victim's mind. This allows you temporary, limited access to this one field of knowledge.

Check: A Drain Knowledge check allows you to sift through a specific target's mind. For a target that is conscious and not resisting, the check is against DC 15. For targets that are unconscious or actively resisting, the check must exceed the target's Will saving throw or DC 20, whichever is higher. The Drain Knowledge check requires 5 minutes, and you must touch the target for the duration of the attempt. (Therefore, you must render an unwilling target unconscious or otherwise immobile before attempting this skill.)

If the Drain Knowledge check is successful, the target temporarily loses 2 points of Intelligence. (The target recovers lost Intelligence points at the rate of 1 per day of rest.) You may then choose one Knowledge skill the target possesses and immediately gain the ability to make untrained skill checks for that skill. (You do not acquire the target's skill points, but you can make Intelligence checks to access that information.) The target doesn't lose the Knowledge skill you have acquired; however,

temporarily lowering his Intelligence temporarily reduces all of his Knowledge skills.

Retry: Yes, but you must continue to touch the target during each attempt. Each successful check allows you to use another of the target's Knowledge skills untrained.

Special: You only have temporary access to the Knowledge skill you have drained. Each time you use the stolen skill, you must attempt a Will saving throw (DC 15). If you fail the Will save, you lose the ability to make untrained skill checks in that skill. If you fail the save by 10 or more, you also temporarily lose 2 points of Intelligence.

Note that the Force Defense skill adds a bonus to the target's Will save.

Vitality Point Cost: 8.

Illusion (Cha)

Trained Only; Requires the Force-Sensitive and Alter feats
You are able to manifest phantasmal images that seem completely real to those who perceive them. Although these illusions cannot cause physical harm, they can, when wielded by a sufficiently skilled practitioner, provoke fatal mistakes in those who do not recognize them as unreal. Each person who perceives the illusion perceives the same event (instead of his or her own slightly different interpretation).

Your Illusion check sets the DC for the target's Will saving throw.

Result	Will Saving Throw DC
5 or less	10
6–15	15
16–25	20
26–35	25
36+	30

The maximum range for this skill is 10,000 meters from the user. The distance of the illusion modifies the vitality point cost.

Distance	Vitality Point Cost/Minute
10 m	3
100 m	5
1,000 m	8
10,000 m	10

Maintaining an illusion for more than a single round requires concentration; the Force-user cannot maintain an illusion while using the rage ability, for instance. Keeping the illusion going requires an attack action each round.

Creating illusions does not in and of itself give the user a Dark Side Point. In fact, the Jedi ability Affect Mind draws from a similar tradition. However, using

FORCE ILLUSIONS

Characters encountering an illusion cannot attempt saving throws to recognize it as illusory until they study it carefully or interact with it in a significant (not casual) fashion. For example, if Luke Skywalker created an illusion of himself to accompany his sister Leia away from danger, Leia would only receive a Will saving throw if she stopped and studied her brother, or if she had a conversation with him. Likewise, if the illusory Luke attempted to restrain Leia, she would receive a saving throw because she would be interacting with the illusion directly. A stormtrooper who simply walked past the illusion would not receive a saving throw.

A successful saving throw against an illusion reveals it to be false, but does not dispel the illusion. For example, a character who makes a successful saving throw against an illusion of a massive starship knows that the starship isn't really there, but cannot actually see the smaller starships hidden inside.

A failed saving throw indicates that a character doesn't notice anything amiss. A character faced with incontrovertible proof that an illusion isn't real needs no saving throw. A character who flies through an illusory starship knows that something isn't right, as does a character who passes a lightsaber through an imaginary person without dealing damage. If any viewer successfully saves against an illusion and communicates this knowledge to other viewers, each of these viewers immediately makes a saving throw with a +4 bonus. ∴

either skill to perform an evil act—such as murdering someone—should give the user a Dark Side Point. This skill is included here because it was developed by the ancient Sith, and they generally used it to harm others.

Note that the Force Defense skill adds a bonus to the target's Will save.

Vitality Point Cost: 3 per round.

Transfer Essence (Cha)

Dark Side; Trained Only; Requires the Force-Sensitive and Sith Sorcery feats
You can transfer your life essence from your own body into the body of another—either an empty vessel (such as a clone) or, in more extreme cases, another developed, intelligent being. Your consciousness then overwrites that other individual's consciousness—leaving your mind in the other body. Your own body disintegrates, leaving behind your clothing and any items you previously held or carried.

Check: Your Transfer Essence check sets the DC for the target's Will saving throw.

Result	Will Saving Throw DC
20 or less	10
21–35	15
31+	20

The target of this skill must be within 10 meters of you. You must expend a Force Point to use this ability. Attempting to use this skill is a full-round action.

If your target makes the Will saving throw, your attempt fails, and you can never attempt to occupy that body again. Instead, you may immediately attempt to occupy a different body in the same 10-meter radius. As long as you have vitality points, you can continue to attempt to use this ability, but you cannot attempt to occupy the same body twice. Furthermore, you lose half your remaining vitality points for each attempt. If all of your attempts fail, your character's consciousness is scattered, and he ceases to exist.

If your target fails his Will save, your Intelligence, Wisdom, and Charisma scores overwrite those of your target, but the target's Strength, Dexterity, and Constitution replace yours. You retain your classes and levels, your feats, and your Dark Side Points. You retain your skills, initiative modifier, base attack bonuses, vitality points, and saving throws, but these may need to be recalculated based on your new ability scores. You lose half of your remaining Force Points and Reputation. Your wound points may change as well if your new body has a different Constitution score. Equipment does not carry over to the new body. The GM should make a note of the original body's abilities, skills, and so on—particularly the body's Will saving throw (see below).

If your attempt succeeded, the consciousness of the original body may still attempt to reassert control at a later time. Whenever you spend a Force Point, you must make another Transfer Essence check. The original consciousness may attempt another Will save against the new DC. If the save is successful, the body's original consciousness forces yours out. You may attempt another Transfer Essence check immediately to occupy a new host body (if one is available within 10 meters), with the same consequences for failure as the original check.

Regardless whether the target succeeds or fails the Will save, you lose half of your remaining vitality points on each attempt. Each attempt also gives you 2 Dark Side Points.

Special: Transferring your consciousness is a decidedly risky business, because it requires that your old body relinquish its grip on your life essence. In other words, you must die. Precisely how this occurs is unimportant, as long as you are able to declare the action and the skill attempt before you expire. (Since doing this requires an action, you cannot attempt Transfer Essence after your wound points drop to 0.)

Your original body only disintegrates when you voluntarily leave it. If you transfer your essence to another body, and the original consciousness asserts control, you are simply forced out, and the original body survives.

Note that the Force Defense skill adds a bonus to the target's Will save.

You can also transfer your life essence from your own body into a specially prepared item, such as a temple, although this is a much more difficult process. This process requires that the user have ranks in Alchemy and that life force other than the user's is expended to help power the transfer. This application of the skill requires a check against DC 30. For every hundred lives that are willingly lost to provide power for this transfer, the DC is reduced by 1, to a minimum of DC 10. Success indicates that the user's essence lives on, trapped within the prepared item until freed by another Force-user. Exar Kun used this application of Transfer Essence at the end of the Sith Wars.

Retry: Yes, but each additional attempt decreases the Will save DC by –5.

Vitality Point Cost: Special; see above.

New Dark Side Feats

Dark side feats can give characters new capabilities or improve capabilities they already have. They also exact a toll of corruption and madness. The new feats described below draw on the power of the dark side. All of the feats herein are Force-based feats. Rules for acquiring Force-based feats can be found in the *Star Wars Roleplaying Game*, Chapter 5: Feats.

Drain Force

You are able to draw life energy from living beings, gradually absorbing it yourself. Draining the Force from others in this fashion provides you with additional Force Points, but each time you attempt this, you gain a Dark Side Point.

Table 2-1: Force-Based Skills

Skill	Type*	Key Ability	Untrained	DSD	DSM	EH	FA	DFW	IN	JC	JG	SA	SL	SW
Affect Mind	Alter	Cha	No	□	3rd	□	□	□	3rd	4th	3rd	□	□	□
Alchemy†	Force**	Int	No	□	□	□	3rd	□	□	3rd	4th	□	□	□
Battlemind	Control	Con	No	5th	□	3rd	4th	3rd	□	3rd	□	3rd	□	□
Control Mind†	Alter**	Cha	No	□	3rd	□	3rd	□	3rd	4th	4th	□	□	□
Drain Energy†	Alter	Con	Yes	□	3rd	□	□	□	3rd	4th	3rd	□	□	□
Drain Knowledge†	Sense	Int	No	3rd	5th	5th	2nd	□	□	□	4th	□	□	3rd
Empathy	Force	Wis	Yes	□	□	□	□	□	□	□	□	□	□	□
Enhance Ability	Force	Con	No	□	□	□	□	□	□	□	□	□	□	□
Enhance Senses	Sense	Wis	No	3rd	5th	5th	2nd	□	□	□	4th	□	□	3rd
Farseeing	Sense	Wis	No	3rd	5th	5th	2nd	□	□	□	4th	□	□	3rd
Fear†	Sense	Wis	Yes	3rd	5th	5th	2nd	□	□	□	4th	□	□	3rd
Force Defense	Control	Con	Yes	5th	□	3rd	4th	3rd	□	3rd	□	3rd	□	□
Force Grip†	Alter	Int	Yes	□	3rd	□	□	□	3rd	4th	3rd	□	□	□
Force Push	Alter	Int	No	□	3rd	□	□	□	3rd	4th	3rd	□	□	□
Force Stealth	Control	Con	Yes	5th	□	3rd	4th	3rd	□	3rd	□	3rd	□	□
Friendship	Force	Cha	No	□	□	□	□	□	□	□	□	□	□	□
Heal Another	Alter	Wis	Yes	□	3rd	□	□	□	3rd	4th	3rd	□	□	□
Heal Self	Control	Con	Yes	5th	□	3rd	4th	3rd	□	3rd	□	3rd	□	□
Illusion	Alter	Cha	No	□	3rd	□	□	□	3rd	4th	3rd	□	□	□
Move Object	Alter	Int	Yes	□	3rd	□	□	□	3rd	4th	3rd	□	□	□
See Force	Sense	Wis	Yes	3rd	5th	5th	2nd	□	□	□	4th	□	□	3rd
Telepathy	Sense	Wis	No	3rd	5th	5th	2nd	□	□	□	4th	□	□	3rd
Transfer Essence†	Force**	Cha	No	□	□	□	3rd	□	□	3rd	4th	□	□	3rd

* *This also indicates the prerequisite feat that a character must have to use or purchase ranks in the skill (Force = Force-sensitive).*

† *Use of this skill gives the character a Dark Side Point.*

** *Additional feats are required to use this skill. See the text of the skill for other prerequisites.*

□ *Class skill.*

2nd, 3rd, 4th: *The level at which the skill becomes a class skill. Before then, it is a cross-class skill.*

All Alter-based, Control-based, and Sense-based Force skills are exclusive to the Force-user classes. Force skills based on the Force-Sensitive feat are class skills for a character of any class who has the Force-Sensitive feat.

Untrained: Yes: *The skill can be used untrained. That is, a character can have 0 ranks in this skill but can make skill checks normally. (You must still have the prerequisite feats to use the skill untrained.)* **No:** *You can't use the skill unless you have at least 1 rank in it.*

Class names are abbreviated as follows: DSD, dark side devotee; DSM, dark side marauder; EH, Emperor's Hand; FA, Force adept; DFW, Dark Force witch; IN, Imperial inquisitor; JC, Jedi consular; JG, Jedi guardian; SA, Sith acolyte; SL, Sith Lord; SW, Sith warrior.

Prerequisite: Force-Sensitive, Alter, Control, Sith Sorcery, Force level 6th+, 6+ Dark Side Points.

Benefit: Once per week, you may attempt to absorb Force energy from another character. This target must be within 10 meters when you make the attempt. In addition, the target must have at least one Force Point for the ability to work. Having this feat does not allow you to know how many Force Points the target has at the time you use the feat. (The character's player—or the GM, in the case of GM characters—is not required to let you know whether the character has any Force Points before you make the attempt.)

When you exercise this ability, the target must immediately attempt a Fortitude saving throw (DC 20). If the save succeeds, you gain nothing. If the save fails, the target loses one Force Point, and you gain one Force Point.

Using this feat doesn't cost you vitality points, but it does grant you a Dark Side Point.

Hatred

You can release all your hatred in a blast of pure Force energy, dealing damage to all those around you.

Prerequisite: Force-Sensitive, Alter, 2+ Dark Side Points.

Benefit: Waves of your hatred buffet everyone within a 10-meter radius of you. This counts as an attack action and costs 4 vitality points. All those within the radius suffer 2d6 damage and receive a –2 penalty on all attacks, skill checks, and ability checks. Each target may attempt a Fortitude save (DC 15 + the user's Charisma modifier) to reduce the damage by half. The effect lasts for 1 round. You may spend 4 additional vitality points as a move action to maintain the effect for that round. Each round you maintain your Hatred, you deal 2d6 damage. (You may not take two move actions in a round to "maintain" this ability twice.)

The effect always centers on you and moves as you move. Activating this ability grants a Dark Side Point; maintaining it does not. (You may, however, gain additional Dark Side Points for evil actions you perform while using Hatred.)

Rage

You can channel your anger into a berserker fury, increasing your battle prowess as you give yourself to the dark side.

Prerequisite: Force-Sensitive, Control, 2+ Dark Side Points.

Benefit: You temporarily gain +4 Strength, +2 vitality points per level, and a +2 rage bonus on Fortitude and Will saving throws, but you suffer a –2 penalty to Defense. While raging, you cannot use skills, feats, or special abilities that require patience

and concentration, such as Move Silently, Expertise, Illusion, or any light side Force-based powers. Your Rage lasts for a number of rounds equal to 5 + your Constitution modifier. At the end of this duration, you lose the bonus vitality points gained from the Rage, as well as 1d4 additional vitality points for every round of the Rage's duration. This vitality point loss cannot result in wound damage.

The benefits granted by this feat are not cumulative with the benefits granted by Wookiee Rage. Using this feat does not cost vitality points (other than as explained above). Activating this ability grants a Dark Side Point; maintaining it does not. (You may, however, gain additional Dark Side Points for evil actions you perform while using Rage.)

Sith Sorcery

You have the ability to channel the spirits of deceased Sith lords, using their power to supplement your own—but at the risk of becoming their puppet.

Prerequisite: Force-Sensitive, Sense, Force level 3rd+, 6+ Dark Side Points.

Benefit: You may use this feat to gain a bonus on attacks, saves, and dark side skill checks for the next minute. You gain a +1 competence bonus for every three Force levels you have attained. This feat costs you 4 vitality points to use and requires a move action to activate.

Special: Whenever you use this ability, in addition to gaining a Dark Side Point, you open yourself to possession by the Sith spirits you have summoned. At the end of the power's duration, you must immediately attempt a Will saving throw (DC 10 + the bonus gained). You cannot activate this ability again before you have resolved this save.

If the save succeeds, there are no side effects. If the save fails, however, a dark side spirit possesses you. (See Dark Side Spirit in Chapter Six.)

Sith Sword Defense

You are adept at blocking incoming attacks with an alchemically sharpened Sith sword.

Prerequisite: Force-Sensitive; Control; level 3rd+ in Sith acolyte, Sith warrior, or Sith Lord; Dex 13+; Exotic Weapon Proficiency (Sith sword).

Benefit: When wielding a Sith sword, you gain a +2 dodge bonus to your Defense against attacks. Note: A condition that makes you lose your Dexterity bonus to Defense (if any) also makes you lose dodge bonuses.

Sith Sword Expert Defense

You are adept at blocking incoming attacks with an alchemically sharpened Sith sword.

Prerequisite: Force-Sensitive; Control; level 5th+ in Sith acolyte, Sith warrior, or Sith Lord; Dex 13+;

Exotic Weapon Proficiency (Sith sword); Sith Sword Defense; base attack bonus +5.

Benefit: When wielding a Sith sword, you gain an additional +2 dodge bonus to your Defense against attacks. Note: A condition that makes you lose your Dexterity bonus to Defense (if any) also makes you lose dodge bonuses. (The benefits of this feat stack with Sith Sword Defense.)

Sith Sword Mastery

You are adept at blocking incoming attacks with an alchemically sharpened Sith sword.

Prerequisite: Force-Sensitive, Control, level 8th+ in Sith acolyte, Sith warrior, or Sith Lord; Dex 13+; Exotic Weapon Proficiency (Sith sword); Sith Sword Defense; base attack bonus +8.

Benefit: When wielding a Sith sword, you gain an additional +2 dodge bonus to your Defense against attacks. Note: A condition that makes you lose your Dexterity bonus to Defense (if any) also makes you lose dodge bonuses. (The benefits of this feat stack with Sith Sword Defense and Sith Sword Expert Defense.)

Summon Storm

You can manipulate the atmosphere to create rain, winds, and lightning.

Prerequisite: Force-Sensitive, Alter, Force level 6+.

Benefit: You may use this feat to create storm conditions in a radius around you equal to your Force-user class level × 100 meters. The user can voluntarily reduce the radius if she desires, but not to less than half of its maximum. (Thus, a 6th-level Force adept with this feat could summon a storm 1,200 meters in diameter—twice the radius of 600 meters. The same Force adept could also shrink the storm down to a 600-meter diameter, if she desired, but no smaller.)

These conditions create rain that reduces visibility, winds that hinder activities, and intermittent lightning. The rain provides nine-tenths concealment to anyone in the area (in addition to thoroughly soaking anything that isn't waterproof). The winds are strong enough to cause foliage to whip about violently and hurl loose leaves and paper about, providing a significant distraction to ordinary activities (a –2 penalty on all attacks, skill checks, and ability checks). The storm is not strong enough to move objects heavier than 1 kg. The lightning strikes are random, as with an ordinary storm; the user cannot direct them. Lightning hits a vessel very rarely, though its presence does provide an additional –2 penalty on Pilot checks for flying vessels through the storm.

Activating Summon Storm requires a full-round action and costs 5 vitality points. Maintaining the power is a free action and costs 5 additional vitality points per 10 minutes (paid at the onset of the 10-minute period). The storm can only be generated outdoors, and the GM may rule that certain effects of this feat do not apply in extreme climates. (This power could not be used to generate rain on Tatooine, for example.) If the effects of this power (blinding rain and driving winds) create dangerous conditions (such as sandstorms on Tatooine or blizzards on Hoth), the GM may also call for Survival checks.

Special: Though most commonly used by darksiders, this ability is not a dark side feat. However, those who use Summon Storm indiscriminately—and thus risk injuring the innocent—may gain a Dark Side Point for unleashing uncontrollable forces and indirectly causing harm. The GM should carefully consider whether the character using Summon Storm showed concern for its effect on the innocent.

Dark Side Prestige Classes

Prestige classes allow characters to diverge from the standard path of their classes into something special. With dark side prestige classes, the character follows a path toward darkness and evil. Characters willing to embrace the dark side may become mysticism-bound acolytes or slaughter-mad marauders. They might ally themselves with the Emperor, serving as his personal assassins or as one of his Jedi-hunting inquisitors. They might learn the secrets of the savage dark Force witches, or perhaps even fall into the foul abyss that is the Sith tradition.

A character cannot begin as a member of a prestige class. Abilities granted by prestige classes are inappropriate for beginning characters. They are acquired only by meeting the requirements specific to each example, which almost always require—in effect—that a character be at least 5th or 6th level (or, in a few cases, 3rd or 4th level). Additionally, there may be requirements that must be met in-game, such as rigorous initiation rituals or the scrutiny of one's proposed peers. With dark side prestige classes, failure to fulfill these latter requirements can mean a gruesome death.

Prestige classes are purely optional, and the decision to allow them is always the purview of the GM. In a dark side campaign, however, few characters can ever hope to achieve their maximum potential as servants of the dark side without access to at least one such class. GMs who allow characters to explore this path should be prepared for characters to adopt any of these new prestige classes.

Dark Side Devotee

The dark side devotee is what the Force adept would have been had he turned to the dark side early on.

JEDI CHARACTERS

Page 59 of the *Star Wars Roleplaying Game* states that a character with one Jedi class may not add another Force-using class when multiclassing. This is true of standard classes. Thus, a Jedi guardian can't add a level of Force adept or a level of Jedi consular. However, a Jedi character can add levels in a Force-using prestige class, provided that character meets all the requirements. Thus, a Jedi guardian can turn to the dark side and add levels of dark side marauder later in his career. ⁙

Pursuing a different path from the Jedi or even the Sith tradition, he regards the Force as something supernatural, fostering that image in the minds of others to make himself seem more mysterious and powerful. His belief system may not recognize the Force as the same tool the Jedi or the Sith use. Dark side devotees are even more rare than Force adepts, although a greater proportion of them take up careers as adventurers or wanderers.

If you select the dark side devotee class, you need to determine how your character views the Force and decide what his beliefs encompass. Dark side devotees can be aliens—though Humans are far more common while the Emperor is in power—and their specific goals and methods can reflect those of a shaman, an occultist, a sorcerer, a priest, or even a scientist grounded in physics and "rational explanations."

Dark side devotees become adventurers because of their quest for power. Often they have exhausted the mystical resources and artifacts of their own world, forcing them to look elsewhere for relics and knowledge to further their ambitions. They often forge alliances with other devotees, either to pursue a common goal or simply to exploit their abilities. But every dark side devotee knows that if he falters, if he rejects the power offered to him by the dark side, others will trample him underfoot in their own rush for power. All dark side devotees follow the dark side of the Force, even if they think of it as something else.

A dark side devotee begins his training in the Force by taking what he wants from others and dominating the world around him, as typified by the Alter feat. Many of his skills and feats—including those that are not directly related to the Force—involve manipulating others.

Dark side devotees discover their power early in life. Frequently, they do not care how the Force works, as long as it

focuses their hatred and anger against those who have wronged them. What little training they receive is generally bestowed by more powerful darksiders,

LB

ERA NOTES: DARK SIDE DEVOTEE

The dark side devotee is common in all eras. Though hardly as open as the Jedi during the Rise of the Empire, they often outnumber Force adepts. They certainly outnumber the Sith, who by this era are reduced to only two. During the Rebellion era, dark side devotees become a bit more open, drawn by the power of the Emperor and their acceptance into his court. They are much easier to find anywhere in the Empire, especially in the Imperial Palace, where their power is focused and augmented by that of the Emperor. As the Empire gives way to the New Republic, dark side devotees are once again driven into the shadows, but they still manage to flourish in the chaos brought on by years of fighting. By the time of The New Jedi Order, dark side devotees are somewhat less common—though this may be because the alien Yuuzhan Vong overshadow their evil. ☼

who may initially think of the dark side devotee as an apprentice or even a slave. There are precious few formal traditions for dark side devotees. Many come from primitive cultures where they are regarded in awe and terror for their ability to manipulate the environment, and they nurture this belief to exploit the weak. They occasionally find themselves tricked into an ever-escalating race for power or lured into pacts with more powerful dark side practitioners—in either case, risking a fate worse than death for a lapse in judgment or a show of ambition.

Vitality: 1d8 per level.

Requirements: To qualify to become a dark side devotee, a character must fulfill the following criteria:

Base Attack Bonus: +2.
Skills: Intimidate 4 ranks, Move Object 4 ranks.
Feats: Force-Sensitive.
Reputation: 1.
Dark Side Points: 3.

Class Skills

The dark side devotee's class skills (and the key ability for each skill) are: Affect Mind (Cha), Craft (Int), Drain Energy* (Con), Empathy (Wis), Enhance Ability (Con), Fear* (Wis), Force Grip* (Int), Force Push (Int), Handle Animal (Cha), Hide (Dex), Illusion (Cha), Knowledge (Int), Listen (Wis), Move Object (Int), Profession (Wis), Sense Motive (Wis), Spot (Wis), and Survival (Wis).

Use of this skill gives the dark side devotee a Dark Side Point.

Skill Points at Each Additional Level: 6 + Int modifier.

Class Features

Weapon Proficiency: The dark side devotee has the feats Weapon Group Proficiency (blaster pistols) and Weapon Group Proficiency (simple weapons).

Alter: The dark side devotee gains the bonus feat Alter at 1st level and gains access to Alter-based class skills.

Dark Side Skill Emphasis: At 1st level and every three levels thereafter (4th, 7th, and 10th), the dark side devotee gains the bonus feat Skill Emphasis. The feat is applied to one of the devotee's class skills, but it must be a dark side skill. The character may not select the same skill twice.

Dark Side Talisman: At 2nd level, a dark side devotee gains the ability to imbue a small item of personal significance with the dark side of the Force. It takes a full day to imbue the item, as well as the expenditure of one Force Point. Once imbued, the item becomes a dark side talisman, providing the dark side devotee with a +2 Force bonus on saving throws made to defend against non-dark side Force skills or Force feats. At 8th level, the same process can increase the power of the dark side talisman; it then provides a +4 Force bonus.

Table 2-2: The Dark Side Devotee

Level	Base Attack Bonus	Fort Save	Ref Save	Will Save	Special	Defense Bonus	Reputation Gain
1st	0	+1	+1	+2	Alter, Dark side Skill Emphasis	+3	+0
2nd	+1	+2	+2	+3	Dark side talisman +2	+4	+1
3rd	+2	+2	+2	+3	Sense	+4	+0
4th	+3	+2	+2	+4	Dark side Skill Emphasis	+4	+1
5th	+3	+3	+3	+4	Control	+5	+0
6th	+4	+3	+3	+5	Force weapon +1d4	+5	+1
7th	+5	+4	+4	+5	Dark side Skill Emphasis	+5	+0
8th	+6	+4	+4	+6	Dark side talisman +4	+6	+1
9th	+6	+4	+4	+6	Force weapon +2d4	+6	+0
10th	+7	+5	+5	+7	Dark side Skill Emphasis	+6	+1

Sense: The dark side devotee gains the bonus feat Sense at 3rd level and gains access to Sense-based class skills.

Control: The dark side devotee gains the bonus feat Control at 5th level and gains access to Control-based class skills.

Force Weapon: At 6th level, the dark side devotee may imbue a nonpowered melee weapon (such as a club, a knife, or a quarterstaff) with the Force. This must be a weapon that the dark side devotee wields personally. Imbuing the weapon with the Force takes a full-round action and costs 4 vitality points. The benefit the weapon gains lasts for a number of rounds equal to the character's dark side devotee level. At 6th level, the weapon's damage increases by 1d4. (So, for instance, a Force-imbued quarterstaff deals 1d6 + 1d4 damage.) At 9th level, the weapon's damage increases by an additional 1d4 (for a total of 2d4).

Dark Side Marauder

Warriors who discover in themselves an ability to wield the Force can become dark side marauders. Like Jedi guardians, dark side marauders combine physical prowess with training in the Force. Unlike Jedi, they bend it to their own violent purposes. Without the mental disciplines and strict code of conduct the Jedi Order provides, these warriors become brutal, living weapons, delighting in inflicting pain and taking lives. The dark side marauder becomes an extension of the dark side of the Force in the same way that her weapons are an extension of her body. She lives in a world where her destiny is entirely dependent on her mastery of her weapons and her strength in the Force. The dark side makes her survival far more likely.

Dark side marauders are the ultimate mercenaries. Adventure, pillage, slaughter, and violence define them. They often live for the joy of battle, the test of arms, and the tempering that only bloody conflict can provide—but they are hardly above taking pleasure in the spoils that victory provides. While the adrenaline rush of combat is a heady drug to them, the thrill of the dark side flowing through their veins is far more intoxicating. To feel that thrill again and again, the dark side marauder seeks out any activity that lets her wield the Force against an opponent. Many can be found acting as bodyguards, gladiators, mob enforcers, mercenaries, street thugs, professional soldiers, or simply adventurers.

Dark side marauders combine the best aspects of the soldier and the Jedi guardian, mixing a well-rounded complement of fighting tools with the ability to wield the Force. The weapons they choose are many and varied. Without a regular tradition, their techniques are just as diverse. As dark side marauders

gain experience, they find that the dark side of the Force offers them far more in the way of destructive potential than any conventional weapon ever could.

When violence touches the life of someone strong in the Force, it can change her forever, especially if she lacks a Jedi mentor to guide her development. If her life *is* violence—such as is the case with warriors—it is almost a foregone conclusion that she will succumb to the temptation of the dark side. A dark side marauder may have turned to the dark side to overcome the horrors of war or the brutality of crime. She may have been trained as a living weapon by a twisted taskmaster, or initiated into an exclusive company of Force-strong soldiers-of-fortune. Few have formal training in the Force, however; they learn by doing.

Vitality: 1d10 per level.

Requirements: To qualify to become a dark side marauder, a character must fulfill the following criteria:

Base Attack Bonus: +3.
Skills: Intimidate 4 ranks.
Feats: Force-Sensitive, Power Attack.
Dark Side Points: 4.

Class Skills

The dark side marauder's class skills (and the key ability for each skill) are: Battlemind (Con), Climb (Str), Craft (Int), Empathy (Wis), Enhance Ability (Con), Force Defense (Con), Heal Self (Con), Intimidate (Cha), Jump (Str), Knowledge (Int), Profession (Wis), Survival (Wis), Swim (Str), and Tumble (Dex).

Skill Points at Each Additional Level: 4 + Int modifier.

Class Features

Weapon Proficiency: The dark side marauder has the feats Weapon Group Proficiency (blaster pistols), Weapon Group Proficiency (blaster rifles),

Weapon Group Proficiency (primitive weapons), Weapon Group Proficiency (simple weapons), and Weapon Group Proficiency (vibro weapons).

Armor Proficiency: The dark side marauder has the feat Armor Proficiency (light).

Control: The dark side marauder gains the bonus feat Control at 1st level and gains access to Control-based class skills.

Rage: The dark side marauder gains the dark side feat Rage at 1st level.

Alter: The dark side marauder gains the bonus feat Alter at 3rd level and gains access to Alter-based class skills.

Sense: The dark side marauder gains the bonus feat Sense at 5th level and gains access to Sense-based class skills.

Bonus Feats: At 2nd level and every two levels thereafter (4th, 6th, 8th, and 10th), the dark side marauder gets a bonus feat. These bonus feats must be drawn from the following list: Ambidexterity,

Table 2-3: The Dark Side Marauder

Level	Base Attack Bonus	Fort Save	Ref Save	Will Save	Special	Defense Bonus	Reputation Score
1st	+1	+2	+2	+0	Control, Rage	+3	+0
2nd	+2	+3	+3	+0	Bonus feat	+3	+1
3rd	+3	+3	+3	+1	Alter	+4	+1
4th	+4	+4	+4	+1	Bonus feat	+4	+2
5th	+5	+4	+4	+1	Sense	+4	+2
6th	+6/+1	+5	+5	+2	Bonus feat	+5	+3
7th	+7/+2	+5	+5	+2		+5	+3
8th	+8/+3	+6	+6	+2	Bonus feat	+6	+4
9th	+9/+4	+6	+6	+3		+6	+4
10th	+10/+5	+7	+7	+3	Bonus feat	+6	+5

Armor Proficiency (medium), Armor Proficiency (heavy), Blind-Fight, Dodge (Mobility, Spring Attack, Whirlwind Attack), Exotic Weapon Proficiency, Hatred, Heroic Surge, Improved Initiative, Martial Arts, Point Blank Shot (Far Shot, Precise Shot, Rapid Shot, Shot on the Run), Power Attack (Cleave, Great Cleave), Quick Draw, Two-Weapon Fighting (Improved Two-Weapon Fighting), Weapon Finesse*, or Weapon Focus*.

Feats dependent on other feats are listed parenthetically after the prerequisite feat. Characters must still meet all prerequisites for each feat, including minimum ability scores and base attack bonuses. See the *Star Wars Roleplaying Game*, Chapter 5: Feats, for descriptions of feats not covered in this book.

Important: These feats are in addition to the feats that a character of any class gets for gaining levels (see the *Star Wars Roleplaying Game*, Table 3–1: Experience and Level-Dependent Benefits). The dark side marauder is not limited to the list given here when choosing those level-based feats.

Emperor's Hand

The Emperor's Hand is an assassin recruited, trained, and employed by Emperor Palpatine himself. To rule the galaxy effectively, Emperor Palpatine sometimes needs certain persons removed from it. These might be ambitious planetary governors, greedy crime lords, highly placed Rebel sympathizers, or disloyal Imperial officers. But too often for the Emperor's taste, these individuals (rather wisely) refuse to come to him, instead making themselves inaccessible. They frequently occupy heavily fortified structures, employ numerous guards, and fill every chamber, corridor, and entrance with security devices. They are determined to survive the Emperor's will. The Emperor is then forced to charge one of his Hands with reaching out and crushing these defiant fools.

The Emperor's Hands operate out of devotion to the Emperor. Though they rightly fear his wrath, they also feel gratitude or even affection for him, for he rewards their service lavishly. They enjoy a freedom shared by precious few in the Empire. The fact that they are murdering people to please the Emperor hardly enters into their thinking; after all, these people are often tyrants and killers themselves. Because their targets are usually a threat to the general public—even if that means the *Imperial* public—the Hands, in a way, protect the public, and thus are doing good. (Of course, the Emperor is not above embellishing the misdeeds of a target to foment a sense of duty in his minions.)

Each Emperor's Hand operates alone, often with the false idea that he or she is the Emperor's only assassin. The Hands are given a great deal of support and authority, with special clearances designed to

allow them access to whatever resources they need. They rarely identify themselves as Hands, however. The Emperor prefers that they exist as rumors—mythic figures whose powers grow with each whispered story. The words "the Emperor has set his personal assassin on your trail" are often far more effective in controlling the unruly than actually dispatching one of the Hands.

Because he or she operates alone, each Hand has a distinctly different method of achieving the Emperor's goals. Some prefer a surgical strike, leaving a corpse in the midst of a crowd; others would just as soon destroy a fortress full of innocents to reach their target. Some refuse to use lethal force except against their actual target. As long as they achieve their goals and leave no witnesses who can properly identify them, the Emperor allows them to work in their own ways. The violence and killing eventually turns every Hand to the dark side. For the Emperor, this is simply an added bonus.

Vitality: 1d8 per level.

Requirements: To qualify to become an Emperor's Hand, a character must fulfill the following criteria:

Base Attack Bonus: +4.

Skills: Bluff 4 ranks, Disable Device 4 ranks, Gather Information 4 ranks, Hide 4 ranks, Move Silently 4 ranks, Sleight of Hand 4 ranks, Survival 4 ranks.

Feats: Alertness, Point Blank Shot, Force-Sensitive.

Reputation: 4 or less.

Dark Side Points: 2.

Species: The character must be Human.

Special: Only the Emperor chooses who can serve as one of his mysterious Hands. To attain this prestigious position, a character must impress the Emperor with his ingenuity, resourcefulness, skill, and loyalty. Typically, the character demonstrates his abilities in some unexpected way, without threatening the Emperor or revealing himself prematurely. This latter requirement is the deciding factor, though; should a character incur the Emperor's wrath in proving his

ingenuity, the Emperor may summon him for an informal chat to discuss the character's skills. The character does not know until he attends the meeting whether he is being genuinely summoned—or merely trapped.

Class Skills
The Emperor's Hand's class skills (and the key ability for each skill) are: Affect Mind (Cha), Bluff (Cha), Computer Use (Int), Craft (Int), Demolitions (Int), Disable Device (Int), Disguise (Cha), Enhance Ability (Con), Escape Artist (Dex), Force Stealth (Con), Gather Information (Cha), Hide (Dex), Intimidate (Cha), Knowledge (Int), Listen (Wis), Move Object (Int), Move Silently (Dex), Pilot (Dex), Profession (Wis), Search (Int), Sleight of Hand (Dex), Spot (Wis), Survival (Wis), and Tumble (Dex).

Skill Points at Each Additional Level: 8 + Int modifier.

Class Features
Weapon Proficiency: An Emperor's Hand has the feats Weapon Group Proficiency (simple weapons), Weapon Group Proficiency (blaster pistols), Weapon Group Proficiency (blaster rifles), and Weapon Group Proficiency (vibro weapons).

Alter: An Emperor's Hand gains the bonus feat Alter at 1st level and gains access to Alter-based class skills.

Resource Access: Beginning at 1st level, an Emperor's Hand has access to nearly the full array of Imperial resources. Once per game session, the Emperor's Hand may make a Charisma check to use those resources during the game session.

The value of the resources gained equals the Hand's class level × the result of the Charisma check × 20. Thus, a 4th-level Emperor's Hand who got a check result of 17 would gain (4 × 17 × 20) 1,360 credits' worth of resources. These resources can take virtually any form the Emperor's Hand chooses

Table 2-4: The Emperor's Hand

Level	Base Attack Bonus	Fort Save	Ref Save	Will Save	Special	Defense Bonus	Reputation Score
1st	+0	+0	+2	+0	Alter, resource access	+1	+1
2nd	+1	+0	+3	+0	Authority, target bonus +1	+2	+1
3rd	+2	+1	+3	+1	Control, sneak attack +1d6	+2	+0
4th	+3	+1	+4	+1	Target bonus +2	+2	+1
5th	+3	+1	+4	+1	Sense	+3	+1
6th	+4	+2	+5	+2	Target bonus +3	+3	+0
7th	+5	+2	+5	+2	Sneak attack +2d6	+4	+1
8th	+6	+2	+6	+2	Target bonus +4	+4	+1
9th	+6	+3	+6	+3	Deadly strike	+4	+0
10th	+7	+3	+7	+3	Target bonus +5	+5	+1

026

The Emperor's Hands exist as such only during the Rebellion era. They do not come into being until the Emperor begins consolidating his control of the galaxy. Previously, he may have used agents as assassins, and even called them his "hands," but they were usually trained by someone else to fulfill a different function. Even Darth Maul was not specifically trained to fulfill the function of assassin—his purpose was to kill Jedi. Darth Maul was so good at eliminating other impediments to Darth Sidious's plans that the Emperor realized his need for assassins that were less like apprentices and more like operatives.

After the death of the Emperor, the Hands survived in other capacities. The most famous of them, Mara Jade, drifted through the galaxy, hooking up with the smuggler Talon Karrde, working with Lando Calrissian, and eventually marrying Luke Skywalker—who was once her primary target. Other Hands found new lives, though often doing the same general kind of work. The major difference during the birth of the New Republic and The New Jedi Order is that no one is actively training new Hands—though it is not out of the realm of possibility that someone sufficiently powerful might revive the practice. ⁘

(within reason) and are his to do with as he pleases. He may keep them, use them, give them away, or sell them as he sees fit.

Authority: Once he has established his skill and loyalty to the Emperor, the Emperor's Hand is granted special privileges within the Imperial bureaucracy to facilitate completing his missions. This allows the Emperor's Hand to add his Intimidate skill rank to Diplomacy checks when dealing with Imperial officers or personnel.

Target Bonus: Beginning at 2nd level, the Emperor's Hand gets a +1 attack bonus against a chosen victim, usually a target chosen by the Emperor himself. The hero gets the same bonus on Bluff, Listen, Search, Sense Motive, and Spot checks when using these skills against or when tracking this specific target. The bonus goes up by 1 at every even-numbered level (4th, 6th, 8th, and 10th).

The target bonus normally applies only to a single individual. The player of the hero must announce the target before the game session begins. (Generally, this target should be someone the Emperor's Hand has taken a contract to track down.) Alternatively, the Hand may select a small group as his target (a number of individuals up to his level in size), or a large group or species (such as the Rebellion, or Wookiees). In such cases, the bonus is one-half or one-third normal, respectively (round fractions down). Whatever the choice, it must be approved by the Gamemaster.

Control: An Emperor's Hand gains the bonus feat Control at 3rd level and gains access to Control-based class skills.

Sneak Attack: The character can sneak attack like a 5th-level scoundrel (see page 46 of the *Star Wars Roleplaying Game*).

Sense: An Emperor's Hand gains the bonus feat Sense at 5th level and gains access to Sense-based class skills.

Deadly Strike: At 9th level, the Emperor's Hand gains the ability to execute a deadly strike with any weapon he wields. Making a deadly strike requires a full-round action. (The Hand can take a 2-meter step, but cannot attempt any other action or movement.) The Emperor's Hand uses his normal base attack bonus (including all relevant modifiers), with an additional +4 competence bonus on the attack. The threat range for a critical hit is doubled, and the attack also deals maximum possible damage (regardless of whether it is a normal or a critical hit).

Dark Force Witch

On all-but-forgotten primitive worlds, where the strong survive by preying upon the weak, those gifted with the Force are the strongest of all. Isolated from the formalized training of the Jedi and the Sith, Force-users on these worlds have developed traditions all their own—traditions that depend upon the dark side. Of all the primitive cultures of dark side Force-users, the Nightsisters of Dathomir are among the most infamous. Priding themselves on their cruelty and barbarism, these dark Force witches and others like them can become remarkably powerful. Fortunately for the rest of the galaxy, their low level of technology prevents most of them from escaping their homeworlds and spreading their evil elsewhere.

To become a dark Force witch, a character must immerse herself not only in the dark side of the Force, but in the traditions and rituals of her primitive culture. If the character can survive those savage customs long enough, she might glean the knowledge necessary to join the ranks of the dark Force witches. The GM should devise some suitably barbaric ritual that the prospective witch must pass, bearing in mind that the consequence of failure should be severe, and the consequence of success should at the very least include gaining one more Dark Side Point. Under no circumstances should the GM allow a character to "join" the sect if she has never actually encountered a witch.

The path of the dark Force witch is fraught with brutality. She is encouraged to dominate her environment, imposing her will on everything weaker while constantly testing the power and resolve of everything stronger. A witch advances in prestige by exerting her influence and defending her territory (literally or figuratively). She earns the respect of her sisters by being at least as powerful as they are. She earns their fear by being twice as ruthless. On Dathomir, regular challenges to personal combat are a way of continually testing each other's might and the will to use it. The number of male slaves owned by a Dathomiri Nightsister is merely an outward display of her ability to keep what she has taken.

Dark Force witches who are born into the culture begin their training in some other class (generally as Force adepts, though fringers and scouts are not uncommon), but they are encouraged to develop their Force powers as soon as they can. Violence and cruelty distinguish their early training. By teaching a Force-strong novice fear and hate, they prepare her for the embrace of the dark side. Those who fail to learn an equivalent ruthlessness can at best hope to be cast out. More commonly, they don't survive. Dark Force witches treat all prospective recruits the same way, regardless of their age or experience. To them, only the strong should survive; the weak are meant to serve. By becoming full-fledged witches, they prove themselves strong.

Vitality: 1d8 per level.

Requirements: To qualify to become a dark Force witch, a character must fulfill the following criteria:

Base Attack Bonus: +1.

Skills: Intimidate 2 ranks, Knowledge (culture–local*) 4 ranks, Move Object 4 ranks.

Dark Side Skills: Fear 4 ranks.

Feats: Force-Sensitive, Alter, Sense.

Reputation: 1.

Dark Side Points: 4.

*This skill must be gained by surviving in a culture dominated by dark Force witches.

Special: Dark Force witches embody a culture as well as a career. Those wishing to become witches must pass traditional initiations, and the price of failure is often death. Commonly, the elders demand a sacrifice of some kind (the slaying of a loved one, for example) to prove one's devotion, or a ritual combat with another witch (to the death) to prove one's worth.

Class Skills

The dark Force witch's class skills (and the key ability for each skill) are: Affect Mind (Cha), Climb (Str), Craft (Int), Drain Knowledge* (Int), Empathy (Wis), Enhance Senses (Wis), Fear* (Wis), Force Grip* (Int), Handle Animal (Cha), Hide (Dex), Intimidate (Cha), Knowledge (Int), Listen (Wis), Move Object (Int), Move Silently (Dex), Profession (Wis), Ride (Dex), Spot (Wis), and Survival (Wis).

*Use of this skill gives the dark Force witch a Dark Side Point.

Skill Points at Each Additional Level: 6 + Int modifier.

Class Features

Weapon Proficiency: The dark Force witch has the feats Weapon Group Proficiency (simple weapons) and Weapon Group Proficiency (primitive weapons).

Inspire Fear: The witch quickly develops the ability to inspire obedience through fear. Her underlings have difficulty taking direct actions against her, resulting in a penalty on attacks and skill checks (including Force-based skill checks) directed against her. At 1st level, the penalty is –1. It increases to –2 at 5th level and –3 at 9th level. For purposes of this ability, "underlings" are those who answer to the witch's authority.

Spider Walk: At 2nd level, the witch gains the ability to adhere to solid surfaces using the Force, allowing her to climb and travel on walls or even traverse ceilings. Her hands and feet must be bare to use this ability. She may climb at half her normal speed. Using this ability costs no vitality points. Someone who wishes to pull the witch off the surface to which she is clinging can attempt a Strength check opposed by her Intelligence check (for those attempting to physically displace her) or an opposed Move Object check (for those using the Force). Additional weight carried by the witch slows her down (see Table 6–10: Carrying Capacity and Table 6–11: Carrying Loads in the *Star Wars Roleplaying Game*), but cannot detach her from the surface.

Control: The witch gains the bonus feat Control at 3rd level and gains access to Control-based class skills.

Summon Storm: At 4th level, the witch gains the bonus feat Summon Storm (described earlier in this chapter).

Enshroud: At 6th level, the witch can summon darkness about herself. The darkness obscures all sight, including darkvision, beyond 5 meters. A character 5 meters away has one-half concealment

ERA NOTES: DARK FORCE WITCH

Throughout the history of the galaxy, there have been primitive worlds and primitive Force-users to rule them. Lacking contact with the Republic and its somewhat more enlightened attitude toward the Force, many of these Force-users find their strength in the dark side. In the Old Republic, countless worlds boast enclaves of dark Force witches. Some are detected and dealt with by the Jedi Order. Others are blissfully unaware that they are not alone in mastery of the Force.

During the Rise of the Empire and Rebellion eras, the Emperor makes a token effort to locate such groups. His searches so frequently end in bloodshed that he is forced to destroy or interdict entire worlds of dark Force witches. The risk of them getting loose and roaming the galaxy is sufficient motivation for Palpatine to continue his search for such powerful darksiders. Still, with unsanctioned scout ships discovering new worlds all the time, especially in the Unknown Regions, dark Force witches frequently manage to escape their backwater worlds and roam the galaxy–though they must work hard to avoid the notice of more powerful Force-users.

During the New Jedi Order era, as the Yuuzhan Vong arrive and the galaxy is thrown into turmoil, more dark Force witches find their way offworld, blending in with endless waves of refugees. Few have yet exerted their power over the rest of the galaxy, but it is only a matter of time.

(attacks have a 20% miss chance). Characters farther away have total concealment (50% miss chance, and the attacker cannot use sight to locate the target). See the *Star Wars Roleplaying Game*, Chapter 8: Combat, for rules on concealment.

Creating this darkness costs 5 vitality points; maintaining it costs 1 vitality point per round. The field of darkness moves with the witch and endures until she ceases to spend vitality points to maintain it.

Force Flight: At 7th level, the witch learns to float or fly by manipulating the Force. She can make a Move Object check (DC 20) to travel at 10

Table 2-5: The Dark Force Witch

Level	Base Attack Bonus	Fort Save	Ref Save	Will Save	Special	Defense Bonus	Reputation Score
1st	+0	+1	+1	+2	Inspire fear –1	+2	+0
2nd	+1	+2	+2	+3	Spider walk	+3	+1
3rd	+2	+2	+2	+3	Control	+3	+0
4th	+3	+3	+2	+4	Summon Storm	+3	+1
5th	+3	+3	+3	+4	Inspire fear –2	+4	+0
6th	+4	+4	+3	+5	Enshroud	+4	+1
7th	+5	+4	+4	+5	Force flight (10 m)	+5	+0
8th	+6	+5	+4	+6		+5	+1
9th	+6	+5	+4	+6	Inspire fear –3	+5	+0
10th	+7	+6	+5	+7	Force flight (20 m)	+6	+1

meters per round, soaring as high above the ground as she wishes. At 10th level, she can increase her speed, traveling at 20 meters per round with a successful Move Object check (DC 20). Using this ability requires that the witch spend vitality points as per the Move Object skill. The witch can carry additional weight if she is willing or able to spend additional vitality points. For each order of magnitude of additional weight (50 kg, 500 kg, and so on), the vitality costs doubles. The DC for the skill check also increases by 5 for each additional order of magnitude of weight.

Imperial Inquisitor

The Imperial inquisitor is a Force-trained hunter charged with seeking out other Force-users and either turning them to the service of the Emperor or eliminating them. Given tools and resources, they range the boundaries of the Empire and beyond, searching for rumors of hidden enclaves of Jedi who might have escaped the great purge of their Order—and clues where to find them. Employing draconian tactics and ruthless violence, an Imperial inquisitor gradually homes in on his quarry, then brings the might of the Empire to bear until his target is broken or dead. An Imperial inquisitor has little time for subtlety. He is a hammer designed to pound the galaxy into a shape the Emperor finds pleasing.

The Emperor created the office of Imperial inquisitor after the purge that destroyed most of the Jedi. He then enlisted inquisitors to help seek out and destroy the last vestiges of the Jedi Order. Armed with the weapons of their fallen enemies, the inquisitors began tracking down every rumor of every Jedi that had somehow escaped the Emperor's notice. As the targets became fewer and fewer, inquisitors drifted into other roles in the Empire, or disappeared altogether. Some fall in battle, while others earn the displeasure of their master and pay the price.

Inquisitors who survive their service to the Emperor receive greater honors, greater resources, and greater assignments to test them even further. Their master places ships, troops, weapons, and money at their disposal, along with sophisticated instruments of torture no living being should ever have to see, let alone suffer.

An Imperial inquisitor's greatest fear is that he will one day incur the Emperor's displeasure and find himself hunted by his erstwhile colleagues. Each inquisitor is intimately acquainted with this possibility from the moment he chooses to seek the position. To prove one's skill, one must convince the Emperor himself of one's ability with the Force, without seeming either too powerful or too critical

of the Emperor's cause. Otherwise the applicant is no different from the quarry he seeks—and thus may prove unreliable.

The potential inquisitor must be carefully tested and examined, first by Imperial Intelligence, then by the Grand Inquisitor, and finally by the Emperor himself. If the inquisitor does not pass, he is executed as a traitor. And this scrutiny does not end with the application process. Each Imperial inquisitor is constantly observed by the watchful eye of the Grand Inquisitor, and frequently tested by Lord Vader as well. An unfortunate few are sometimes called to make reports to the Emperor himself—with potentially fatal repercussions.

Vitality: 1d10 per level.

Requirements: To qualify to become an Imperial inquisitor, a character must fulfill the following criteria:

Base Attack Bonus: +4.

Skills: Intimidate 4 ranks, Knowledge (Jedi lore) 4 ranks, See Force 4 ranks, Telepathy 4 ranks.

Dark Side Skills (any): 8 ranks total.

Feats: Force-Sensitive, Sense, Track.

Reputation: 3.

Dark Side Points: Equal to or greater than half the character's Wisdom score.

Species: The character must be Human.

Special: A character wishing to become an Imperial inquisitor must first demonstrate his loyalty and devotion to Imperial Intelligence. When Imperial Intelligence is satisfied that the character is a loyal citizen of the Empire, the candidate passes to the judgment of the Grand Inquisitor. He must prove his detection abilities by ferreting out secrets and arriving quickly at the correct solution to a test devised by the Grand Inquisitor. If he is again successful, the character is granted an audience with the Emperor, who tests the character's skill in the Force—and his moral character. Those

who fail to pass this scrutiny, at any step of the way, are destroyed.

Class Skills

The Imperial inquisitor's class skills (and the key ability for each skill) are: Bluff (Cha), Computer Use (Int), Craft (Int), Drain Knowledge* (Int), Enhance Senses (Wis), Fear* (Wis), Gather Information (Cha), Intimidate (Cha), Knowledge (Int), Profession (Wis), See Force (Wis), Sense Motive (Wis), Survival (Wis), Telepathy (Wis), and Tumble (Dex).

*Use of this skill gives the Imperial inquisitor a Dark Side Point.

Skill Points at Each Additional Level: 4 + Int modifier.

Class Features

Weapon Proficiency: The Imperial inquisitor has the feats Weapon Group Proficiency (simple weapons), Weapon Group Proficiency (blaster pistols), and Exotic Weapon Group Proficiency (lightsaber).

Control: The Imperial inquisitor gains the bonus feat Control at 1st level and gains access to Control-based class skills.

Lightsaber: As an agent of the Emperor, the Imperial inquisitor is given the weapon most suited to her job: a lightsaber. The lightsaber is almost invariably from the Emperor's private collection—and certainly belonged to a Jedi at some point in the past.

Resource Access: Beginning at 2nd level, an Imperial inquisitor has access to nearly the full array of Imperial resources. Once per game session, the Imperial inquisitor may make a Charisma check to use those resources during the game session.

The value of the resources gained equals the Imperial inquisitor's class level × the result of the Charisma check × 50. Thus, a 4th-level inquisitor who got a check result of 17 would gain (4 × 17 × 50) 3,400 credits' worth of resources. These

Table 2-6: The Imperial Inquisitor

Level	Base Attack Bonus	Fort Save	Ref Save	Will Save	Special	Lightsaber Damage*	Defense Bonus	Reputation Score
1	+0	+2	+1	+2	Control, lightsaber	–	+3	+1
2	+1	+3	+2	+3	Resource access	–	+4	+1
3	+2	+3	+2	+3	Alter	–	+4	+1
4	+3	+4	+2	+4	Authority	+1d8	+5	+0
5	+4	+4	+3	+4	Favored enemy	+1d8	+5	+1
6	+5	+5	+3	+5	High Inquisitor	+1d8	+6	+1
7	+6	+5	+4	+5		+1d8	+6	+1
8	+7	+6	+4	+6	Favored enemy	+2d8	+7	+0
9	+8	+6	+4	+6		+2d8	+7	+1
10	+9	+7	+5	+7	Grand Inquisitor	+2d8	+8	+1

* The additional damage dealt by the Imperial inquisitor's lightsaber.

Like the Emperor's Hands, the post of Imperial inquisitor does not come officially into being until Palpatine's rise to power. Specifically, the Emperor creates his cadre of Imperial inquisitors to eradicate the Jedi from the galaxy, ensuring that the only users of the Force are those loyal to him. Thus, Imperial inquisitors only exist in the latter part of the Rise of the Empire era and throughout the Rebellion era. Afterward, they gradually disappear from the face of the galaxy, bereft of the support and resources provided by the once-mighty Galactic Empire. By the arrival of the Yuuzhan Vong, the Imperial inquisitors are just an unpleasant memory.

The role of Imperial inquisitor is one of the hardest positions to achieve. A character must walk a thin line between proving one's ability as a Force-user and proving one's loyalty, for the position requires precisely the kind of power the Emperor wishes to erase—though, of course, not the same mentality. Even the darkest of darksiders must beware the Emperor's whim, for if she seems too powerful or ambitious, she could easily find herself the target of an inquisition. ⁘

resources can take virtually any form the Imperial inquisitor chooses (within reason) and are hers to do with as he pleases. She may keep them, use them, give them away, or sell them as she sees fit.

Alter: The Imperial inquisitor gains the bonus feat Alter at 3rd level and gains access to Alter-based class skills.

Authority: In pursuit of her duties to the Emperor, an Imperial inquisitor is granted special privileges within the Imperial bureaucracy to facilitate her missions. This allows the inquisitor to add her Intimidate skill rank to Diplomacy checks when dealing with Imperial officers or personnel.

Favored Enemy: The purpose of the Imperial inquisitor is to hunt those strong in the Force—especially Jedi. Extensive study of the Force, and those who wield it, grants the Imperial inquisitor a +2 attack bonus against Force-using victims. The Imperial inquisitor gets the same bonus on Bluff, Intimidate, See Force, Sense Motive, Survival, and Telepathy checks when using these skills against or when tracking this specific kind of target.

At 5th level, the Imperial inquisitor must choose either Force adept, Jedi consular, or Jedi guardian as her favored enemy. At 8th level, the Imperial inquisitor's bonus against this favored enemy increases to +4. She can then choose a second favored enemy, against which she has a +2 bonus.

High Inquisitor: At 6th level, the Imperial inquisitor is promoted to the rank of High Inquisitor and gets a bonus feat. This bonus feat must be drawn

from the following list: Burst of Speed, Deflect Blasters, Dissipate Energy, Force Lightning, Lightsaber Defense, Throw Lightsaber, or Weapon Focus (lightsaber). The Imperial inquisitor must meet the prerequisite for the feat to select it.

Grand Inquisitor: At 10th level, the Imperial inquisitor is promoted to the rank of Grand Inquisitor and gets a bonus feat. This bonus feat must be drawn from the following list: Deflect Blasters, Dissipate Energy, Force Lightning, Knight Defense, Knight Speed, Throw Lightsaber, or Weapon Focus (lightsaber). The Imperial inquisitor must meet the prerequisite for the feat to select it. The only exception to this rule is that the Imperial inquisitor may substitute her Imperial inquisitor levels for Jedi levels for purposes of qualifying for Knight Defense and Knight Speed.

Sith Acolyte

The Sith acolyte is a Force-using adherent of the Sith tradition. Descended from a rogue Jedi faction, the Sith tradition dominated a corner of the galaxy for millennia before being discovered—and ultimately decimated—by Old Republic forces and the Jedi Knights. Their survivors eventually succumbed to internal conflict, leaving only one Sith: Darth Bane, who established the rules by which the Sith tradition managed to survive another thousand years. Although Sith acolytes came and went in fits and spurts during this time, they were far more common when the Sith were strong, before Bane.

Jedi who turn away from the light side to become Sith are especially prized by the dark side. A Jedi who takes on any of the Sith prestige classes gains one level in the new class for each level of Jedi consular or Jedi guardian he trades in. For example, a character who has 12 levels of Jedi guardian can immediately become a 10th-level Sith warrior with all the Sith warrior's class abilities if he chooses to lose 10 levels of Jedi guardian. The character's character level does not change.

There are two restrictions to this rule (in addition to the normal "rule of two," if the campaign is set after the time of Darth Bane). First, the character may not "mix and match" Sith prestige class levels; that is, he cannot exchange 6 levels of a Jedi class for 3 levels of Sith acolyte, 2 levels of Sith warrior, and 1 level of Sith Lord. He may only choose levels in the class he has just entered.

Second, a character can only trade in a maximum of 9 levels for the Sith Lord class; the character cannot become a Sith Master immediately upon taking on the Sith Lord class. ⁘

Every Sith acolyte delves deep into the mysteries of the Sith, learning how to wield the Force in ways that draw upon the dark side. They are dark sorcerers and fell priests, practitioners of living sacrifices and base deception. They come to the Sith tradition from the ranks of the Force adepts, the dark side devotees, and in ancient times, from the Sith species itself. During the past thousand years, others sensitive to the Force discovered the Sith tradition and were seduced by it, resulting in warriors, merchants, smugglers, explorers, ambassadors, rogues, and even famous political figures becoming Sith acolytes. But Darth Bane's "rule of two" ensured that their existence—or at least, their true loyalties—remained a secret. Those who become Sith acolytes accept that there can never be more than two of them, and that for another to begin following the tradition, one of the existing acolytes must die.

People who become Sith acolytes often do so simply out of naked ambition. The Sith path teaches the power of the dark side of the Force, and such a weapon is often irresistible to those without power of their own. Victims and subordinates make excellent Sith acolytes. Those with more authority and control make even better Sith acolytes.

The Sith acolyte proceeds from a position of weakness, even within the ranks of the Sith. Sith warriors are far more physically capable, and Sith Lords combine the best aspects of both the cultist and the warrior. Therefore the Sith acolyte comes to rely on cunning and subterfuge, advancing more through assassination and betrayal than conquest and domination. For those who perform well, the role of acolyte is only the beginning. For those who perform poorly, the dark side is a yawning abyss of madness. The path of the Sith acolyte should never be traveled lightly.

Vitality: 1d8 per level.

Requirements: To qualify to become a Sith acolyte, a character must fulfill the following criteria:

Base Attack Bonus: +3.

Skills: Knowledge (Sith lore) 6 ranks, Read/Write Sith, See Force 6 ranks.

Dark Side Skills (any): 6 ranks total.

Feats: Force-Sensitive, Alter, Sense.

Reputation: 4.

Dark Side Points: 4.

Special: During the Golden Age of the Sith, the Sith proliferated in their own corner of the galaxy, with plenty of opportunities for Sith acolytes and warriors to flourish. But since the days of Darth Bane, the rule of the Sith has mandated that there be only two Sith at any one time—a master and an apprentice. For a character to become a Sith acolyte

Only during the Golden Age of the Sith are Sith acolytes truly plentiful, sprawling across Sith-controlled worlds like so many carrion insects. But with the great Sith wars and the rise of Darth Bane, the Sith tradition is reduced to two practitioners: a master and an apprentice. When the master expires—sometimes at the hand of an ambitious apprentice—the apprentice becomes the new master and seeks out a new student. The best students are those who already have some training in the Force, but who are still malleable enough to fall to the dark side.

The Rise of the Empire era carries out this silently observed tradition, culminating in the return of the Sith in the form of Darth Sidious. After the Emperor's death at the end of the Rebellion era, Sith acolytes are nonexistent. Therefore, unless the GM wishes to allow the campaign to diverge from the events of the *Star Wars* films, the class of Sith acolyte is prohibited in the Rebellion era and The New Jedi Order era. However, certain portions of the Old Republic era could certainly allow for Sith acolyte characters—especially before the events of *The Phantom Menace*. ☽

in a future era, an existing Sith must die and the Sith Master must seek out the character as an apprentice. Certainly a character can aspire to such a position, but it falls to the GM to decide if the campaign will take this particular path—and if the Sith Master will approach the character and offer the apprenticeship.

Class Skills

The Sith acolyte's class skills (and the key ability for each skill) are: Alchemy* (Int), Bluff (Cha), Computer Use (Int), Craft (Int), Diplomacy (Cha), Empathy (Wis), Enhance Senses (Wis), Farseeing (Wis), Fear* (Wis), Force Grip* (Int), Gather Information (Cha), Illusion (Cha), Intimidate (Cha), Knowledge (Int),

Move Object (Int), Profession (Wis), Read/Write Language (None), See Force (Wis), Sense Motive (Wis), and Speak Language (None).

*Use of this skill gives the Sith acolyte a Dark Side Point.

Skill Points at Each Additional Level: 6 + Int modifier

Class Features

Weapon Proficiency: The Sith acolyte receives Weapon Group Proficiency (simple weapons) and Weapon Group Proficiency (blaster pistols) at 1st level.

Sith Sorcery: The Sith acolyte gains the dark side feat Sith Sorcery, provided he fulfills the prerequisites.

Preferred Weapon: The Sith acolyte receives a Sith sword or the lightsaber.

Exotic Weapon Proficiency: The Sith acolyte begins training in the proper use of the preferred weapon of the Sith. In ancient times, this would be the Sith sword (see Chapter Four). In modern times, however, this is the lightsaber. If the Sith acolyte wishes to use a double-bladed lightsaber, he must take the proficiency as one of his level-based feats.

Control: The Sith acolyte gains the bonus feat Control at 4th level and gains access to Control-based class skills.

Bonus Feat: At 6th level, and again at 8th and 10th, the Sith acolyte gains a bonus feat. These bonus feats must be drawn from the following list: Deflect Blasters, Dissipate Energy, Drain Force, Force Mind (Knight Mind, Master Mind), Frightful Presence, Hatred, Infamy, Lightsaber Defense, Prolong Force, Rage, and Throw Lightsaber.

Feats dependent on other feats are listed parenthetically after the prerequisite feat. Characters must still meet all prerequisites for each feat, including minimum ability scores and base attack bonuses. See the *Star Wars Roleplaying Game*, Chapter 5: Feats, for descriptions of feats not covered in this book.

Table 2-7: The Sith Acolyte

Level	Base Attack Bonus	Fort Save	Ref Save	Will Save	Special	Lightsaber Damage*	Defense Bonus	Reputation Score
1st	+0	+2	+1	+2	Sith Sorcery, preferred weapon	—	+2	+1
2nd	+1	+3	+2	+3	Exotic Weapon Proficiency	—	+3	+1
3rd	+2	+3	+2	+4	Control	—	+3	+0
4th	+2	+4	+2	+4		+1d8	+4	+0
5th	+3	+4	+3	+5		+1d8	+4	+1
6th	+4	+5	+3	+6	Bonus feat	+1d8	+5	+1
7th	+4	+5	+4	+6		+1d8	+5	+0
8th	+5	+6	+4	+7	Bonus feat	+2d8	+6	+0
9th	+6	+6	+4	+8		+2d8	+6	+1
10th	+6	+7	+5	+8	Bonus feat	+2d8	+7	+1

* The additional damage dealt by the Sith acolyte's lightsaber.

Important: These feats are in addition to the feats that a character of any class gets for gaining levels (see the *Star Wars Roleplaying Game*, Table 3–1: Experience and Level-Dependent Benefits). The Sith acolyte is not limited to the list given here when choosing those level-based feats.

Sith Lord

The Sith Lord is the pinnacle of the Sith tradition. His most sacred tasks include preserving the lore and glory of the Sith and plotting their eventual ascendance to their place as rulers of the galaxy. The Sith Lord must allow nothing to stand in the way of this goal: not all the forces of the Republic military, nor the entirety of the Jedi Order. When the time comes, the Sith Lord must be prepared to ruthlessly crush all opposition, leaving no traces behind. This has been the way of the Sith for a thousand years.

Most Sith Lords begin as Sith acolytes or Sith warriors. The Sith Lord cultivates individuals with the potential for both great power and great evil, training them from childhood, when possible, to be every bit as ruthless as he is himself. The training can be better described as physical and mental torture, but it is designed to create someone strong, fast, cunning, and deadly. The Sith Lord passes on his knowledge of the dark side of the Force, instilling in his apprentice both a lust for power and a fear of failure.

Arguably, only the truly ambitious or deeply twisted ever seek to become Sith Lords. Following the path of the Sith dominates one's destiny, requiring a constant devotion to engineering the reascendance of the Sith. A Sith Lord cannot afford the luxury of friends, mercy, or even rest. The dark side sustains him through decades of scheming and planning, of masterminding plots subtle and grandiose. Even then, a Sith Lord may meet his end without ever seeing his contributions to the Sith grand scheme come to fruition. Each must content himself with knowing that his apprentice, or a descendant of his apprentice a hundred generations down the line, will one day honor his sacrifice by destroying the Jedi Order and replacing it with the dark empire of the Sith.

Vitality: 1d10 per level.

Requirements: To qualify to become a Sith Lord, a character must fulfill the following criteria:

Base Attack Bonus: +6.

Skills: Battlemind 6 ranks, Knowledge (Sith lore) 8 ranks, Intimidate 8 ranks, Read/Write Sith, Speak Sith.

Dark Side Skills (any): 8 ranks total.

Feats: Force-Sensitive, Alter, Control, Sense, Exotic Weapon Proficiency (Sith sword, lightsaber, or double-bladed lightsaber).

Reputation: 10.

Dark Side Points: Equal to or greater than the character's Wisdom score.

Special: During the Golden Age of the Sith, the Sith proliferated in their own corner of the galaxy, with plenty of opportunities for Sith acolytes and warriors to flourish and become one of the rare Sith Lords. But since the days of Darth Bane, the rule of the Sith has mandated that there be only two Sith at any one time. For a character to become a Sith Lord when there are already two Sith, one of them must expire. An ambitious character engineers this turn of events. The customary Sith method is to vanquish a Sith acolyte, Sith warrior, or a Sith Lord in combat. Once there is only one Sith in existence, a character can adopt the Sith Lord class—even if the other surviving Sith is a Sith Lord.

Class Skills

The Sith Lord's class skills (and the key ability for each skill) are: Alchemy* (Int), Battlemind (Con), Bluff (Cha), Computer Use (Int), Craft (Int), Diplomacy (Cha), Empathy (Wis), Enhance Ability (Con), Enhance Senses (Wis), Farseeing (Wis), Fear* (Wis), Force Defense (Con), Force Grip* (Int), Force Stealth (Con), Gather Information (Cha), Illusion (Cha), Intimidate (Cha), Knowledge (Int), Move Object (Int), Profession (Wis), Read/Write Language (None), See Force (Wis), Sense Motive (Wis), Speak Language (None), and Telepathy (Wis).

*Use of this skill gives the Sith Lord a Dark Side Point.

Skill Points at Each Additional Level: 6 + Int modifier.

Class Features

Weapon Proficiency: The Sith Lord has the feats Weapon Group Proficiency (simple weapons), Weapon Group Proficiency (blaster pistols), and Weapon Group Proficiency (vibro weapons).

Resource Access: Beginning at 2nd level, the Sith Lord has access to an array of resources. Once per game session, the Sith Lord may make a Charisma check to use those resources during the game session.

The value of the resources gained equals the Sith Lord's class level × the result of the Charisma check × 50. Thus, a 4th-level Sith Lord who got a check result of 17 would gain (4 × 17 × 50) 3,400 credits' worth of resources. These resources can take virtually any form the Sith Lord chooses (within reason) and are his to do with as he pleases. He may keep them, use them, give them away, or sell them as he sees fit.

Sith Battle Prowess: At 3rd, 6th, and 9th level, the Sith Lord gets a bonus feat associated with combat. This bonus feat must be drawn from the following list: Knight Defense, Lightsaber Defense, Master Defense, Sith Sword Defense, Sith Sword Expert Defense, or Sith Sword Mastery. The Sith Lord must meet the prerequisite for the feat to select it.

Sith Secrets: The Sith Lord plunges boldly into the abyss of Sith knowledge. At 4th level, then again at 7th level, the Sith Lord gains a bonus feat involving Sith lore. This bonus feat must be drawn from the following list: Drain Force, Force Lightning, Force Mastery, Force Mind, Hatred, Rage, or Sith Sorcery.

Minions: Beginning at 5th level, a Sith Lord can add his Sith Lord level to any Reputation checks made to attract followers. (See Followers, page 106 of the *Star Wars Roleplaying Game*.)

Exceptional Minions: Beginning at 8th level, the level limit of the Sith Lord's minions is twice his Reputation score.

Sith Master: At the pinnacle of his ability, the Sith Lord is able to bolster the Force abilities of his minions with his own. The Sith Lord may grant temporary ranks in any skill he possesses to any Force-sensitive being. The maximum number of ranks that can be granted in this fashion is the number of ranks the Sith Lord possesses in the skill

Table 2-8: The Sith Lord

Level	Base Attack Bonus	Fort Save	Ref Save	Will Save	Special	Lightsaber Damage*	Defense Bonus	Reputation Score
1st	+1	+2	+2	+2		—	+2	+1
2nd	+2	+3	+2	+2	Resource access	+1d8	+2	+1
3rd	+3	+3	+3	+3	Sith battle prowess	+1d8	+3	+0
4th	+4	+4	+3	+3	Sith secrets	+1d8	+3	+1
5th	+5	+4	+4	+4	Minions	+2d8	+4	+1
6th	+6	+5	+4	+4	Sith battle prowess	+2d8	+4	+0
7th	+7	+5	+5	+5	Sith secrets	+2d8	+5	+1
8th	+8	+6	+5	+5	Exceptional minions	+2d8	+5	+1
9th	+9	+6	+6	+6	Sith battle prowess	+3d8	+6	+0
10th	+10	+7	+6	+6	Sith Master	+3d8	+6	+1

* The additional damage dealt by the Sith Lord's lightsaber.

in question. While the Sith Lord is exercising this power, he loses that number of ranks from the skill. The Sith Lord can grant skill ranks to any number of targets—but the more skill ranks he grants to others, the more he weakens himself.

Using this ability requires a daily expenditure of 1 vitality point per skill rank granted, beginning at the moment the ranks are initially granted. Vitality points spent in this fashion are recovered normally. The Sith Lord can alter the precise number granted to the target at the same time that he spends vitality points. He may also completely withdraw bonus ranks at this same time, regaining them immediately. Should he withdraw all granted ranks from a target at any time, that target immediately becomes fatigued (–2 to Strength and Dexterity rolls, cannot run or charge). If the Sith Lord should perish, the transferred ranks remain with the target until the time they would ordinarily be renewed the next day.

To bestow the skill ranks, a target must be within 2 meters of the Sith Lord. But afterward, the target can range as far as he or she likes; the bonus remains for as long as the Sith Lord continues to expend vitality on the target's behalf.

The target can only gain skill ranks in his or her class skills in this fashion. If the target does not meet the requirements of the skill—generally, by not possessing the proper feats—he or she gains no benefit from the transfer of skill ranks.

Example: A 10th-level Sith Lord has 13 ranks in Affect Mind. By expending 6 vitality points, he can transfer 6 ranks to his favorite assassin, a Dark Jedi with the Alter feat. The Sith Lord now effectively has only 7 ranks in Affect Mind, and the Dark Jedi has 6 ranks (which are added to his Charisma modifier and any ranks in Affect Mind he may already have). If the Dark Jedi had not yet taken the Alter feat, he would not gain any ranks in Affect Mind. The Sith Lord would be wasting vitality and lowering his own ability with the skill for no reason.

ERA NOTES: SITH LORD

In the early days of the Sith, only one of their rank could ever gain the title "Dark Lord of the Sith." Seizing this prestigious position generally required the support of a significant portion of the Sith—and the death of the previous Sith Lord.

With the twilight of the Sith and the rise of Darth Bane, the rules of the old Sith were supplanted by new rules. There could only be two Sith at any time: One was the master, and the other was the apprentice. While both of these could be Sith Lords, neither could take on an apprentice until the other was dead. Sometimes this resulted in vicious battles between master and student. But more commonly, a Sith Master would pass on all he knew before expiring, leaving his former apprentice to take on an apprentice of his own, and thus continue the tradition of the Sith.

Unless the GM wishes to diverge from *Star Wars* canon, he should not allow characters to adopt this class. The only Sith Lords in *The Phantom Menace* are Darth Maul and Darth Sidious. During the Rebellion era, Darth Vader and the Emperor fill the role of Sith Lords. With the deaths of the Emperor and Vader, the Sith tradition comes to an effective end. However, the centuries—even millennia—before the events of the films are wide open for characters who want to battle for a Sith Lord's title.

Sith Warrior

The Sith warrior combines combat mastery with the power of the dark side to create a living embodiment of rage and savagery. Physical conditioning and punishing discipline make the Sith warrior into a formidable opponent, and facility with the powers of the dark side add a wicked barb to an otherwise deadly weapon. The Sith warrior is dedicated to the conquest and subjugation of any obstacle to the Sith tradition. Throughout history, a single Sith warrior has usually been more than a match for most Jedi.

Table 2-9: The Sith Warrior

Level	Base Attack Bonus	Fort Save	Ref Save	Will Save	Special	Lightsaber Damage*	Defense Bonus	Reputation Score
1	+1	+2	+2	+1	Preferred weapon	—	+2	+1
2	+2	+3	+2	+2	Bonus feat	—	+2	+1
3	+3	+3	+3	+2	Sense, enemy bonus +1	+1d8	+3	+0
4	+4	+4	+3	+3	Bonus feat	+1d8	+3	+1
5	+5	+4	+4	+3	Uncanny dodge (Dex bonus)	+1d8	+4	+1
6	+6	+5	+4	+4	Bonus feat, enemy bonus +2	+2d8	+4	+0
7	+7	+5	+5	+4	Uncanny dodge (flanking)	+2d8	+5	+1
8	+8	+6	+5	+5	Bonus feat	+2d8	+5	+1
9	+9	+6	+6	+5	Enemy bonus +3	+2d8	+6	+0
10	+10	+7	+6	+6	Bonus feat	+3d8	+6	+1

* The additional damage dealt by the Sith warrior's lightsaber.

When Sith warriors gathered in numbers, as they did four thousand years before the days of Darth Maul and Darth Sidious, the galaxy trembled.

But those times are gone, and the few Sith warriors to appear since the rule of Darth Bane have worked in secrecy to preserve the Sith tradition and prepare for their ultimate conquest of the galaxy. Throughout the thousand years since Bane established the rule of one master and one apprentice, footsoldiers, outlaws, warlords, mercenaries, pirates, fighter pilots, survivalists, duelists, and even the occasional Jedi Knight have turned to the dark side and embraced the way of the Sith, becoming mighty warriors or dying brutal deaths—often both. The way of the Sith warrior is a constant, unforgiving test of will and ability, honing each into a blade fearsome enough to cut through the heart of the hated Jedi Order. Every Sith warrior dreams of being the one who will destroy this ancient enemy of the Sith.

Where other Sith focus on plots and deceptions, the Sith warrior devotes himself to the art of violence. The two complement each other perfectly, with the Sith warrior often delivering the final blow to a foe laid low by the machinations of a Sith acolyte or Sith Lord. When the plans of the Sith hinge on a crime boss or a senator or a military officer dying a vicious death, the Sith warrior is in his element. His is the last face the enemies of the Sith ever see—if they see him at all.

The training of a Sith warrior is always one of deprivation and hardship. Mercy and forbearance create a weak weapon, and such a weapon is useless. The Sith warrior is subjected to endless conditioning and drilling. Displays of fear or uncertainty are rewarded with painful and educational punishment. Displays of strength and ruthlessness are rewarded with another day's survival. The Sith warrior learns to live for the precious few words of encouragement his master gives, and the dream that he will one day stand atop a pile of slain Jedi. For the Sith warrior, battle is its own reward.

Vitality: 1d10 per level.

Requirements: To qualify to become a Sith warrior, a character must fulfill the following criteria:

Base Attack Bonus: +4.

Skills: Battlemind 4 ranks, Knowledge (Sith lore) 4 ranks, Intimidate 6 ranks, Read/Write Sith.

Dark Side Skills (any): 4 ranks total.

Feats: Force-Sensitive, Alter, Control, Exotic Weapon Proficiency (Sith sword or lightsaber).

Reputation: 4.

Dark Side Points: 6.

Special: During the Golden Age of the Sith, the Sith proliferated in their own corner of the galaxy, with plenty of opportunities for Sith acolytes and warriors to flourish. But since the days of Darth Bane, the rule of the Sith has mandated that there be only two Sith at any time. For a character to become a Sith warrior when there are already two Sith, one of them must expire. An ambitious character engineers this turn of events himself. The customary Sith method is vanquishing a Sith acolyte, Sith warrior, or (considerably less likely) a Sith Lord in combat. Once there is only one Sith in existence, a character can adopt the Sith warrior class.

Class Skills

The Sith warrior's class skills (and the key ability for each skill) are: Battlemind (Con), Climb (Str), Computer Use (Int), Craft (Int), Enhance Ability (Con), Force Defense (Con), Force Grip* (Int), Force Push (Int), Force Stealth (Con), Intimidate (Cha), Jump (Str), Knowledge (Int), Move Object (Int), Profession (Wis), Swim (Str), and Tumble (Dex).

Use of this skill gives the Sith warrior a Dark Side Point.

Skill Points at Each Additional Level: 4 + Int modifier.

Class Features

Weapon Proficiency: The Sith warrior has the feats Weapon Group Proficiency (simple weapons), Weapon Group Proficiency (blaster pistols), and Weapon Group Proficiency (vibro weapons).

Preferred Weapon: The Sith warrior begins to wield the weapon he has been trained to use—either the Sith sword or the lightsaber.

Bonus Feats: At 2nd level and every other level thereafter (4th, 6th 8th, and 10th), the Sith warrior gains a bonus feat. These bonus feats must be drawn from the following list: Ambidexterity, Armor Proficiency (medium), Armor Proficiency (heavy), Blind-Fight, Dodge (Mobility, Spring Attack, Whirlwind Attack), Exotic Weapon Proficiency, Hatred, Heroic Surge, Improved Initiative, Martial Arts, Point Blank Shot (Far Shot, Precise Shot, Rapid Shot, Shot on the Run), Power Attack (Cleave, Great Cleave), Quick Draw, Rage, Sith Sword Defense, Sith Sword Expertise, Sith Sword Mastery, Two-Weapon Fighting (Improved Two-Weapon Fighting), Weapon Finesse*, and Weapon Focus*.

Feats dependent on other feats are listed parenthetically after the prerequisite feat. Characters must still meet all prerequisites for each feat, including minimum ability scores and base attack bonuses. See the *Star Wars Roleplaying Game*, Chapter 5: Feats, for descriptions of feats not covered in this book.

Important: These feats are in addition to the feats that a character of any class gets for gaining levels

ERA NOTES: SITH WARRIOR

As with other Sith prestige classes, the Sith warrior is relatively unknown for a thousand years before the rise of Emperor Palpatine. Because the Sith tradition is such a closely guarded secret, the Sith warriors who exist never divulge their origins, and are often mistaken for Dark Jedi. The first Sith warrior identified as such is Darth Maul. By the time he is discovered, he has actually made the transition to Sith Lord.

Only during the Golden Age of the Sith, four thousand years prior to the events of *The Phantom Menace,* do Sith warriors proliferate. Even then, they are confined to a relatively small corner of the galaxy, where the Sith had millennia earlier fled to escape extinction at the hands of the Jedi. But after the new Sith tradition imposed by Darth Bane, only two Sith exist at any given time, meaning that the GM must approve any character who wishes to choose this prestige class. Even then, if there are already two Sith of any class in existence, one must die for the character to make the transition. ∴

(see the *Star Wars Roleplaying Game*, Table 3–1: Experience and Level-Dependent Benefits). The Sith warrior is not limited to the list given here when choosing those level-based feats.

Sense: The Sith warrior gains the bonus feat Sense at 3rd level and gains access to Sense-based class skills.

Enemy Bonus: As the Sith warrior advances in training, he learns to focus his aggression against the traditional oppressors of the Sith: the Jedi. When fighting Jedi opponents, the Sith warrior gains a +1 attack bonus against a chosen Jedi opponent. If there is more than one Jedi involved in a battle, the player of the Sith warrior must announce which is his target before his first action. Even if that opponent is removed from the fray (by death or by escape), the Sith warrior cannot nominate a new target enemy for the remainder of the combat. The bonus increases to +2 at 6th level and +3 at 9th level.

Uncanny Dodge: Starting at 5th level, the Sith warrior gains the extraordinary ability to react to danger before his senses would normally allow him to do so. At 5th level and above, the Sith warrior retains his Dexterity bonus to Defense (if any) regardless of being caught flat-footed or struck by a hidden attacker. (He still loses his Dexterity bonus to Defense if immobilized.) Note that this level of uncanny dodge does not negate flank attacks.

At 7th level, the Sith warrior can no longer be flanked, since he can react to opponents on opposite sides of him as easily as he can react to a single attacker. This ability denies scoundrels the opportunity to use flank attacks to sneak attack the Sith warrior.

Chapter Three:
Gamemastering the Dark Side

If you play in or run a *Star Wars* campaign, you'll eventually need to deal with the dark side of the Force. Villains knowingly or inadvertently embrace the dark side. Heroes often face the temptations that the dark path offers. By way of example, one of the main characters of the *Star Wars* films goes through the entire cycle of light and dark over the course of the six movies. Anakin Skywalker begins as an untrained Force-sensitive character who's strong in the Force. (He may even be the Chosen One of Jedi prophecy, but that's another story.) He joins the Jedi Order, becomes a Jedi Knight, then succumbs to temptation and falls to the dark side. As one of the predominant darksiders and Sith Lords of his age, Skywalker (now called Darth Vader) serves as the Emperor's right hand and helps rule over the galaxy. In the end, Vader turns back to the light when he destroys the Emperor and risks his own life to save his son.

Not every hero's story will involve this level of far-reaching or dramatic action, but the potential for this kind of epic tale lies within every campaign. Achieving that potential depends, in part, on the direction the Gamemaster sets for his or her campaign.

This chapter deals with the various issues revolving around incorporating dark side characters into a campaign. It provides hard and fast game mechanics to adjudicate a character's journey along the dark path, as well as advice for GMs and players alike. It also contains plenty of examples and adventure ideas to use as a model for introducing a dark side character into an existing campaign, or to help kick-start a dark side campaign.

The Gamemaster ultimately decides which elements of this book are available to players and their heroes. A GM might decide that most of this material is only available to Gamemaster characters. That's the GM's call. But if the GM wants to add a touch of the dark side to the game, we suggest starting slowly. Introduce a new rule here or a new item there to see how it fits into the game. If the campaign doesn't fall apart around you, add another element. Just as in the *Star Wars* universe, the dark side can be extremely tempting and hard to control; be careful not to overdo it.

Rules for the Dark Side

This chapter provides additional rules for dealing with dark side characters, especially Force-users who habitually call upon the dark side of the Force. We recommend using these additional rules if you plan to incorporate any of the material in this book into your campaign.

When Is a Character Dark?

A character achieves the distinction of falling to the dark side in two stages: tainted and dark.

When a character attains a number of Dark Side Points equal to half his Wisdom score, that character is considered to be tainted. A tainted character tempts fate with each appeal to the dark side, but also has the option of working his way back to the light through heroic deeds, the use of Force Points, and by atoning for past misdeeds. Effectively, the character accomplishes this by reducing his number of Dark Side Points to one less than half his Wisdom score.

When a character attains a number of Dark Side Points equal to his Wisdom score, that character is considered to be dark. (A tainted character can also become dark by failing a Wisdom check, as described under Dark Side Templates in Chapter Two.) This character is now effectively lost to the dark side. Even if the character finds a way to reduce his Dark Side Points total to one less than his Wisdom score, the dark template remains in place. Only a truly epic act of heroism and atonement can return a dark character to the light.

Long-Term Effects of Using the Dark Side

While the dark side offers a quick path to power for those who feel the flow of the Force, it also extracts a high price from those who dip into the well too frequently. This price takes the form of a long-term withering of the character's physical attributes. Early in a darksider's career, the ratio of power to negative effect runs in favor of the power the dark side provides. Each time a Force-sensitive character calls on the dark side, however, the urge to again feel that electric flow of power grows stronger. It becomes easier to gain Dark Side Points, to fall deeper and deeper into the darkness. In the middle stages of a character's career, as the character becomes first tainted and then dark in nature, the power the dark side provides begins to collect what is owed to it. With great effort, a balance can be maintained—for a while. As a character reaches higher levels, the long-term effects of dark side use begin to show. The character grows weaker in body, all the while growing stronger and stronger in the dark side of the Force. Eventually, the darksider's body begins to fail as it is corrupted and rotted away by the darkness and evil flowing through it.

Corruption and Tainted Characters

Whenever a hero with the tainted template attains a new character level, he or she must check to see if the corruption of the dark side has had a permanent, lasting effect. To do this, the character makes a Fortitude saving throw against a DC of 10 + the number of Dark Side Points the character possesses at the time of the level advancement.

If the save succeeds, the character has managed to stave off the debilitating effects of the dark side for the time being.

If the save fails, the character immediately and permanently reduces Strength, Dexterity, or Constitution by 1 point. The character's player chooses which ability withers. The only way to offset this effect is to replace the lost point with an ability increase at the appropriate level (as described on Table 3–1: Experience and Level-Dependent Benefits in the *Star Wars Roleplaying Game*).

No ability can be reduced two times in a row by dark side corruption. So, if Jog Saveen, a tainted Force adept, fails her saving throw at 6th level and reduces her Strength score from 14 to 13, then if she fails her save at 7th level she must reduce either her Dexterity or Constitution score. She can't decrease her Strength score two times in a row.

Even if a tainted character later returns to the light, any ability decreases due to the corrupting effects of the dark side remain. The memory of this deadly touch remains long after the effects are applied.

Corruption and Dark Characters

Whenever a hero with the dark template attains a new character level, he or she immediately and permanently reduces Strength, Dexterity, or Constitution by 1 point. There is no saving throw for a dark character. The only way to offset this effect is to replace the lost point with an ability increase at the appropriate level (as described on Table 3–1: Experience and Level-Dependent Benefits in the *Star Wars Roleplaying Game*).

As with tainted characters, no ability can be reduced two times in a row by dark side corruption.

If a dark character eventually finds redemption, any ability decreases due to the corrupting effects of the dark side remain.

Gaining Force Points

Characters who have acquired either the tainted or dark template have a limited ability to gain Force points. Dramatic heroism is no longer an option for characters who have taken the path of corruption. Instead, a tainted or dark character gains Force Points in the following ways:

- Each time a tainted or dark character gains a level, he or she gains one Force Point.
- A tainted or dark character, once per level, can gain one Force Point by accepting one Dark Side Point.

In addition, the Drain Force feat allows a character to gain one Force Point by stealing it from another character.

Gaining Dark Side Points

Characters can gain Dark Side Points in any of three ways;

- Using a Force Point to call on the dark side.
- Using a dark side Force-based skill or feat.
- Performing an evil act.

A character can use the Force to increase his chance of success on any d20 roll (ability checks, skill checks, saving throws, and attacks). Calling upon the dark side of the Force, however, is sometimes far more effective than calling upon the light side. When a character calls upon the dark side of the Force in this fashion, he gains a Dark Side Point. The hero's intent doesn't matter. Good or evil, he gains a Dark Side Point. It also makes no difference if the check ultimately fails; the dark side promises much, but sometimes delivers nothing.

Example: Set Harth, a Jedi guardian with a penchant for solving situations with violence, is losing a battle with a Sith warrior. Fearing for his life, he decides to throw everything he has into an all-or-nothing attack. But he suddenly doubts that the 2d6 bonus dice he'll get for calling on the Force will be enough; he needs a little extra power. Set Harth decides to call on the dark side instead, gaining 3d6 bonus dice rather than 2d6. He tells himself that he'll never do it again, and that a single Dark Side Point won't hurt him.

Characters may be intrigued by a number of options in the form of skills and feats that draw on the power of the dark side of the Force. Examples include Drain Knowledge, Fear, Force Lightning, and Hatred. Many of these dark side skills can be used untrained—making them that much more tempting for Force-users to employ in desperate situations. But, as with calling on the dark side of the Force, the success or failure of the task and the hero's intent when employing the skill do not figure into the hero's Dark Side Point gain.

Example: Although Set Harth defeated the Sith warrior, the battle left him weakened—and the warrior had anticipated just such a turn of events. As Set Harth returns to his ship, an assassin droid ambushes him. Knowing that he is too weak to fight it, he tries to use the Force to switch it off. Unfortunately, the Sith warrior has disabled the droid's power switch, and Set Harth realizes that the only way to deactivate the assassin droid is to drain its power cells. He reaches out with the Force and finds a sort of energy void—a conduit to the dark side—into which he can empty the droid's store of energy. Using the Drain Energy skill untrained, however, is too much for Set, and the droid continues to attack him. Now Set Harth has gained another Dark Side Point—and he still must contend with the droid.

Acts of anger or hatred give the dark side a hold on a character. Acts of revenge and cruelty strengthen that grip. Using the Force to perform evil acts is innately an evil act—and even when a Force-wielding character performs such an act without calling upon the dark side, he risks corruption. While one or two such acts may not imperil a Force-user, doing evil without apparent repercussions teaches the character that he can do so as often as he likes. The dark side has seduced many Force-users this way.

The Gamemaster may wish to remind characters of the repercussions of taking such an action, particularly when dealing with inexperienced players. "You know, killing that helpless enemy would be an evil act," the GM might warn, for example.

Example: Backed into a corner by the assassin droid, all looks bleak for Set Harth. Then, a little old man appears and commands the droid to shut down. The wizened man explains that he was the Sith warrior's servant, and that he will share what he knows of the Sith if Set Harth transports him off the planet. Set Harth agrees, but only if the old man tells him what he knows first. The old man refuses and becomes evasive. Tired, hurt, and frustrated, Set Harth ignites his lightsaber and threatens the servant. "Tell me now or you'll die here!" he says. Once again the old man refuses, and Set Harth gives in to his anger and cuts the old man down. He gains another Dark Side Point and is beginning to feel that adhering to the Jedi Code is only slowing him down.

Note that all three of these conditions are cumulative with one another. If Set Harth had spent a Force Point to call upon the dark side while using Force Grip to choke the old servant, he would gain 3 Dark Side Points at once.

Acts of Evil

Evil is not always easy to recognize. An innocent act may ultimately result in great suffering. An act of revenge may save the lives of millions of people. The pure at heart can lash out in anger. Evil may lurk beneath a mask of virtue. Whether an act is evil or not often boils down to a question of motivation, and motivations can be hard to identify.

When a Gamemaster is in doubt about whether to award a Dark Side Point to a character, he or she should consider the character's motives: Did the character act out of anger? Hatred? Cruelty? Vengeance? Pride? Did the character choose an option simply because it would allow her to spill an enemy's blood? Was greed or envy involved? Jealousy?

The Gamemaster should always remember that simply feeling anger, fear, bloodlust, or any other similarly negative emotion is not in and of itself of the dark side. The journey to the dark side begins when a character allows such negative emotions to determine his actions *rather than the will of the Force.* A Jedi may hate a Sith, but if he kills the Sith in self-defense he does not necessarily gain a Dark Side Point.

Knowing when a character allows base emotions to sway her actions can be difficult. When questions arise as to the motive behind a character's actions—and whether or not the character should receive a Dark Side Point—the GM should look for certain hallmarks that identify these emotions.

Fear

"Fear is the path to the dark side . . ."
   —Yoda

All sentient creatures experience fear at some point in their lives; it is a defense mechanism designed to impel creatures away from danger. Characters feel fear when they believe they may lose something valuable to them. Fear for their own lives is the most common motivator, but the fear can be for the lives of friends or loved ones, or even for something as trivial as the loss of a possession or an opportunity.

A character acts out of genuine fear when he abandons reason and logic in order to eliminate or escape a threat. Unreasoning fear is characterized by desperation and frantic attempts to escape the danger at any cost. Characters who use the most lethal weapon available (regardless of their proficiency with it), attack all-out without first determining the actual degree of danger, or abandon threatened allies to save their own lives are almost certainly acting out of fear. Their journey to the dark side has begun.

Example: Bal Serinus visits a planet in the Corporate Sector. She notices a local following her and decides to confront him. She corners the stranger in an alley, and he responds by reaching into his jacket for something. Bal Serinus draws her lightsaber and attacks before he reveals his weapon. As he falls to the ground, she discovers that he was reaching for a datapad. Bal Serinus acted out of fear—fear that the stranger was a threat—without actually waiting to see if he really posed a danger to her.

Anger

". . . fear leads to anger . . ."
—Yoda

Like fear, anger is almost unavoidable for sentient beings. It is symptomatic of frustration—stress without a suitable means of release. Such tension results in violent behavior, aimed at relieving the frustration all at once. It can be brought on by a variety of factors, but most commonly relates to fear. The fear of the consequences of failure can create tremendous surges of anger in sentient beings.

Characters acting in anger lose the ability to show mercy; the target of the character's anger must feel his wrath. A character gripped by anger often takes unnecessary risks in order to punish or destroy the target of his ire. Victory is not good enough if the foe is still moving. The character does not wish to address the situation when he is more rational; he needs to vent his fury *now*, while his blood is boiling and his enemy is within reach. Such a character deliberately gives his anger free rein, and thus gives in to the dark side.

Example: Set Harth finds himself at odds with a dark side marauder. Both want the same Sith artifact. While fighting over it, they become separated by a falling column. The column traps the dark side marauder, and Set Harth easily claims the artifact. But in the grip of anger, Set dashes through a hail of falling masonry to personally finish off the trapped marauder. His anger is so great that he cannot accept his own victory.

Hatred

". . . anger leads to hate . . ."
—Yoda

Stress can also result in a more subtle kind of anger: hatred. Hatred is a simmering resentment, the outward expression of which may start small but gradually escalates into full-scale acts of violence. Hatred festers inside a character until eventually she comes to believe that the target of her hatred somehow has less right to exist than she does. In her own mind, she reduces her enemy to a nebulous menace, the source of all the things she despises and of all the ills that plague her. To her thinking, the object of her hatred consciously attempts to thwart her. But it is not a personal vendetta; her enemy clearly threatens all that he touches. She has a right and

even a duty to destroy him and, what's more, to undo all that he has wrought.

Hatred is often identifiable by an accompanying sense of righteousness; the character feels that she is morally bound to eliminate the thing she hates. For her, considerations such as perspectives and mitigating circumstances are not a factor. Lenience is not an option. Justice is hers to administer, and she does so with the assurance that anyone can plainly see the correctness of her decision. But whether she is right or wrong, the very fact that she chooses to act on her belief and nothing else brings her one step closer to the dark side.

Example: In killing the stranger, Bal Serinus angered a local Hutt crime lord, because the stranger was his messenger. Now his bounty hunters chase after her, and Bal Serinus is filled with indignation. She feels completely justified in having killed the man with the datapad—how was she to know who he was? As the first bounty hunters close in on her, she decides to teach them a lesson about trifling with her. She could present her side of the story and smooth things over with the Hutt, but she decides that anyone who would put a price on her head over a misunderstanding is beneath her contempt. She'll kill all the bounty hunters, then the Hutt, for the crime of inconveniencing her.

Suffering

". . . hate leads to suffering."
   —Yoda

Hatred often springs from a position of inferiority; what one cannot control, one frequently hates. But when a character has the power of life and death over the object of his hatred—a single individual, or even an entire galaxy—he can cause suffering. Mental, verbal, and physical abuse are his tools; through these methods, the character denigrates and depersonalizes his victims—making them no more significant than objects, to be used or destroyed as he likes.

Malice is the ultimate expression of hatred, because the object of such hate invariably suffers. A character who wishes to cause suffering has no sense of pity. He callously causes pain, injury, and anguish, because he knows that no one has the power to stop him—he is in command. But he has graduated beyond the need to destroy that which he hates; to him, keeping his victims alive but always in fear of death reminds them of his authority over them. As long as he can continue to exert control over them, they feed his contempt for them. But should they challenge him, they present a threat, and the character must destroy them. Thus, he returns to fear, and traces his path to the dark side all over again.

Example: With the Sith artifact in his control, Set Harth returns to his hideout on Nar Shaddaa to unlock its secrets. He soon learns that he can use it to control the nervous systems of others, moving their limbs by remote control—pulling their strings like puppets. In no time, he has assembled a group of helpless citizens and petty criminals, all forced to walk, dance, grovel, or otherwise serve him purely for his amusement. That manipulating them with the artifact causes them excruciating pain isn't important to Set; anyone who objects joins his troop of unwilling servants. And if one of them becomes too weak to continue—well, Nar Shaddaa's deepest levels are full of such useless refuse.

Pride

Some characters build their self-image and their ego on uncertain foundations. Their sense of self-worth is predicated on beliefs that may or may not be true. When others challenge those beliefs, these characters feel their self-worth deteriorating, and they do whatever they feel necessary to protect the foundations of their fragile self-image. Wounded pride can be just as dangerous as a wounded animal.

Pride runs the gamut of fear, anger, and hatred, because a character whose pride is at stake fears the judgment of others, becomes angry at those who attack her self-image, and grows to hate those who force her to face unpleasant truths. She feeds her pride when she becomes defensive and gives in to her pride when she becomes quarrelsome—because if denial isn't good enough, she must silence the source of her frustration. Simple denial isn't particularly dangerous, but the way to the dark side passes through aggressive pride.

Example: Bal Serinus carved her way through the crime lord's court, only to be felled effortlessly by a mysterious alien—her life spared so that she can become the Hutt's servant. Bal Serinus is terrified. Never before has she been beaten so easily—the alien is an unknown quality, and as far as she knows, he can defeat her again and again. She angrily defies the Hutt's wishes, refusing to be humbled, but when she fights back too hard, he turns the alien loose on her. Her days and nights are filled with seething hatred for the Hutt and his alien servant. Bal vows that when she does finally escape, she will kill everyone in the Hutt's court—coincidentally, everyone who witnessed her defeat.

Aggression

"A Jedi uses the Force for knowledge and defense, never for attack."
   —Yoda

Sometimes characters act out of a desire simply to see blood. This is definitely a trait of the dark side.

827EZA

Such a character may be overcompensating for a perceived personal weakness, because he believes that by taking the offensive, he masks his poor defenses. The faster and harder he strikes, the less chance that his opponent will discover his weak spot.

Aggression manifests as an eagerness to fight. The character has no patience for more peaceful solutions, and consciously engineers situations so that he can respond with his favorite element: violence. He may not always strike the first blow, but the provocation can almost always be traced directly back to him. He is most dangerous when he encounters another being who is also motivated by aggression, because both feel the need to test themselves. Once the fighting starts, an aggressive character can easily fall to the dark side.

Example: Emboldened by his success with the artifact, Set Harth begins carrying it hidden on his person as he ventures into the worst clubs and gambling dens Nar Shaddaa has to offer. He challenges every perceived slight and forces every issue, in hopes that someone will try to best him—so that he can crush that individual with the power of his artifact. In seedy bar after seedy bar, he goads thugs and toughs into drawing their weapons—then forces them to turn those weapons on themselves.

Vengeance

"At last we will have our revenge."
—Darth Maul

A combination of hatred and anger, vengeance impels a character to administer what she considers "justice"—though ultimately, that justice only serves herself. The character acts out of a need for compensation, often to redress wrongs she feels she has suffered. Whether she actually has or not is immaterial; to her, the scales must be balanced. But she may overcompensate, inviting vengeance directed at herself. Vengeance is a dangerous motivator because it frequently replicates itself, continuing the cycle.

Acts of vengeance are usually obvious. The character suffers a blow to her pride or her person and seeks to visit an "equal but opposite" blow on the perpetrator. What constitutes "equal" is generally open to the character's interpretation, but "opposite" is always clear. Without practicing forbearance, the character demands that the loss of pride be repaid with the loss of pride, the loss of limb be repaid with the loss of limb, and the loss of life be repaid with the loss of life. When she takes revenge, the character takes a step farther toward the dark side.

Example: Bal Serinus finally has a chance to free herself from the Hutt. The alien bodyguard attends to business elsewhere, and the Hutt foolishly leaves Bal Serinus alone long enough to recover her strength and break loose from her chains. A gruesome bloodbath

ensues, until the Hutt's bodyguard returns. By this time, though, Bal Serinus has learned the alien's secret: He secretes a nerve-paralyzing toxin from his fingertips. Having recovered her lightsaber, the Dark Jedi severs the alien's hands, leaving him defenseless. But rather than kill him, she hauls him off in chains, selling him as a slave to another Hutt—a rival to the one who had captured her.

Greed

"Greed can be a powerful ally . . . if it's used properly."
—Qui-Gon Jinn

Sometimes a character refuses to be satisfied with what he has already attained. He wants whatever there is to be had, and if he cannot have it, he becomes bitter and resentful. His greed drives him to acquire anything that seems valuable, even if he cannot perceive its value himself. He can be persuaded to part with his acquisitions—but only for something of greater value. This character has no real concern for how his avarice affects those around him. To him, other sentient beings are merely ambulatory showrooms, to be picked clean or disdained according to his whim.

Greed manifests as a desire to take what cannot easily be earned. A character acting out of greed may make a token effort to acquire some coveted object by conventional means, but resorts to more extreme means if he is thwarted. He is often unconcerned that he cannot actually use what he gains. His real goal is exclusive ownership; if someone else values it, he must have it. His obsession may override his sense of fairness, and thus lead to the suffering of others—the summit of the dark side.

Example: Though he has completely mastered the Sith artifact, Set Harth begins to feel that controlling people in this fashion just isn't enough. He begins using the artifact to torture information out of smugglers, crime lords, and art collectors, hoping to hear news of other, similar artifacts. Finally, his efforts pay off, and he journeys to Nal Hutta to "negotiate" with a Hutt crime lord for another relic of the Sith rumored to be in the Hutt's collection. But the Hutt refuses to part with what he considers an amusing toy. Confident that he can take what he wants using the artifact he already owns, Set Harth demonstrates his Sith artifact on the Hutt's pet rancor, and the Hutt wisely accedes to Set's demands.

Jealousy

Where the greedy character covets material things, the jealous character covets intangibles. She resents the attention or honor afforded to others, and whether she has earned the same treatment or not, she feels she is worthy of it. She may in fact be deserving—but her jealousy dictates that she receive more recognition, greater accolades, or more support. Deprived of this attention, her hatred festers within her, until she decides she should simply eliminate her competition.

A character moved by jealousy acts to weaken the opposition. She attacks whatever makes the other person her "rival." It may be the other's skill, or beauty, or reputation, but the character simply wants her own qualities to seem better by comparison—and reducing the other is easier than improving herself. The character may steal a ship or weapon, attempt to disfigure her rival, or attempt to besmirch her rival's good name. How she attacks is not so important as what she attacks, for it reveals her jealous nature and empowers the dark side.

Example: Bal Serinus is selling her alien prisoner to a Hutt when another Dark Jedi, Set Harth, arrives to negotiate for some treasure in the Hutt's possession. After Set demonstrates his power, the Hutt hands over the trinket. But then, in a foul mood, the Hutt refuses to bargain with Bal Serinus for the alien slave. Bal knows that if she could impress the Hutt with a display of her own power, the Hutt would acquiesce, but she can't top Set Harth's stunt with the rancor. Infuriated, she attacks the other Dark Jedi and tries to destroy the Sith artifact. Without it, she tells herself, Set Harth is doubtless far less powerful than he appears.

Love

While not itself of the dark side, love can create an opening for the dark side to insinuate itself in a character's heart. Love is delicate, and can be upset by the merest touch of doubt, anger, or jealousy. When a character feels love, he feels fulfilled. If something intrudes on that feeling of well-being, he fears losing the fulfillment—the absence of which is an aching emptiness. All alone in that void, he can give in to anger, hatred, suffering, pride, or vengeance—any emotion that fills the emptiness and takes the pain away.

Characters acting out of love are in no danger of falling to the dark side. But a character who acts out of the *need* for love risks everything.

Example: Set Harth's battle with Bal Serinus leaves them both exhausted and weak—and easy prey for the Hutt's enforcers. Soon, they find themselves locked in his deepest dungeons. Set Harth uses his powers of telepathy to communicate with Bal Serinus—at first to plan their escape, but as they languish for days, then weeks, simply to have someone to talk to. He begins to depend on their daily communications and, seeing inside her mind as he does, recognizes a kindred spirit. One day, inexplicably, Bal Serinus resists his mental contact, and Set is devastated—not because he has

no one to talk to, but because, he finds, he misses *her* specifically. As the days go by and she refuses to let him read her thoughts, Set Harth wonders what he has done wrong. Eventually he decides that Bal Serinus is avoiding him out of simple, malicious spite—and he decides that if she can show such hatred toward him, he can throw it right back at her. When he escapes, he tells himself, he'll leave her behind.

Atoning

When a hero has not yet fully turned to the dark side, he can begin a period of meditation and absolution in order to atone for his evil deeds. He can decrease his number of Dark Side Points by expending Force Points specifically for this purpose—in effect, erasing his Dark Side Points. The character is most likely out of contact with other characters during this period as he reflects on his misdeeds—though the GM and the player can certainly work together to make this process part of the campaign, or part of a specific adventure.

An atoning character can also divest himself of Dark Side Points by performing acts of dramatic heroism. Should the character choose this route, he reduces his Dark Side Point total by 1 rather than gaining a Force Point. Of course, if the character performs an act that would gain him a Dark Side Point in the process, the effort is wasted, because his Dark Side Point total remains the same.

Running Dark Side Heroes

Let's look at the dark side hero and what the player of such a character needs to consider before, during, and after the character steps onto the dark path of corruption.

In a campaign based on the traditional model, in which the heroes fight for freedom and goodness (at least most of the time), deciding to let your character fall to the dark side has a number of repercussions that must be considered first. Of course, even if you decide you want to take this route, you need your GM's permission. After all, taking the dark path means more work for the GM, and not every GM wants to deal with the group division that such a choice may create. (We recommend that the GM not allow more than one hero to explore the dark side at a time. If a significant number of players in the group want to try this path, it might be time to consider starting a dark side campaign, as described below.)

Even if your Gamemaster agrees, the path to the dark side that looms before you contains a number of hazards. The character who dabbles in the dark side must keep his or her true goals a secret. If the other player characters determine that your hero wants to fully embrace the dark side, then the group dynamic may suffer. Heroes dedicated to stopping evil won't want an evil character in their midst. They won't trust that character. The players might even argue about the situation outside the game. This kind of divisiveness can destroy a gaming group, so it falls to the player of the dark side character and the GM to diplomatically work through any such problems that arise.

To best develop a dark side character in a group of otherwise good heroes, make the character good at heart with a flaw or two that leads him or her toward the dark side. The other heroes work to keep the dark side character on the side of good, or attempt to pull the dark side character back if he or she strays too far into the shadows. Flaws include impatience, a tendency to quick anger, or a desire for revenge that gives the seductive call of the dark side its opening.

At some point, the other heroes succeed at drawing the dark side character away from the abyss, or the dark side character embraces the dark side and betrays them. This moment becomes a turning point for the campaign. If the other heroes redeem the dark side character, that character finds the strength to completely turn away from corruption, and the shadow of doom that hung over the group evaporates. If instead the dark side character

succumbs to the siren call, therein lie the seeds that could destroy the campaign.

When one or more player characters come into conflict, the resulting stress might reflect outside the game and cause hard feelings or worse. Even experienced roleplayers sometimes have trouble keeping events in the game from affecting their feelings toward the other players. If you want to play a dark side character and you plan to eventually betray the other heroes who called you ally and friend, you have to be prepared to deal with the fallout. In cases where the GM and players worked together to reach this stage, the timing and change in events can be exciting and stimulating. But when it comes as a complete surprise, the wrath of the heroes might descend fully upon the dark side character's head. Player characters might die in the resulting backlash, and some heroes might not be satisfied with anything less than the death of the betrayer. Either way, once the dark side character breaks the trust of the other heroes, the campaign becomes much more difficult to manage. Now the GM must run a split campaign, with the dark side character on his own and operating at odds with the other player characters. Instead of leading to a fun and fulfilling game, this situation usually causes frustration and complexity that makes it hard to run compelling adventures.

The Dark Side Hero: One Method for Success

One way to run a dark side hero and keep the campaign going strong involves following a more or less good-aligned character through the ongoing battle to curb dark impulses and desires. Perhaps the character faces a situation in which to save a life he calls upon the dark side for a burst of power. The character works to atone and eliminate Dark Side Points, but often finds it easier to resort to the dark side when a problem looms. The character believes that he is in control, and that he can step back from the dark side at any time. The other heroes worry about the dark side character, but everyone is convinced that although the situation is unpleasant, it is not necessarily dangerous.

Then the character achieves a number of Dark Side Points equal to half his Wisdom score. The character seems darker to the other heroes, a little too quick to resort to anger and violence. He's still the friend they have all come to know and rely upon, though, and they plan to be there to help when the need arises. No one can deny the power the dark side character brings to the group, however. The heroes refuse to see the rising evil in their friend, blinded by his newfound abilities.

When the character falls completely to the dark side, he either betrays the group and becomes their enemy or departs to keep from having to face old friends in combat. To keep the character viable for a while longer, the player decides to have the dark side character disappear. The player creates a new hero character to join the group while continuing to work with the Gamemaster to keep the dark side character current and active off screen. At some point, the dark side character returns to help the heroes face some greater menace, or asks for help from the heroes to advance his own goals. The heroes can now see how far down the dark path their old companion has gone, and they may even be more than a little frightened by the change. They agree to work together, however, convinced that the greater good will be served—this time.

Eventually, the dark side character must become an enemy of the group, perhaps even the group's nemesis. The player may allow the GM to control the dark side character from this point on, but that isn't necessary. It all depends on the dynamics of the group and how comfortable the players and GM are with a player-controlled villain. In the end, the heroes either find a way to help the dark side character atone and return to the light, or they are forced to destroy him—if they can. The confrontation should be one of the key events in the campaign, so neither side should be sure of a victory.

The Price of Darkness

However you approach a character who flirts with the dark side, be aware that a number of real costs are associated with following the dark path. The distrust and animosity of onetime friends, the attention of agencies of power (both the forces of light and more powerful agents of evil), and the social implications of turning to evil all provide difficulties for the character through roleplaying situations. Following the dark side also has a game mechanic cost. This long-term negative effect is described earlier in this chapter.

Running Dark Side GM Characters

Perhaps the best use of dark side characters in a campaign is as foes the Gamemaster creates to challenge the heroes. Dark side characters make the most memorable and truly evil opponents the heroes will ever face, and it could be argued that such power must only reside in the hands of the GM. That's a decision that each GM must make for his or her group.

Whether you allow players to develop dark side characters or not, you will still find it advantageous to use dark side characters in the game. Not all opponents of the heroes are dark side characters. Most thugs, Imperial operatives, pirates, smugglers, bounty hunters, and other types of opposition for the heroes aren't necessarily inherently evil and of the dark side. When you have a dark side character oppose the heroes, everyone should realize exactly what sort of character they are facing. A dark side villain should appear more evil and dangerous than the typical thug or pirate. And remember that not every dark side character has to be a Force-user.

Bad Guys

Any character who has a number of Dark Side Points equal to or greater than half his Wisdom score is considered a true bad guy. A bad guy relishes his wickedness and isn't afraid to use his abilities to his best advantage. Unlike a hero, however, a bad guy seeks personal gain at every opportunity—no matter who gets hurt as a result. Bad guys don't have to be Force-sensitive characters. They make excellent lieutenants and major henchmen for the main villain of the campaign. A bad guy is out for himself and has no qualms about doing anything necessary to achieve his goals. Remember that a bad guy's actions have a selfish and self-serving purpose, however. Save the evil for evil's sake for the character who has completely embraced the dark side.

Bad guys make great nemeses for lower-level heroes. Sometimes the heroes can show the bad guy the error of his ways and help him back to the straight and narrow with a modicum of effort. The heroes can always simply beat the bad guy into submission, but the added opportunity for redemption gives the bad guy a different feel from most other villains.

True Evil

When a character gains a number of Dark Side Points equal to her Wisdom score, that character has totally succumbed to the dark side and can be considered Evil with a capital E. Again, such a character can either be Force-sensitive or not. She just needs to have committed enough acts of darkness to attain a large number of Dark Side Points. In some ways, it's easier for a Force-sensitive character to achieve true evil, because the dark side provides Dark Side Points to its Force-using followers in so many ways. That makes a character without the Force who achieves true evil even more terrifying.

This kind of dark side character functions as a nemesis for mid- to high-level groups of heroes and often serves as the main villain for at least a portion of the campaign. Lesser bad guys and opponents answer to the truly evil character, and just the whisper of her name should make the heroes tremble.

A dark side character who has surrendered to corruption might be immoral, amoral, or even psychotically insane. Mass murderers, megalomaniacs, tyrants, evil dictators, and intelligent, motivated characters who enjoy hurting and killing and stop at nothing to gain power and infamy fall into this category. Redemption may not be possible for this type of villain, at least not without a lot of effort and sacrifice on the part of the heroes. Indeed, in many cases the heroes may never directly encounter the true evil of their campaign. Instead, true evil works through lackeys, minions, and other agents of destruction. When and if the heroes eventually meet up with true evil, should they even recognize it for what it is, the situation should be appropriately dramatic and full of the seeds that can inspire the next part of the campaign—or destroy it utterly if the heroes fail to survive the encounter.

Luke Skywalker met true evil in the form of the Emperor at the climax of *Return of the Jedi*. That encounter contained the possibility of continuing adventures as well as the very real threat of destroying the campaign if Luke either fell to the dark side or was destroyed. Fortunately, Luke and Darth Vader managed to withstand and even destroy the Emperor, setting the stage for the destruction of the Empire and the birth of the New Republic.

Darksiders

Take either a bad guy or a character of true evil and add the ability to manipulate the Force. This kind of GM character, the darksider, becomes an even greater menace for the heroes to deal with. Don't overuse darksiders, however. Not every threat needs to involve a Dark Jedi or a Sith Lord. When you do decide to throw a dark Force-user at the heroes, make every encounter dangerous and memorable. Certainly, you can create different levels of evil Force-users. They don't all have to be on the same scale as Darth Vader, Darth Maul, or the Emperor. But even the weakest of darksiders should pose a real and deadly threat to the heroes.

How should you use dark Force-users in your campaign? Sparingly, of course. In the early stages of a campaign, when the heroes develop from starting characters of 1st level and progress to about 5th level, a dark Force-user threat should be the culmination of a long series of adventures. Hints concerning the nature of the enemy might be liberally sprinkled throughout the adventures, but the penultimate encounter should take place sometime during the heroes' 4th or 5th level. This first darksider should be a dark adept or other minor Force-user—deadly in his or her own right, but only a hint of the dangers to come.

Between 6th and 10th level, the heroes might encounter more dangerous and powerful darksiders. Some of these definitely attempt to corrupt the heroes, enticing any Force-using heroes with offerings of power. At this point, heroes may struggle with their own temptation to employ the dark side of the Force. A Dark Jedi or other powerful Force-user waits at the heart of whatever dark plot drives the campaign, and victory might require a death on the part of the heroes. Obi-Wan Kenobi, for example, watched his master fall to Darth Maul before he managed to defeat the Sith Lord.

From 11th level to 15th level, the heroes are ready to tackle the biggest problems in the galaxy. Undoubtedly, some of these problems relate to evil Force-users with various goals and methods of operation. Trying to hinder an evil character who's well on his way to becoming a Sith Lord might fall to a group of heroes at this stage of the campaign. From the evil character's point of view, the heroes must be corrupted, destroyed, or otherwise persuaded to find other plots to overturn. The evil character doesn't want to waste time or energy on those he or she considers to be his inferiors.

In the final stages of a campaign, as heroes work their way through levels 16 to 20, they struggle to save the galaxy from unimaginably huge threats—including a power-mad darksider seeking to control or destroy civilization as we know it. If this darksider is someone from earlier in the campaign, so much the better, but a new evil works just as well as one who has developed over many months of campaign play. This pivotal encounter could very well set the stage for your next *Star Wars* campaign, determining the fate of the galaxy and the seats of power for the next set of heroes your players dream up.

In the end, darksiders make great opponents, villains, and evil masterminds to set against the heroes. Make sure that each new darksider you create has his or her own personality, method of operation, and style of dress and speech. This way each one is memorable and unique, no matter how many times you resort to the dark side of the Force to provide an enemy. Play darksiders intelligently, using every power and ability in their repertoire, and the players will always remember these encounters.

Running Dark Side Campaigns

We've talked about dark side characters from the player's point of view. A dark side campaign centers on a group of evil characters. They don't all have to be Force-sensitive characters. In fact, you can run a respectable dark side campaign without any Force-using heroes at all. On the other hand, your group can consist of nothing but Force-sensitive and Force-using characters who have no qualms about calling on the dark side of the Force whenever they feel the need or desire. The ultimate dark side campaign, however, revolves around a mixed group of Force-sensitive characters and their non-Force-using allies, all determined to walk the path of corruption to see what levels of power they can attain.

The Evil Campaign

A campaign for evil characters can take many forms. The characters might work for a crime lord, intent on clawing their way to the top of the galactic underworld. They might be minions of the secretive Sith Lords, sowing hatred and confusion throughout the crumbling Old Republic. Maybe the group takes on bounty hunter assignments for whoever pays the most credits, sometimes working for the forces of good but usually doing the bidding of evil employers (they pay better).

During the Rebellion era, a group in this kind of campaign works for the Empire, doing everything in its power to crush the Rebellion and end the Galactic Civil War. If the campaign takes place after the fall of the Empire during the formative years of the New Republic, a dark side group might take the role of rebels working to restore the glory of the Emperor's New Order. Or they might be ex-Imperials seeking to carve out their own kingdom as infamous warlords or crime lords in the tradition of Zinj and Prince Xizor of Black Sun.

By the time of The New Jedi Order, evil campaigns can develop in a variety of intriguing new ways. The group could consist of rogue Jedi who have broken away from Luke Skywalker's leadership to follow a more active, darker path. They could be dark Force-users of no discernible tradition, using the confusion of the Yuuzhan Vong invasion to make their own place in the galaxy while the Jedi are too busy to try to stop them. Another option allows the group to side with the invaders, earning a profit while selling out the Republic and the Imperial Remnant. For something really different, you could allow the players to take on the roles of evil Yuuzhan Vong warriors and priests, letting them direct a portion of the invasion.

You might even decide to travel farther back into the *Star Wars* timeline. With a little work and a lot of imagination, a dark side campaign set in the time of the ancient Sith opens up a great many possibilities and provides a lot of freedom in the direction of the campaign's storyline. In the end, it all depends on what you want to run and what kinds of characters your players want to develop.

Beware the Dark Side

While we recommend that players run good or at least neutral characters, we know that the lure of the dark side is strong and persistent. Playing on the dark side provides too many temptations to assume players won't want to try it—at least for a change of pace.

Campaigns built around evil characters face a host of challenges that rarely disturb heroic campaigns. The biggest challenge relates to the players and how they develop their characters. Evil tends to be argumentative, divisive, and out for itself. This sometimes compels players to run their characters as selfish and distrustful, making it difficult to foster teamwork and cooperation. In the hands of a strong GM and good roleplayers, these kinds of characters can create compelling and powerful stories. More often, however, playing evil characters leads to arguments, hard feelings, and, in extreme circumstances, the eventual breakup of the gaming group. You and the players should seek some common ground and a focus for a party of evil characters. As long as the entire group benefits by working together for a shared goal, then the campaign should be able to sustain itself. Even so, at some point, the temptation to take advantage of the other characters may overwhelm an evil character. What happens then depends on the skills of the GM and the players. Will story and character development win out, or will the players be unable to overcome the deception and betrayal of the evil character?

The best way to approach a dark side campaign may be as a limited arc of adventures with a planned ending. This works especially well if you've never run this type of campaign before, or if your players have never created or developed evil characters. If everyone knows that the dark side campaign is an experiment with a finite life span, this makes it easier to walk away from if things go awry. If the campaign thrives and everyone enjoys approaching the game from this direction, you can always keep the campaign going. But if the players allow hard feelings from the game to influence friendships outside the game, then it's time to bring the dark side experiment to an end and return to the play style that works best for your group.

Stepping onto the Dark Path

So you've thought through the possible problems and conferred with your players. Everyone wants to give the dark side campaign a try. The first thing you, as the GM, need to do is determine the basis of the campaign. Talk to your players and let them give you their ideas. You might want to present a few options that you're comfortable with as a starting point to the discussion to help shape the campaign.

The Underworld Campaign

Do you want to explore the galaxy's underworld? The players can create characters who would fit in at Jabba's palace or within Prince Xizor's criminal

organization. In the underworld campaign, the player characters are criminals of one sort or another. Smugglers, thugs, pirates, outlaws, spice runners, bounty hunters, slicers, and other not-so-law-abiding citizens fall into this category.

The player characters start out working for (or trying to break into) a criminal organization. The organization may be as small as a neighborhood gang or as large as an intergalactic crime syndicate, but in the early adventures the heroes are definitely at the bottom of the food chain. Later, as the campaign develops, the heroes should be given a chance to rise within the organization or to find a more powerful group to join. One or two heroes might even want to add levels of crime lord or some other prestige class to eventually make a play for control of the organization.

In an underworld campaign, the chief adversaries for the heroes include rival criminal organizations and various law-enforcement agencies. The law can be local (such as the Corporate Sector Espos or a planetary constabulary) or galaxywide (such as Imperial or Republic inspectors and custom officials, or even Jedi Knights if the crime syndicate is particularly large and influential).

Player characters don't have to be full-fledged, Force-using darksiders in an underworld campaign.

In fact, this kind of evil campaign works best if only one or two players have Force-using characters, and it works just fine without any Force-users at all.

Examples of criminal organizations that player characters can join include Jabba the Hutt's operation, Prince Xizor's Black Sun crime syndicate, and crime lord Ploovo Two-For-One's gang. The GM can also create totally new underworld organizations—violent mercenaries who sell their services to credit-rich crime lords, bounty hunter guilds in the service of a mob boss, or pirate chiefs who run smuggling operations on the side.

The Imperial Campaign

What's it like on the other side of the Galactic Civil War? Let your players create characters devoted to the Emperor and his New Order and find out. In an Imperial campaign, the player characters are Imperial operatives of one sort or another. They start out as low-ranking soldiers or starship crewers who eventually prove their worth and gain the notice of a powerful Imperial officer or official. From that point on, with a moff or general or admiral as their patron, the heroes begin advancing through the ranks while doing their part to crush the Rebellion once and for all.

To give them mobility and the freedom to take on a variety of missions, the heroes might be a team of special operatives working for the Imperial Security Bureau (the ISB) or Imperial Intelligence. The group should have a variety of skills and classes, including nobles, soldiers, scouts, and scoundrels. As in the underworld campaign, no actual dark side Force-users are required for this campaign to run effectively. Indeed, the Empire consists of a mix of evil characters who knowingly promote tyranny and those who believe that the New Order is not only the legal government but the best hope for the galaxy. How each player decides his or her character views the situation depends on the depth to which the characters are immersed in the shadier doings of the Empire.

If characters in an Imperial campaign experiment with the dark side of the Force, they eventually come to the attention of the Emperor or one of his Force-using servants. Force-sensitive heroes in this campaign should decide early on if they want to keep their Force abilities secret (as so many Force-sensitive characters in the Rebellion era did) or if they want to demonstrate their powers in hopes of being noticed. After all, you can't gain prestige as an Emperor's Hand or Imperial inquisitor unless the Emperor sees you in action.

In an Imperial campaign, the heroes take on the Rebel Alliance. Finding Rebel bases, assassinating Rebel leaders, cutting off Rebel supply lines, locating Rebel cells and spy networks, encouraging Rebel sympathizers to change their allegiance, and promoting the tenets of the New Order all fall into the Imperial operative's purview. For a change of pace, Imperial operatives squelch alien uprisings, shake down underworld organizations, or deal with those within the Empire who have shown disloyalty to the Emperor or his chosen servants.

Missions usually come from a superior somewhere higher up in Imperial Command, though a team of special operatives might have the freedom to seek out their own assignments. Of course, failure usually means a loss of status—and, in some cases, death at the hands of a higher authority. If the heroes become too powerful or make one too many enemies among the moffs and senators, they might be targeted for elimination.

The Darksider Campaign

What might a group of Force-users dedicated to the dark side accomplish if set loose on the galaxy? That's the question you can explore in the darksider campaign. How this type of campaign develops depends on the era it's set in.

A campaign situated in the distant past, during the golden age of the Sith Empire, allows Sith characters to fully test the limits of the dark side without any interference from troublesome Jedi Knights. In fact, depending on when you set the campaign, the Sith Empire might not even know of the Old Republic yet—and vice versa. Adversaries are instead found among rival Sith as everyone seeks greater power and influence. With rivals to best and potential new minions to subjugate, the ancient Sith revel in their corruption. With luck and careful plotting, a hero may even gain the prestigious title of Sith Lord, carving out a piece of the Empire for his or her own. This could lead to a series of Sith Wars as the followers of the dark side seek to overthrow each other. Eventually, however, the Jedi discover that the dark side has tainted a portion of the galaxy, and they arrive to challenge their ancient enemies. Or, given the right series of events, perhaps a Sith player character learns the location of a new region of space ripe for conquest: a region called the Republic. Then the Hyperspace Wars can begin.

A campaign set during the Rise of the Empire era, as shown in *The Phantom Menace*, demands that the Sith path to power be closed to the player characters (unless you plan to deviate from the storyline in the films). Therefore, Force-users dedicated to the dark side must be minions of the Sith Lords or independent operatives seeking their own path to glory and power. They could be members of a separate dark side cult with a different tradition. They could be Force-users who were never recruited by the Jedi Order, or failed Jedi who turned their backs on the Code and their honor.

The corruption and confusion of this time, categorized by the slow, decaying death of the Republic, provides ample opportunity for a group of darksiders to form their own power base in a remote section of the galaxy. Of course, such a group will meet opposition from both the Jedi and the Sith at some point. Darth Sidious often used his apprentice, Darth Maul, to eliminate adversaries once they came to his attention.

A campaign set in the Rebellion era has some of the same elements as one that takes place during the Rise of the Empire. The difference is that the Emperor employs a number of darksiders during this period to help him maintain control of the galaxy and wipe out opposition. Whether the group has ties to the Prophets of the Dark Side, serves an Imperial inquisitor, or even receives training from the Emperor's dark adepts, there are plenty of assignments for Force-users loyal to the New Order. Note that few independent darksiders roam the galaxy during this era. The Emperor and his minions work exceedingly hard to destroy Force-users—or corrupt them into serving the Emperor.

Later, after the fall of the Empire, dark side player characters have a wealth of options. They might seek to return the Emperor to life or to avenge his death by destroying the New Republic. They might see an opportunity to take the Emperor's place as the ultimate evil in the galaxy, perhaps by locating the Emperor's secrets from vaults hidden across the galaxy. By the time of The New Jedi Order, Luke Skywalker has started to lose control over a faction of the Jedi Knights. Darksiders in this era might be former Jedi who break away from Skywalker and decide to follow the darker path to power. Either way, opposition comes from Jedi still loyal to the ideals of the light side, the New Republic, various crime syndicates that compete for the same spheres of power as the characters, and the Yuuzhan Vong invaders who want to destroy the abominable Force and its servants—no matter what path they follow.

Controlling the Dark Side

To help you avoid losing control of your campaign, it's important that you make sure the player characters know who they must answer to early in their careers. Certainly, as the heroes gain levels, they should be encouraged to grab power and authority as warranted. At low levels, however, it serves the campaign best if the group has a central figure or authority from which goals and assignments emanate. Underworld and Imperial campaigns provide built-in authority figures to draw upon. Members of a crime syndicate must expect to take direction from one of the crime lord's lieutenants or

even directly from the crime lord at higher levels. Imperial operatives, likewise, must follow the chain of command and handle whatever tasks are placed before them. The darksider campaign might prove problematic in this regard, unless you establish background to provide the group with an authority figure (such as the shadowy Darth Sidious if the group serves as minions of the Sith Lord during the Rise of the Empire era).

As long as you keep some level of authority over the group, you should be able to control the campaign. The moment the heroes break away from the central authority or find a way to put themselves in positions of authority, the freedom to openly compete among themselves can spell the end of the campaign. It all depends on your players and their personal objectives for the game.

In cases where the campaign lacks a central authority, opponents can serve to keep the dark side group functioning as a team. There's strength in numbers, and no dark side character wants to have to face the Rebellion or the Jedi Order alone. Self-preservation is as strong a motivation as wealth and power, especially among evil characters.

Every Dark Side Campaign Needs a Little Light

The dark side works best when contrasted against its antithesis—the light side. Just as good-aligned heroes require great villains to oppose them and make their adventures memorable and meaningful, so too does a group of dark side characters need great heroes to challenge them. The evil Darth Maul fought Jedi Knights Qui-Gon Jinn and Obi-Wan Kenobi to the death. The villainous Darth Vader eventually met his match in Luke Skywalker. In the same tradition, groups dedicated to the dark side must be opposed, hounded, and eventually confronted by worthy heroes. Otherwise, there's no tension or drama. Good roleplaying game adventures, like good stories, need drama and tension to make the challenges worthwhile.

Memorable opponents for dark side characters must be powerful and worthy of their hatred and respect. A group of good characters, such as a team of Rebel operatives in the tradition of Rogue Squadron, must start out more powerful than the players' dark side characters. This gives the dark side characters something to build toward—they seek to thwart the good characters in subtle ways until they are ready to confront them directly. The player characters should advance at a faster pace than their GM-controlled opponents do, so that at some point in the campaign the two groups can meet on more or less equal footing and determine the outcome of their long struggle.

In the case of a single good-aligned opponent, you want a character who stands head and shoulders above the player characters and has allies he or she can call on when the going gets tough. A high-level Rebel operative, bounty hunter, or Jedi Knight makes a worthy opponent for any dark side group. The single adversary must always maintain some advantage over the evil group so that he or she can challenge them in the eventual final battle. Let the single adversary remain one or two levels above the average level of the party throughout the campaign. You might want to create an even higher-level adversary if the evil party consists of mostly Force-users and their opponent doesn't have Force abilities.

Why have a good-aligned character or group serve as a nemesis for your evil heroes? Because in the *Star Wars* universe, good eventually triumphs over evil. It's your job as the GM to challenge the evil player characters and demonstrate how good manages to defeat evil every so often throughout the campaign. There must always be a real and tangible cost for choosing the dark path. This price takes the form of defeat at the hands of the champions of the light, as well as various societal pressures. The law eventually catches up with those who break it. In addition, those who follow evil never feel safe, never trust those around them, and never know from which direction the next betrayal will come. (The Emperor, for example, never anticipated that his loyal apprentice Darth Vader would turn on him. Vader betrayed the Emperor, and the Emperor paid the ultimate price for turning his back on his former servant.)

Evil player characters must be able to grow, advance, and succeed at some of their goals. They must be thwarted the rest of the time and suffer setbacks as good characters apply pressure and leverage against them. This should build up over a series of adventures until the evil heroes meet their nemesis in a final confrontation.

Ending a Dark Side Campaign

Eventually, even the best dark side campaign must come to an end. You should plan toward this ending so that you can show the cost of following the path of corruption. No matter what you intend, however, be prepared to make course corrections based on what the player characters accomplish over the course of the campaign.

Every dark side campaign has two possible endings. The heroes can turn away from the dark side and find redemption, or they can meet their nemesis in a final battle and go out in a blaze of glory. The details are up to you, but here are the basics for your grand conclusion.

Redemption

The story of Anakin Skywalker is a great example of a dark side campaign. In the end, he finds redemption and turns back to the light—saving himself, his son, and the galaxy in the process. One way to end a dark side campaign (or to evolve it into an ongoing campaign) is to allow the player characters to redeem themselves and turn away from the corrupt path.

Of course, this isn't something the Gamemaster can plan. Watch how the player characters develop in the course of the game and determine if they might eventually decide to oppose the evil plans of their superiors. In some cases, the evil plans may have been devised by the player characters, and then they'll need to have a change of heart and try to stop the terrible plot they've set in motion. Either way, as the final scenes of the climactic adventure unfold, the player characters change allegiance and actively work to stop whatever nefarious master plan they helped develop.

Redemption should not come cheaply. Betraying their former superiors and allies puts the heroes in deadly peril. To stop the ultimate plan often requires life-and-death choices as the heroes put their lives on the line. There might not be any conscious thought of personal redemption. Instead, the player characters simply want to foil the plan before more innocent lives are lost (or whatever terrible consequences are attached to the plan's outcome).

If the threat is great enough and the sacrifice is genuine and accomplished at great risk, you can determine that the heroes have redeemed themselves and turned away from the dark side. If their redemption doesn't end in death (which often happens in such situations), then reduce each character's Dark Side Point total to one less than half the character's Wisdom score. The threat of the dark side continues to loom over the characters, but for the time being they have found a way off the dark path. If you want to continue the campaign, it can now take on a more heroic style as the characters strive to keep the dark side in themselves at bay.

Examples of redeemed characters appear often in the *Star Wars* universe. Certainly Darth Vader/Anakin Skywalker demonstrates the character who finds redemption in a sacrifice that ends in death. Mara Jade defies the Emperor's last command to kill Luke Skywalker and redefines her own destiny. In the comic *Tales of the Jedi*, the fallen Jedi Ulic Qel-Droma eventually trains the next great Jedi Knight and also finds redemption in death.

Blaze of Glory

Another way to end a long-running dark side campaign involves making the characters pay for their crimes and evil ways. As in a book or movie, evil characters eventually reach a point where everyone

054

CONTROL, SENSE, AND ALTER

A Force-sensitive individual can train and become a Force-user if opportunity and desire combine. While different Force traditions handle training in different ways, all students eventually focus on the three aspects of understanding and manipulating the Force: Control, Sense, and Alter. These represent stages of learning, and only a select few ever truly master all three.

Control represents the Force as it relates to the individual Force-user. By learning Control, a Force-user can access her inner Force and better utilize and enhance her natural abilities. With Control, the Force-user can unleash the Force within herself to improve her battle skills and physical coordination, to defend herself against the Force when manipulated by opponents, to hide herself in a cloak of Force, and even heal herself with the living Force. At this stage of learning, the Force-user meditates and concentrates on her connection to the inner Force, becoming one in body and spirit with the Force inside her.

Sense represents a connection to the universal Force that binds everything together. By meditating on the eddies and currents of the Force, a Force-user learns to interpret each and every vagary of its restless flow. By expanding his consciousness into the currents, the Force-user becomes aware of other places, other times. He can feel others in the connection, whether they are bright beacons of Force concentration or those with only the normal, living ties to the Force that all things share. At this stage of learning, the Force-user gains the skills necessary to link to the Force around him and gather information as others simply see and hear.

Alter represents the ability to manipulate the Force around you. With the Alter-based skills, a Force-user can grip physical objects—living or not—in tentacles of energy. A Force-user learns to pluck the invisible lines of Force and send reverberations to others in the omnipresent mist that binds all things together. The Force-user can even manipulate the Force in more tangible ways, gathering it around herself to enhance leaps and bounds, or using it as a battering ram to knock others out of the way.

This stage of learning is a dangerous time for Force-users. While there are ways to use Control and Sense in a negative fashion, Alter can easily lead the Force-user to the dark side. It is through Alter that a Force-user learns to directly affect those around him, gaining the abilities to change others' thoughts and perceptions, to move them against their will, and to even injure or kill them with only the power of the Force. During this stage of learning, the dark side tries to seduce the Force-user, promising a quicker path to mastery, urging the Force-user to revel in the power that comes with being able to manipulate others and hold their very lives in his or her hand. Most temptations appear during this stage of learning, and it is a time when mentors and instructors work hardest to keep their students focused on the light side. ⁖

wants to stop their activities. When the forces of light finally corner the evil characters, the only choice left to those characters is to determine how they want the situation to end. In real life, surrender is the appropriate option, but in heroic fiction—and heroic roleplaying games—evil characters often go out in a blaze of glory.

Two scenarios come to mind for the blaze of glory climax. One has the evil characters choosing to run their ship into a sun or bringing about some other kind of spectacular doom. This way, they escape capture and determine their own ending. Alternatively, the evil characters draw their weapons and make a final stand against their enemies. For a roleplaying game, this is probably the most satisfying way to end an evil campaign. The battle should be exciting and complex, set against a unique backdrop, and full of special effects. In the end, the evil characters face death in a spectacular and memorable fashion—and may even wind up taking out one or two of their hated enemies along the way.

When the blaster fire clears, the evil characters have met with a spectacular and well-deserved end. The dark side experiment was a fun diversion. Now the GM and his or her players can return to a heroic campaign more in the tradition of Luke Skywalker and his companions.

Four Stages of the Dark Side

There are four stages that Force-users experience when stepping onto the dark path: Temptation, imperilment, submission, and atonement or redemption. Every Force-user eventually goes through at least one stage of the dark side in his efforts to become one with the Force. It is the power-hungry, hate-filled, ambitious, tragic, or evil character, however, who experiences two or more of these stages of corruption. Anakin Skywalker, for example, went through each of these stages over the course of his life, finally achieving redemption with the help of his son, Luke Skywalker.

The Gamemaster can use these stages in various ways. Obviously, for characters committed to walking the dark path, these stages provide vital adventure and campaign ideas for helping the characters on their way. In more traditional campaigns, these stages provide opportunities for testing Force-using characters, to gauge their commitment to the Jedi Code or their own sense of morality. Both Anakin and Luke often faced the temptations of the dark side, but each took a very different path. Anakin, obviously, gave in to the siren call and embraced his anger and hatred. Luke, on the other hand, struggled to keep off the dark path and eventually managed to defeat the darkness and redeem his father. What stories will you tell? That's up to you and your players, but remember that nothing accentuates the heroic like a good dose of evil's urgings and dark whispers.

Temptation

The Force offers unimaginable powers to those who can feel its connection to the galaxy around them and manipulate its subtle lines of energy. Those who are sensitive to the Force live in a larger, more vibrant galaxy than those who can't perceive the omnipresent energy field. The Force-sensitive character sees and experiences the universe from a different, larger perspective. Because of this bond, the Force-sensitive character has the ability to gain incredible powers using the Force—but also risks the untold dangers of the dark side.

Through the Sense, Control, and especially Alter stages of learning to manipulate the Force, a character opens himself to the first seductive tendrils of dark side power. While any character must be careful of temptation, those who believe that might makes right or that shoot first and ask questions later are particularly susceptible to the lure of the dark side. If a character prefers to act instead of wait, to give in to fear and anger, to proceed from an aggressive posture instead of a passive one, that character must be wary of attracting the dark side.

Force-sensitive characters with no Dark Side Points, as well as characters with points equal to half their Wisdom score, are susceptible to the temptations of the dark side. As the Gamemaster, you should feel obliged to ask a player every so often if his character wants to call upon the dark side. "This task sounds pretty tough," you might say. "Do you want to call on the dark side for a little extra boost?" Don't overstate the point, and certainly don't try to trick the player, but it isn't unfair for you to sometimes remind the player of the various options available to the heroes.

The dark side is quick to join a Force-user in a fight, offering skills especially suited for injuring or even killing an opponent. At lower levels, who wouldn't at least consider calling upon the dark side when spending a Force Point in order to get a bigger boost? In a situation where the hero feels that he must succeed, then the benefit of the dark side might seem to outweigh the negative aspects—at least for a while.

It's up to the Gamemaster to present ethical dilemmas and situations in which the hero has to make a hard decision—whether or not to call upon the dark side or use a Force skill in such a way as to gain a Dark Side Point. The first steps onto the path of corruption are easy. One or two Dark Side Points don't mean very much, so most characters can easily ignore the taint they provide. The trouble is that

once a hero gets used to calling on and using the dark side, it's hard to stop. The player gets used to his character succeeding, and to suddenly have to give up an edge can be frustrating. Therein lies the lure and danger of the dark side.

The trick for the GM is to set up situations that involve these ethical dilemmas in such a way as to not make them stand out. It's easy for a hero to avoid an obvious ethical trap; make it harder by incorporating such situations into the normal course of play. For example, set up situations that demand that the heroes contemplate their options. Should they kill the prisoners? Doing so may be the most expedient option, but it probably isn't the most ethical one. Should the hero use violence to solve a problem, or should the hero seek a more peaceful solution—such as discussion and negotiation—first?

Of course, there are other ways to present ethical dilemmas. Here are a few options to consider when setting up your adventures:

- ➔ Present the heroes with two choices that clearly fall into that gray realm between good and evil, perhaps having both lean a little closer to the evil side. In such cases, how the heroes handle the situation and whether or not they decide to accept the lesser of the two evils firmly places them on the shaky ground of the dark side. For example, the heroes must cut a deal to save themselves. Do they make the deal with the Imperials or with the Hutt crime lord? Neither choice is a clear winner, but how they approach their choice can help you determine whether or not a Dark Side Point is warranted.

- ➔ Make the heroes choose between acting and waiting. In most cases, heroes want to act first and figure out the details later. This can easily lead a character down the path to corruption if the impulse to attack is clearly the wrong way to go. That menacing-looking alien, for example, might wind up being an innocent bystander and not the thug the hero was sent to find, so cutting him down with a lightsaber before determining his identity means that innocent blood has been shed.

- ➔ Sometimes the heroes need help, and sometimes the best help comes from an evil crime lord. Do the ends justify the means? Should a hero use evil to battle evil? If the character believes in this method, then he or she probably has no problem calling on the dark side every once and a while.

- ➔ Another type of dilemma revolves around manipulation. The hero might be put into a no-win situation by an authority figure. If the hero trusts that figure, or believes that the figure is good and just, then the hero might be willing to perform an evil action in what he feels is the cause of goodness. A well-respected Senator who happens to really be the epitome of evil can easily manipulate a hero who trusts him.

Imperilment

A Force-user who has allowed the dark side into her life may eventually gain enough Dark Side Points to reach the brink of total corruption. Such a character has already become tainted and is a failed saving throw or a single Dark Side Point away from becoming a dark character. In most cases, this character has accepted the dark side of the Force as a means to power and probably isn't too concerned about taking that next, fateful step. Some heroes, however, will struggle not to give in, to walk that razor's edge and maintain at least some semblance of remaining in the light. These are the heroes who constantly weigh the moral consequences, who obsess about doing the right thing no matter what the personal cost may be. To these characters, the dark side presents another weapon in their arsenal against evil, regardless of the fact that each use pushes them closer and closer to the very evil they hope to oppose. Eventually, the dark side will consume them; the path to corruption is paved with good intentions.

For such an imperiled character, the Gamemaster sometimes must act as the character's conscience by asking the questions that should be in the imperiled character's mind. Do you want to call upon the dark side in this situation? What are the pros and cons of using the Force in this manner? The GM should also feel free to warn the character: "That action will earn you a Dark Side Point." The hero, of course, is free to ignore the troubling voice of conscience, but it should be an active voice throughout the period of imperilment.

During this part of a campaign, the GM is encouraged to employ Gamemaster characters to drive home the perilous situation the tainted hero has gotten into. Present a dark character as an example of what awaits the hero. This dark character might be an adversary of the hero, or perhaps an associate trying to lure the hero deeper into corruption. The dark character provides someone for the hero to measure against. It's still up to the hero's player whether or not the hero completes the journey to the dark side, but it's up to the GM to provide guideposts along the way.

Another option allows a GM character from the hero's past to reappear. Nothing demonstrates the depths to which a hero has fallen than to see herself through another's eyes. The GM character knows the hero from happier times and is genuinely dismayed by the hero's new outlook. This character can be a family member, an old friend, a mentor—someone who knew the hero well and whose opinion the hero once held in high esteem.

You might also provide an innocent to play the tainted hero's march to darkness off of—a student or an apprentice. The hero will often be forced to reprimand the student, encouraging the student to "Do as I say, not as I do." This situation can lead to all sorts of meaty debates and arguments about the nature of the Force and each character's place therein. Through the words of the student, the GM can ask the hero to explain her actions, to justify her journey to the dark side. If you want to approach the hero from the other direction, and if you have an authority figure to which the hero is responsible (such as the Jedi Council or Alliance High Command), you can have the hero report in to her superiors and discuss her actions with them. None of these devices should be used to necessarily discourage the hero from following the dark path, but instead to make sure the hero at least considers her actions and beliefs.

Throughout the imperilment stage, a character might be interested in playing the angles. Using Force Points to maintain a certain level of Dark Side Points can be a losing proposition in the long run, but for a while it can allow a tainted hero to stave off full darkness.

Submission

When a hero gives himself over to the dark side and becomes a dark character, suddenly the rules change. From the dark character's point of view, there are no more restrictions, no more dangers to worry about. In a way, it can be liberating and exhilarating to give one's self fully to the dark side. You obviously don't have to worry about getting any more Dark Side Points, at least from a certain point of view. The dark hero does have to watch out for the corruption of his physical body, as represented by the loss of Strength, Dexterity, or Constitution points with each level increase.

The character who submits to the dark side has a hard time remaining with a group of good heroes. Eventually, the dark character's true nature becomes apparent and he is forced to battle his onetime friends and companions. More than likely, the dark character leaves to pursue his own agenda, sometimes returning to come in conflict with the heroes or to work beside them to accomplish a mission that benefits both parties.

Once the dark character accepts the corrupt path, there is no longer any need to justify actions. Now power becomes the admitted goal, and through the use of the dark side all obstacles can be pushed aside. Forget past attachments and former codes of conduct. Now the dark character considers himself a law unto himself, and life is considered to have begun when the character submitted fully to the darkness inside him. This is the character who can become the

major villain of the campaign or a catalyst for dark changes in the universe.

Darth Vader, for example, no longer cares what his past masters think, and he obviously has forgotten those parts of his past life that focused on the good man he used to be. He is literally reborn in the dark side, a personification of darkness and evil. So, too, should the dark hero in your campaign shun her past in favor of a dark future. The dark hero isn't impetuous or misunderstood or misguided. The dark hero is evil, pure and simple.

Of course, even a character like Darth Vader had a chance at redemption. If the player and GM want to explore paths back from the dark side, then they have to consider methods for redemption, since atoning is not available to them.

Atonement and Redemption

In many cases, the dark hero doesn't want or need the help of the other player characters. Indeed, the dark hero has no desire to give up the power of the dark side and return to the light—at least not at any conscious level. Darth Vader actively worked against Luke Skywalker's efforts to redeem him, going so far as to help the Emperor's attempt to turn Luke to the dark side. This same kind of struggle probably occupies the characters in your campaign. Even so, while the dark hero may feel this way, the dark hero's player might want to work with the other players and the Gamemaster to find a way to bring the character back to the light.

A tainted character can atone, spending Force Points to reduce the number of Dark Side Points he possesses. For each Force Point sacrificed in this manner, the tainted hero reduces his Dark Side Point total by 1. This represents a period of meditation, reflection, and absolution on the part of the character.

A dark character can't atone. He must find redemption by turning away from the dark side and performing an act of dramatic heroism without calling upon the dark side of the Force. This act requires extreme personal cost and must be made in a selfless manner, thus providing a significant benefit to the galactic balance. This act does not gain the character a Force Point.

If the dark hero finds redemption (and doesn't die in the attempt), then his Dark Side Point total is reduced to one less than half his Wisdom score. He has been redeemed, but the threat of the dark side continues to loom until he also atones (to further reduce his Dark Side Point total). A dark hero who finds redemption must "trade in" levels of dark side prestige classes for levels of Force adept, Jedi consular, or Jedi guardian on a one-for-one basis. This must be done at the time of redemption to show that the character is committed to returning to the light.

Chapter Four: Dark Side Equipment

While the Force makes a powerful ally—and the dark side a vicious one—no dark side devotee relies entirely on the Force alone. Arms, armor, transports, poisons, and even droids can be tainted in some fashion by the power of the dark side, lending a wicked edge to the abilities of anyone trained in their use. More powerful still, ancient relics of long-forgotten origin can amplify the abilities of their wielders—while drawing the unwary deeper into the dark side with promises of power.

Obtaining Dark Side Equipment

Those who wish to buy or sell equipment tainted by the dark side should tread cautiously. Dealing in such items is frequently illegal (due to the lethality of the items). Potential buyers are often not inclined to pay full price, preferring instead to simply take what they want from the weak and ill-prepared. Sellers of these commodities generally conduct business under heavy guard in places where the authorities are either unable or afraid to go.

For each of the items described below, a note indicates which eras they can be acquired in, either by sale or manufacture. Prior to the era listed, an item might exist in prototype form (at the Gamemaster's discretion), but it won't function precisely as listed. Such an item should have quirks that make it unreliable at best—if not outright dangerous. In later eras, the same item becomes an antique. Perhaps it retains some potency, but it is also so rare and valuable as to be traded only among collectors, and never on the open market. Certainly, such antiques are no longer manufactured anywhere in the galaxy.

Weapon and Armor Descriptions

The Sith and other followers of the dark side have, over the centuries, devised, built, and used a wide range of deadly weapons. All are difficult to master, but extremely deadly in the hands of an expert.

Lanvarok

The Sith lanvarok is a short-range weapon worn on the forearm and designed to hurl a flurry of thin but solid disks in an unpredictable "spray" pattern. Though the weapon is time-consuming to reload, the surprise factor of a sudden hail of whirling projectiles often leaves an opponent completely unprepared for the Sith's follow-up attack. Coupled with the Sith's ability to wield the Force to guide the disks to their target, the lanvarok is an extremely effective weapon.

Because of the way the disks fan out upon being launched, the lanvarok gains a +1 equipment bonus on attacks made at 10 meters or less. A Force-user with the Alter feat can extend this bonus to the weapon's full range. Reloading the lanvarok requires a full-round action. The weapon is specifically designed for either the right or left forearm. Any given lanvarok is not interchangeable from right to left.

According to Sith legend, the lanvarok was developed by the ancient Sith as a hunting weapon. Details of its construction can be found in Sith holocrons. The mutated Massassi of Yavin 4 used a more primitive version of this weapon, a two-handed polearm that required brute strength rather than mechanical action or the Force to launch the disks. After its disks are launched, the polearm itself could be used as a slashing weapon.

Era Notes: After the rise of Darth Bane and the New Sith, the lanvarok falls out of use and becomes harder and harder to find. Examples remaining from ancient times are usually sold as collector's items, although a rare Sith holocron could provide schematics for initiates devoted enough to build one.

Lightsaber, Double-Bladed

The Sith-invented double-bladed lightsaber maximizes the potential of the weapon and provides an added surprise in battles against Jedi Knights. The double-bladed lightsaber can be ignited from either end or both ends simultaneously. On some models,

Table 4-1: Weapons

Weapon	Cost	Damage	Critical	Range Increment	Weight	Stun Damage /Fort DC	Type	Size	Group
Lanvarok, Sith	4,000	3d4	20	10m	5.8 kg	—	Bludgeon	Medium	Exotic
Lanvarok, Massassi	250	3d4	20	5m	9.8 kg	—	Bludgeon	Large	Exotic
(as polearm)		2d8	19–20	—	same	—	Slashing	Large	Primitive
Lightsaber, double	7,000	2d8/2d8	19–20	—	2 kg	—	Energy	Medium	Exotic
Sith sword	6,000	2d6	19–20	—	6.5 kg	—	Slashing	Large	Exotic

the handle can be disconnected at the middle to become two separate weapons.

Sith double-bladed lightsabers are impossible to find on the open market. When a Sith constructs a double-bladed lightsaber, he does not do so for profit. The weapon is for his own use, and Sith rarely lose their weapons. The construction process resembles the process for creating a Jedi's lightsaber, but requires plans available—from the time of the Old Republic and afterward—only in Sith holocrons.

Despite this limitation, a few double-bladed lightsabers exist in the galaxy, apparently created by Jedi as experiments. The Jedi Council disapproves of such experiments, though, noting that the only reason to carry such a weapon is to kill more effectively. Jedi who have become lost to the dark side, obviously, care nothing for the concerns of the Jedi Council.

With only one blade ignited, this variety of lightsaber requires the Exotic Weapon Proficiency (lightsaber) feat to use without suffering the usual –4 penalty on attacks. With both blades ignited, the double-bladed lightsaber becomes a sort of lightsaber staff. While the Exotic Weapon Proficiency (lightsaber) feat suffices to wield it, a character with this feat effectively uses it just like a lightsaber, dealing 2d8 damage (plus class and level modifiers).

To be truly effective as a double weapon—that is, to gain the extra attack for additional damage—the wielder must also possess the Two-Weapon Fighting feat. The table below duplicates the relevant information from page 138 of the *Star Wars Roleplaying Game* as it applies to the double-bladed lightsaber:

Circumstances	Single Blade	Double Blade
Two lightsabers	–6	–10
Lightsaber and light weapon or double-bladed lightsaber	–4	–8
Double-bladed lightsaber and Ambidexterity feat	–4	–4
Double-bladed lightsaber and Two-Weapon Fighting feat	–2	–6
Double-bladed lightsaber and Ambidexterity feat and Two-Weapon Fighting feat	–2	–2

A double-bladed lightsaber requires two special energy cells to operate. The cost of each cell is ten times that of an ordinary energy cell.

Era Notes: Double-bladed lightsabers, like Jedi lightsabers, must be taken from their creators, discovered at ancient sites, or created using plans found only in rare Sith holocrons. They can never be purchased on the open market.

MASSASSI LANVAROK

SITH SWORD

DOUBLE-BLADED LIGHTSABER

SITH LANVAROK AND DISC

Sith Sword

An alchemically altered blade attached to an ordinary sword hilt, the Sith sword was often a match for a lightsaber when wielded by a trained Sith warrior. The alterations allow the blade to deflect blaster bolts and lightsabers, just as lightsabers themselves do. The blade also focuses the Force energy of the user, giving the edge an unnatural sharpness. As the wielder grows more proficient in the power of the dark side, the blade becomes more deadly.

To simulate this, when a dark side character who wields a Sith sword calls upon the dark side of the Force, he may choose to add his dark side bonus dice to the sword's damage, rather than adding it to his attack roll with the weapon. The damage bonus lasts for 10 rounds + 1 round per Force level of the wielder. (This bonus cannot be added to any other rolls during that time, such as attack rolls or skill rolls.)

In addition, Sith swords are effective against lightsabers because of the way their alchemically altered metal refracts the lightsaber's energy. Sith swords retain their hardness against attacks from lightsabers, instead of having it reduced to 0 as with ordinary weapons. (See the Lightsabers and Hardness sidebar on page 117 of the *Star Wars Roleplaying Game*.) Sith swords do not require power packs or energy cells.

Era Notes: During the Golden Age of the Sith, these weapons were only available in areas of space controlled by the Sith. After this time, they become available in the rest of the galaxy as rarely seen relics of a dead civilization.

Dark Armor

Those who fall to the dark side know that their greatest enemies will be Jedi. Any given Jedi might be a match for the darksider, so to tip the scales of battle, the darksider needs an edge—a way to withstand damage better than his Jedi opponent can. For many, armor provides the best advantage.

Dark armor is nearly always created to meet the specific needs of the wearer. The material and design varies from wearer to wearer. Some suits are crude and heavy, while others are elegant and light. A few seem almost decorative. Almost all of them are alchemically treated during their construction to achieve certain effects desired by the wearer, from additional protection against blasters and lightsabers to extra resistance against certain forms of attack.

Dark armor is never simply found; those who wear it almost always take it with them to the grave. It is often destroyed when they are. The Gamemaster should only allow characters to find dark armor in ancient burial vaults, or at least require them to loot it from the bodies of vanquished foes. In either case, taking the armor should not be a simple task. Burial vaults have traps and guards, and the foe should have been enough of a challenge to make the acquisition of his armor a difficult proposition. Alternatively, though, the GM may allow characters to construct their own dark armor (see sidebar).

Creating Dark Armor

Characters who have begun the journey to the dark side may wish to construct their own dark armor. This requires the Craft (armor) skill, though some other skills are needed to create certain components the character may desire to incorporate (see below). The character chooses one of the armor types listed on Table 7–3: Armor in the *Star Wars Roleplaying Game* as the basis for his or her dark armor, then creates that armor using the Craft rules (as described on pages 72–73 of the rulebook). Additional features can then be chosen from the table below (or designed with the cooperation of the GM) and constructed using the rules in this section. Many suits of dark armor also incorporate ordinary technological devices, such as breath masks, comlinks, and motion sensors; these can all be installed after the armor has been constructed and modified.

Cortosis Weave: This substance is made using the Craft skill rules in the *Star Wars Roleplaying Game,* Chapter 4: Skills. A character decides whether to incorporate Cortosis weave into armor when he begins crafting it. (This modification cannot be added to a completed suit of armor.) This increases the cost of the armor by 15,000 credits and adds 5,000 credits to the cost of raw materials. The character then makes a Craft roll for each week of work; on a failed roll, half of the raw materials—including the materials for the original armor—are ruined and must be replaced.

Damage Reduction: A character cannot add damage reduction to a completed suit of armor. He must decide whether to incorporate it when he begins crafting the armor. The price of materials on Table 4–2 doesn't add to the work-value of the suit of armor. Instead, after building the suit of armor, the character buys 10,000 credits (for damage resistance 5) or 25,000 credits (for damage resistance 10) of alchemical materials and makes a final Alchemy check. This last Alchemy check represents one week of work; on a failed roll, half of the materials are ruined—including those used in the original suit of armor—and must be replaced.

Special Price: Some dark armor special qualities have a special price: They require dark side energy.

Table 4-2: Dark Armor Special Qualities

Special Quality	Effect	Price	Skill, DC
Cortosis weave	Deactivates any lightsaber that damages the wearer	15,000	Craft (armor)*, DC 25
Damage reduction 5	Not cumulative with other DR	10,000	Alchemy, DC 20
Damage reduction 10	Not cumulative with other DR	25,000	Alchemy, DC 30
Dark side energy	+2 Force bonus on saves against light side Force powers or any Force power augmented by a light side Force Point	Special	Alchemy, DC 20
Dark side stealth	+2 equipment bonus on saves against See Force and Telepathy	Special	Alchemy, DC 25
Increased might	+2 Force bonus to Strength	Special	Alchemy, DC 25

*Originally, cortosis alloys were only possible through the Alchemy skill, and in Old Republic era campaigns the GM might rule that the skill check should be Alchemy rather than Craft (armor). But since the Rise of the Empire, various technicians have unraveled the exceedingly arduous methods by which cortosis fibers can be woven into certain alloys, though the process is still extremely expensive and time-consuming.

To add these features, the character forging the dark armor spends 1 Force Point and makes an Alchemy check against the DC given on Table 4-2. This represents one week of meditation and arcane alchemical processes; on a failed roll, the raw materials aren't ruined, but the Force Point is still lost.

Examples of Dark Armor

Some examples of dark armor are described below.

Dark Combat Jumpsuit: Worn by the ancient Sith warrior Larad Noon, this heavily padded jumpsuit incorporated Cortosis weave that wreaked havoc with any lightsaber audacious enough to slice into it. Its +5 defense bonus was augmented with dark side stealth, providing Larad Noon with a +2 equipment bonus on saves made against See Force and Telepathy. The total cost for this suit of dark armor was 16,500 credits and 1 Force Point.

Dark Padded Battle Armor: Worn and crafted by the dark side marauder Kaox Krul around the time of the Battle of Ruusan, its protective padding and composite plates provided a defense bonus of +6 and damage reduction 5. The armor was also imbued with dark side energy, granting a +2 Force bonus on saves made against light side Force powers or any Force power augmented by a light side Force Point. The total cost for this suit of dark armor was 12,000 credits and 1 Force Point.

Dark Heavy Battle Armor: Worn and crafted by the fearsome Belia Darzu—one of the Sith Lords who kept the Sith cult alive before the Battle of Ruusan—this heavily plated armor provided a defense bonus of +9 and damage reduction 10. Darzu also imbued her armor with dark side stealth to keep her hidden (+2 equipment bonus on saves made against See Force and Telepathy) and increased might (+2 Force bonus to Strength) to boost her physical power. The total cost for this suit of dark armor was 37,000 credits and 2 Force Points.

Vehicles and Starships

During the time of the Old Republic, most Sith vehicles were built around ancient schematics stored in Sith holocrons (see below) by the Sith themselves. A few were constructed by well-paid manufacturers who worked from blueprints delivered—and later collected, along with any copies—by dark, mysterious figures whose will could not be denied. Many of those who worked on such ships later suffered from terrible nightmares, and many died under mysterious circumstances.

Sith Speeder

The small, fast, Sith speeder personal transport carries a lightsaber-wielding warrior into battle. It utilizes a high-acceleration repulsorlift engine that allows it to reach punishing speeds and take corners with frightening ease. (The rider receives a +4 equipment bonus on Pilot checks for Turn, Extreme Turn, and Bootlegger Turn maneuvers.)

It possesses no particular sensor systems, since the Sith generally prefer to rely on the Force to warn them of approaching dangers. Similarly, not all Sith speeders possess weaponry. While the speeder can mount blaster cannons, many Sith prefer to rely on their lightsabers and personal skills when going into battle.

Before the coming of Darth Bane, the Sith were infamous for decorating their speeders with mystic Sith runes and grisly trophies of past victories. Sith gave their speeders suitably intimidating names, usually those of predators with which the riders identified. Darth Maul's speeder was named *Bloodfin*, after a particularly vicious aquatic hunter Maul had encountered on a storm-shrouded ocean world of the Outer Rim.

The controls for Maul's speeder also included a "safe release" system. If Maul released the handlebars for any reason, the speeder immediately slowed, reducing speed by half each round until Maul retrieved the grips. This enabled him to avoid violent crashes if he was stunned while piloting the vehicle. If he had to leap off the vehicle, he could easily retrieve it later. (This feature gives the rider a +2 equipment bonus on Pilot checks for Regain Control maneuvers.)

Sith Speeder

Craft: Scratch-built custom speeder bike; **Class:** Ground (Speeder); **Cost:** 8,000 (new), 2,500 (used); **Size:** Medium (2.15 m long); **Crew:** Varies (1 pilot); **Passengers:** None; **Cargo Capacity:** 2 kilograms; **Speed:** 210 m (max. speed 650 km/h); **Altitude:** up to 15 meters; **Defense:** 13 (+3 armor); **Hull Points:** 18; **DR:** 5.

Weapons: None.

Sith Infiltrator

Built from heavily modified designs based on the Republic Sienar Systems' Star Courier, the Sith Infiltrator is a long-range reconnaissance ship built specifically to carry the influence of Darth Sidious to the far-flung worlds of the Old Republic. Sidious had the Infiltrator, dubbed *Scimitar*, constructed for his apprentice Darth Maul, so that Maul could travel undetected to and from Coruscant on errands for his Sith Master.

Although the ship is a completely new design (of which Sienar Systems claims complete ignorance), it actually carries on a long-standing Sith tradition of small, virtually undetectable ships used by the Sith during their thousand years of hiding. Many mysterious hyperspace accidents that coincidentally claimed the lives of Jedi can no doubt be attributed to Sith Infiltrators.

The extremely effective—and shockingly expensive—stygium crystal cloaking device built into *Scimitar's* fuselage enables the ship to come and go without interference. This is a vital necessity for Maul and Sidious, who both have constant business on Coruscant. The cloak—more powerful than ordinary Republic cloaking devices—makes *Scimitar* impossible to detect from longer than medium range using sensors, conferring a –10 penalty on Spot, Listen, Search, and Computer Use checks made to find it. Even if the ship is successfully located, its indistinct lines mean that any successful attack still has a 40% miss chance, as though the ship were always nine-tenths concealed.

Where others are blind to Maul's ship, *Scimitar* is more than adequately equipped to detect theirs. *Scimitar* boasts a state-of-the-art tracking system (providing a +4 equipment bonus on Computer Use checks to detect or monitor objects). The ship also possesses an experimental sublight ion drive that, despite requiring extremely large radiator panels to

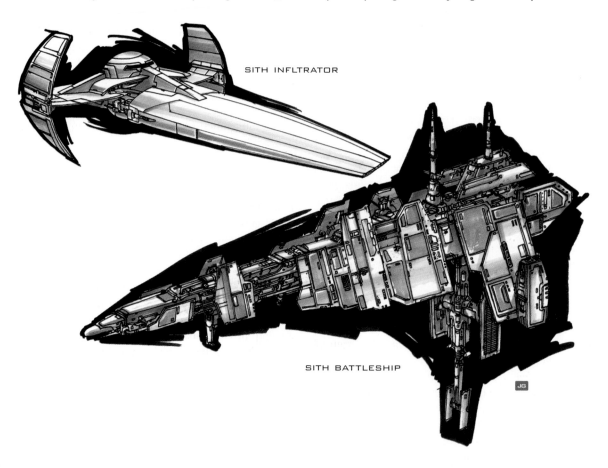

SITH INFLTRATOR

SITH BATTLESHIP

JG

vent excess heat, makes *Scimitar* faster and more maneuverable than any ship of a comparable class, and even many starfighters.

In addition to enough provisions to keep Maul (and up to six passengers—or captives) alive for a short jaunt through hyperspace, *Scimitar* features equipment a Sith Lord might need in the pursuit of his duty: bombs, mines, poisons, drugs, caustic chemicals, weapons, survival gear, implements of torture, a trio of Dark Eye probe droids, and Maul's Sith speeder. The ship also includes an escape pod—though Maul's vanished under unknown circumstances between the time he left Coruscant for Tatooine and the moment his ship was recovered by the Republic authorities on Naboo after his death.

Sith Infiltrator

Craft: Heavily modified Republic Sienar Systems Star Courier; **Class:** Space transport; **Cost:** Not available for sale; **Size:** Small (26.5 m long); **Initiative:** +5 (+1 size, +4 crew); **Crew:** 1 (Skilled +4); **Passengers:** 6; **Cargo Capacity:** 2.5 metric tons; **Consumables:** 30 days; **Hyperdrive:** ×1.5 (backup ×12); **Maximum Speed:** Ramming; **Maneuver:** +5 (+1 size, +4 crew); **Defense:** 21 (+1 size, +10 armor); **Shield Points:** 60; **Hull Points:** 90; **DR:** 5.

Weapon: 6 light laser cannons (fire-linked); **Fire Arc:** Front; **Attack Bonus:** +7 (+1 size, +6 fire control); **Damage:** 3d10×5; **Range Modifiers:** PB +0, S −2, M/L n/a.

Sith Battleship

While the Sith after Darth Bane stressed stealth and secrecy, the ancient Sith challenged the Old Republic in a war that carried the Sith armada to Coruscant itself. This armada consisted primarily of troopships and the Sith battleship, a massive, heavily armored strike cruiser built to withstand the best the Republic could throw at it. Though the Sith were ultimately defeated and only one battleship escaped (eventually resurfacing on Yavin 4), for a short time Sith battleships were the most fearsome power in the galaxy.

Though fairly small, slow, and ungainly by modern galactic standards, the Sith battleship was capable of inflicting heavy damage from its two rows of blaster cannons and its close-range concussion missile launchers. The heavy armor plating on the battleship's hull also meant that the Old Republic fleet had to bring to bear the guns of at least a half-dozen of their own ships against a battleship to bring it down. Even then, the Sith could expect to cripple or destroy at least one of their enemy's ships.

The Sith Empire turned out about one hundred battleships prior to the invasion of the Republic. All were destroyed before the end of the war, except for the Sith flagship under the command of Sith Lord

Naga Sadow. Sadow sacrificed his fleet to escape the Republic's counterattack. His ship lay hidden beneath a massive temple on Yavin 4 for a thousand years. Former Jedi Exar Kun, having turned to the dark side, arrived to take possession of Sadow's long-forgotten refuge. Exar Kun eventually used Sadow's flagship to escape Yavin 4 and wage war on the Jedi Order.

Sith Battleship

Craft: Sith battle cruiser; **Class:** Capital; **Cost:** Not available for sale; **Size:** Large (215 m long); **Initiative:** +3 (−1 size, +4 crew); **Crew:** 25 (Skilled +4); **Passengers:** 850; **Cargo Capacity:** 5,000 metric tons; **Consumables:** 1 year; **Hyperdrive:** ×4 (backup ×12); **Maximum Speed:** Cruising (maneuverability −2); **Maneuver:** +1 (−1 size, +4 crew, −2 engines); **Defense:** 23 (−1 size, +14 armor); **Shield Points:** none; **Hull Points:** 420; **DR:** 20.

Weapon: 6 blaster cannons; **Fire Arc:** 3 left, 3 right; **Attack Bonus:** +2 (−1 size, +3 fire control); **Damage:** 4d10×2; **Range Modifiers:** PB +0, S −2, M/L n/a.

Weapon: 3 concussion missile launchers; **Fire Arc:** Front; **Attack Bonus:** +0 (−1 size, +1 fire control); **Damage:** 8d10×2; **Range Modifiers:** PB +1, S/M/L n/a.

Droids

While not even the Sith could imbue droids with the power of the dark side, they could certainly create automatons to aid them in their vile work. The most simplistic dark side droids are merely spies: mechanicals designed to seek out targets. More sinister are those droids programmed to inflict suffering at the command of their controller, either for interrogation or for a Dark Lord's amusement.

Interrogator Droid, Mark III

Although in frequent use among the Emperor's Inquisitors (and on occasion by Darth Vader himself), the IT-0 Interrogator droid was originally devised by the ancient Sith as a means of torturing prisoners—though not necessarily for information. The IT-3, a newer, more refined model, saw more use late in the Rebellion era, and was especially popular with Ysanne Isard, the Emperor's former Director of Imperial Intelligence. During the New Republic era, she was the guiding force for what was left of the Empire.

Like the IT-0 upon which it was based, the IT-3 Interrogator droid is a half-meter sphere of black durite bristling with instruments of torture. The IT-3 improves upon its predecessors by incorporating more manipulators and injectors and sports a much glossier shine—presumably so that victims can see in their reflections what precisely is being done to them.

064

The IT-3's equipment includes a laser scalpel, three sets of power shears, a sonic warbler, an electroshock probe, and a trio of long hypodermic syringes on extendable tool mounts. The syringes are filled from internal reservoirs with a variety of truth agents and stimulants. An additional syringe, normally kept enclosed within a hidden compartment, contains Sith poison (see below), the source of which is unknown.

Unlike its predecessors, the IT-3 can and does speak Basic—in a pleasant, mothering tone. The designers who made this modification believed that an interrogation droid that spoke soothingly to its victim—even as it did its grisly work—would be far more unnerving than one that remained absolutely silent. Sources inside the design laboratory said that they had actually grown queasy listening to the prototype calmly negotiating with its victims for the severity of their injuries.

Thankfully, most of the IT-3s were dismantled when Coruscant was liberated from the Empire.

IT-3 Series: Hovering interrogation droid, Expert 5; Init −1; Defense 11 (+1 class, +1 size, −1 Dex); Spd 4m; VP/WP 0/8; Atk +3 melee (1d3−1, claw; or 2d6, power shears; or 2d4, laser scalpel; or 1d2, hypodermic needle; or 2d6, electroshock probe), +2 ranged; SV Fort +0, Ref +0, Will +6; SZ S; Rep 0; Str 8, Dex 8, Con 8, Int 10, Wis 14, Cha 14. Challenge Code: C.

Equipment: Sonic torture device, electroshock probe, syringes (4), tool mounts (6), telescopic appendage (3), recording unit (video), locked access, Sith poison.

Skills: Diplomacy +9, Knowledge (Life sciences [biology]) +8, Knowledge (Physical sciences [chemistry]) +8, Knowledge (Scholar [psychology]) +8, Sense Motive +9, Speak Basic, Treat Injury +10.

Unspent Skill Points: 0.

Feats: Skill Emphasis (Diplomacy), Skill Emphasis (Sense Motive).

Cost: Restricted to Imperial use only.

Sith Probe Droid

Constructed from schematics provided in ancient Sith holocrons, Sith probe droids are silent, effective stalking machines designed to quickly locate targets using parameters programmed by their master. When desired, these droids can also be fitted with weapons, though most Sith are loath to do this, since they prefer to kill targets themselves.

The Dark Eye model has seen centuries of use, and the Sith have incorporated a number of improvements and modifications in that time. The model used by Darth Maul during the time of the Old Republic includes several imaging devices but generally goes without the added weaponry. Every version has a

scan-absorbing outer shell designed to foil electronic scans, providing a +4 equipment bonus on the droid's Hide checks. In concert with its +8 size modifier on Hide checks, the antiscan shell makes the Dark Eye extremely difficult to locate.

When it does mount weapons, the Sith probe droid generally carries a low-profile laser cannon (with a 20-meter range increment due to the short muzzle), a stun blaster (with a maximum range of 10 meters), and a needler gun loaded with poisoned darts. These darts can be filled with any kind of liquid poison. Darth Maul prefers a nerve toxin that mimics the effects of the paralytic poison described on page 219 of the *Star Wars Roleplaying Game*.

The statistics below are for a fully armed Dark Eye probe droid.

Dark Eye: Hovering military droid, Scout 6; Init +1; Defense 18 (+5 class, +2 size, +1 Dex); Spd 10m; VP/WP 20/8; Atk +2 melee, +5 ranged (4d8/19–20, laser cannon; or 1d6 stun, save DC 15; or 1, special, poison dart); SQ Skill mastery (Spot), trailblazing, uncanny dodge; SV Fort +2, Ref +4, Will +5; SZ T; Rep 0; Str 6, Dex 13, Con 8, Int 13, Wis 14, Cha 8. Challenge Code: C.

    Equipment: Laser cannon, stun blaster, poison-dart needler, antiscan shell (+4 Hide), comlink, improved sensor package (+2 Listen, Search, Spot), infrared vision, low-light vision, motion sensors (+2 Spot), recording unit, self-destruct system, sonic sensors (+2 Listen), telescopic vision, weapon mounts (3).

    Skills: Hide +22*, Knowledge (Jedi lore) +10, Listen +17, Move Silently +10, Search +16, Spot** +20, Survival +11.

    Unspent Skill Points: 0.

    Feats: Alertness, Sharp-Eyed, Skill Emphasis (Spot), Track, Weapon Group Proficiency (blaster pistols), Weapon Group Proficiency (blaster rifles), Weapon Group Proficiency (simple weapons).

    Cost: Not available for sale.

*Includes +8 size modifier for Hide checks.

**Mastered skill.

Equipment

Some items used by darksiders are not strictly weapons, though they frequently enable characters to make more effective use of their dark powers. Primary among these are the tools—and the products—of Sith alchemy.

Alchemical Apparatus

Sith alchemy usually requires a significant amount of equipment: machines, chemicals, and generators that power the processes of altering the physical properties of matter, both living and nonliving. The

cost of the most basic such equipment—assuming one lives in an era when it is available—is around 10,000 credits. Additional raw materials cost even more. (See the rules for the Alchemy skill in Chapter Two: Playing the Dark Side.)

More complex and efficient alchemical apparati exist. For ten times the base cost, a character can procure either more specialized or more versatile equipment. A specialized apparatus lowers the DC of any Alchemy skill check by 5, but can only be used on a single species. A generalized apparatus can be used on any species, adding a +2 equipment bonus on any use of the Alchemy skill. The materials cost for making the skill check remains unchanged.

Sith Poison

Among the secrets revealed by dabbling in Sith alchemy is the formula for Sith poison. This toxin is more accurately described as a disease, however, because once in the system of a Force-using being, it remains there, gradually weakening the character's resistance to the dark side of the Force.

Sith poison is introduced into the victim's system either by ingestion or injury. If the victim fails his Will saving throw (DC 20), the character immediately suffers 1d6 damage to his Constitution score. (This damage is neither temporary damage nor permanent drain; see below.) Thereafter, the poison feeds the character's anger, drawing him closer to the dark side. Whenever the character uses a Force Point, he must attempt another Will save (unless he calls upon the dark side). If the save fails, the character is overcome with his anger and calls upon the dark side regardless—and thus gains a Dark Side Point.

Overcoming the poison is a lengthy process. Each time the character uses a Force Point, he must attempt a Will save (as described above); when the character successfully makes a total of five of these rolls, the poison is forced from the character's system. The Treat Injury skill cannot heal a character of this particular variety of poisoning. Only Heal Another or Heal Self can alleviate the character's suffering and drive the toxin out. Every time the poisoned character makes a Will save to resist the poison, the character can attempt a Heal Self check, or the healer can attempt a Heal Another check. The poisoned character may then use the result of the Heal Self or Heal Another check in place of the saving throw if the skill check result is higher.

Sith poison is extremely rare and can only be created by an Alchemy skill check (DC 25). For every 5 points by which the check exceeds the DC, the character creates one additional dose. Whether the attempt succeeds or fails, the character concocting the poison must expend 1 Force Point and gains 1 Dark Side Point.

066

Artifacts

Some dark side items are so rare and powerful that they are treasures of incalculable worth, sought after by dark side devotees and fortune-seekers alike in every corner of the galaxy. The secrets of their construction are lost in antiquity, though the foremost among them—the enigmatic Sith holocron—is presumably the key to unlocking these mysteries, at least for anyone who has the ambition to delve so deeply into the dark side.

Sith Holocron

A holocron is an extremely rare, crystalline storage device that serves as a repository of information. Embedded within the crystal, primitive holo-technology allows the device to display moving images of the data stored within it, usually in the form of teachers who contributed their knowledge to the creation of the device. The interactive technology enables the "teacher" to hold conversations with the holocron's user. Only a Force-user can activate a holocron, but once it is activated, anyone can communicate with the teacher.

The construction of holocrons is a lost technology, forgotten by the time Darth Bane came to power. The only existing holocrons are centuries or even millennia old. Jedi holocrons tend to be crystalline cubes, while Sith holocrons are pyramidal.

The information stored on Sith holocrons includes data and schematics for Sith weapons, armor, droids, vehicles, and starships. Using this information grants the holocron user a +2 competence bonus on related Knowledge checks, or on Craft checks to create any of these items. The storage medium allows for massive amounts of data; the user can consult the same holocron to build a suit of armor or a Sith battleship.

Each Sith holocron is imprinted with the personalities of multiple ancient Sith. These simulacra try to corrupt otherwise innocent beings who access their knowledge. They can only exert verbal influence, of course, but this still gives them plenty of opportunities to mislead their "students," drawing them down the path to the dark side. These personalities often withhold information until they deem the "student" is sufficiently steeped in the ways of the dark side. The GM should require a Knowledge (Sith lore) check (DC 20) to access most of the data. The character using the Sith holocron should receive a bonus on his check equal to his current number of Dark Side Points; the more a character experiences the power of the dark side, the more he understands which questions to ask.

Remember that consulting a Sith holocron is not by itself an evil act. The holocron is a tool—nothing

SITH HOLOCRON PERSONALITIES

The GM who makes a Sith holocron available to the characters should create at least a few personalities that inhabit the holocron. The "person" they first meet when activating the holocron should be the primary personality; the others are secondary personalities that can only be spoken to by specifically asking the primary for permission. For example, a Sith holocron might contain the following personalities:

- Kla, the "gatekeeper": An ancient Jedi consular who turned to the ways of the Sith long before the coming of Darth Bane, Kla is an exotic humanoid with an encyclopedic knowledge of the Sith Empire under Naga Sadow. He lies to those who access the holocron, telling them that they can only access specific knowledge by physically attaching the holocron to ancient devices sealed in burial vaults on the Sith graveyard world of Korriban. His true intention is to lure naive Force-users to a place where they can be possessed by Sith spirits—including his own.

- Komok-Da, the armorer: Komok-Da is descended from the original Sith, the species conquered by the corrupted Jedi who founded the Sith tradition. A master of weapons and armor, he can provide detailed instructions on building any Sith weapon, including double-bladed lightsabers and Sith poison. He seems almost academic about his approach, apparently uncaring as to who uses his knowledge or how. In truth, he is obsessed with the killing power of his designs. He only discloses full information to those who demonstrate their ability to kill without mercy—an act that garners at least one Dark Side Point for every design he reveals.

- Bo Vanda, the alchemist: Bo Vanda is plainly insane—and just as plainly brilliant. She eagerly and happily displays graphic representations of alchemical processes working on helpless subjects, explaining in gleeful terms how the victim responded to the treatment. Should the holocron's user express a desire to stop viewing the material, Vanda shrieks her anger and derision that only the weak fear what they requested to see. She essentially dares the user to see each process through to the end and duplicate the experiments. Otherwise, she simply refuses to confer with the user, berating him mercilessly whenever she is called.

more. However, the GM should be prepared to award Dark Side Points to characters who use the knowledge in Sith holocrons to construct tools of pain and suffering—for example, building torture devices and concocting Sith poisons.

Sith Amulet

Sith amulets are ancient relics created to focus and amplify a darksider's power. They are occasionally found in the burial tombs of the ancient Sith, or in the hands of Sith servants like the Massassi. Built in the form of crystal-studded gauntlets, the amulets radically enhance the user's telekinetic abilities—at the cost of leading the character to the dark side.

A Force-user with the Alter feat can use a Sith amulet to project focused blasts of dark side energy. The target of the blast must make a Reflex saving throw. The DC depends on the level of the Force-user wielding the amulet.

Force-User's Level	Target's Save DC
5th–10th	15
11th–16th	20
17th–20th	25

The blast deals 6d6 points of damage (half damage if the Reflex save succeeds). The maximum range of this blast is 20 meters. Unleashing this energy requires an attack action, costs 6 vitality points, and gives the wielder a Dark Side Point.

Sith Talismans

Created by the same dark alchemy used to create Sith amulets, Sith talismans provide the wearer with defense against blaster bolts, lightsaber blades, and even the Force itself. Whenever the wearer would suffer damage from energy weapons or Force-based attacks, he can attempt a Will saving throw to negate an amount of damage equal to his current number of Dark Side Points. The DC for the save is 10 (for energy attacks such as blasters and ion guns), 15 (for Force powers such as Force Grip or Force Lightning), or 20 (for lightsabers).

For every 3 points of damage negated in this fashion, the talisman's wearer gains 1 temporary vitality point. The amount of vitality gained is calculated per attack; fractions are lost, not carried over to the next attack. The gain of these vitality points may not increase the wearer's total beyond his maximum.

Orbalisk Armor

Orbalisk armor cannot truly be considered an artifact of the dark side—it is not so much constructed as hosted. An orbalisk is a type of hard-shelled parasite that attaches to living beings and feeds off their energies. Although orbalisks' venomous secretions are generally fatal to host organisms, a host can form an ongoing symbiotic relationship with the orbalisks if he is strong in the dark side. The host feeds the orbalisks, and the hard-shelled orbalisks provide armored protection.

When an orbalisk attaches to a host, it can be removed by making an opposed Strength check or by killing the orbalisk. If the orbalisk is not removed, it injects its poison into the victim once per day. (See the Orbalisk entry in Chapter Six for more information.) If multiple orbalisks attach to the same host, and they include a mated pair, they will produce two more orbalisks every four days, which will also inject their poison into the host—and breed, even as the original pair continues breeding. If a Small host does not remove the parasites within 13 days, it will be entirely covered. Orbalisks can cover a Medium-size host within 17 days and a Large host in 21 days. A single full-grown orbalisk weighs 1 kilogram.

JG

If the orbalisks are allowed to completely cover the host (100% coverage)—including the host's eyes, ears, and mouth—the host is subject to blindness, deafness, and suffocation. (See the *Star Wars Roleplaying Game,* page 217, for rules on suffocation.) The host (or another interested party) can prevent this from occurring in one of two ways. The first is by diligently reducing the number of orbalisks. The alternative method involves creating some kind of helmet or barrier to prevent the orbalisks from growing over the host's eyes, ears, and mouth (or the species equivalent thereof).

A host's size determines how many orbalisks it takes to cover its entire body. (See Table 4–3.) The host must keep the number at 90% or less to avoid complete coverage.

The amount of the host's body covered by orbalisks determines the armor bonus to the host's Defense (as shown on Table 4–4). The armor bonus provides more protection against lightsaber damage, as noted on the table.

Once a host has formed a stable relationship with the symbiotes, a secondary benefit comes into effect. The orbalisks heal damage that the host has been dealt every round. The amount of damage healed depends on the number of orbalisks, as shown on Table 4-4.

In addition to providing armor, the intermingling of orbalisk venom and dark side energy actually creates a biochemical reaction simulating the effects of adrenaline. If a host with Dark Side Points can survive the venom of the orbalisks, for every 20% of coverage, the venom and dark side energy add +1 vitality points per level and +1 to the host's Strength score. So, if a host has 90% coverage, the orbalisks provide +4 vitality points per level and an increase of +4 to the host's Strength score.

The percentage of coverage also provides increased healing every round, as shown on Table 4–4. This healing factor stops being applied when the orbalisk's cover 100% of the host's body and suffocation begins.

Table 4-3: Host Size and Number of Orbalisks

| Percentage of Coverage | Host Size | | | | | |
	Tiny	Small	Medium	Large	Huge	Gargantuan
10%		1	2	6	9	12
20%		2	4	12	18	24
30%	1		6	18	27	36
40%		4	8	24	36	48
50%		6	12	30	45	60
60%	2		14	36	54	72
70%		8	16	42	63	84
80%			20	48	72	96
90%	4	10	24	54	81	108
100%	6	12	28	60	90	120

Table 4-4: Orbalisks and Defense

Percentage of Coverage	Defense Bonus	Maximum Dex Bonus	Armor Check Penalty	Speed (10m)	(6m)	Vitality/Wounds Healed per Round
10%	+1/+2*	+6	−1	10	6	1/1
20%	+2/+4*	+5	−2	10	6	2/1
30%	+3/+6*	+5	−2	10	6	4/2
40%	+4/+8*	+4	−4	8	4	6/3
50%	+5/+10*	+4	−4	8	4	8/4
60%	+6/+12*	+2	−4	8	4	16/5
70%	+7/+14*	+2	−6	6	2	20/6
80%	+8/+16*	+1	−6	6	2	25/7
90%	+9/+18*	+1	−6	6	2	30/8
100%	+9/+18*	+0	−8	2	1	−/−

* Defense bonus against lightsaber attacks.

Chapter Five: Dark Side Traditions

The *Star Wars* galaxy can be a dark place. Worse than the void between the stars is the void found in the hearts of those who turn to evil—for power, lust, greed, or pride. Few beings in the galaxy are completely without the stain of the dark side, and when evil people are gifted with the power of the Force, they can ruin lives, topple empires, or spread the evil in their spirits across the entire galaxy.

Just as the dark side is known by many names in countless cultures, those who revere and draw upon it are known by many different names. The most famous of these are the Sith, originally a species of primitive beings subjugated by Jedi renegades, but eventually the name of an entire tradition devoted to the power of its adherents—and the suffering of its victims.

The Sith Empire

Thousands of years before the Empire dominated the galaxy, a renegade group of Jedi challenged the Masters of their Order for the freedom to explore the dark side. When they were refused, defeated, and finally forced into exile, they crossed the galaxy to find a place where they could live and learn as they chose without the interference of the Jedi Order. They came at last to a planet inhabited by a barely civilized people who called themselves the Sith. The primitive, superstitious Sith, seeing these visitors from the stars, declared the outcasts gods and promptly devoted themselves to worshiping their new masters.

For thousands of years the renegade Jedi ruled the Sith, expanding their empire to include nearby worlds, though they managed to avoid contact with their ancient enemies. Through continued campaigns of conquest they honed their battle arts, while simultaneously adding to the fortune and glory of their empire. When they ran out of foes, they fought among themselves in bloody wars of succession. After another thousand years, the Sith Empire was dangerously close to extinction through self-annihilation. Finally, after the death of the infamous Lord of the Sith, Marka Ragnos, a Republic scout ship stumbled onto the Sith necropolis world of Korriban. This single accident of hyperspace travel set off a chain of events that would eventually see the Sith return to nearly conquer the Old Republic—and planted the seeds for the return of the Sith, millennia later.

Marka Ragnos, Sith Lord

Five thousand years before Emperor Palpatine ordered the construction of the first Death Star, the Sith Empire was ruled by a powerful Sith named Marka Ragnos, who held the exalted title Dark Lord of the Sith. Ragnos was a half-breed Sith, a warlord of tremendous physical power and a frightening grasp of the dark side of the Force. He rose to prominence through a series of short, ruthless campaigns against his enemies. Once he gained control of the Sith Empire, he maintained dominance by pitting his detractors against one another, manipulating them into challenging him, or simply assassinating them. Among the Sith, Marka Ragnos was feared, obeyed, and admired.

Marka Ragnos retained power for over a century, crushing all resistance—but he expanded the Sith Empire only slightly in all that time. Marka Ragnos was one of the few Sith alive who had researched the history of his people and knew of the Old Republic and its defenders, the Jedi Order. Ragnos knew that if the Sith Empire were to expand too far toward their ancestral home, they would encounter the Republic. He believed the Sith were not yet ready to enter into a protracted war with the forces of the Republic, especially if the Jedi were still as strong as they had been when they defeated his ancestors.

Obviously, his views were not shared by all the Sith. Many saw his lack of expansion as a sign of weakness and took it as an opportunity—a justification, even—to unseat the Dark Lord of the Sith. At first irate that the other Sith would so blindly endanger his empire with their ambition, over time Ragnos

RENEGADE JEDI

Because the renegade Jedi were exiled from the Old Republic before the development of personal blaster technology, Sith of this period do not receive the feats Weapon Group Proficiency (blaster pistols) or Weapon Group Proficiency (vibro weapons); instead, they receive the feats Armor Proficiency (light) and Armor Proficiency (medium), respectively.

Similarly, when these Jedi left the Old Republic, Jedi Knights armed themselves with ordinary swords. While the Old Republic developed lightsaber technology, the Sith Empire explored alchemical metallurgy, resulting in the mystically honed Sith sword. Thus, Sith of this period cannot take the feat Exotic Weapon Proficiency (lightsaber). They must take Exotic Weapon Proficiency (Sith sword) instead when it becomes available through their class abilities. (If Sith characters come across lightsaber technology—perhaps from vanquished Jedi foes—and the Gamemaster allows it, Sith characters can take Exotic Weapon Proficiency (lightsaber) as one of their level feats.)

070

came to realize that while they were focusing their efforts on him, they were not actually expanding the borders of the Sith Empire, and thus, not precipitating contact with the Republic. Marka Ragnos elected to play to the aggression of the other Sith, to distract them from making a mistake that could bring the Sith Empire to ruin.

Marka Ragnos: Male Sith (near-Human), Force Adept 4/Sith Acolyte 8/Sith Lord 8; Init +0; Defense 25 (+15 class); Spd 10m; VP/WP 159/17; Atk +20/+15/+10/+5 melee (2d6+3/19–20, Sith sword) or +16/+11/+6/+1 ranged (3d4, lanvarok); SV Fort +19, Ref +11, Will +18; SZ M; FP 12; DSP 30; Rep 15; Str 16, Dex 11, Con 17, Int 15, Wis 15, Cha 13. Challenge Code: I.

   Equipment: Sith sword, Sith lanvarok, Sith amulet, Sith talisman, dark armor, Sith battleship, alchemical apparatus.

   Skills: Bluff +13, Craft (Sith swords) +12, Intimidate +19, Knowledge (Jedi lore) +10, Knowledge (Sith lore) +22, Read/Write Basic, Read/Write Sith, Sense Motive +9, Speak Basic, Speak Massassi, Speak Sith, Survival +12.

   Force Skills: Affect Mind +8, Alchemy +22, Battlemind +17, Control Mind +19, Enhance Ability +19, Force Defense +18, Move Object +10, See Force +12, Telepathy +9.

   Feats: Armor Proficiency (light), Armor Proficiency (medium), Exotic Weapon Proficiency (Sith sword), Exotic Weapon Proficiency (Sith lanvarok), Force-Sensitive, Great Fortitude, Power Attack, Weapon Focus (Sith sword), Weapon Group Proficiency (primitive weapons), Weapon Group Proficiency (simple weapons).

   Force Feats: Alter, Control, Drain Force, Force Lightning, Force Mastery, Force Mind, Rage, Sense, Sith Sorcery, Sith Sword Defense, Sith Sword Expertise, Sith Sword Mastery.

Naga Sadow, Sith Lord

When Marka Ragnos, the Dark Lord of the Sith, finally expired after a century of iron-fisted rule, two powerful Sith Lords were in a position to claim his title as supreme ruler of the Sith Empire. Ludo Kressh had the popular support of most of the Sith, but Naga Sadow had the military might. Together they could have made a powerful combination—but naturally, they hated one another. Ragnos's body had only been interred on the tomb-world of Korriban for a few minutes when the two began to fight over leadership. Their combat was fierce, but short, for the

spirit of Marka Ragnos appeared to them, telling them of their ancient ties to the Republic and the Jedi Knights and warning them to make their decisions for the future wisely.

   At that moment, a Republic scout ship appeared in the sky over Korriban. *Starbreaker 12*, piloted by brother and sister explorers Gav and Jori Daragon, arrived in Sith space by accident. Seeing the funeral procession and the riches of the tombs below them, they decided to set down and make contact. The Sith immediately took them prisoner. In private council, the assembled Sith Lords argued over how to deal with the two Republic explorers, with Ludo Kressh proposing to kill the Daragons, thus preventing the Republic from learning of the Sith Empire and invading. Naga Sadow, however, welcomed an invasion, hoping to stir the Sith out of their complacency. He jump-started the Sith–Republic war by secretly freeing Gav and Jori Daragon from their imprisonment, allowing Jori to return to the Republic while keeping Gav behind to teach him the Sith arts. Jori Daragon fled back to her home world of Cinnagar, unaware that Naga Sadow had planted a tracer on *Starbreaker 12*.

   Meanwhile, Sadow planted evidence that the Republic had rescued the Daragons, thus forcing the other Sith to address the "threat" posed by a Republic invasion fleet. With this ruse he convinced the other Sith Lords to declare

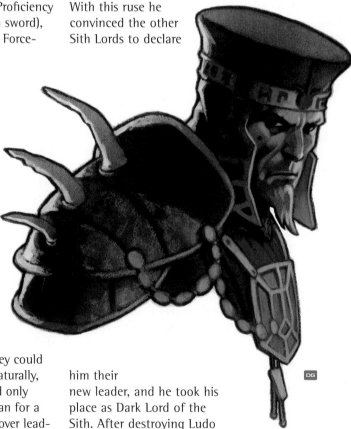

him their new leader, and he took his place as Dark Lord of the Sith. After destroying Ludo Kressh's flagship—with Kressh presumably on board—Sadow marshaled the Sith Lords and set off for Republic space with a vast battle fleet. His strike was swift and brutal, and world after world fell before his might. Soon he threatened Coruscant itself, but was ultimately defeated and forced to retreat.

Naga Sadow paid the price for his ambition. When he returned to Sith space, he discovered that Ludo Kressh had used his empty flagship to stage his own death. Now Kressh had his own fleet, and he fell upon Sadow's badly damaged ships. Though Naga Sadow destroyed Ludo Kressh for certain this time, he could not enjoy his victory. A Republic fleet had followed him back to the Sith Empire and attacked while he was still recovering from his battle with Kressh's fleet. Sadow sacrificed the remainder of his fleet so that he could escape in his flagship. Taking a cue from Kressh, he staged his own death while simultaneously destroying his pursuers between binary suns.

His force reduced to only a handful of Sith followers and a small Massassi crew, Naga Sadow searched out a new home for the Sith Empire. Eventually he chanced upon a small, unnamed jungle moon orbiting the yellow-orange gas giant Yavin and began construction of a permanent fortress there. In time the Republic forgot about him, and it would be almost a thousand years before anyone ventured to the small moon again. This new visitor was Jedi Knight Exar Kun, who, guided by the dark spirit of Freedon Nadd, would reclaim the ancient artifacts Naga Sadow left behind and subjugate the descendants of Sadow's original Massassi, now devolved into barbaric savages.

Naga Sadow: Male Sith (near-Human), Force Adept 4/Sith Acolyte 5/Sith Lord 5; Init +1; Defense 23 (+12 class, +1 Dex); Spd 10m; VP/WP 126/18; Atk +14/+9/+4 melee (2d6+3/19–20, Sith sword) or +12/+7/+2 ranged; SQ Minions, resource access; SV Fort +14, Ref +10, Will +15; SZ M; FP 8; DSP 24; Rep 12; Str 17, Dex 13, Con 18, Int 15, Wis 15, Cha 14. Challenge Code: F.

Equipment: Sith sword, Sith amulet, Sith talisman, dark armor (damage reduction 5), Sith battleship, alchemical apparatus.

Skills: Bluff +15, Computer Use +6, Diplomacy +13, Intimidate +16, Knowledge (Sith lore) +14, Listen +4, Read/Write Sith, Sense Motive +8, Speak Basic, Speak Massassi, Speak Sith, Spot +4, Survival +11.

Force Skills: Affect Mind +9, Alchemy +12, Battlemind +12, Control Mind +17, Enhance Ability +14, Force Defense +12, Force Grip +10, See Force +10.

Feats: Armor Proficiency (light), Armor Proficiency (medium), Exotic Weapon Proficiency (Sith sword),

Force-Sensitive, Infamy, Persuasive, Sith Sword Defense, Sith Sword Expertise, Trustworthy, Weapon Focus (Sith sword), Weapon Group Proficiency (primitive weapons), Weapon Group Proficiency (simple weapons).

Force Feats: Alter, Control, Drain Force, Force Mind, Sense, Sith Sorcery.

Ludo Kressh, Aspiring Sith Lord

The most powerful of the Sith to oppose Naga Sadow's rise to power was Ludo Kressh, a conservative among the Sith Lords, who believed that the Sith Empire must grow strong within itself before looking for new foes to conquer. After the death of Marka Ragnos, Ludo Kressh was fully prepared to accept the reins of power. With the unexpected arrival of Gav and Jori Daragon, hyperspace explorers from the Republic, his plans were thrown into chaos. The safest plan, Kressh knew, would be to execute the brother and sister. Before he could convince the other Sith Lords, Naga Sadow outmaneuvered him, abducting the Daragons and making it appear as though the Republic had mounted a rescue mission. If the Republic had entered Sith space, war was inevitable—so the Sith Lords transferred their support to Naga Sadow, and Ludo Kressh was forced to retreat to his fortress world with his few remaining allies.

Determined not to allow the Sith Empire to fall into ruin under the leadership of Naga Sadow, Ludo Kressh mounted an attack on Sadow's stronghold—only to be outmaneuvered again when the fortress turned out to be a decoy. Sadow counterattacked Kressh's meager fleet, and Kressh was forced to retreat. Learning a harsh lesson from his failures, Kressh sent his flagship—empty, of course—to attack Sadow at his actual stronghold. Predictably, Naga Sadow destroyed the decoy. Thinking Ludo Kressh dead, Naga Sadow assembled his war fleet and embarked for the worlds of the Republic.

Meanwhile, Kressh rallied the Sith Lords who remained behind, promising them wealth and power if they allied with him against Naga Sadow. With their support, Ludo Kressh declared himself the new Dark Lord of the Sith. When Sadow's badly damaged battle fleet returned, Kressh was waiting. His ships devastated Sadow's ships, but Sadow was the better strategist. Sadow ordered one of his own damaged ships to ram Kressh's new flagship. Both ships were destroyed, along with Ludo Kressh's dreams of ruling the Sith Empire.

Ludo Kressh: Male Sith (near-Human), Force Adept 4/Sith Acolyte 10; Init +1; Defense 22 (+11 class, +1 Dex); Spd 10m; VP/WP 122/17; Atk +13/+8 melee

072

(2d6+3/19–20, Sith sword) or +10/+5 ranged; SV Fort +12, Ref +8, Will +16; SZ M; FP 6; DSP 14; Rep 10; Str 16, Dex 12, Con 17, Int 16, Wis 14, Cha 15. Challenge Code: E.

Equipment: Sith sword, Sith talisman, Sith amulet, Sith armor (damage reduction 5), Sith battleship, alchemical apparatus.

Skills: Bluff +15, Computer Use +6, Diplomacy +10, Intimidate +17, Knowledge (Sith lore) +12, Listen +5, Read/Write Sith, Sense Motive +12, Speak Basic, Speak Massassi, Speak Sith, Spot +6, Survival +6.

Force Skills: Affect Mind +10, Alchemy +13, Battlemind +13, Drain Knowledge +8, Enhance Ability +10, Fear +8, See Force +9.

Feats: Armor Proficiency (light), Armor Proficiency (medium), Exotic Weapon Proficiency (Sith sword), Force-Sensitive, Infamy, Iron Will, Persuasive, Power Attack, Weapon Focus (Sith sword), Weapon Group Proficiency (primitive weapons), Weapon Group Proficiency (simple weapons).

Force Feats: Alter, Control, Dissipate Energy, Drain Force, Rage, Sense, Sith Sorcery.

Freedon Nadd, Jedi Expatriate

The legend of the Dark Lords of the Sith was often an enticing lure to young Jedi apprentices, and more than a few dreamed of the kind of power a Sith Lord could wield. One such Jedi was Freedon Nadd, who slew his own master to pursue his dream of exploring the dark side of the Force.

Nadd tracked down rumors about the Sith, eventually arriving at the jungle moon Yavin 4. There, he convinced the primitive Massassi to take him to the temples of their ancestors' Sith Master, Naga Sadow. Awakening Sadow's dark spirit, Freedon Nadd learned all that he could about Sith sorcery, plundering Sadow's treasure vaults for whatever Sith artifacts and teachings he could haul away. But without a kingdom, Freedon Nadd knew that he could never truly be the new Dark Lord of the Sith. He set out to find himself a world to conquer.

Freedon Nadd came to Onderon, a world beset by ravaging monsters from its moon of Dxun. Using his dark side powers, Nadd deposed the existing rulers and declared himself king, arming his people against Dxun's monsters and banishing criminals and other malcontents to the harrowing wilds of the primitive moon. Under his rule, Onderon became a prosperous, if tainted, world. When Freedon Nadd died, his dark spirit lived on, instructing his offspring in the use of the dark side of the Force. His descendants became the royal family of Onderon's walled city of Iziz, and ruled as he had—with the dark side. As centuries passed, his sarcophagus, deep in the subterranean vaults under the royal palace, became a focal point of dark side energies.

Nadd died a second death a few hundred years later, ironically at the hands of another Jedi student questing after knowledge of the Sith. Freedon Nadd extended his aid—albeit with his own interests in mind—to Exar Kun, an ambitious and powerful Jedi who hoped to bend the dark side to his own will. But in turning Exar Kun to the dark side, he had pushed the young Jedi too far, and once Exar Kun had the power and the knowledge how to use it, he turned on Freedon Nadd. On Yavin 4, where Nadd had gotten his start in the ways of the Sith, his spirit was destroyed forever.

Freedon Nadd: Male Human, Jedi Guardian 5/Sith Acolyte 10; Init +1; Defense 24 (+13 class, +1 Dex); Spd 10m; VP/WP 118/14; Atk +6 melee* (5d8+2/19–20, lightsaber) or +5 ranged; SV Fort +4, Ref +4, Will +3; SZ M; FP 6; DSP 18; Rep 10; Str 14, Dex 13, Con 14, Int 16, Wis 14, Cha 13. Challenge Code: F.

Equipment: Lightsaber*, Sith swords, dark armor (+2 Force bonus to Strength).

*Freedon Nadd has constructed his own lightsaber.

Skills: Bluff +13, Craft (lightsaber) +11, Diplomacy +9, Intimidate +11, Knowledge (Onderon) +7, Knowledge (Sith lore) +15, Read/Write Basic,

Read/Write Sith, Sense Motive +10, Speak Basic, Speak Sith.

Force Skills: Affect Mind +9, Alchemy +19, Battlemind +14, Fear +14, Force Defense +14, Force Grip +9, Move Object +15, See Force +10.

Feats: Armor Proficiency (light), Exotic Weapon Proficiency (lightsaber), Exotic Weapon Proficiency (Sith sword), Force-Sensitive, Infamy, Iron Will, Two-Weapon Fighting, Weapon Group Proficiency (blaster pistols), Weapon Group Proficiency (simple weapons).

Force Feats: Alter, Control, Deflect Blasters, Lightsaber Defense, Hatred, Rage, Sense, Sith Sorcery.

Queen Amanoa of Onderon, Sith Sorceress

Amanoa ruled Onderon in the absence of her husband, King Ommin, whose dark side studies left him a withered husk. Queen Amanoa was a powerful darksider in her own right, a woman whose fascination with the power of the long-dead Freedon Nadd bordered on a twisted infatuation.

Queen Amanoa had been married to King Ommin for many years before she realized that he was delving into dark side mysteries. Gifted in the Force herself and devoted to Ommin, Amanoa attempted to redeem her husband, but Ommin refused to be turned. Out of love, Amanoa agreed to help Ommin with his studies, hoping to gradually lead him back to the light. Instead, King Ommin turned his young wife to the dark side.

As their knowledge in the dark side grew, their love faded, replaced with mistrust, loathing, and outright hatred—little realizing that they were being manipulated all along by the dark spirit of Freedon Nadd. Nadd wanted to return from the grave to the physical world, and hoped that if his two students became powerful enough, they would find a way to bring him back. And to his thinking, the best way to ensure that Ommin or Amanoa attained that power was to put them in competition with one another. When the dark side began to consume King Ommin's strength, Nadd knew that he had failed; without her husband's competition to drive her, Queen Amanoa was content to merely rule the Onderonian city of Iziz and let her dark side studies fall by the wayside.

More concerned now with temporal power—perhaps having learned from Freedon Nadd himself that after death she would be relatively powerless—Queen Amanoa sought to expand the rule of Iziz to include all of Onderon. But the beast-riders of Onderon, barbaric warriors descended from Iziz's early outcasts, were a major obstacle to this plan. Queen Amanoa attempted to wipe them out, but the beast-riders, led by the charismatic warrior Oron Kira,

struck back in kind. Soon Iziz was on the brink of war with the beast-riders. Amanoa consulted the spirit of Freedon Nadd for advice, and he told her that if war broke out, she would die. Nadd tried to convince Amanoa to return to her dark side studies, but Amanoa mistook his meaning and decided to defuse the war with the beast-riders. Amanoa called in the Jedi Knights.

Once the Jedi—led by Ulic Qel-Droma—arrived and investigated, they resolved to side with the beast-riders to overthrow Queen Amanoa and put her daughter Galia on the throne of Iziz. War broke out despite Amanoa's plans. While the army of the beast-riders attacked Iziz, the Jedi Knights and their allies fought their way into Amanoa's private chambers. There they discovered the secret source of her power in the deepest tombs of the palace: Freedon Nadd's sarcophagus, filled with the dark power of the ancient Sith warrior. Confronted by the light side strength of Jedi Master Arca Jeth, Freedon Nadd withdrew his strength from Amanoa, and she collapsed, lifeless, to the floor.

Queen Amanoa: Female Human, Noble 3/Dark Side Devotee 6; Init +1; Defense 20 (+9 class, +1 Dex); Spd 10m; VP/WP 54/12; Atk +6 melee or +6 ranged; SQ Call in a favor (2), dark side talisman +2, Force weapon +1d4, inspire confidence +1; SV Fort +5, Ref +6, Will +11; SZ M; FP 2; DSP 18; Rep 10; Str 12, Dex 12, Con 12, Int 15, Wis 15, Cha 16. Challenge Code: E.

Equipment: Dark side talisman, various Sith tomes and artifacts.

Skills: Bluff +10, Diplomacy +8, Intimidate +9, Knowledge (Jedi lore) +6, Knowledge (Onderon) +6, Knowledge (nobility) +6, Knowledge (Sith lore) +14, Profession (bureaucrat) +12, Profession (merchant) +6, Read/Write Basic, Read/Write Onderonian, Read/Write Sith, Sense Motive +6, Speak Basic, Speak Onderonian, Speak Sith.

Force Skills: Fear +9, Force Grip +7, Force Stealth +5, Heal Self +7, Illusion +7, Move Object +6.

Feats: Force Sensitive, Frightful Presence, Iron Will, Dark Side Skill Emphasis (Fear), Dark Side Skill Emphasis (Force Grip), Weapon Group Proficiency (blaster pistols), Weapon Group Proficiency (simple weapons).

Force Feats: Alter, Control, Rage, Sense, Sith Sorcery.

King Ommin of Onderon, Sith Sorcerer

As a direct descendant of Freedon Nadd, King Ommin of the planet Onderon was heir to all of Nadd's legacy—including a trove of Sith artifacts and a body of Sith lore that eventually lured

074

Ommin to the dark side. But while Ommin secretly developed his dark side skills, his body withered and his bones decayed until he was barely able to move without the aid of a complex mechanical exoskeleton. Only his sheer willpower—aided by the dark spirit of his ancestor, Freedon Nadd—enabled Ommin to persist where lesser beings would have failed.

Ommin came to the dark side the same way as his father, and his father's father: the legacy of Freedon Nadd, passed down from generation to generation in the royal family of the vast Onderonian city of Iziz. Ommin initially thought of the dark side lore his father taught him as just another lesson in the use of power, much like the tutoring he received in diplomacy and etiquette. But he came to realize that the dark side offered so much more. He studied the ways of Sith sorcery, until after he assumed the throne of Iziz he was able to call forth the spirit of Freedon Nadd himself.

Nadd taught Ommin far more than Ommin's father ever had, schooling him not only in the power of the dark side but in the traditions of the Sith. Ommin's meager knowledge grew by leaps and bounds, until he was immersed in the darkness—bound by it, strengthened by it, but unable to ever escape it. His corruption tainted his new wife, Amanoa, who became a powerful Sith sorceress in her own right. Ommin looked forward to the day when they could indoctrinate their daughter Galia into the ways of the Sith as well.

But before Ommin could realize his dream, Jedi Knights came to Onderon to settle a dispute between the Onderonians and the barbaric beast-riding warriors who lived in Onderon's wilderness. Investigating, the Jedi learned that the beast-riders were fighting for their survival against the tyranny of Queen Amanoa, and aided them against her. After a fierce battle, the Jedi confronted Amanoa, who called upon the spirit of Freedon Nadd for aid—only to be defeated by the light side power of the Jedi Master Arca Jeth. Nadd's spirit was driven off, and Amanoa was killed.

King Ommin joined her in death only a short time later, after his loyalists attempted to steal the sarcophagi of Amanoa and Freedon Nadd and to depose Galia and her husband, Oron Kira. Though Ommin overcame Master Arca with his dark side power, he himself was beaten when the Jedi Ulic Qel-Droma severed the connection to his support exoskeleton, leaving King Ommin barely able to speak or move, let alone draw upon the power of the dark side. Freedon Nadd claimed King Ommin's corrupted spirit and departed, only to return some time later to corrupt the Jedi Knight Exar Kun.

King Ommin: Male Human, Noble 6/Dark Side Devotee 8/Sith Acolyte 2; Init +0; Defense 24 (+14 class); Spd 10m; VP/WP 21/13; Atk +12/+7 melee (2d6+1/19–20, Sith sword) or +11/+6 ranged; SQ Call in a favor (3), command +2, dark side talisman +4, Force weapon +1d4, inspire confidence +2; SV Fort +10, Ref +9, Will +18; SZ M; FP 4; DSP 24; Rep 15; Str 13 (1*), Dex 11 (1*), Con 13 (4*), Int 15, Wis 15, Cha 14. Challenge Code: F.

*Without support exoskeleton.

Equipment: Sith swords, Sith talisman, Sith amulet, Sith tomes, support exoskeleton.

Skills: Bluff +14, Diplomacy +21, Intimidate +12, Knowledge (Onderon) +6, Knowledge (nobility) +6, Knowledge (Sith lore) +17, Profession (bureaucrat) +8, Read/Write Basic, Read/Write Onderonian, Read/Write Sith, Speak Basic, Speak Onderonian, Speak Sith.

Force Skills: Affect Mind +7, Alchemy +16, Drain Knowledge +10, Enhance Ability +6, Enhance Senses +6, Farseeing +10, Fear +11, Force Defense +5, Force Stealth +5, Heal Self +5, Move Object +6, See Force +15, Telepathy +10.

Feats: Dark Side Skill Emphasis (Alchemy), Dark Side Skill Emphasis (Drain Knowledge), Dark Side Skill Emphasis (Fear), Exotic Weapon Proficiency (Sith sword), Force-Sensitive, Iron Will, Weapon Group Proficiency (blaster pistols), Weapon Group Proficiency (simple weapons).

Force Feats: Alter, Control, Dissipate Energy, Drain Force, Force Lightning, Hatred, Prolong Force, Sense, Sith Sorcery.

Satal and Aleema Keto, Sith Acolytes

Aleema Keto and her cousin Satal Keto, son of the ruler of the Empress Teta system and heir to the corrupt government, were spoiled, bored, and rich. Along with their friends, the pair dabbled in Sith magic and amused themselves with artifacts from the time of the Great Hyperspace War. To gain more power, Aleema persuaded Satal to steal an ancient book of Sith secrets from a Coruscant museum, but they couldn't read the text. They went in search of someone who could.

Armed with rumors of Sith practitioners on Onderon, the two aristocrats used their money and novice dark side skills to reach King Ommin. The delighted ruler gave Satal a Sith amulet and had a scribe start work on translating the arcane tome.

The specter of Freedon Nadd had been assisting King Ommin, but decided that Satal and Aleema held the key to resurrecting the golden age of the Sith. The dark side avatar appeared before the pair and offered to guide them in their rise to power. Spurred on and encouraged by the spirit's attention,

Satal and his cousin extracted a wealth of Sith artifacts and returned to the Empress Teta system.
Nadd's spirit, meanwhile, was trapped within an
armored tomb on the moon of Dxun.

With the artifacts and Sith tome in hand, Satal
and Aleema quickly grew in dark side power. They
led a rebellion against the government of the
Empress Teta system, killing Satal's parents and
delighting in the use of their newfound abilities.
Barbaric, evil, and totally despotic, the pair spread
fear and suffering throughout the system as the
inhabited worlds revolted.

Republic forces, assisted by Jedi Knights Ulic Qel-
Droma and Nomi Sunrider, tried to put an end to the
violence, but Aleema used powerful Sith illusions to
confuse and confound the unwanted intruders.

Later, Ulic disguised himself as a fallen Jedi and
made his way to Satal and Aleema's stronghold in
the city of Cinnagar. An assassin threatened to end
Aleema's life, but Ulic intervened. He killed the
assassin and was accepted into the usurper's sect by
the beautiful Aleema. Satal, jealous and suspicious of
Ulic, tortured the Jedi, seeking to make him confess
to being a spy. Even under the influence of Sith
poison, Ulic denied the charges, though his mind
was clouded by the foul substance. Aleema scoffed
at Satal's suspicions and made Ulic general of their
military forces—and her personal pet Jedi. When
Satal Keto eventually discovered Ulic's true plans, he
confronted the fallen Jedi in a great duel that had
terrible repercussions: Ulic unleashed his fury, killing
Satal but completing his slide to the dark side.

Aleema allowed Ulic to claim his place beside her
as the new ruler of their dark side sect. Ulic's military
genius, combined with Aleema's Sith illusions,
allowed the sect to gain a number of victories
against the Republic. In the end, however, a brave
band of Jedi Knights captured Ulic and stripped him
of his power. Aleema escaped, leaving her onetime
pet to his fate.

Later, the treacherous Aleema's ambition would
be the end of her. She triggered an ancient Sith
weapon—at the behest of Ulic and Exar Kun—that
killed her as it destroyed the star systems of the
Cron cluster.

Satal Keto: Male Human, Noble 2/Dark Side
Devotee 4; Init +1; Defense 19 (+8 class, +1 Dex);
Spd 10m; VP/WP 29/10; Atk +5 melee (2d6+1, Sith
sword) or +5 ranged (3d6, blaster pistol); SQ Call in
a favor, dark side talisman +2, inspire confidence +1;
SV Fort +3, Ref +5, Will +7; SZ M; FP 2; DSP 6; Rep
6; Str 13, Dex 13, Con 10, Int 14, Wis 11, Cha 14.
Challenge Code: D.

Equipment: Sith amulet, Sith sword, Sith talisman,
blaster pistol, Sith tomes and artifacts.

Skills: Appraise +8, Computer Use +9, Diplomacy
+7, Knowledge (Sith lore) +4, Hide +5, Listen +3,
Pilot +3, Read/Write Basic, Sense Motive +5, Speak
Basic, Spot +6.

Force Skills: Alchemy +7, Drain Energy +9,
Empathy +4, Fear +5, Force Grip +7, Illusion +6.

Feats: Dark Side Skill Emphasis (Alchemy), Dark
Side Skill Emphasis (Drain Energy), Force-Sensitive,
Heroic Surge, Power Attack, Weapon Group
Proficiency (blaster pistols), Weapon Group
Proficiency (simple weapons).

Force Feats: Alter, Control, Sense, Sith Sorcery.

Aleema Keto: Female Human, Noble 2/Dark Side
Devotee 5; Init +3; Defense 22 (+9 class, +3 Dex);
Spd 10m; VP/WP 41/11; Atk +4 melee (1d3, punch)
or +7 ranged (3d6, blaster pistol); SQ Barter, dark
side talisman +2; SV Fort +6, Ref +8, Will +7; SZ M;
FP 5; DSP 9; Rep 8; Str 10, Dex 16, Con 11, Int 16,
Wis 12, Cha 17. Challenge Code: E.

Equipment: Sith amulet, Sith talisman, blaster
pistol, Sith tomes and artifacts.

Skills: Appraise +7, Astrogate +5, Bluff +8,
Computer Use +7, Diplomacy +8, Gather
Information +6, Intimidate +8, Knowledge (Sith lore)
+11, Pilot +5, Read/Write Basic, Read Sith, Sense
Motive +7, Speak Basic, Speak Sith, Spot +3.

Force Skills: Affect Mind +8, Alchemy +5,
Empathy +6, Fear +9, Force Grip +11, Force Push
+8, Illusion +13, Move Object +6.

Feats: Dark Side Skill Emphasis (Fear), Dark Side
Skill Emphasis (Force Grip), Force-Sensitive, Iron Will,
Persuasive, Weapon Group Proficiency (blaster
pistols), Weapon Group Proficiency (simple
weapons).

Force Feats: Alter, Control, Sense, Sith Sorcery.

Ulic Qel-Droma, Former Jedi Knight, Sith Lord

Almost four thousand years before the coming of
Darth Vader, two other Jedi Knights embraced the
dark side, eventually challenging and almost decimating the ranks of the Jedi Order they once
loyally served. One, Exar Kun, turned to the dark
side in a quest for knowledge long forbidden by
the Order. The other, Ulic Qel-Droma, sought to
destroy the dark side sect of Satal and Aleema Keto
from the inside, only to be turned to evil himself
by dark side poison. By the time he was finally
defeated, Ulic Qel-Droma had become a formidable
Dark Lord of the Sith, second only to his partner
Exar Kun.

Ulic and his brother Cay Qel-Droma trained under
Jedi Master Arca Jeth on the world of Arkania,
alongside a Twi'lek Jedi named Tott Doneeta. Master
Arca sent the three Jedi students to the world of

Onderon to settle the dispute between Iziz and the beast-riders of Onderon. Ulic encountered the dark side spirit of Freedon Nadd in the Sith storehouses below the royal palace. Nadd foretold that Ulic would one day be a great Sith Lord, equal to the mightiest Jedi masters. Though Ulic brushed off Freedon Nadd's prophecy, it also chilled him. He was a devoted follower of the light side; how could he become a Sith Lord?

The beginning of the answer came when a dark side sect led by Satal and Aleema Keto, heirs to the throne of Cinnagar in the Empress Teta system, seized control of the entire system. The Tetans suffered under the pair's cruel dark side rule. The Republic finally intervened, sending a small group of Jedi led by Ulic Qel-Droma to deal with the crisis. During the space battle Ulic was injured, and the wound—inflicted by a twisted shred of alchemically altered metal— refused to heal. When the Jedi Order convened on the world of Deneba to discuss a solution to the problem of the dark side sect, Satal and Aleema sent a battle force of warships and droids to attack them. During the fight Arca Jeth was killed, and the loss of his master gave Ulic all the incentive he needed to carry out his plan to infiltrate the sect and destroy it from within.

LB

Ulic journeyed to the Empress Teta system, where he presented himself to Satal and Aleema, who promptly imprisoned him. Though Ulic explained that he had come to join them, Satal did not trust the Jedi. He injected the Jedi with potent Sith poisons to ensure that whether Ulic was lying or not, he would still turn to the dark side. Ulic became a member of the sect, using his Force powers to help crush all resistance to their rule, even though it brought him into conflict with his old friends—including Nomi Sunrider, the Jedi woman with whom he had fallen in love. Armed with Aleema's Sith talisman, Ulic was able to drive off his former allies, but he was not prepared for the arrival of Exar Kun.

While Ulic infiltrated the dark side sect, Exar Kun had been learning the secrets of the Sith directly from the source. He journeyed to the tomb of Freedon Nadd on Dxun, the moon of Onderon, then followed Nadd's spirit to the Sith tomb world of Korriban and finally to the temple of the exiled Sith Lord Naga Sadow on Yavin 4. Now armed with powerful Sith artifacts and accompanied by a force of Massassi warriors, Exar Kun battled his way into the royal palace of Cinnagar, where Ulic and Aleema had just repulsed the Jedi group. Exar Kun and Ulic fought, but they were too evenly matched for either

to gain the upper hand. Their battle might have gone on for hours but for the macabre manifestation of a host of Sith spirits, led by the shade of Marka Ragnos. Ragnos told Ulic and Exar Kun that they would restore the Sith Empire to its former glory, proclaiming Exar Kun the new Dark Lord of the Sith, and Ulic Qel-Droma his first apprentice.

Together, Exar Kun and Ulic Qel-Droma assembled vast armies with which to destroy the Jedi Order and establish the Sith as the rulers of the galaxy. While Exar Kun corrupted Jedi students with the dark side and sent them to assassinate their former masters, Ulic led an assault of warships against Coruscant, the heart of the Republic, where he was captured by his former Jedi allies and forced to stand trial for his crimes. With Exar Kun's help, Ulic escaped, and the dark side sect then moved against the Jedi learning center on Ossus, unleashing a supernova that destroyed vast storehouses of Jedi relics and lore.

Before the shock waves reached the planet, Cay Qel-Droma confronted his brother, attempting once again to free Ulic from the grip of the dark side. He failed, and Ulic killed him. Overcome with grief by this heinous action, Ulic offered no resistance when his former love Nomi Sunrider attacked, using her unique Force powers to block Ulic's connection to the Force. Having lost his onetime master, his brother, and his powers, Ulic surrendered to the Jedi and led them to Exar Kun's secret stronghold on Yavin 4. The Jedi arrived too late to confront Exar Kun—who by then had joined with the dark side—but still managed to cleanse Yavin 4 with their combined Jedi powers.

Broken and defeated, Ulic began wandering the galaxy, finally making his home on the frozen world of Rhen Var. Vima Sunrider—the daughter of his former love—approached Ulic, who had been in solitude for many years, and begged him to teach her about the Force. Unable to comply with her wishes without his own connection to the Force, Ulic nonetheless taught Vima about the concepts of honor and duty—speaking as someone who had had both once, and lost them. When Nomi Sunrider and another former Jedi compatriot arrived to rescue Vima, they realized that Ulic had long since paid for his crimes against them and the Republic. But a down-on-his-luck scoundrel who brought the two Jedi to Rhen Var, hoping to make a new reputation for himself, shot Ulic Qel-Droma from behind, killing him. Nevertheless, Ulic found redemption thanks to young Vima, and became one with the Force upon his death.

Ulic Qel-Droma: Male Human, Jedi Guardian 11/Sith Lord 5; Init +3; Defense 26 (+13 class, +3 Dex); Spd 10m; VP/WP 141/16; Atk +21/+16/+11/+6 melee* (6d8+3/19–20, lightsaber), +19/+14/+9/+4 ranged; SQ Minions, resource access; SV Fort +14, Ref +14, Will +11; SZ M; FP 8; DSP 14; Rep 12; Str 16, Dex 16, Con 16, Int 14, Wis 14, Cha 14. Challenge Code: G.

Equipment: Lightsaber*, Sith amulet.

*Ulic Qel-Droma has constructed his own lightsaber.

Skills: Astrogate +6, Bluff +4, Craft (lightsaber) +6, Diplomacy +6, Intimidate +12, Knowledge (Sith lore) +12, Knowledge (Outer Rim systems) +3, Pilot +8, Read/Write Basic, Read/Write Sith, Repair +8, Ride +5, Speak Arkanian, Speak Basic, Speak Ryl, Speak Sith.

Force Skills: Battlemind +15, Drain Knowledge +7, Enhance Ability +9, Enhance Senses +6, Farseeing +8, Force Defense +11, Force Grip +12, Force Push +8, Heal Self +8, Move Object +14, See Force +11, Telepathy +10.

Feats: Exotic Weapon Proficiency (lightsaber), Force-Sensitive, Heroic Surge, Infamy, Power Attack, Starship Operation (space transports), Weapon Focus (lightsaber), Weapon Group Proficiency (blaster pistols), Weapon Group Proficiency (simple weapons).

Force Feats: Alter, Burst of Speed, Control, Deflect Blasters, Knight Defense, Lightsaber Defense, Rage, Sense.

Exar Kun, Former Jedi Knight, Sith Lord

Tempted by the promise of powers he arrogantly believed he could control, Exar Kun went from promising Jedi apprentice to formidable Sith Lord with barely a backward glance. Filled with curiosity and convinced there was nothing he could not handle, he heeded the advice of the Dark Jedi spirit Freedon Nadd, who found in Exar Kun an apt and willing pupil. But even Freedon Nadd was surprised at how eagerly Exar Kun embraced the dark side.

Consumed by pride and ambition, Jedi student Exar Kun had a dark place in his heart that even his vaunted master, Vodo-Siosk Baas, could not reach. An excellent student and a master swordsman, Exar Kun was fascinated with the powers of the ancient Sith Lords. Supremely confident, Kun felt that he could separate out the dark side from the abilities used by the Sith and use those abilities to greatly expand the Jedi Order's understanding of the Force. But Kun was stymied by Master Vodo, who constantly warned his student to heed only the lessons Vodo himself taught him. Impatient and irritated, Exar Kun abandoned Master Vodo's training and went in search of darker power.

His travels brought him to Onderon, where he learned of the Sith tomb of Freedon Nadd on Onderon's moon, Dxun. Encountering Freedon Nadd's spirit, Exar Kun learned of the Sith crypts on Korriban and journeyed there to continue his search. On Korriban, he again spoke with Freedon Nadd's spirit, who tricked Kun into at first accepting the dark side, then embracing it. Under Nadd's ghostly tutelage, Kun traveled on to Yavin 4, the last stronghold of the Sith Empire, where a thousand years before Naga Sadow went into exile. Captured there by the primitive descendants of Sadow's Massassi warriors, Exar Kun escaped his own execution and seized a dark side amulet from among Sadow's treasures, using it to escape the gargantuan dark side beast that the Massassi brought forth to devour him. He then turned the weapon on Freedon Nadd, destroying the dark side spirit forever.

Now the master of the Massassi rather than their captive, Exar Kun sought out the ancient relics Naga Sadow brought to Yavin 4 and discovered among them the instruments of Sith alchemy. Turning these devices on his now-loyal Massassi subjects, Exar Kun transformed them into mighty warriors, then set out in Naga Sadow's ancient battleship to track down others who Kun sensed had the dark side training to usurp his power. He found them on Cinnagar—the Sith acolyte Aleema Keto and her Dark Jedi lover, Ulic Qel-Droma. He and Ulic fought for supremacy, but their battle was cut short by the appearance of a group of Sith spirits led by none other than Marka

Ragnos—Naga Sadow's predecessor. Ragnos declared that Exar Kun would be the new Dark Lord of the Sith, and that Ulic Qel-Droma would be his first apprentice. Together, the two would conquer the galaxy and build a new Sith Empire.

Exar Kun began his part of the work by recruiting several impressionable Jedi students from the Jedi learning center on Ossus, bringing them to Yavin 4, then using the power of a Sith holocron to turn them to the dark side. After sending them out on missions to assassinate their former masters, Kun traveled to Coruscant to secure the release of Ulic Qel-Droma, who had brashly attacked the center of the Republic in hopes of a swift victory. In the process he once more faced his former master, Vodo-Siosk Baas, this time armed with a double-bladed lightsaber of his own construction. Master Vodo did not have a chance, and fell to his former student.

Kun and Ulic escaped back to Yavin 4, where they planned their next attack against the Jedi learning center on Ossus. Arranging for Aleema Keto to use a Sith artifact to trigger a supernova, the two launched their forces at the evacuating Jedi, while they went in search of Jedi relics to plunder. While Ulic battled his brother Cay Qel-Droma, Exar Kun returned with his treasure to Yavin 4—only to be betrayed by Ulic. Blocked from using the Force—light or dark—by his former paramour Nomi Sunrider, Ulic Qel-Droma surrendered to the Jedi and told them where to find Exar Kun's secret base.

Seeing that the Jedi fleet in the skies above him was poised to destroy him, Exar Kun opted for a somewhat risky escape. Utilizing the alchemical apparatus he used to mutate the Massassi, Exar Kun divested himself of his physical body and took refuge within one of his temples, knowing that his spirit would live forever and waiting for the day when he could take his vengeance on the Jedi.

Exar Kun: Male Human, Jedi Guardian 9/Sith Lord 8; Init +3; Defense 27 (+14 class, +3 Dex); Spd 10m; VP/WP 158/17; Atk +21/+16/+11/+6 melee (5d8+3/19–20 plus 5d8+3/19–20, double-bladed lightsaber) or +20/+15/+10/+5 ranged; SQ Exceptional minions, resource access; SV Fort +15, Ref +15, Will +10; SZ M; FP 8; DSP 18; Rep 12; Str 17, Dex 16, Con 17, Int 14, Wis 11, Cha 13. Challenge Code: H.

Equipment: Double-bladed lightsaber, Sith amulet, dark armor (+2 equipment bonus on saves against light side powers), Sith battleship, alchemical apparatus.

Skills: Computer Use +4, Craft (lightsaber) +8, Intimidate +13, Knowledge (Jedi lore) +12, Knowledge (Sith lore) +17, Read/Write Basic, Read/Write Sith, Speak Arkanian, Speak Basic, Speak Ryl, Speak Sith.

Force Skills: Affect Mind +13, Alchemy +24, Battlemind +18, Enhance Ability +13, Force Defense +21, Force Push +14, Move Object +14, See Force +12.

Feats: Ambidexterity, Exotic Weapon Proficiency (double-bladed lightsaber), Exotic Weapon Proficiency (lightsaber), Force-Sensitive, Heroic Surge, Two-Weapon Fighting, Weapon Focus (lightsaber), Weapon Group Proficiency (blaster pistols), Weapon Group Proficiency (simple weapons), Weapon Group Proficiency (vibro weapons).

Force Feats: Alter, Control, Deflect Blasters, Force Lightning, Knight Defense, Lightsaber Defense, Master Defense, Rage, Sense, Sith Sorcery.

The New Sith

The Sith species had died out two thousand years earlier, but their teachings lived on to be studied and absorbed by new darksiders. The word "Sith" itself came to mean a sect devoted to the dark side, though true students of Sith teachings were few and far between.

One such student was a rogue Jedi who absconded from the Jedi temple with a rare Sith holocron. Armed with its corrupt knowledge, this Jedi founded a new order of Sith, who flourished over the next thousand years. Though the Sith were strong enough to threaten their ancient Jedi enemies, they began fighting among themselves, and a great many of them were destroyed. The survivors, united under Sith Lord Kaan, gathered together to found a new Sith empire, but were driven back over the course of several battles to the planet Ruusan. There, Kaan's Sith warriors made their final stand, constructing a Force-powered "thought bomb." When the Jedi arrived for the final conflict, Lord Kaan detonated the device, destroying himself, his Sith army, and the Jedi Knights. The Jedi grieved at their losses, but also rejoiced that the Sith threat was finally ended.

Unfortunately, this was not so. One Sith Lord, Darth Bane, survived.

Darth Bane

Darth Bane, the last surviving Sith from the devastating Battle of Ruusan, devised a different path to power and darkness. The old system failed time and time again, and Bane decided that it was time for a new Sith Order to emerge, with a new philosophy and approach to conquest and vengeance. Where his now-dead associates craved power to such an extent that they even fought among themselves, Bane came to appreciate the need for patience and stealth. He would develop a new code of conduct. But first, he had to find refuge in the wake of the titanic battles between the forces of light and dark.

Forced to crash-land on Dxun, a moon of Onderon, by the spirit of Dark Lord Qordis, Bane encountered a strange life form. Hard-shelled, parasitic creatures called orbalisks attached themselves to Bane's body. He struggled to remove the creatures, but to no avail. After a time, he came to accept the creatures and realized that the symbiotic relationship they formed with him would be mutually beneficial. The creatures bred, multiplying and forming a living suit of armor that offered amazing protection, as well as giving him extraordinary strength and recuperative powers. He fashioned a cagelike helmet to keep the orbalisks from covering his face and inadvertently suffocating him, accepting that every advantage had a price.

With his own master killed in the Battle of Ruusan, Bane was forced to continue training on his own. He discovered a concentrated region of dark side power on the moon and a Sith holocron, and used these resources to build his own power. In the years spent communing with the dark side, with only orbalisks and the other monsters of Dxun for company (and the occasional appearance of a dark side spirit), Darth Bane developed the philosophy that would govern the Sith for the next millennium.

Control was the key, control and patience. Thus was born the most important rule of the new Sith Order. From now on, there could be only two Sith at any one time. There would always and only ever be a master and an apprentice.

With his strength returned, his philosophy determined, and his dark side powers enhanced and improved, Darth Bane subjugated a flying beast and used it to travel from Dxun to Onderon.

He would find an apprentice.

The legacy would live on.

Eventually, the Sith would have their revenge.

Darth Bane: Male Human, Jedi Guardian 4/Sith Warrior 2, Sith Lord 10; Init +4; Defense 23/32* (+9/+18* orbalisk armor, +4 Dex); Spd 10m; VP/WP 188/14; Atk +22/+17/+12/+7 melee** (5d8+3, lightsaber), +20/+15/+10/+5 ranged; SQ Exceptional minions, resource Access, Sith Battle Prowess, Sith Master; SV Fort +16, Ref +16, Will +14; SZ M; FP 12; DSP 24; Rep 18; Str 21, Dex 18, Con 14, Int 14, Wis 18, Cha 11. Challenge Code: G.

*Defense against lightsaber attacks.

Equipment: Orbalisk armor (90%), lightsaber**. Bane's armor enables him to heal 30 vitality points and 8 wound points per round.

**Darth Bane has constructed his own lightsaber.

Skills: Bluff +6, Computer Use +6, Craft (lightsaber) +12, Diplomacy +10, Gather Information +7, Intimidate +10, Knowledge (Sith lore) +8,

Read/Write Basic, Read/Write Sith, Sense Motive +8, Speak Basic, Speak Sith, Tumble +1.

Force Skills: Alchemy +15, Battlemind +13, Empathy +6, Enhance Ability +10, Farseeing +14, Force Defense +14, Force Grip +14, Force Push +4, Force Stealth +16, Heal Self +6, Move Object +7, See Force +7, Telepathy +7.

Feats: Armor Proficiency (light), Armor Proficiency (medium), Armor Proficiency (heavy), Cleave, Exotic Weapon Proficiency (lightsaber), Force-Sensitive, Power Attack, Weapon Group Proficiency (blaster pistols), Weapon Group Proficiency (simple weapons).

Force Feats: Alter, Control, Drain Force, Force Lightning, Hatred, Knight Defense, Lightsaber Defense, Rage, Sense, Sith Sorcery, Sith Sword Defense.

Sorcerers of Tund

For thousands of years before the Battle of Yavin, the Sorcerers of Tund studied the mystical arts in their monastic enclaves on their homeworld of Tund, seeking a better understanding of the galaxy and the powers that held it together. While members of the Jedi Order would recognize their field of study as training in the Force, the Sorcerers saw their abilities as a kind of magic, and presented themselves to the galaxy at large as powerful wizards.

The Jedi Council knew of the Sorcerers, and periodically sent representatives to Tund—at first to try to convince the Sorcerers to join the Jedi Order and study the Force without the trappings of mysticism and magic. But as the Sorcerers demonstrated power oftentimes at least as great as that of the Jedi sent to recruit them, the Jedi Council discreetly chose to allow the Sorcerers to study the Force in their own way—provided, of course, they did not delve into the teachings of the dark side. Later representatives came only to observe and evaluate, seeking signs that the Sorcerers had become corrupted. Satisfied that they were not, the Jedi Order developed a comfortable détente with the Sorcerers of Tund. But roughly one thousand years before the Battle of Yavin, the Jedi Order became preoccupied with the Sith Lord Kaan, and following the terrible battle on Ruusan, the depleted ranks of the Jedi ceased visiting Tund and eventually the Jedi all but forgot about the Sorcerers.

Rokur Gepta

The enigmatic figure known as Rokur Gepta was the last of the Sorcerers of Tund. Gepta was a master of illusion, able to create images directly in the minds of his enemies, torturing them with their past mistakes and agonies.

CROKE ILLUSORY PRESENCE

The natural ability of Crokes to create personal illusions allows the creatures to create extremely convincing disguises. This illusion is so complete that onlookers are only allowed a Will save (DC 25) to penetrate the disguise when the Croke is stunned or unconscious (and thus not concentrating on maintaining the illusion). Because the illusion is a manifestation of the Force, the Force Defense skill can add a bonus to this Will saving throw.

A Croke's natural facility with illusions also grants it a +2 species bonus on Disguise and Illusion checks.

Of all the Sorcerers, only he seemed interested in expanding his dominion and pursuing power in the galaxy at large. Eager to extend his reach beyond the tiny world of Tund, Gepta exploited the Sorcerers' knowledge for his own plans of galactic domination. After learning all the Sorcerers could teach him, Gepta killed the last of the Sorcerers and laid waste to their planet.

Rokur Gepta wore the heavy, deep gray robes of the Sorcerers of Tund, completely concealing his body from view. With his head and face wrapped in a turbanlike headdress and cowl, only Rokur Gepta's eyes were visible—and those who looked into them likened the sorcerer's eyes to swirling nebulas of darkness. Thanks to his illusions, to some he appeared as a giant, and to others a malign dwarf, but Gepta's greatest secret was that he was not humanoid at all. Gepta was actually a Croke—a grayish, snaillike creature, no bigger than a Wookiee's fist, with thousands of tiny, hairy legs. Crokes—able to survive in vacuum and renowned for their naked ambition—were naturally adept at illusory disguises, enabling them to blend in unnoticed with the other sentient species of the galaxy.

At some point roughly five years before the destruction of the first Death Star at the Battle of Yavin, Rokur Gepta allied himself with the Empire—at least, insofar as it was necessary to obtain Imperial materiel for his own use. Gepta acquired *Wennis*, a decommissioned Imperial Cruiser, an Imperial-trained crew, and a license to operate more or less at his own discretion. His plots to usurp the Emperor's throne and rule the galaxy, however, went awry when he vied with the famous smuggler Lando Calrissian, and Rokur Gepta forgot his goals when his own overriding hatred caused him to pursue Calrissian from star system to star system. Eventually, Gepta challenged the smuggler to single combat. He lost and was squeezed to a greasy slime in Calrissian's gloved hands, thus ending his dreams of galactic domination.

Rokur Gepta: Male Croke, Force Adept 12; Init –2; Defense 24 (+8 class, +8 size, –2 Dex); Spd 10m; VP/WP 54/6; Atk +13/+8/+3 melee (1d3–4, punch) or +15/+10/+5 ranged (3d6, blaster pistol); SQ Illusory presence, +2 species bonus on Disguise and Illusion checks, Force weapon +1d4, Comprehend speech, Force talisman +2; SV Fort +4, Ref +4, Will +11; SZ F; FP 7; DSP 18; Rep 15; Str 2, Dex 6, Con 6, Int 16, Wis 16, Cha 18. Challenge Code: F.

Equipment: Blaster pistol, small menagerie of lethal pets, decommissioned Imperial Cruiser (*Wennis*).

Skills: Bluff +13, Diplomacy +8, Disguise +16, Handle Animal +10, Intimidate +15, Knowledge (Sith lore) +7, Knowledge (Tund Sorcerers) +9, Read/Write Basic, Read/Write Sith, Read/Write Tundan, Sense Motive +9, Speak Basic, Speak Tundan.

Force Skills: Affect Mind +12, Empathy +11, Fear +22, Illusion +24, Move Object +18, See Force +11.

Feats: Force-Sensitive, Infamy, Persuasive, Skill Emphasis (Disguise), Skill Emphasis (Illusion), Weapon Group Proficiency (blaster pistols), Weapon Group Proficiency (primitive weapons), Weapon Group Proficiency (simple weapons).

Force Feats: Alter, Control, Force Mastery, Sense.

Nightsisters of Dathomir

Dathomir is an all but unknown world living in a state of barbarism. Six hundred years before the Battle of Yavin, a failed Jedi named Allya found herself exiled to an obscure prison colony on Dathomir. Using her meager Force training, she rose up against the overseers, subjugated the other prisoners, and learned to tame the planet's fierce natural predators, the rancors. Allya's female descendants became the ruling class on Dathomir, and, like her, they were strong in the Force. Allya taught her children what little she knew about the Force, and they passed it on to their children, and to their children, until Dathomiri understanding of the Force came to resemble shamanistic magic, and its users "witches."

Over the centuries, Dathomiri Force witches occasionally fell to the dark side and were exiled from their clans for their evil acts. Such dark Force witches came to be known as Nightsisters and practiced more violent forms of Force "magic." Where light side Force witches learned to work with their environment, the Nightsisters bent the environment to their will, and were able to call forth rain, wind, and lightning, to climb spiderlike on vertical surfaces, and to control the weak-minded like virtual puppets.

The most powerful of the Nightsisters was an aged crone named Gethzerion.

Gethzerion the Nightsister

The ancient hag Gethzerion was once an extremely beautiful and ambitious young Dathomiri witch with a promising future. Gethzerion was the second daughter of Augwynne, the Clan Mother of the Singing Mountain Clan. But Gethzerion and Augwynne frequently clashed on interpretations of *The Book of Law*, the text passed down to the witches of Dathomir by the original Force witch, Allya. Gethzerion believed that the more dangerous spells mentioned in Allya's writing were not meant never to be used, but to be used only by the most skilled witches. No matter how well reasoned Gethzerion felt her arguments were, the final decision always rested with Augwynne—who never failed to rule against using the powerful and destructive magic. Eventually, Gethzerion realized that the only way she would change the interpretation of *The Book of Law* would be when Augwynne was dead, and she, Gethzerion, was the final authority in the Singing Mountain Clan. The only problem was that Augwynne was healthy and strong—and Gethzerion was impatient.

Gethzerion sought out another malcontent in the clan, a Force witch named Baritha. The two began plotting to murder Augwynne. With her mother out of the way, Gethzerion believed, she was the natural choice to replace lead the clan. Then Gethzerion and Baritha could begin studying

THE BOOK OF LAW AND THE BOOK OF SHADOWS

Before the original Force witch Allya died, she created a book of advice, based loosely on the Jedi Code, to guide her children in the safe and sane use of the Force. As generations passed and her descendants scattered, each new clan made a copy of Allya's "book of law" to share with their new clansisters and to add to as they learned new lessons about the Force.

The central message of *The Book of Law* is that the magic it describes must always be used wisely—that a Force witch must never surrender to evil, lest she be consumed by it. (In her own way, Allya was warning her followers to avoid the dark side.) But as the book was handed down through the generations, other Force witches added information to it, including examples of dark side magic. And though they included similar warnings to avoid such uses of the Force, they also unintentionally created enticements for those eager to expand their power.

Any given copy of *The Book of Law* contains a primitive, abbreviated version of the Jedi Code, as well as a few references to dark side applications of the Force. Reading the book allows the reader to gain either 2 ranks in Knowledge (Dathomir magic) or 1 rank in Knowledge (Jedi lore).

When Gethzerion created the Nightsister Clan, she decided that they needed their own book of lore to pass down through the generations—if only to tell the story of how their clan was formed. *The Book of Shadows* goes into quite a bit of detail about the dark side of the Force as well, providing the reader with advice on using dark side powers. Reading *The Book of Shadows* allows the reader to ignore the Knowledge (local culture) requirement for taking the dark Force witch prestige class, but the reader automatically gains a Dark Side Point when he or she enters the dark Force witch class (above and beyond the 4 or more Dark Side Points required to take the class).

the more powerful rituals in *The Book of Law* at their leisure. Unfortunately, their plan went awry, and it was Gethzerion's younger sister, Kara'Teel, who died—not Augwynne. When Augwynne learned that Gethzerion planned the "accident"—and why—she was left with no choice but to exile Baritha and Gethzerion. Though it broke her heart to do so, she knew it was the only way to separate Gethzerion from *The Book of Law*, and give her daughter a chance to cleanse her spirit and return peacefully to her clan.

But circumstances conspired to drive a wedge even farther between the two exiled Force witches and the Singing Mountain Clan. Attacked by three other outcast Force witches, Baritha and Gethzerion managed to prevail, slaying two of the three attackers. The survivor begged to be spared, and promised her loyalty in exchange for mercy. Though Baritha wanted to kill the third one as well, Gethzerion realized that she did not need to rule the Singing Mountain Clan if she were leader of her own clan, a clan more powerful than Augwynne's—one that could take *The Book of Law* by force.

Gethzerion and Baritha began seeking out other exiled Force witches to join their new clan, which they called the Nightsisters. The Nightsisters explored the forbidden magic that Gethzerion could recall from *The Book of Law*, and through trial and error learned to master the dark arts of Dathomir. They fought periodic battles with the other clans of Dathomir, and whenever possible, they promised to spare captives if they would forswear their old clan and join the Nightsisters. In some cases, other Force witches tried to use their

own dark magic against them. While they enjoyed a certain amount of success, their brush with the dark side of the Force pulled them down the same evil path that Gethzerion and Baritha followed, and they too became Nightsisters. Even Gethzerion's surviving sister, Baruka, foolishly surrendered herself to the Nightsisters, hoping to turn Gethzerion away from the dark side—only to be corrupted by it herself. The ranks of the Nightsisters swelled, while the ranks of the traditional Force witches dwindled.

Though already strong, the Nightsisters became even stronger when Imperial ships arrived on Dathomir to recreate the old prison colony. Gethzerion approached the Imperial commander and offered the services of her clan to control prisoners. He was not entirely sure why she made the offer, but the commander readily accepted her offer. Gethzerion and her dark compatriots became a familiar sight in the Imperial compound, and no one thought to question why they were so curious about the workings of the short-range shuttles berthed at the base.

But the Emperor, who sensed Gethzerion's power through the Force, realized that once Gethzerion mastered the controls of a shuttle, she could reach the orbiting docking facility, and from there spread her influence to the rest of the galaxy, one day perhaps even challenging him. The Emperor ordered the orbital docks destroyed, abandoning the Imperial forces of the penal colony to Gethzerion and the Nightsisters. Ships were assigned to periodically visit the planet and make orbital scans to ensure that the Nightsisters were still confined to Dathomir, but were given strict orders never to land.

This state of affairs continued for many years, until the death of the Emperor. Imperial Commander Zsinj, now a power-hungry warlord, returned to Dathomir pursuing the smuggler turned war hero Han Solo, who had kidnapped Leia Organa to prevent her from marrying the Hapan ambassador Prince Isolder. Learning of Solo's presence on Dathomir—and Zsinj's interest in him—Gethzerion offered her services in capturing the smuggler, if Zsinj would in turn give her a hyperspace-capable transport. Zsinj reluctantly agreed, but their mutual plans were thwarted when Organa's brother, the new Jedi Knight Luke Skywalker, arrived on Dathomir with Prince Isolder and helped the Force witches of the Singing Mountain Clan defeat the numerically superior Nightsisters. At the controls of Solo's ship, the *Millennium Falcon*, Luke Skywalker fired the missile barrage that destroyed Gethzerion's transport before she could escape into hyperspace, thus ending the threat of Gethzerion and her dark side followers.

Gethzerion: Female Human, Force Adept 7/Dark Force Witch 10; Init +2; Defense 24 (+12 class, +2 Dex); Spd 10m; VP/WP 122/15; Atk +13/+8/+3 melee (1d6+1, quarterstaff) or +14/+9/+4 ranged; SQ Force weapon +1d4, comprehend speech, inspire fear −3, spider walk, Force flight (20m), enshroud; SV Fort +12, Ref +11, Will +16; SZ M; FP 10; DSP 21; Rep 10; Str 12, Dex 14, Con 15, Int 16, Wis 14, Cha 16. Challenge Code: G.

  Equipment: Tattered exotic robes, original copy of *The Book of Shadows*, Imperial-issue comlink.

  Skills: Bluff +7, Climb +5, Diplomacy +9, Handle Animal +11, Hide +6, Intimidate +13, Jump +5, Knowledge (Dathomir) +9, Knowledge (shadow magic) +15, Pilot +6, Read/Write Basic, Read/Write Paecian, Ride +12, Speak Basic, Speak Paecian, Survival +10.

  Force Skills: Affect Mind +12, Drain Energy +12, Empathy +10, Enhance Senses +10, Farseeing +8, Fear +14, Force Defense +12, Force Grip +12, Force Push +8, Heal Self +8, Illusion +13, Move Object +18, See Force +12, Telepathy +10.

  Feats: Force-Sensitive, Frightful Presence, Infamy, Iron Will, Skill Emphasis (Move Object), Weapon Group Proficiency (blaster pistols), Weapon Group Proficiency (primitive weapons), Weapon Group Proficiency (simple weapons).

  Force Feats: Alter, Control, Force Lightning, Force Whirlwind, Rage, Sense, Summon Storm.

The Dark Jedi

Since the founding of the Jedi Order, thousands of years before the Battle of Yavin, only a small number of Jedi Knights have turned completely from the path of light to the path of darkness. To the Order, each Dark Jedi's story is a tragic tale, filled with ambition, passion, and mortal weaknesses. Although the Jedi do not like to dwell on these failures, every Jedi who takes on a Padawan is expected to meditate on the lessons provided by the Dark Jedi Knights.

Set Harth, Dark Jedi

Had Set Harth remained true to the Jedi Code, he could one day have become a powerful Jedi Knight. But from the beginning, Harth felt that the shortest distance between opposing viewpoints was violence, preferring fighting to talking. For this reason, his Jedi master, Aru-Wen, instructed Set Harth to remain at the Jedi Temple on Coruscant while he joined Jedi Master Hoth's Army of Light as they did battle with Lord Kaan's Sith forces. When the Sith thought bomb destroyed the Jedi and Sith armies alike, Set Harth was left without an instructor. Rather than seek a new master from the surviving Jedi, Set preferred the freedom of independent training.

Harth began by seeking out knowledge unavailable to him through the Jedi Temple. He tracked down rumors of a Sith artifact from the battlefields of Ruusan, eventually dueling for its possession with a powerful dark side warrior in an abandoned Sith armory. During this combat, Set Harth gave in to his anger, opening himself to the dark side and completing a journey he began years before when he battled one of Sith Lord Kaan's warriors. Winning the artifact, Harth began to explore its uses, little realizing that its evil was infecting him and drawing him even farther down the dark path.

Eventually, Set Harth grew disenchanted with the power of the artifact, and from his base on Nar Shaddaa, began investigating rumors of other Sith artifacts that survived the destruction on Ruusan. His search led him to a Hutt slaver who, to Harth's surprise, was simultaneously dealing with another Dark Jedi—a woman named Bal Serinus. For some reason, Harth's presence infuriated Bal Serinus, and she attacked him in the Hutt's palace. The battle left both Jedi exhausted and helpless, and they were captured by the Hutt slaver.

While imprisoned, Set Harth slowly learned to use the Force to communicate with Bal Serinus in the next cell. Desperate for companionship in the Hutt's dungeons, Set Harth forged a bond with the Jedi woman and promised himself he would protect her from harm. But when Bal Serinus suddenly rebuffed Harth's telepathic contact with no explanation, he grew bitter and angry all over again, and his pledge of protection turned to a vow of vengeance.

Set Harth: Male Human, Jedi Guardian 8; Init +2; Defense 20 (+8 class, +2 Dex); Spd 10m; VP/WP

70/15; Atk +10/+5 melee* (3d8+2/19–20, lightsaber) or +10/+5 ranged (3d6, blaster pistol); SV Fort +8, Ref +8, Will +4; SZ M; FP 5; DSP 8; Rep 8; Str 13, Dex 14, Con 15, Int 12, Wis 11, Cha 12. Challenge Code: D.

Equipment: Lightsaber*, blaster pistol.

*Set Harth has constructed his own lightsaber.

Skills: Computer Use +3, Craft (lightsaber) +5, Intimidate +5, Knowledge (Jedi lore) +5, Knowledge (Sith lore) +3, Pilot +3, Read/Write Basic, Tumble +6, Speak Basic, Speak Huttese.

Force Skills: Affect Mind +4, Battlemind +12, Enhance Ability +6, Force Defense +8, Force Push +5, Move Object +9, See Force +2, Telepathy +8.

Feats: Dodge, Exotic Weapon Proficiency (lightsaber), Force-Sensitive, Heroic Surge, Weapon Group Proficiency (blaster pistols), Weapon Group Proficiency (simple weapons).

Force Feats: Alter, Control, Deflect Blasters, Knight Defense, Lightsaber Defense, Sense.

Xanatos, Former Jedi Padawan

Before Jedi Qui-Gon Jinn selected young Obi-Wan Kenobi as his Padawan learner, Xanatos was his apprentice. Qui-Gon discovered Xanatos as a child. The boy, strong in the Force, was the son of Crion, leader of a powerful family on Telos. Qui-Gon convinced his father to place the boy in Jedi training. Growing up in the Jedi Temple on Coruscant, young Xanatos had a genuine desire to learn and an excellent aptitude for Jedi training. His lightsaber skills were unsurpassed in his class, and he was a leader among the other students.

But Xanatos wasn't perfect. He constantly fought with the other students. He loved to taunt his opponents, to play mind games on friends and foes alike. With fierce intellect and a quick, agile mind, he was destined for greatness within the Jedi Order—if he didn't succumb to his driving ambition and seething anger first.

Indeed, it was Xanatos's anger and ambition that led to his undoing. Qui-Gon Jinn watched Xanatos grow and was sure he was ready to graduate from Padawan learner to Jedi Knight. Yoda, however, wasn't convinced. "One more test," Yoda insisted. He sent Qui-Gon and his apprentice to investigate disturbing reports of trouble in Xanatos's home star system. On Telos, Xanatos saw the power and riches that his father commanded. Crion was leading the star system to civil war, and he urged his son to join him.

Qui-Gon understood Xanatos's final test. The young man had to make a choice: embrace the Jedi Code or grab the material wealth and power offered by his corrupt and scheming father. Xanatos came to the conclusion that the Jedi Order and Qui-Gon in particular had deprived him of his heritage, and he

hated them for it. When Qui-Gon was forced to battle and kill Crion, his lightsaber sliced through the man's ring of office. Steaming hot, the piece of cut metal clattered to the floor. Xanatos picked it up, ignoring the searing heat, and pressed it to his face. That scar would forever remind him of his hatred for Qui-Gon and the Jedi. Master and apprentice battled as well, and though Qui-Gon won the fight, he let his former student live. Xanatos failed his final test, disgracing the Jedi and betraying Qui-Gon.

Years later, as Qui-Gon was deciding whether to accept Obi-Wan Kenobi as his apprentice, the pair met Xanatos. Strong in the dark side of the Force, Xanatos had pale skin and dark blue eyes. Black hair flowed to his shoulders, and the broken circle scar marred his cheek. He was dressed all in black, and he carried a lightsaber. The Jedi's solemn rule was that if you left the Order, you did not retain your lightsaber. Xanatos blatantly broke that rule.

"Qui-Gon is the worst kind of master," Xanatos told young Obi-Wan. "He denies you his trust yet demands everything of you." He was a master manipulator, feeding doubt by twisting the truth. A technological genius with a lust for power and wealth, he was merciless in seeking vengeance against the Order and his former Master.

Qui-Gon and Obi-Wan confronted Xanatos a number of times. In Xanatos's last bid for revenge, he invaded the Jedi Temple itself and corrupted a young student named Bruck. He set the fusion furnace to explode, hoping to wipe out the Temple and its occupants, but Qui-Gon and Obi-Wan foiled this plot. The pair met Xanatos in final battle on Telos. When Xanatos realized he could not win, he told Qui-Gon, "I am your biggest failure. Live with that. And live with this." He then stepped into a pool of black acid, presumed to have killed himself instead of surrendering.

Xanatos: Male Human, Jedi Guardian 6/Dark Side Marauder 4; Init +3; Defense 24 (+11 class, +3 Dex); Spd 10m; VP/WP 61/11; Atk +14/+9 melee* (3d8+3, lightsaber) or +13/+8 ranged; SV Fort +9, Ref +12, Will +5; SZ M; FP 4; DSP 13; Rep 8; Str 17, Dex 16, Con 11, Int 16, Wis 12, Cha 13. Challenge Code: E.

Equipment: Lightsaber*, datapad, tool kit.

*Xanatos has constructed his own lightsaber.

Skills: Bluff +7, Computer Use +11, Craft (lightsaber) +7, Repair +12, Tumble +9.

Force Skills: Battlemind +9, Enhance Ability +7, Fear +5, Force Defense +7, Force Stealth +8, Heal Self +8, Move Object +10, See Force +5, Telepathy +5.

Feats: Exotic Weapon Proficiency (lightsaber), Force-Sensitive, Weapon Group Proficiency (blaster pistols), Heroic Surge, Power Attack, Weapon Group Proficiency (simple weapons).

Force Feats: Alter, Control, Rage, Sense.

The Return of the Sith

After centuries of quiet plotting, the time finally came for the Sith to return to their rightful place as rulers of the galaxy. Careful manipulation of the tradition-bound Republic allowed the current Sith Lord, Darth Sidious, to infiltrate a Senate weakened by corruption and apathy, and to slowly undermine public confidence in the Jedi Order. The first, most telling blow came when the Trade Federation blockaded the small world of Naboo. In the ensuing battle for control of the planet, a Sith warrior appeared for the first time in a thousand years. This Sith, Darth Maul, slew Jedi Master Qui-Gon Jinn—reminding the complacent Jedi that they were not the only Force wielders in the galaxy.

Suddenly, the Jedi had a new enemy to fear.

Darth Sidious

When the Sith finally emerged from a thousand years of watching and waiting, they numbered—in accordance with the tradition set down by Darth Bane—only two. The most powerful of these was Darth Sidious, an ice-cold, diabolically calculating genius equipped with the strength of the dark side of the Force, as well as an enormous wealth of Sith artifacts, equipment, and knowledge. Perhaps the best weapon in his arsenal was his keen understanding of galactic politics, and his seemingly unlimited ability to engineer situations that ultimately served to further empower the Sith.

Sidious's origins are unknown. He may already have been on the dark path when he began studying Sith teachings, or his discovery of ancient Sith artifacts might have unlocked his dark side potential and brought him to the attention of an existing Sith. Whatever the case, Darth Sidious learned his craft well. Possessed of malevolent cunning and sustained by the dark side, he presented a pleasant—even trustworthy—face to the public, while also working in secret to undermine the foundations of the Republic.

Darth Sidious planned to turn the Republic against the Jedi, since he knew that he could not single-handedly destroy the entire Jedi Order—especially after having lost his apprentice Darth Maul during the Battle of Naboo. Ideally, he desired to watch the Jedi die one by one, but he could not bring about that particular turn of events until he found a new apprentice.

Darth Sidious: Male Human, Noble 3/Dark Side Devotee 3/Sith Acolyte 3/Sith Lord 9; Init +0; Defense 27 (+17 class); Spd 10m; VP/WP 124/13; Atk +16/+11/+6 melee* (4d8/19–20, lightsaber) or +15/+10/+5 ranged; SQ Call in a favor (2), inspire confidence +1, dark side talisman +2, resource access,

exceptional minions; SV Fort +13, Ref +11, Will +19; SZ M; FP 9; DSP 32; Rep 16; Str 11, Dex 11, Con 13, Int 18, Wis 16, Cha 15. Challenge Code: I.

Equipment: Lightsaber*, Sith holocron, private transport.

*Darth Sidious has constructed his own lightsaber.

Skills: Bluff +12, Computer Use +9, Craft (lightsaber) +6, Diplomacy +18, Gather Information +18, Intimidate +17, Knowledge (Jedi lore) +10, Knowledge (Naboo) +6, Knowledge (politics) +17, Knowledge (Sith lore) +15, Read/Write Basic, Read/Write Bothan, Read/Write Sith, Sense Motive +13, Speak Basic, Speak Bothan, Speak Sith.

Force Skills: Affect Mind +13, Alchemy +17, Control Mind +12, Empathy +17, Farseeing +23, Fear +16, Force Defense +16, Force Grip +16, Heal Self +14, Move Object +12, See Force +18, Telepathy +20.

Feats: Exotic Weapon Proficiency (lightsaber), Force-Sensitive, Skill Emphasis (Farseeing), Skill Emphasis (Fear), Skill Emphasis (Knowledge: politics), Skill Emphasis (Telepathy), Trustworthy, Weapon Group Proficiency (blaster pistols), Weapon Group Proficiency (simple weapons).

Force Feats: Alter, Control, Dissipate Energy, Drain Force, Force Lightning, Force Mastery, Force Mind, Sense, Sith Sorcery.

Note to Gamemasters

The statistics presented here differ from those presented in the *Star Wars Roleplaying Game*. While these statistics provide a much more holistic interpretation of Darth Sidious's abilities, either version of Darth Sidious works perfectly well for most roleplaying purposes.

Darth Maul

Where Darth Sidious was a strategist, his fearsome apprentice Darth Maul was a blazing lightsaber aimed directly at the heart of the Jedi Order. A Zabrak born on the world of Iridonia, the child who would one day be known as Darth Maul was taken offworld and indoctrinated into the ways of the dark side, trained by Darth Sidious in not only Sith lore, but in the Jedi arts. Any display of fear on his part was punished with vicious retribution. Any hint of mercy in his character was rewarded with severe cruelty. One those rare occasions when he relaxed his guard, his master nearly killed him to remind him that a Sith can never afford a moment of rest. After years of this kind of treatment, Darth Maul was absolutely ruthless—a perfect Sith weapon. By the time he reached adolescence, Darth Maul was already a hardened, remorseless killer.

Maul's final test as a Sith apprentice occurred on an isolated Outer Rim world. Abandoned there by Darth Sidious, he was told that he had to survive on his own until Sidious returned a month later, all the while being hunted by hordes of deadly assassin droids. Maul fought as best as he could, but exhaustion and hunger finally took their toll, and one of the tireless droids finally wounded him badly enough that he felt he could not go on. At that point, Darth Sidious returned and challenged his apprentice to a lightsaber duel, telling Maul that he had secretly been training a second apprentice in case Maul failed his final test—which, by failing to kill Sidious in the duel, he just had.

Anger and hatred welled up in Maul, and he drew renewed strength from the dark side. Hurling himself at Darth Sidious, he nearly bested his master with a flurry of deadly lightsaber blows. Sidious barely deflected them all. Eventually Maul spent his fury, and Darth Sidious still stood. Maul prepared himself for death—but Sidious only laughed. By giving in to his rage and hatred to kill his own master—by *wanting* to kill his own master—Maul had in fact passed the final test. Now he was a Sith Lord—Darth Maul, Dark Lord of the Sith.

Taking Darth Maul to a secret facility on Coruscant, Sidious gave his protégé funds and materiel, along with detailed schematics with which to construct the weapons of a Sith. Maul built vehicles, droids, and weapons, including his

preferred weapon, a double-bladed lightsaber modeled on the ancient weapon of the Sith Lord Exar Kun. He began to pursue missions of terror and assassination for Darth Sidious, following some terrible plan known only to his master. He fought—and slaughtered—countless foes, including politicians, warlords, merchants, and even all but destroying the fledgling Black Sun criminal cartel. The foes he longed to face were the Jedi, the ancient enemy of the Sith. When Darth Sidious sent him to Tatooine to capture the missing queen of Naboo, Darth Maul got his first chance. Queen Amidala was guarded by two Jedi Knights—Qui-Gon Jinn and his apprentice, Obi-Wan Kenobi.

Though he failed on Tatooine, Darth Maul enjoyed partial success later, on Naboo, when the two Jedi returned with Amidala to retake Naboo from Sidious's pawns, the Trade Federation. Though he managed to slay the older Jedi, Qui-Gon Jinn, the death of his master seemed to give Obi-Wan Kenobi renewed strength, and Darth Maul perished, sliced in two by the younger Jedi's lightsaber.

Darth Maul: Male Zabrak, Soldier 1/Dark Side Marauder 3/Sith Warrior 6/Sith Lord 2; Init +4; Defense 26 (+12 class, +4 Dex); Spd 10m; VP/WP 120/16; Atk +15/+10/+5 melee (1d6+3, martial arts)

or +17/+12/+7 melee* (5d8+3/19–20 plus
5d8+3/19–20, double-bladed lightsaber) or
+16/+11/+6 ranged (3d4, Sith lanvarok); SQ Enemy
bonus +2, uncanny dodge (retain Dex bonus),
resource access; SV Fort +16, Ref +13, Will +7; SZ
M; FP 6; DSP 14; Rep 7; Str 17, Dex 19, Con 16, Int
14, Wis 11, Cha 12. Challenge Code: F.

   Equipment: Double-bladed lightsaber*, lanvarok,
3 "Dark Eye" probe droids, wrist link, electrobinocu-
lars, Sith speeder, Sith Infiltrator (*Scimitar*).

   *Darth Maul has constructed his own lightsaber.

   Skills: Computer Use +7, Craft (lightsaber) +7,
Intimidate +10, Jump +5, Knowledge (Jedi lore) +6,
Knowledge (Sith lore) +8, Read/Write Basic,
Read/Write Sith, Repair +5, Speak Basic, Speak
Huttese, Speak Sith, Survival +4, Tumble +15.

   Force Skills: Affect Mind +3, Battlemind +13,
Force Defense +11, Force Grip +13, Force Push +8,
Force Stealth +5, Move Object +12, See Force +8

   Feats: Armor Proficiency (light), Exotic Weapon
Proficiency (double-bladed lightsaber), Exotic
Weapon Proficiency (lightsaber), Expertise, Force-
Sensitive, Heroic Surge, Power Attack, Two-Weapon
Fighting, Weapon Finesse (double-bladed light-
saber), Weapon Group Proficiency (blaster pistols),
Weapon Group Proficiency (blaster rifles), Weapon
Group Proficiency (heavy weapons), Weapon Group
Proficiency (simple weapons), Weapon Group
Proficiency (vibro weapons).

   Force Feats: Alter, Control, Deflect Blasters,
Lightsaber Defense, Rage, Sense.

Note to Gamemasters

The statistics presented here differ from those
presented in the *Star Wars Roleplaying Game.*
While these statistics provide a much more holistic
interpretation of Darth Maul's abilities, either
version of Darth Maul works perfectly well for
most roleplaying purposes.

Jedi Hunters

Though many of the galaxy's citizens think of Jedi
as undefeatable warriors, the sad truth is that Jedi
frequently fall in battle. Even more tragic is when
one of them turns against the others, or when a
misguided individual takes it as a personal crusade
to destroy the Jedi wherever they are found. These
"Jedi-hunters" are dangerous in the extreme, not
only because they threaten the guardians of peace
and justice in the galaxy, but because in doing so
they flirt dangerously with the dark side.

Aurra Sing

Aurra Sing is a predator who hunts the most
dangerous type of prey: Jedi Knights. As a freelance

bounty hunter, she accepts commissions for a variety of tasks, not all of which revolve around the
Jedi. One of her most prized possessions, however,
is a carrying case in which rest the lightsabers of
five defeated Jedi. The case has room for two more,
and she wears another lightsaber at her belt. Her
most potent weapon is her hatred of the Jedi, and
whenever she wields it, she draws slowly closer to
the dark side.

   Had Aurra Sing's life worked out differently, she
might have been a Jedi herself. Born to a spice
addict on Nar Shaddaa, Aurra Sing was discovered by
the Jedi Master known as the Dark Woman and
taken away from the smuggler's moon to be trained
as a Jedi. She spent the next seven years of her life
in the Jedi Temple on Coruscant. At age nine, while
offworld, Aurra Sing was captured by pirates. The
pirates told her that the Dark Woman had sold her
to them—beginning Aurra Sing's lifelong hatred for
all Jedi, and her former master in particular.

   She learned piloting and astrogation—and how to
stage an ambush and take a life—from the pirates,
until their captain grew worried that she would
someday ambush and kill him. He sold her to a
Hutt named Nooga, who in turn handed her over to
the Anzati, alien vampires who owed him a favor.
They trained Aurra Sing as Nooga's private enforcer,
altering her biomechanically to overcome the short-
comings of her "weaker" species, but were in turn
stunned by how eagerly she adapted their ways: the
hunt, the kill, and the amoral mentality that made
both so easy. When her training was complete, the
Anzati returned her to Nooga the Hutt, and Aurra
Sing promptly assassinated him.

   Without a master for the first time in her life,
Aurra Sing was at a loss. She had trained as a Jedi.
She had trained as a pirate. She had trained to
become one of the finest assassins in the galaxy. Her
options were nearly limitless, but she decided that
what she really wanted to do was hurt the people
who had hurt her the most: the Jedi.

   Aurra Sing embarked on a career of paid assassi-
nations and bounty hunting, always keeping an eye
out for contracts, or even merely opportunities, to
fight Jedi. Since Jedi die just like anyone else, she
soon acquired a lightsaber. She accumulated a
collection of them, mementos of her victories over
the best warriors the galaxy had to offer. Her
exploits earned her notoriety in the galaxy's underworld, and she received commissions from a number
of Outer Rim luminaries, including the Hutts, Jabba
and Gardulla. (She despises the dry, desert air of
Tatooine, but the money is good.)

   Over the years, Aurra Sing has obtained a number
of tools useful to her quest, including the Rhen-
Orm biocomputer that the Anzati implanted in her

skull, a Corellian corvette, a heavily modified ion-repulsorlift swoop, and a half-dozen lightsabers. Aurra Sing is a deadly foe, more than a match for most opponents, but she still has not gone completely over to the dark side. Properly approached and guided, she could be led back to the path of the Jedi—but no Jedi has survived her onslaughts long enough to make the attempt.

Aurra Sing: Female near-Human, Jedi Guardian 2/Scout 6/Bounty Hunter 4: Init ı6; Defense 24 (+12 class, +2 Dex); Spd 10m; VP/WP 92/14; Atk +11/+6 melee (1d3+1, punch) or +11/+6 melee (2d8+1/19–20, lightsaber) or +12/+7 ranged; SQ Trailblazing, uncanny dodge (retains Dex bonus to Defense), skill mastery (Survival), target bonus +2, sneak attack +2d6; SV Fort +7, Ref +8, Will +5; SZ M; FP 5; DSP 7; Rep 8. Str 12, Dex 15, Con 14, Int 13, Wis 12, Cha 12. Challenge Code: E.

　　Equipment: Lightsabers (several), slugthrower rifle, blaster pistols (2), utility vest, protective bodysuit, Rhen-Orm biocomputer, ion-repulsorlift swoop, Corellian blockade runner, jumpsuit.

　　Skills: Astrogate +5, Computer Use +5, Gather Information +6, Hide +12, Intimidate +7, Jump +3, Knowledge (Anzati lore) +7, Knowledge (streetwise) +6, Knowledge (Jedi lore) +6, Move Silently +12, Pilot +7, Read/Write Basic, Speak Basic, Speak Huttese, Spot +7, Survival +11, Tumble +8.

　　Force Skills: Battlemind +8, Force Push +7, Move Object +5, See Force +13.

　　Feats: Exotic Weapon Proficiency (lightsaber), Expertise, Force-Sensitive, Improved Initiative, Track, Two-Weapon Fighting, Weapon Group Proficiency (blaster pistols), Weapon Group Proficiency (blaster rifles), Weapon Group Proficiency (simple weapons).

　　Force Feats: Alter, Control, Sense.

Del Korrot

In the aftermath of the Clone Wars, in the months after the Jedi Purge, Del Korrot emerged from the shadows to offer a singular service to the Emperor and his newly empowered Empire. The Cerean psychopath promised to hunt down and destroy any Jedi Knights or Force-sensitive individuals who managed to survive the brutal period that marked the end of the Jedi Order. Grudgingly, the Emperor accepted Korrot's offer and awarded him limited authority to operate within the confines of the Empire. What the Cerean did outside Imperial borders was of no concern to the Emperor—as long as Korrot succeeded in his hunts.

　　The Jedi hunter traveled from world to world within his modified light transport, a starship he called *Shadow I*, in search of rumors that would put him on the trail of a Force-user. For travel across planetary surfaces, Korrot utilized a powerful speeder bike. Though he wasn't opposed to assaulting a powerful Force-user from a distance with either his heavy blaster pistol or blaster rifle, he preferred to fight on a more personal level, pitting his vibroblade against the foe's lightsaber or other weapon of

RHEN-ORM BIOCOMPUTER

Aurra Sing's abilities were formidable, but the Anzati realized that she was "blind" to many of the sensations that were second nature to them. To correct this shortcoming, they surgically implanted a biocomputer in her skull, giving her a greater range of awareness than ordinary beings. The computer processes information from the long antenna protruding from her forehead, enabling her to home in on what the Anzati call "luck."

　　Though not precisely the same thing, this characteristic is related to the Force, and so those who use the Force possess it in a greater degree than those who do not (there are notable exceptions—Han Solo was an extremely tasty prospect to the Anzati). Thus, the number of Force points an individual has acts as a bonus on Aurra Sing's ability to track the individual with a Survival check.

choice. He loved to watch the lightsaber wielder's face when the energy blade made contact with his cortosis-weave armor and sputtered out. Then he was free to employ his most cruel and torturous attacks, reveling in the burst of dark side energy that always seemed to join him in those situations.

Of course, not every death attributed to Korrot resulted in one less Force-user in the galaxy. The sadistic and mean-spirited Jedi hunter often killed whenever the mood struck him, later justifying it (if he needed to) by claiming that the victim was a latent Force-sensitive. As time passed and more and more of Korrot's kills fell into this nebulous category, the Emperor finally grew tired of the mad Cerean's antics. The Emperor ordered Darth Vader to destroy Del Korrot.

The Jedi hunter welcomed the challenge. After all, what was Darth Vader but the last of the Jedi Knights? But Vader proved to be much too power-ful for Del Korrot. Vader destroyed each of the Cerean's weapons with his lightsaber in turn, then used his furious Force Grip ability to strangle Korrot, thus rewarding the Jedi hunter for his many months of service to the Empire with a slow and painful death.

Del Korrot: Male Cerean, Soldier 3/Dark Side Marauder 6; Init +5 (+3 Dex, +2 species); Defense 18 (+5 combat jumpsuit, +3 Dex); Spd 10m; VP/WP 61/15; Atk +11/+6 melee (2d6+2, vibroblade) or +12/+7 ranged (3d8, heavy blaster pistol); SQ +2 species bonus to Initiative; SV Fort +9, Ref +9, Will +2; SZ M; FP 4; DSP 12; Rep 6; Str 14, Dex 16, Con 12, Int 11, Wis 9, Cha 9. Challenge Code: E.

Equipment: Heavy blaster pistol, vibroblade, combat jumpsuit augmented by cortosis weave, comlink, blaster rifle, thermal detonator, medpacs (2), macrobinoculars, speeder bike, light transport (*Shadow I*).

Skills: Intimidate +5, Knowledge (Jedi lore) +6, Pilot +9, Treat Injury +5.

Force Skills: Battlemind+7, Enhance Ability +5, Force Defense +7, Heal Self +4, See Force +1.

Feats: Armor Proficiency (light) Armor Proficiency (medium) Armor Proficiency (heavy), Cleave, Dodge, Force-Sensitive, Heroic Surge, Point Blank Shot, Power Attack, Toughness, Weapon Group Proficiency (blaster pistols), Weapon Group Proficiency (blaster rifles) Weapon Group Proficiency (heavy weapons), Weapon Group Proficiency (simple weapons), Weapon Group Proficiency (vibro weapons).

Force Feats: Alter, Control, Hatred, Rage, Sense.

The New Order

With the rise of Senator Palpatine to the position of Supreme Chancellor of the Galactic Senate, the stage was set for the cruel tyranny of the Galactic Empire. The Jedi disappeared, replaced as a peacekeeping force by the new Imperial stormtroopers. Planets were bombarded. Entire cultures were exterminated. The Emperor's vaunted "New Order" suddenly seemed a bleak and terrible blight on the freedom of the galaxy.

As the last fragments of the Senate were ground under the Emperor's iron fist, systems began to rise up against the Empire, paving the way for the Alliance to Restore the Republic—the Rebel Alliance. Unknown to the Rebels, the Emperor had already laid the groundwork for the perpetual rule of his New Order. He had turned a Jedi into his new dark apprentice, the terrifying Darth Vader. Vader himself trained apprentices. And the Emperor created a corps of loyal, Force-skilled minions to maintain his rule.

Most powerful of all, of course, was the Emperor himself.

The Emperor

Possessed of the boundless power of the Force and adept in the ways of the dark side, Emperor Palpatine was one of the most dangerous and evil Humans in galactic history. As his corruption grew stronger, the Emperor became physically weaker, but he was never helpless. To the galaxy at large, he

presented the image of an enfeebled old man, maintaining order in the Empire through sheer force of will. To those who knew him better, the Emperor was a cunning, sadistic tyrant, concerned only with squeezing the life out of the universe that spawned him.

Palpatine began his career of evil so subtly that no one noticed. Certainly no outward change evidenced the darkness in his heart. Those who encountered him considered Palpatine a kindly fellow, perhaps even a bit outclassed by the pace and magnitude of the political arena into which he had been thrust when he became a senator. But even then, Palpatine was scheming, forging alliances with influential figures in the Senate and the great learning centers. Political science students pored over his speeches. Military science students absorbed his philosophies. Palpatine even had the ear of a powerful Jedi Master. His circle of supporters and confidants seemed at times to dwarf the power of the Galactic Senate itself.

When Palpatine was elected Supreme Chancellor of the Senate, he made use of its potential. Gradually his sphere of influence grew, his opinions became the Republic's opinions, and his decisions became the Republic's laws. In time, the Republic became an Empire, ruled by the most evil man in the galaxy.

Historians disagree on when and how the Emperor managed to first hobble, then utterly destroy the Jedi Knights. The fact remains that by the time the first Death Star was under construction, the only Jedi still alive remained in hiding, and the galaxy as a whole thought them extinct. Even the Force, once a thriving belief throughout nearly every star system, became an outdated myth, a superstition worthy only of ridicule—though the Emperor seemed particularly intent on stamping out any resurgence of the defunct order. Those who displayed any sign of facility with the Force either learned to hide their ability, or were arrested by Imperial stormtroopers and never heard from again. Those who questioned the fate of those arrested were arrested themselves, until they finally learned to scoff at any mention of an "all-powerful energy field" that bound the galaxy together and controlled their destinies.

Without the Jedi Order to protect peace and justice, Imperial stormtroopers became a common sight. The dagger-shaped Imperial Star Destroyers and a vast fleet of smaller ships supported them. However, with the resources of a million worlds at his disposal, and an endless supply of political malcontents to serve as slave labor, the Emperor dreamed of greater and greater engines of destruction. He authorized the construction of massive Super Star Destroyers and, even more terrible, the planet-destroying Death Star. His designers worked in secret research laboratories, dreaming up plans to help the Emperor dominate the galaxy, and his technicians labored in well-guarded factories, assembling the tools the Emperor would use to enforce his reign of terror.

Such superweapons were insignificant toys compared to the power of the Force, and the Emperor undertook that research personally. He turned a young Jedi Knight, Anakin Skywalker, into his personal enforcer. Skywalker turned to the dark side and became the dreaded Darth Vader, the Dark Lord of the Sith, feared by the entire galaxy. With his assistance, the Emperor also formed a group of inquisitors, Force-trained agents who tracked down any rumor of Force-strong individuals—or surviving Jedi—and either brought them into the Emperor's fold or destroyed them. Between Lord Vader and the Imperial inquisitors (and a handful of independent Jedi hunters), the dark side grew stronger and stronger.

Even with their combined might, Vader and the inquisitors were still public figures—hammers used to crush resistance. The Emperor also needed scalpels to cut into the heart of his enemies, and so created a cadre of Force-trained assassins—known as the Emperor's Hands—who answered only to him. Their effectiveness depended on their remaining anonymous, even to each other. Few of the Hands knew that they were not the Emperor's only covert assassins.

The Emperor foresaw the return of the Jedi Knights in the form of Luke Skywalker, the son of his apprentice, Darth Vader. He did not foresee, however, that young Skywalker would find the tiny spark of good still left within Anakin Skywalker and draw it out long enough for Vader to forsake the Emperor. Aboard the second Death Star, in orbit over the forest moon of Endor, the Emperor met his doom, hurled by his erstwhile student into the radioactive depths of the Death Star's power core.

Emperor Palpatine: Male Human, Noble 3/Dark Side Devotee 3/Sith Acolyte 3/Sith Lord 10; Init +0; Defense 27 (+17 class); Spd 6m; VP/WP 124/13; Atk +16/+11/+6/+1 melee* (4d8–1/19–20, lightsaber) or +16/+11/+6/+1 ranged; SQ Call in a favor (2), inspire confidence +1, dark side talisman +2, resource access, exceptional minions, Sith Master; SV Fort +14, Ref +12, Will +19; SZ M; FP 9; DSP 32; Rep 16; Str 9, Dex 11, Con 12, Int 18, Wis 16, Cha 16. Challenge Code: 1.

Equipment: Lightsaber*, Sith holocron, private transport.

*Emperor Palpatine has constructed his own lightsaber.

Skills: Bluff +13, Computer Use +9, Craft (lightsaber) +6, Diplomacy +19, Gather Information +19, Intimidate +16, Knowledge (Jedi lore) +10, Knowledge (Naboo) +6, Knowledge (politics) +17, Knowledge (Sith lore) +15, Read/Write Basic, Read/Write Bothan, Read/Write Sith, Sense Motive +13, Speak Basic, Speak Bothan, Speak Sith.

Force Skills: Affect Mind +14, Alchemy +17, Control Mind +15, Empathy +17, Farseeing +23, Fear +18, Force Defense +16, Force Grip +16, Heal Self +14, Move Object +12, See Force +18, Telepathy +20, Transfer Essence +17.

Feats: Exotic Weapon Proficiency (lightsaber), Force-Sensitive, Skill Emphasis (Farseeing), Skill Emphasis (Fear), Skill Emphasis (Knowledge: politics), Skill Emphasis (Telepathy), Trustworthy, Weapon Group Proficiency (blaster pistols), Weapon Group Proficiency (simple weapons).

Force Feats: Alter, Control, Dissipate Energy, Drain Force, Force Lightning, Force Mastery, Force Mind, Sense, Sith Sorcery.

Note to Gamemasters

The statistics presented here differ from those presented in the *Star Wars Roleplaying Game*. While these statistics provide a much more holistic interpretation of the Emperor's abilities, either version of the Emperor works perfectly well for most roleplaying purposes.

Darth Vader, Dark Lord of the Sith

Clad in his gleaming black armor, Darth Vader, the Dark Lord of the Sith, was the mighty fist with which the Emperor maintained his grip on the scattered systems of the Empire. When his subjects forgot who ruled the Empire, the Emperor sent Darth Vader to remind them. His mere presence inspired dread; his visage inspired terror. Few could stand in his presence and not feel the terrible emanations of his power.

Fewer still knew that the formidable Darth Vader was once an idealistic little boy who wanted little more than to play with his friends and to make his mother proud. The future Dark Lord of the Sith was born Anakin Skywalker, the son of a slave woman named Shmi. He labored as an assistant to an irascible Toydarian merchant on Tatooine, until fate—or the Force—intervened and introduced Anakin to Qui-Gon Jinn, a Jedi Master. Qui-Gon noted the boy's extraordinary Force potential and believed him to be a "vergence" in the Force—a locus of power.

Securing Anakin's freedom (but not his mother's), Qui-Gon took Anakin to the Jedi Temple on Coruscant to be tested, and hopefully trained. Although the Jedi Council agreed that Anakin Skywalker was indeed powerful, they also sensed that his destiny was clouded. He had already been exposed to hardship and cruelty, and held much anger in his heart. The Jedi Council refused to allow Qui-Gon to train Anakin. But when Qui-Gon died fighting the Sith Lord Darth Maul, his final request of his own apprentice, Obi-Wan Kenobi, was for Kenobi to train Anakin. The wisest of the Jedi Council disagreed with the decision but finally relented, and Obi-Wan took Anakin Skywalker as his apprentice.

Unfortunately, Obi-Wan Kenobi was not the teacher Qui-Gon Jinn had been, though he did his best to train Anakin. Over time, Obi-Wan and Anakin became enemies and met in a climatic battle. Anakin was mortally injured in the battle, but he was sustained by his rage—the dark side kept him alive. It also changed him, stripping away the last vestiges of his idealistic youth. When he was finally healed, Anakin Skywalker was gone. In his place was Darth Vader, Sith Lord.

But Skywalker had not turned to the dark side purely on his own. His mentor had been the man whom the galaxy would one day learn to fear: the Emperor. Under the Emperor's dark tutelage, Skywalker learned the ways of the Sith and rejected his Jedi training. In exchange, he gave the Emperor his loyalty and service—including betraying the Jedi Order to the Emperor. On the Emperor's command, Vader hunted down the last of the Jedi Knights and destroyed them. Now Darth Vader was a being of pure evil, like his master.

Vader became an important part of the Emperor's New Order. As the Empire expanded, systems resisted the Emperor's rule and needed to be brought into line. Darth Vader provided object lessons for those foolish enough to express belief that the Empire should still be a democracy. Placed in command of some of the Empire's best forces, Vader traveled about the galaxy enforcing the Emperor's will. He was feared and hated wherever he went—even by his own troops, whom he frequently executed if they failed him—but he was also extremely effective.

Darth Vader also spent some of his time training others in the Force and, when possible, turning them to the dark side. He personally schooled Lord Hethrir, who became Vader's Procurator of Justice. He oversaw the Force training of the Emperor's Royal Guard and Sovereign Protectors. He worked with the Imperial inquisitors to hunt Force-users, either to wipe them out or bring them into the Emperor's fold. He also discovered and subjugated the deadly Noghri of the planet Honoghr, making them his personal strike force.

When the Emperor authorized Grand Moff Tarkin to begin the construction of a new weapon—one that would demonstrate once and for all that no

planet could ever be a safe place for the Emperor's enemies to hide—he put Darth Vader under Tarkin's command. This "Death Star" was a hyperdrive-capable battle station as large as a small moon, equipped with a powerful superlaser that could destroy an entire planet with a single blast. The evil Tarkin demonstrated the battle station's power to Rebel leader Princess Leia Organa by destroying her homeworld of Alderaan.

The mission to rescue Princess Leia and bring the plans of the Death Star to the Rebellion also brought an old foe back to Darth Vader: Obi-Wan Kenobi, his old master. Vader and Kenobi battled one last time, and in the end, Kenobi sacrificed himself so that his new apprentice Luke Skywalker—Vader's own son, though he did not realize it at the time—could escape with the princess. Luke later returned as part of the force that defended the Rebellion's base on Yavin 4 from the Death Star, and fired the fateful shot that destroyed the Death Star. Due to the timely intervention of Han Solo, the smuggler captain who helped Luke rescue Leia from the Empire's clutches, Vader was unable to stop Skywalker and was forced to retreat aboard his personal starfighter.

Vader sensed the strength of the Force in the young pilot who destroyed the Death Star, but didn't know his name. He sent a brief report back to the Emperor and then did everything in his power to track down this new hero of the Rebellion. After torturing a captured Rebel, Vader learned the name of the pilot, and realized that Luke Skywalker was his own son. His path crossed his son's several times over the next few years, but it wasn't until the fall of Bespin that Vader confronted Luke and told him that he was his father. Vader made an attempt to turn Luke, inviting him to join his father in service to the Emperor, but Luke refused and escaped Vader's clutches.

While Vader would have continued his search for Luke, fate intervened, and he found himself otherwise occupied battling Prince Xizor and his Black Sun criminal empire. After Xizor's death, the Emperor foretold that Luke Skywalker would come to them willingly, and he and Vader set a trap for the Rebels, tricking them into attacking the Emperor's new Death Star while it was still under construction in the Endor system. While the Rebels fought the battle in space outside, the Emperor pitted Vader against Skywalker, trying to arouse feelings of rage and hatred in Skywalker and turn him to the dark side.

Skywalker refused the temptation of the dark side, and his bravery in facing the Emperor's dark side powers fanned the tiny spark of heroism still alive in Darth Vader. Overwhelmed with compassion for his son, Vader turned on the Emperor, hurling him screaming into the depths of the Death Star. Vader redeemed himself—but at the cost of his own life. Although Luke Skywalker tried desperately to save him from the doomed Death Star, his father died in his arms—but he died Anakin Skywalker. Anakin became one with the Force, joining his former teacher Obi-Wan Kenobi, and Kenobi's teacher, Yoda.

Darth Vader: Male Human, Fringer 1/Jedi Guardian 11/ Sith Lord 6; Init +3; Defense 19 (+6 armor, +3 Dex); Spd 8m; VP/WP 122/17; Atk +18/+13/+8/+3 melee** (6d8+3/19–20, lightsaber) or +16/+11/ +6/+1 ranged; SQ Resource access, minions, damage reduction 10; SV Fort +17, Ref +15, Will +11; SZ M; FP 10; DSP 16; Rep 10; Str 16*, Dex 16, Con 17*, Int 17, Wis 11, Cha 12. Challenge Code: H.

*Strength and Constitution boosted by chemicals provided by life support apparatus in armor.

Equipment: Lightsaber**, dark armor (padded battle armor with damage reduction and life support apparatus, as well as Sith alchemical Strength and Constitution boosters).

**Darth Vader has constructed his own lightsaber.

Skills: Climb +0, Craft (lightsaber) +10, Intimidate +10, Knowledge (Jedi lore) +7,  Knowledge (Podracing) +7, Knowledge (Tatooine) +7, Pilot +15, Repair +5, Search +7, Read/Write Basic, Read/Write Huttese, Read/Write Sith, Speak Basic, Speak Huttese, Speak Sith, Spot +6, Survival +2, Tumble +1.

Force Skills: Affect Mind +8, Battlemind +8, Enhance Ability +11, Farseeing +6, Force Defense +13, Force Grip +15, Force Push +7, Move Object +20, See Force +13, Telepathy +14.

Feats: Exotic Weapon Proficiency (lightsaber), Force-Sensitive, Skill Emphasis (Pilot), Starship Operation (starfighters), Weapon Group Proficiency (blaster pistols), Weapon Group Proficiency (simple weapons), Weapon Group Proficiency (vibro weapons).

Force Feats: Alter, Burst of Speed, Control, Deflect Blasters, Knight Defense, Lightsaber Defense, Force Whirlwind, Prolong Force, Rage, Sense, Weapon Focus (lightsaber).

Note to Gamemasters

The statistics presented here differ from those presented in the *Star Wars Roleplaying Game*. While these statistics provide a more holistic interpretation of Darth Vader's abilities, either version of Darth Vader works perfectly well for most roleplaying purposes.

Lord Hethrir

Lord Hethrir was the Emperor's Procurator of Justice, charged with carrying out death sentences imposed by the Emperor on individuals, or even entire worlds.

DARTH VADER'S ARMOR

Darth Vader wears a unique suit of dark armor. It is the equivalent of padded battle armor (Defense +6, armor check penalty −4), imbued with dark side power through Sith alchemical techniques. The dark armor provides Vader with damage reduction 10, and it contains various life-support apparatus that maintains Vader's breathing and his shattered body.

In addition to these attributes, the life-support system is irrigated with Sith-crafted chemicals that enhance Vader's Strength and Constitution. The Dark Lord needs to regularly receive treatments of these chemicals in his specially designed meditation chambers (such as his personal sanctum aboard the Star Destroyer *Executor*). The Emperor has his dark side adepts prepare these chemicals for Vader, and he personally doles out a supply to his apprentice as he sees fit.

Without his helmet, Vader's life-support begins to fail, and he loses 1 point of Constitution each round. Without his armor, his Strength and Constitution scores are immediately reduced by 4 points as the Sith chemical infusion stops flowing. Within his personal meditation chambers, however, Vader can remove his armor and find comfort within its pressurized, life-supporting shell as though he were still wearing his full suit of armor.

Personally trained as a Dark Jedi by Darth Vader, Hethrir wielded tremendous power—at least until the Emperor's death at Endor, when the Empire began to fall apart. Hethrir departed the Empire for the Outer Rim Territories, hoping to rebuild the Empire. To fund his plans, Hethrir sold former political prisoners as slaves.

Hethrir and his mate Rillao underwent Vader's training, but only Hethrir developed the kind of dark side abilities that Vader needed. He proved his loyalty to the Empire by destroying his own homeworld of Firrerre. In the process he alienated Rillao, who fled with her unborn son into hiding. Eventually Hethrir found them and brought them back—Rillao to be tortured, and his son Tigris (who to his disappointment had no Force potential whatsoever) to be Hethrir's personal slave.

Ten years after the Battle of Endor, Lord Hethrir encountered an extradimensional intelligence called Waru. This creature was brought into existence by Hethrir's scientists, and consumed the life essences of others in order to survive. For Waru to return to his own reality, he needed the life energy of someone strong in the Force. Hethrir saw an opportunity to both appease the powerful Waru and to weaken the New Republic. He kidnapped the children of Han and Leia Organa Solo, and planned to sacrifice Anakin Solo—the grandson of Darth Vader—but was prevented by Anakin's parents and Luke Skywalker. The enraged Waru took out its anger on Hethrir, and the two of them vanished from the known universe.

Lord Hethrir: Male near-Human, Noble 2/Jedi Councilor 5; Init +1; Defense 18 (+7 class, +1 Dex); Spd 10m; VP/WP 49/14; Atk +5 melee (2d8+1/19–20, lightsaber) or +5 ranged; SQ Call in a favor, inspire confidence +1; SV Fort +6, Ref +6, Will +9; SZ M; FP 3; DSP 10; Rep 8; Str 13, Dex 13, Con 14, Int 14, Wis 14, Cha 15. Challenge Code: D.

Equipment: Lightsaber, personal transport.

Skills: Appraise +7, Bluff +7, Computer Use +3, Diplomacy +16, Gather Information +9, Intimidate +7, Knowledge (Firrerre) +7, Knowledge (Jedi lore) +4, Knowledge (Sith lore) +6, Profession (merchant) +7, Read/Write Basic, Read/Write Firrerreo, Search +4, Sense Motive +9, Speak Basic, Speak Firrerreo.

Force Skills: Affect Mind +10, Empathy +7, Force Grip +6, Force Stealth +7, Friendship +7, Move Object +7, See Force +8.

Feats: Force-Sensitive, Sharp-Eyed, Trustworthy, Weapon Group Proficiency (blaster pistols), Weapon Group Proficiency (simple weapons).

Force Feats: Alter, Control, Deflect Blasters, Sense.

Prophets of the Dark Side

During the height of the Empire, a handful of dark side devotees loyal to the Emperor used their powers and abilities to look into the dark side of the Force and predict the outcome of specific events. The Emperor consulted the Prophets of the Dark Side almost as often as he looked into the dark side himself, making sure that no possibility that he had not foreseen would occur.

Of the Prophets of the Dark Side, the most powerful were Kadann, the Supreme Prophet, and Jedgar, the High Prophet. Few beyond the Emperor's most trusted advisors knew of the existence of the Prophets, as the Emperor maintained a public face that provided no hint of his Force-born powers and abilities. There were rumors in the upper echelons of Imperial Command, but few attempted to find the truth for fear of angering the Emperor.

As the Battle of Endor drew closer, the Emperor refused to acknowledge any prediction that revealed less than total victory for the Empire. Whether he saw such revelations during his own meditations, or if his military advisors offered scenarios in which the Rebellion attained the upper hand, he dismissed such dire predictions. He preferred to hold onto the whispers and urgings of the dark side that assured him that he would crush the Rebellion and corrupt young Luke Skywalker. When Kadann brought his own prophecy from the Force, one in which balance was returned to the galaxy, the Emperor laughed at him.

Later, after the destruction of the second Death Star, a fraudulent group revealed itself as the Prophets of the Dark Side. Imperial Intelligence established this ploy to help certain moffs retain power in the face of the Emperor's demise. They even procured a false Kadann and Jedgar to carry out their plans, citing fake prophecies and using various mundane influences to make these predictions come true. Meanwhile, the true Prophets remained hidden, waiting for a sign that they should once again involve themselves in galactic affairs.

Kadann

The true Supreme Prophet of the Dark Side, Kadann was a black-bearded dwarf who wore dark robes that appeared to be cut from the fabric of space itself, with stars gleaming in its inky depths. During the time of the Republic, Kadann was a Jedi Knight. More of a thinker and philosopher than a man of action, Kadann strove to understand the ancient prophecies that concerned the balance of the Force.

To these ends, Kadann struggled to reconcile balance with adhering to only the light side of the Force. He came to believe that dark and light in equal measures were needed to truly master and understand the Force. In time, he turned away from the Jedi Code and started to experiment with dark side powers. While his intentions may have been good, Kadann still managed to stray onto the path of corruption. He traveled the galaxy, exploring his theories and meditating on the dark side.

Soon, Kadann discovered that he had a special bond with the dark side of the Force. It revealed secrets to him, opening his mind to the streams of time and the possible outcomes of important events. These insights served him well, even if the revelations didn't always come true. He saw various paths opened to him, various futures waiting to be grasped. He struggled to decide if he should accept the things the dark side was offering him, for to do so would not serve balance any better than if he remained loyal to the Jedi Code.

Prior to the destruction of the Jedi Order, by Darth Sidious visited Kadann. The Dark Lord of the Sith was intrigued by Kadann and his unique view of the Force. After many long conversations and debates, Sidious revealed Kadann's true purpose. "The future you see isn't yours," the Dark Lord said. "You are merely the messenger. Serve me. Become my prophet. Reveal the will of the Force as you see it and I will make your predictions come true."

Kadann became the Supreme Prophet of the Dark Side, leading a small group of dark side devotees with a particular talent for seeing portents and omens in the mists of the Force. By the time the Empire was established, Kadann had become one of the Emperor's most trusted advisors. He and his group worked in secret, hidden from the galaxy at large. They searched the Force for signs and warnings, passing on what they saw to the Emperor and his adepts. Throughout this period of service, Kadann continued his own studies, contemplating the idea of balance and seeking to achieve a state that was neither fully light nor fully dark.

When Kadann looked deep into the dark side prior to the Battle of Endor, he saw a myriad of possibilities. One

of the strongest was the return of balance to the Force and the end of the Empire. The Emperor dismissed his warnings, for he had not seen anything of the sort during his own meditations. Kadann wasn't certain which path the galaxy would find itself on after the events played out, but he trusted his own visions and instincts. He gathered his loyal assistants and left Imperial Center. It was time to find a new place in the galaxy, a place of safety from which the Prophets could watch the unfolding events. Kadann led the Prophets into hiding, where they stayed, watching and waiting for a sign that the time was right to once again let their presence be known.

Kadann: Male Human, Jedi Consular 8/Dark Side Devotee 5; Init –1; Defense 20 (+11 class, –1 Dex); Spd 6m; VP/WP 55/10; Atk +9/+4 melee* (3d8–1, lightsaber) or +8/+3 ranged (3d4, hold-out blaster); SQ Healing, dark side talisman +2; SV Fort +9, Ref +6, Will +16; SZ M; FP 4; DSP 11; Rep 7; Str 9, Dex 8, Con 10, Int 16, Wis 18, Cha 14. Challenge Code: F.

   Equipment: Lightsaber*, dark side talisman, hold-out blaster.

   *Kadann has constructed his own lightsaber.

   Skills: Bluff +8, Computer Use +7, Craft (light-saber) +7, Diplomacy +17, Gather Information +10, Hide +3, Intimidate +4, Knowledge (Force lore) +12, Listen +10, Read/Write Basic, Sense Motive +14, Speak Basic, Spot +10, Treat Injury +9.

   Force Skills: Affect Mind +8, Empathy +10, Farseeing +18, Fear +16, Force Defense +6, Force Grip +14, Force Stealth +10, Heal Another +7, Heal Self +5, Move Object +8, See Force +12, Telepathy +11.

   Feats: Alertness, Dark Side Skill Emphasis (Fear), Dark Side Skill Emphasis (Force Grip), Exotic Weapon Proficiency (lightsaber), Force-Sensitive, Iron Will, Weapon Group Proficiency (blaster pistols), Weapon Group Proficiency (simple weapons).

   Force Feats: Alter, Control, Dissipate Energy, Force Mastery, Force Mind, Knight Mind, Hatred, Sense.

Jedgar

Tall, bald, and bearded, Jedgar was the true High Prophet of the Dark Side. As a youth studying at the Jedi Temple on Coruscant, he was troubled by dark dreams that had a frightening habit of coming to pass. He had nightmares of the Clone Wars and the Jedi Purge years before either event occurred. Though filled with a talent for seeing the future, Jedgar frightened the other students and could find no Jedi Knight to accept him as an apprentice. He was assigned to the Agri-Corps on his thirteenth birthday, but refused to accept such a menial occupation. Jedgar ran away and followed his dreams to the dark side.

   Years later, Jedgar's visions led him to Kadann, a Jedi Knight who also left the Order behind. "I foresaw this meeting," Kadann told the young man. "So did I," replied Jedgar. On that day, Jedgar found a master and Kadann found an apprentice. Using his dark musings to help Kadann see and understand the motion of the future, Jedgar also served as the dwarf's bodyguard. The post was more for show than anything else, for Jedgar knew his master could more than protect himself from any danger.

   When the Empire reached its height of power, Kadann and Jedgar led the Prophets of the Dark Side. This mysterious and secret group advised the Emperor with their omens and predictions. Everything was going fine until Kadann saw a future that didn't agree with what the Emperor or the other Prophets had foreseen. Still, Kadann was their leader, the most powerful among them, and they trusted his visions. Jedgar and the others agreed to follow Kadann into hiding, and from their secret temple they watched as the Emperor was destroyed and balance returned to the Force—just as Kadann predicted.

   In the months following the Battle of Endor, Imperial Intelligence gathered a band of impostors to pretend to be the Prophets of the Dark Side. There was even a false Jedgar proclaiming himself the High Prophet. The true Jedgar saw these lies and falsehoods in his dark visions, but Kadann refused to let him leave their place of hiding to do anything about it.

   "Let them pretend," Kadann told him. "Their false prophecies will not come to pass, and the time is not yet right for the true Prophets to appear."

   And so Jedgar and his Master wait and watch, biding their time until the signs and portents direct a new course of action.

Jedgar: Male Human, Force Adept 3/Dark Side Devotee 5; Init +1; Defense 20 (+9 class, +1 Dex); Spd 10m; VP/WP 60/15; Atk +8/+3 melee (2d8+3, lightsaber) or +7/+2 ranged; SQ Dark side talisman +2; SV Fort +7, Ref +6, Will +8; SZ M; FP 3; DSP 10; Rep 4; Str 16, Dex 13, Con 15, Int 12, Wis 13, Cha 10. Challenge Code: E.

   Equipment: Lightsaber, dark side talisman.

   Skills: Hide +8, Intimidate +6, Jump +9, Spot +9.

   Force Skills: Affect Mind +5, Battlemind +5, Drain Energy +14, Empathy +6, Enhance Ability +7, Farseeing +10, Fear +10, Force Grip +14, Force Push +5, Illusion +4, Move Object +5, See Force +6.

   Feats: Dark Side Skill Emphasis (Drain Energy), Dark Side Skill Emphasis (Force Grip), Force-Sensitive, Heroic Surge, Power Attack, Weapon Group Proficiency (blaster pistols), Weapon Group Proficiency (primitive weapons), Weapon Group Proficiency (simple weapons).

   Force Feats: Alter, Control, Deflect Blasters, Hatred, Sense.

Azrakel the Dark Warrior

The mysterious darksider called Azrakel was an experiment born in the mind of the Emperor and given life by the High Prophet Kadann. The Emperor found the young man, strong in the Force, and decided to expose him to the full force of the dark side. For weeks on end, the Emperor conducted his dark side experiments, hoping to see how long it would take for an unprepared mind to shatter. Time passed, and

097

could create his own apprentice—a tool to use when and if he made his own play for control of the Empire.

In secret and with the raw power of the dark side, Kadann recreated Azrakel. He trained the young man as he had been taught, providing him with the mentoring necessary to harness his power and strengthen his abilities. As Azrakel, the young man grew strong in body and in the Force. He became Kadann's secret weapon, his tool for performing covert acts that increased his own power and prestige.

Azrakel's mind was broken by the ordeal he underwent at the hands of the Emperor. Azrakel was nothing more than raw hatred and anger, the dark side personified. He hated the Emperor, and Kadann taught him to also hate Darth Vader, the Emperor's most trusted servant (and perhaps Kadann's most powerful enemy, if the darksider ever decided to make his play for power). In time, Azrakel even grew to hate Kadann, and eventually cut himself off from both the Prophets and the Empire.

When Kadann went into hiding after the death of the Emperor, Azrakel had already left his service. Kadann knew the dark warrior still lived, for he could feel his hatred as a beacon in the Force. But he trained Azrakel too well. The dark warrior was highly skilled and possessed powerful survival instincts. He would appear again, Kadann knew, but at a time and place of his own choosing. And with the objects of his hatred gone, Kadann assumed that Azrakel's anger would turn toward him. Kadann was disappointed, but he wasn't afraid. He would be ready when the confrontation came.

Azrakel, meanwhile, hid his Force powers from the galaxy at large. He claimed to be a mercenary, selling his skills to anyone with the money to pay and a cause that allowed him to unleash the full extent of his anger. He possessed no mercy, and sliced through his targets with a passion that disturbed even his most ruthless employers. If anyone asked him where he learned to use the double-bladed lightsaber, he simply shrugged and said he found it on a dead man. Usually, no one pressed for further explanation.

Azrakel operated far from the Core worlds, trying to hide himself in the Outer Rim Territories, the Corporate Sector, and even Wild Space. He lost his direction and focus for a time when the two most powerful objects of his hatred died at Endor. His anger toward Kadann could sustain him for a time,

the Emperor grew bored and moved on to other matters. He left the youth to wither and die in one of his hidden retreats, forgetting all about him.

High Prophet Kadann, who assisted the Emperor in a few of these experiments, decided to take the young man and nurse him back to health. The youth had been opened to the dark side, but his mind had been wiped clean. He was a blank slate upon which Kadann but Azrakel found a new target for his hatred: Luke Skywalker, the son of Darth Vader. Someday, if his passions don't get him killed first, Azrakel plans to return to the heart of the galaxy and hunt down the Jedi Knight. On that day, there will be a reckoning.

Azrakel: Male human, Jedi Guardian 3/Dark Side Marauder 3; Init +1; Defense 17 (+6 armor, +1 Dex); Spd 10m; VP/WP 48/14; Atk +8/+3 melee (2d8+2 plus 2d8+2, double-bladed lightsaber) or +7/+2 ranged (3d6, blaster pistol); SV Fort +8, Ref +7, Will +3; SZ M; FP 3; DSP 9; Rep 5; Str 15, Dex 13, Con 14, Int 10, Wis 11, Cha 12. Challenge Code: D.

   Equipment: Padded battle armor, double-bladed lightsaber, blaster pistol.

   Skills: Intimidate +6, Jump +1, Tumble +1.

   Force Skills: Battlemind +12, Enhance Ability +8, Force Defense +7, Force Stealth +7, Heal Self +8.

   Feats: Armor Proficiency (light), Armor Proficiency (medium), Exotic Weapon Proficiency (lightsaber), Exotic Weapon Proficiency (double-bladed lightsaber), Force-Sensitive, Power Attack, Weapon Group Proficiency (blaster pistols), Weapon Group Proficiency (simple weapons).

   Force Feats: Alter, Control, Hatred, Rage, Sense.

The Emperor's Minions

To exercise his power and guarantee his safety, the Emperor employed many operatives, ranging from simple military soldiers and Imperial stormtroopers to trained assassins and genetically altered mutants.

Royal Guard

Those members of the Imperial stormtroopers who showed particular expertise were recruited into the Imperial Royal Guard, the red-garbed personal bodyguards of the Emperor himself. But each was also tested for Force potential, and those who displayed an aptitude for wielding the Force were singled out for special training on the isolated world of Yinchorr. There, these stormtroopers honed their battle prowess so that they were almost a match for the formidable Darth Vader himself. As a final test, they were paired off with their closest companions among the other trainees and ordered to fight to the death—for without absolute loyalty to the Emperor, they were useless to him.

   Upon successfully passing the Emperor's test, the recruits were given the ceremonial armor of the Royal Guard and assigned to his personal staff. Their primary duty was to protect the Emperor from any threat—but failing that, they were trained in Force techniques that could sustain the Emperor until help arrived. In all its history, the Royal Guard was never called upon to perform the latter duty.

Royal Guard: Human Thug 6/Soldier 3/Force Adept 3; Init +7; Defense 20 (+7 armor, +3 Dex); Spd 10m; VP/WP 56/14; Atk +14/+9 melee (2d8+2/19–20, force pike) or +14/+9 ranged (3d8, heavy blaster pistol); SQ Immunities (see page 278 of the *Star Wars Roleplaying Game*); SV Fort +10, Ref +5, Will +6; SZ M; FP 2; DSP 4; Rep 5; Str 14, Dex 16, Con 14, Int 11, Wis 12, Cha 12. Challenge Code: E.

   Equipment: Ceremonial armor, force pike, heavy blaster pistol.

   Skills: Intimidate +9, Knowledge (nobility [Emperor]) +6, Listen +7, Read/Write Basic, Speak Basic, Spot +7, Survival +7.

   Force Skills: Enhance Ability +8, Force Defense +8, Heal Another +8, See Force +4.

   Feats: Armor Proficiency (heavy), Armor Proficiency (light), Armor Proficiency (medium), Armor Proficiency (powered), Force-Sensitive, Improved Initiative, Weapon Focus (Force pike), Weapon Group Proficiency (blaster pistols), Weapon Group Proficiency (blaster rifles), Weapon Group Proficiency (heavy weapons), Weapon Group Proficiency (simple weapons), Weapon Group Proficiency (vibro weapons).

   Force Feats: Alter, Control, Sense.

Imperial Sovereign Protector

While the Royal Guard was trained in rudimentary Force techniques, the Imperial Sovereign Protectors were trained in the use of the dark side of the Force. Their methods of recruitment and advancement were almost identical to those of the Royal Guard—but in the process, their propensity for aggression and brutality was identified and encouraged. Those who could find their way to the dark side were rewarded with status and authority—and given the enviable task of policing the ranks of the Imperial Royal Guard. They were answerable only to Darth Vader or to the Emperor himself.

Imperial Sovereign Protector: Human Thug 6/Soldier 3/Force Adept 3/Dark Side Devotee 2; Init +7; Defense 20 (+7 armor, +3 Dex); Spd 10m; VP/WP 56/14; Atk +15/+10 melee (2d8+2/19–20, force pike) or +14/+9 ranged (3d8, heavy blaster pistol); SQ Immunities (see page 278 of the *Star Wars Roleplaying Game*); SV Fort +14, Ref +10, Will +10; SZ M; FP 2; DSP 4; Rep 5; Str 14, Dex 16, Con 14, Int 11, Wis 12, Cha 12. Challenge Code: E.
    Equipment: Ceremonial armor, force pike, heavy blaster pistol.
    Skills: Intimidate +9, Knowledge (nobility [Emperor]) +6, Listen +7, Read/Write Basic, Speak Basic, Spot +7, Survival +7.
    Force Skills: Enhance Ability +7, Force Defense +7, Force Grip +4, Move Object +7, See Force +6.
    Feats: Armor Proficiency (heavy), Armor Proficiency (light), Armor Proficiency (medium), Armor Proficiency (powered), Force-Sensitive, Improved Initiative, Skill Emphasis (Force Grip), Weapon Focus (Force pike), Weapon Group Proficiency (blaster pistols), Weapon Group Proficiency (blaster rifles), Weapon Group Proficiency (heavy weapons), Weapon Group Proficiency (simple weapons), Weapon Group Proficiency (vibro weapons).
    Force Feats: Alter, Control, Sense.

Imperial Sentinel

Towering monsters seemingly made of pure muscle, Imperial sentinels were giant brutes who served the Emperor on Byss. Their existence was all but unknown outside the secret facility on Byss, but whispered rumors in the Imperial court suggested that the sentinels were members of a species that opposed the Emperor in the formative years of the Empire. They were, the rumors insisted, electronically and chemically altered to serve the Emperor they once rebelled against.

    The truth was somewhat more sinister. Imperial sentinels were potent products of dark side alchemy, mute giants created from tissue stock and shaped into loyal, unquestioning warriors by the Emperor's dark side adepts as part of their training. Few of

these creatures existed, and those were found only on Byss. Periodically, when one of the dark side adepts or Executor Sedriss undertook a high-priority mission for the Emperor, one or more of these lumbering behemoths accompanied him offworld—often to the surprise, and terror, of the Emperor's enemies.

Imperial Sentinel: Male Soldier 6; Init +3; Defense 11 (+9 armor, +3 Dex, –1 size); Spd 6m; VP/WP 86/22; Atk +11/+6 melee (1d3+6, punch) or +12/+7 melee (2d10+6, vibro-ax) or +9/+4 ranged (3d8/19–20, blaster rifle); SQ Immunities (see page 278 of the *Star Wars Roleplaying Game*); SV Fort +11, Ref +5, Will –1; SZ L; FP 0; DSP 3; Rep 5; Str 20, Dex 16, Con 22, Int 5, Wis 5, Cha 10. Challenge Code: E.
    Equipment: Vibro-ax, heavy battle armor.
    Skills: Climb +9, Intimidate +6, Understand Basic.
    Feats: Armor Proficiency (heavy), Armor Proficiency (light), Armor Proficiency (medium), Armor Proficiency (powered), Cleave, Endurance, Great Cleave, Power Attack, Weapon Focus (vibro-ax), Weapon Group Proficiency (blaster pistols), Weapon Group Proficiency (blaster rifles), Weapon Group Proficiency (heavy weapons), Weapon Group Proficiency (simple weapons), Weapon Group Proficiency (vibro weapons).

Mara Jade, Emperor's Hand

As one of the Emperor's personal Force-trained assassins—and to her knowledge, the *only* one—Mara Jade walked a thin line between the light side and the dark side. Although she killed, she did not kill out of malice. To her way of thinking, she was protecting the citizens of the Empire by eliminating threats to their safety—no more an evil act than a court-ordered execution. The Emperor, of course, did not disillusion her; if Mara Jade had reason to question the morality of her actions, she would have been less effective. Even so, she occasionally complied with orders that did not sit well with her conscience, trusting the wisdom of the Emperor.

    Most courtiers in the Imperial Palace did not even realize that Mara was anything more than a pretty decoration. But Mara Jade trained in combat alongside the Imperial Royal Guard and was schooled in infiltration techniques by the Emperor's spymasters. From the Emperor's advisors she learned the art of political intrigue. And from the Emperor himself, Mara Jade learned to develop her Force powers. She learned to listen for his telepathic "voice," even across the galaxy, and to draw strength from his own vast reserves of power.

    Mara Jade performed dozens of successful missions for the Emperor, earning his appreciation and his occasional indulgence for the missions she failed. One such was her mission to assassinate Luke

099

DG

100

Skywalker, the Jedi hero of the Rebellion who destroyed the first Death Star and escaped Darth Vader's clutches on Bespin. Mara intercepted Skywalker on Tatooine, in the desert palace of the depraved Hutt crime lord Jabba, but was prevented from fulfilling her mission. Skywalker escaped, and though the Emperor was disappointed, he ordered Mara to give up the chase for the time being.

When the Emperor next contacted her, he was dying—slain by Darth Vader at the Battle of Endor. His final telepathic command thundered in Mara Jade's mind: "**You will kill Luke Skywalker.**" But in the turmoil following news of the Emperor's death, it was all Mara could do to arrange passage away from Imperial Center without being captured and executed by the Emperor's Director of Intelligence, Ysanne Isard.

Mara fled to the anonymity offered by the Outer Rim Territories. Though the Emperor's final command still pounded in her skull, she managed to live a relatively quiet life—with the occasional wild adventure brought about by her past position in the Empire. Eventually, she joined the smuggler baron Talon Karrde and served with him as a mechanic and, after a time, as an advisor. She managed to keep her past from him, but the arrival of Luke Skywalker d Mara to reveal who she really was. Torn een her loyalty to the Emperor and to Talon

Karrde, Mara allowed Skywalker to live and eventually even aided him in resolving the threat of Grand Admiral Thrawn, in the process discharging her duty to the Emperor by slaying a clone of Skywalker.

Though Mara could have easily joined Skywalker's new Jedi academy on Yavin 4 and instantly become his best student, she opted instead to explore the galaxy on her own for a while. She crossed paths with Skywalker periodically, and over time, the two admitted that they had romantic feelings for one another. Eventually they married, and the former Emperor's Hand became Mara Jade Skywalker.

Mara Jade: Female Human, Scoundrel 6/Emperor's Hand 5; Init +2; Defense 22 (+10 class, +2 Dex); Spd 10m; VP/WP 78/15; Atk +10/+5 melee* (2d8+2/19–20, lightsaber) or +9/+4 ranged (3d6, blaster pistol); SQ Illicit barter, better lucky than good, sneak attack +3d6, resource access, authority, target bonus +2; SV Fort +5, Ref +11, Will +4; SZ M; FP 4; DSP 4; Rep 5; Str 14, Dex 15, Con 15, Int 13, Wis 12, Cha 14. Challenge Code: F.

Equipment: Lightsaber*, blaster pistol, yacht (*Jade's Fire*), Z-95 Headhunter, assorted weapons and gear, assorted disguises and fake IDs.

*Mara Jade has constructed her own lightsaber.

Skills: Bluff +6, Computer Use +7, Craft (lightsaber) +5, Demolitions +6, Disable Device +9, Disguise +10, Entertain (dance) +8, Gather Information +10, Hide +7, Intimidate +6, Knowledge (Jedi lore) +5, Knowledge (streetwise) +5, Move Silently +7, Pilot +10, Read/Write Basic, Repair +4, Sleight of Hand +7, Speak Basic, Speak Huttese, Survival +5.

Force Skills: Affect Mind +4, Enhance Ability +8, Move Object +9, See Force +11, Telepathy +6.

Feats: Exotic Weapon Proficiency (lightsaber), Force-Sensitive, Heroic Surge, Martial Arts, Point Blank Shot, Skill Emphasis (Disguise), Weapon Group Proficiency (blaster pistols), Weapon Group Proficiency (blaster rifles), Weapon Group Proficiency (simple weapons), Weapon Group Proficiency (vibro weapons).

Force Feats: Alter, Control, Sense.

High Inquisitor Tremayne

A former Jedi Knight, High Inquisitor Tremayne followed a path similar to Darth Vader's, being seduced by the dark side and serving the Emperor in hunting down and destroying other Jedi. Unlike Vader, however, Tremayne is subtle, even delicate, in his activities.

Tremayne has at his disposal an Imperial II Star Destroyer, *Interrogator*, and its crew and complement of support ships and weapons. With *Interrogator*, High Inquisitor Tremayne goes anywhere he wishes, answerable only to the Emperor, Darth Vader, and certain high-ranking

give way—and, of course, given his superior position by the time such a conversation takes place, it will not be Tremayne's.

Like Lord Vader, High Inquisitor Tremayne has also undergone reconstructive cybernetic surgery to repair damage inflicted upon him by a Jedi. Tremayne once dueled a Jedi named Corwin Shelvay, who defeated Tremayne with a vicious lightsaber cut that took Tremayne's right arm and part of his face. Now Tremayne has a cybernetic arm and a metallic plate over the right side of his face, giving him an eerie, inhuman appearance. Despite these startling disfigurements, Tremayne is actually a fairly attractive fellow, which makes the evil in his heart all the more tragic.

Tremayne: Male Human, Jedi Guardian 8/Imperial Inquisitor 7; Init +3; Defense 27 (+14 class, +3 Dex); Spd 10m; VP/WP 121/14; Atk +17/+12/+7 melee (4d8+1/19-20, lightsaber) or +17/+12/+7 ranged (3d6, blaster pistol); SQ Jedi Knight, resource access, authority, favored enemy (Jedi guardian) +2, High Inquisitor; SV Fort +11, Ref +10, Will +11; SZ M; FP 7; DSP 12; Rep 15; Str 13, Dex 16, Con 14, Int 14, Wis 13, Cha 13. Challenge Code: G.

Equipment: Lightsaber, blaster pistol, encrypted comlink, datapad, robes.

Skills: Bluff +8, Gather Information +11, Intimidate +10, Knowledge (The New Order) +6, Knowledge (Jedi lore) +9, Knowledge (Imperial space) +5, Profession (bureaucrat) +8, Read/Write Basic, Read/Write Sith, Search +5, Speak Basic, Speak Sith, Survival +9.

Force Skills: Affect Mind +6, Battlemind +10, Drain Knowledge +6, Enhance Senses +5, Farseeing +7, Fear +7, Force Defense +8, Force Grip +8, Heal Self +8, Move Object +10, See Force +10, Telepathy +5.

Feats: Exotic Weapon Proficiency (lightsaber), Force-Sensitive, Frightful Presence, Iron Will, Track, Weapon Finesse (lightsaber), Weapon Group Proficiency (blaster pistols), Weapon Group Proficiency (simple weapons).

Force Feats: Alter, Control, Deflect Blasters, Dissipate Energy, Knight Defense, Lightsaber Defense, Sense.

Jerec, Dark Jedi Master

The blind Jedi Knight Jerec was one of a handful of Jedi located and turned to the dark side by High Inquisitor Tremayne. Jerec had been part of a small task force of Jedi charged by the Jedi Council with recovering lost artifacts, and was stunned to discover on his return to the Republic that in his absence it had become an Empire—and Jedi were being hunted down like wild animals. He fled back to the Unknown Regions, but to no avail; Tremayne followed his trail,

members of the Inquisitorium—the Force-trained secret division of Imperial Intelligence. Though attached in this fashion to Imperial Intelligence, the Inquisitorius might as well be a separate organization. Imperial Intelligence calls so rarely upon the inquisitors that Tremayne has a great deal of free time with which to search for Force-users. He conducts most of these searches in the Outer Rim Territories, where isolated communities produce enough Force adepts, village shamans, dark side devotees, and alien students of the Force to keep Tremayne busy for several lifetimes.

Despite his role in the Emperor's New Order, High Inquisitor Tremayne is cultured, polite, and composed—disarmingly so. Partly this is his strategy for unnerving his subjects, but Tremayne also knows that once someone becomes his subject, he has all the time in the galaxy. His subjects cannot escape from his interrogation chambers or holding cells, and only a brute tries to break a subject's mind by starting with his body. (He secretly thinks of Vader as such a person, in fact.) Tremayne believes that intelligent subjects can be convinced through logic that they will be much better off opening up to him, rather than resisting long enough to be painfully tortured first. He tries to reinforce this belief by being cordial and even friendly. Tremayne wants his subjects to know that he regrets that fate has brought them together in such a fashion. He frequently takes some time to explain that when two opposing ideologies intersect, one must captured him and his few companions, and turned Jerec to the dark side.

Jerec immediately offered his services to the Emperor, explaining that he knew of a handful of other Jedi students who were on long-range missions and knew nothing of the fall of the Jedi Order. Jerec sought them out and turned them to the dark side, then with their aid gathered a few more Force-users, until finally Jerec had a cadre of six Dark Jedi under his command.

The Emperor charged Jerec with a task similar to the one the Jedi Council assigned him: locate artifacts of the Jedi—and the Sith—and bring them to Imperial Center. Jerec and his Dark Jedi pursued the task with fanatical devotion, but when the Emperor died at the Battle of Endor, Jerec decided to apply his work toward expanding his own power. He researched the existence of the legendary Valley of the Jedi, which he believed to be the repository of vast power, just waiting to be claimed by someone brave enough to unlock it and strong enough to control it.

Jerec learned that a Jedi named Qu Rahn was also seeking the Valley of the Jedi, and that Qu Rahn learned which planet it was on from a Rebel named Morgan Katarn. Jerec slew Rahn and Katarn and eventually discovered the location of the Valley of the Jedi on Ruusan. Pursued by Katarn's vengeful son, Kyle Katarn, Jerec and his Dark Jedi hurried to Ruusan. Jerec's followers held Kyle off long enough for Jerec to access the Valley's secrets and gain phenomenal Force powers. But even with his increased might, Jerec was unable to defeat Kyle or to prevent him from freeing the Valley's trapped Jedi spirits.

Jerec: Male Human, Jedi Guardian 15; Init +2; Defense 23 (+11 class, +2 Dex); Spd 10m; VP/WP 108/15; Atk +17/+12/+7 melee (5d8+2/19–20, light-saber) or +17/+12/+7 ranged; SV Fort +11, Ref +11, Will +8; SZ M; FP 7; DSP 15; Rep 8; Str 14, Dex 15, Con 15, Int 14, Wis 13, Cha 14. Challenge Code: G.

Equipment: Lightsaber.

Skills: Computer Use +6, Intimidate +10, Knowledge (Jedi lore) +8, Knowledge (Sith lore) +6, Read/Write Basic, Read/Write Sith, Speak Basic, Speak Sith.

Force Skills: Affect Mind +10, Battlemind +14, Enhance Ability +10, Enhance Senses +9, Force Defense +16, Force Grip +12, Force Push +14, Move Object +17, See Force +18.

Feats: Blind-Fight, Exotic Weapon Proficiency (lightsaber), Force-Sensitive, Weapon Group Proficiency (blaster pistols), Weapon Group Proficiency (simple weapons).

Force Feats: Alter, Burst of Speed, Control, [Deflec]t Blasters, Dissipate Energy, Force Lightning, [Han]d, Knight Defense, Lightsaber Defense, Master [Defe]nse, Sense.

Executor Sedriss

One of Emperor Palpatine's many dark side warriors was Sedriss, a young mercenary who displayed an aptitude for using the Force, if not any particular desire to join the ranks of the Imperial military. Various Imperial organizations tried to recruit Sedriss but found him insolent, insubordinate, and violently opposed to authority. He was awaiting execution for the deaths of a handful of Imperial officers when he was spirited away by members of the Inquisitorium, and dragged before the Emperor himself, who asked Sedriss simply: "Would you like to kill me?"

The Emperor looked inside Sedriss's heart and in his own way cut to the core of Sedriss's problem. Sedriss could not respect anyone whom he knew he could easily kill—which included most of his superiors in the military. The Emperor made a bargain with Sedriss: They would duel, and if Sedriss won, he could take the Emperor's life. But if Sedriss lost, he would serve the Emperor with unquestioning loyalty, or suffer the most terrible, lingering, ignominious death he could imagine. Confident of his chances against the frail old man, Sedriss agreed—and was promptly crushed to the ground by the Emperor's power. Sedriss admitted that the Emperor had defeated him and promised to honor their agreement. The Emperor didn't desist. Sedriss felt his ribs collapsing, and *swore* that he would serve the Emperor. Still the Emperor did not stop, until Sedriss felt his heartbeat slowly coming to a stop and begged to serve the Emperor. When he was finally able to stand, he instead knelt—convinced that this was a superior who was truly superior to him.

Sedriss underwent extensive training under the Emperor, learning to develop his Force talents to wield power the way the Emperor himself did. All the while, he wondered to what task the Emperor intended to put him. The Emperor never discussed the subject. Then the Emperor died, killed at the Battle of Endor. Like most of the Empire's dark side adepts, Sedriss retreated to the worlds of the Deep Core, where he oversaw the military defense of Byss. Without leadership, other Imperial military commanders fought among themselves for control of the Empire, but Sedriss knew that for Palpatine's Empire to endure, his facilities on Byss would need to remain under the control of those loyal to Palpatine.

When the Emperor was reborn five years later, he rewarded Sedriss's service by naming him his Executor. Sedriss's job would be to ensure that, should the Emperor again suffer an extended absence—which, considering the condition of his new body, he felt was quite likely—no supposedly loyal Imperial agency would seize control of the Emperor's clone vats on Byss and make it impossible for the Emperor to return. Furthermore, the Emperor placed Sedriss in command of Operation Shadow

Hand. This military operation aimed to retake the Empire in a series of lightning-fast assaults, using the latest weapons of war and stopping only when its targets begged, as Sedriss had, to be allowed to serve the Emperor.

Just as the Emperor predicted, he was forced to leave his new body for another, and when that one was destroyed aboard his flagship, *Eclipse*, Sedriss set Operation Shadow Hand into motion. Seizing powerful new weapons and taking control of weapons factories, Sedriss returned to Byss to discover that some of the Emperor's dark side adepts had turned traitor and were attempting to destroy the Emperor's remaining clones. Unknown to them, they missed one, and the Emperor had already been reborn again. Sedriss slew the saboteurs, then accepted new orders from the Emperor: Capture Luke Skywalker and bring him to Byss.

Sedriss followed Skywalker and another Jedi Knight, Kam Solusar, to the devastated world of Ossus, once a Jedi stronghold. There, Skywalker hoped to retrieve ancient Jedi artifacts, but before he could uncover much, Sedriss confronted him. Sedriss found himself overwhelmed by Skywalker's control of the Force. Desperate, he seized a hostage—only to be grappled by Ood Bnar, an ancient plantlike Jedi Master who survived the destruction of Ossus and had stood guard over the Jedi treasures for the intervening four thousand years. Ood Bnar had been reawakened by the presence of the dark side warrior. In a devastating blast of Force energy, he destroyed both Sedriss and himself.

Executor Sedriss: Male Human, Sol 6/Dark Side Marauder 8; Init +1; Defense 21 (+10 class, +1 Dex); Spd 10m; VP/WP 106/14; Atk +16/+11/+6 melee (2d8+2/19–20, lightsaber) or +14/+9/+4 ranged (3d6, blaster pistol); SV Fort +13, Ref +9, Will +7; SZ M; FP 5; DSP 14; Rep 10; Str 14, Dex 12, Con 14, Int 13, Wis 12, Cha 13. Challenge Code: F.

Equipment: Lightsaber.

Skills: Bluff +5, Computer Use +5, Demolitions +9, Intimidate +9, Knowledge (Emperor) +5, Knowledge (Imperial forces) +9, Knowledge (Sith lore) +3, Pilot +9, Read/Write Basic, Read/Write Sith, Speak Basic.

Force Skills: Affect Mind +9, Battlemind +12, Force Grip +11, Force Push +5, Move Object +11, See Force +7.

Feats: Armor Proficiency (heavy), Armor Proficiency (light), Armor Proficiency (medium), Armor Proficiency (powered), Cleave, Dodge, Exotic Weapon Proficiency (lightsaber), Expertise, Force-Sensitive, Heroic Surge, Iron Will, Mobility, Power Attack, Spring Attack, Weapon Focus (lightsaber), Weapon Group Proficiency (blaster pistols), Weapon Group Proficiency (blaster rifles), Weapon Group Proficiency (heavy weapons), Weapon Group Proficiency (primitive weapons), Weapon Group Proficiency (simple weapons), Weapon Group Proficiency (vibro weapons).

Force Feats: Alter, Control, Deflect Blasters, Rage, Sense.

Dark Side Adepts

The courtesans and advisors loyal to the Emperor, who traveled the galaxy at his side and filled the halls of the Imperial palace, were Palpatine's dark side adepts. Followers in the dark side of the Force, they had great intelligence as well as some ability to manipulate the Force.

Most people thought that the adepts were simply cronies who craved whatever crumbs of power were available by hanging onto the Emperor's robes. They dismissed the adepts as fools and yes-men, but the truth was much more sinister.

The adepts served the Emperor's will, and he trained them to eventually replace the moffs and planetary governors so that they could rule at the Emperor's whim. One group trained secretly in the hidden facility on Byss, awaiting orders to unleash the various experiments that were coming to fruition deep in the galactic core.

Dark Side Adept: Male Human, Force Adept 3/Dark Side Devotee 3; Init +0; Defense 18 (+8 class); Spd 10m; VP/WP 27/10; Atk +4 melee (1d3, punch) or +4 ranged (3d4, hold-out blaster); SQ Dark side talisman +2; SV Fort +4, Ref +4, Will +8; SZ M; FP 2; DSP 15; Rep 5; Str 10, Dex 11, Con 10, Int 16, Wis 14, Cha 12. Challenge Code: D.

Equipment: Hold-out blaster pistol, dark side talisman.

Skills: Hide +8, Knowledge (dark side lore) +8, Listen +6, Move Silently +5, Sense Motive +6, Spot +8. **Force Skills:** Affect Mind +8, Alchemy +8, Drain Energy +5, Empathy +8, Fear +6, Force Grip +10, Force Push +9, Heal Another +8, Illusion +8, Move Object +9.

Feats: Force-Sensitive, Stealthy, Weapon Group Proficiency (blaster pistols), Weapon Group Proficiency (primitive weapons), Weapon Group Proficiency (simple weapons).

Force Feats: Alter, Control, Sense, Sith Sorcery.

The Shadow Academy

When Luke Skywalker felt that he had learned all he could of the ancient Jedi, he decided that he should share his knowledge with others who might be strong in the Force. He converted the old Rebel Alliance base on Yavin's fourth moon into a school for Jedi—the new Jedi academy—and invited students from all over the galaxy.

Master Skywalker was not entirely certain that he was ready to teach others the Jedi arts. He remembered all too well that his first mentor, Obi-Wan Kenobi, tried and failed to tutor his father, Anakin Skywalker—and thus contributed to Anakin's fall to the dark side and eventual transformation into the monstrous Darth Vader. Of course, some of Luke's new students were not yet ready to become Jedi, or were only interested in becoming Jedi to pursue their own plans.

Some fell to the dark side influence of Exar Kun—whose spirit haunted Yavin 4 since his defeat by the Jedi of the Old Republic four thousand years earlier. Others, like the twisted Dolph and the Imperial spy Brakiss, turned their backs on Luke's training and set off to find their fortunes elsewhere. Still others never came to Luke's school at all but studied the Force on their own, giving the dark side easy targets.

Kyp Durron, Fallen Jedi

As a young boy, Kyp Durron watched in horror as Imperial stormtroopers invaded his home on the Deyer Colony in the Anoat sector. Kyp's older brother was taken away for training to become a [st]rooper himself, while Kyp and his politically [br]oken parents were dragged off in shackles to [sp]ice mines of Kessel. When the Empire finally

collapsed and the Imperial facility fell into the control of its administrator Moruth Doole, Kyp's parents were executed, leaving Kyp alone.

Eventually, Kyp encountered a mysterious old woman named Vima-Da-Boda, who recognized Kyp's facility with the Force. She taught him a few rudimentary Force techniques before she, too, was dragged away, and Kyp continued toiling in the pitch-black mines, still unaware of his true potential. When Han Solo and his Wookiee first mate Chewbacca were imprisoned on Kessel and forced to mine spice, they befriended the young man, and when they escaped they took him with them. Though their escape took them into the nearby top-secret weapons development facility, the Maw Installation—and into the clutches of the malevolent Imperial Admiral Daala—they finally managed to get to safety, in the process discovering that Kyp was strong in the Force.

Kyp became one of Luke Skywalker's first students at the new Jedi academy on Yavin 4. But unknown to Luke, Kyp tasted the power of the dark side during his escape from Kessel, and this made him a ripe target for the spirit of Exar Kun. Kun was already preying upon the academy's trainees, and managed to convince Kyp that he could teach him more and faster than Master Skywalker could. To his credit, Kyp resisted, but when offered a chance to strike back at the Empire that had persecuted him for so long, Kyp resolved that he would become the new Dark Lord of the Sith.

With Exar Kun's guidance, Kyp Durron stole a ship and left the Jedi academy. He returned after having torn the technical information on the Sun Crusher, an Imperial superweapon, from the mind of its designer, an alien researcher named Qwi Xux. Again with Exar Kun's help, Kyp recovered the Sun Crusher from its resting place in the gassy core of Yavin, then set out to use its power to punish the Empire. In the process, he joined with Exar Kun to defeat his erstwhile master, Luke Skywalker, sundering Luke's spirit from his physical form and leaving him an immaterial, invisible ghost.

Aboard the Sun Crusher, Kyp Durron destroyed system after system, seeking his vengeance. Armed with nova-inducing resonance torpedoes and covered with impenetrable armor, the Sun Crusher was invincible, and only when Han Solo and Lando Calrissian sought him out to appeal to his better nature did he finally relent. Even then, it took the defeat of Exar Kun, back on Yavin 4, before Kyp could bring himself to surrender the Sun Crusher.

Returning to the new Jedi academy, Kyp swore to Master Skywalker that—despite the majority of the New Republic crying out for his blood—he would try to atone for his misdeeds. Skywalker, having been seduced by the dark side once or twice himself, agreed to give Kyp a second chance. But even so, the dark side has still left its mark on Kyp Durron, and resisting its siren call again might be even more difficult for him.

Kyp Durron: Male Human, Jedi Guardian 4/Fringer 2; Init +1; Defense 19 (+8 class, +1 Dex); Spd 10m; VP/WP 47/15; Atk +8 melee* (2d8+2/19–20, light-saber) or +5 ranged (3d6, blaster pistol); SQ Barter; SV Fort +7, Ref +6, Will +2; SZ M; FP 2; DSP 3; Rep 5; Str 15, Dex 13, Con 15, Int 12, Wis 13, Cha 13. Challenge Code: C.

Equipment: Lightsaber*, blaster pistol, datapad, Jedi robes, cape.

*Kyp Durron has constructed his own lightsaber.

Skills: Bluff +3, Computer Use +3, Craft (light-saber) +3, Diplomacy +2, Hide +6, Intimidate +3, Knowledge (alien species) +3, Knowledge (Kessel) +5, Listen +3, Move Silently +3, Pilot +5, Read/Write Basic, Repair +2, Search +3, Speak Basic, Speak Sullustese, Spot +3, Survival +5, Treat Injury +2.

Force Skills: Affect Mind +3, Battlemind +6, Drain Knowledge +3, Enhance Ability +5, Enhance Senses +3, Force Stealth +4, Heal Self +4, Move Object +3, See Force +5.

Feats: Alertness, Endurance, Exotic Weapon Proficiency (lightsaber), Force-Sensitive, Starship Operation (starfighters), Weapon Group Proficiency (blaster pistols), Weapon Group Proficiency (simple weapons).

Force Feats: Alter, Control, Deflect Blasters, Sense.

Exar Kun, Dark Side Spirit

Cornered in his lair by an ancient Jedi battle fleet, Exar Kun chose to shed his physical form and preserve his spirit. After millennia of waiting for his revenge, he was rewarded with an opportunity too perfect to believe: The new Jedi Master, Luke Skywalker—the last Jedi in the galaxy—chose the Massassi ruins on Yavin 4 as the site of his school for training new Jedi. Skywalker's new Jedi acad-emy would be located in the Great Temple—the very place where Exar Kun once mutated the prim-itive Massassi and planned the overthrow of the Old Republic.

But as a nonphysical spirit, there was little Kun could do directly. He contented himself with corrupting Skywalker's students, starting with the temperamental youth Gantoris. Under Exar Kun's dark tutelage, Gantoris's anger grew, until finally he assembled his own lightsaber and challenged Skywalker to a duel. Gantoris failed to defeat the Jedi Knight, however, and Kun was forced to punish him. The other students found Gantoris's blackened corpse the next morning.

Next Exar Kun turned his attention to Kyp Durron, whose own experiences with the dark side made him an ideal candidate for corruption. Convincing Kyp that he would be able to study the dark side without being tainted by it, Exar Kun drew the young Jedi apprentice farther and farther away from the light. He tempted Kyp into leaving the new Jedi academy and taking his revenge on Imperial Admiral Daala, who had imprisoned and tortured Kyp after he escaped the Kessel spice mines. For the best revenge—to ensure that Daala's evil was eradicated from the galaxy—Kyp used her own superweapon against her: the Sun Crusher, a ship capable of launching nova-triggering resonance torpedoes and destroying entire systems with one shot.

Meanwhile, Exar Kun ensured that Luke Skywalker would be unable to oppose him. In acquiring the Sun Crusher, Kyp returned to Yavin 4, where he faced Skywalker in a duel that left the Jedi Master comatose, his spirit forced out of his body. So while Kyp Durron embarked on a reign of terror with the Sun Crusher, Exar Kun continued to launch attacks against Skywalker, sending dark side creatures to attack the Jedi's helpless body or possessing his students and using their powers to attack Skywalker somewhat more directly.

Exar Kun might have ultimately succeeded, had Skywalker's students not eventually realized that their true enemy was a malevolent, nonphysical spirit. Combining their power—along with that of Kun's long-dead former Jedi Master, Vodo-Siosk Baas—Skywalker's Jedi students destroyed Exar Kun's spirit and enabled Luke Skywalker's spirit to return to his body.

Exar Kun: Male Human (Dark Side Spirit), Jedi Guardian 9/Sith Lord 8; Init +3; Defense 27 (+14 class, +3 Dex); Spd 10m; VP/WP 140/17; Atk +21/+16/+11/+6 melee or +20/+15/+10/+5 ranged; SQ Nonphysical, manifestation, possession, Force travel, exceptional minions, resource access; SV Fort +15, Ref +15, Will +10; SZ M; FP 3; DSP 22; Rep 12; Str 17, Dex 16, Con —, Int 14, Wis 11, Cha 17. Challenge Code: G.

Equipment: None.

Skills: Computer Use +4, Craft (lightsaber) +8, Hide +11, Intimidate +13, Knowledge (Jedi lore) +12, Knowledge (Sith lore) +17, Listen +8, Read/Write Basic, Read/Write Sith, Search +10, Speak Arkanian, Speak Basic, Speak Ryl, Speak Sith, Spot +8.

Force Skills: Affect Mind +13, Alchemy* +20, Battlemind* +18, Enhance Ability* +13, Force Defense* +21, Force Push* +14, Move Object* +14, See Force +12.

Feats: Ambidexterity, Exotic Weapon Proficiency (double-bladed lightsaber), Exotic Weapon

Proficiency (lightsaber), Force-Sensitive, Heroic Surge, Two-Weapon Fighting, Weapon Focus (lightsaber), Weapon Group Proficiency (blaster pistols), Weapon Group Proficiency (simple weapons), Weapon Group Proficiency (vibro weapons).

Force Feats: Alter, Control, Deflect Blasters*, Force Lightning*, Knight Defense, Lightsaber Defense, Master Defense, Rage, Sense, Sith Sorcery.

*As a dark side spirit, Exar Kun is unable to employ these skills and feats.

Irek Ismaren

The son of a former Emperor's Hand—and, some said, the Emperor himself—Irek Ismaren is also the product of a strange mix of technology and the dark side. Implanted as a child with a subelectronic converter, Irek developed the ability to access schematics of nearly any computerized device and to seize control of it. For the most part Irek used this ability on droids—which could be quite devastating, considering the power of some droids—but when he came to the attention of the New Republic, it was because he used his power to summon a long-dormant Imperial battle station called the *Eye of Palpatine*.

The scheme to use the *Eye of Palpatine* against the New Republic originated with Irek's mother, Roganda Ismaren, who served the Emperor as an assassin while masquerading in Imperial City as a courtesan. After the Emperor's death at Endor, Roganda fled to the remote world of Belsavis, where as a child she was trained in the use of the Force by a reclusive Jedi Master named Plett. Posing as a fruit-packer, Roganda used the Jedi's former home as a nursery and school for Irek, employing the same educational toys that Plett used to teach her son about controlling the Force. They also experimented with Irek's unique ability by manipulating some of Belsavis's many worker droids.

The ambitious Roganda was not content with merely teaching her son in the ways of the dark side. She contacted powerful lords of the Juvex and Senex sectors, forging an alliance with them. She would deliver the *Eye of Palpatine*, and between it and them, the Juvex and Senex Lords could overthrow the New Republic government and reinstitute the Empire—with her son Irek as the new Emperor.

There were two problems with her plan. First, Han Solo and his wife, Leia Organa Solo, had come to Belsavis to investigate a rumor of lost Jedi children, and they discovered Roganda Ismaren's plot. Second and more dire, her son did not truly have control of the *Eye of Palpatine*. In fact, he had only been able [to su]mmon it to Belsavis. When it arrived, it would [carry out] its last set of orders, given almost half a [centu]ry before: Destroy Belsavis.

IREK ISMAREN'S SCHEMATIC IMPLANT

The subelectronic computer implanted in Irek Ismaren's brain allows him a unique perspective on computerized devices. He can mentally visualize their programming, and through the Force, he can override it. He uses this ability to control the actions of droids and computers. The implant gives Irek Ismaren the ability to use his Affect Mind skill on droids—an application not normally possible, since droids are not organic beings and therefore not part of the Force.

A similar process performed on another individual could allow that person to also use her Affect Mind skill in the same fashion—though it would permanently drain 1 point each from Intelligence and Wisdom, and take many months of practice to master.

Fortunately, Luke Skywalker, having been abducted by the battle station's automatic systems, was already aboard the *Eye of Palpatine*. With the aid of a former Jedi Knight whose spirit was trapped in the station's computers, Luke managed to rig the station to detonate before he escaped with the other abductees the station picked up. In the confusion, Roganda and Irek Ismaren escaped and have not been seen since.

Irek Ismaren: Male Human, Force Adept 4; Init +1; Defense 15 (+4 class, +1 Dex); Spd 10m; VP/WP 27/13; Atk +3 melee (2d8/19–20, lightsaber) or +3 ranged; SQ Schematic implant (see sidebar); SV Fort +3, Ref +3, Will +5; SZ M; FP 3; DSP 8; Rep 4; Str 11, Dex 13, Con 13, Int 15, Wis 12, Cha 12. Challenge Code: C.

Equipment: Lightsaber, assortment of Force "training toys."

Skills: Computer Use +8, Craft (droids) +9, Disable Device +5, Intimidate +6, Knowledge (Jedi lore) +6, Read/Write Basic, Read/Write Binary, Repair +5, Speak Basic, Speak Binary.

Force Skills: Affect Mind +8, Enhance Senses +6, Move Object +5, See Force +7, Telepathy +7.

Feats: Exotic Weapon Proficiency (lightsaber), Force-Sensitive, Gearhead, Skill Emphasis (Computer Use), Weapon Group Proficiency (blaster pistols), Weapon Group Proficiency (simple weapons).

Force Feats: Alter, Control, Sense.

Kueller

Kueller was a vengeance-driven despot, fueled in his hatred by the dark side of the Force. Wearing his grim Hendanyn death mask and imposing body armor, Kueller presented the image of a new Darth Vader. He ruled the world of Almania—the homeworld of the people who slew his parents and set him on the path to the dark side.

Kueller was originally a student of Luke Skywalker's new Jedi academy, where he went by the name of Dolph. He learned only a little there before moving on, unable to reconcile the hatred he carried within himself for the Je'har, the rulers of Almania. As his spite grew, he swore to conquer Almania. Before long he realized his goal, taking the planet and exterminating the Je'har. Then he turned his attention to the New Republic.

The New Republic held a special place of hatred in Kueller's heart. Because the New Republic Senate long ignored the atrocities committed by the Je'har, Kueller felt that they too should pay for the suffering he endured. At his droid factory on Telti, he persuaded Brakiss, another failed student from the new Jedi academy, to install potent bombs in droids bound for the New Republic, and used one of these to attack the Senate Hall during an address by Leia Organa Solo, the New Republic Chief of State.

Doing so attracted the attention of Luke Skywalker, who followed the trail of clues back to Almania, where he was forced to bail out of his sabotaged X-wing fighter, leaving him injured and easy prey for a lightsaber duel with Kueller. Kueller vowed to kill Skywalker if Leia Organa Solo did not step down from her position. The Chief of State resigned, leaving former Chief of State Mon Mothma in charge, to go to her brother's rescue. On Almania, Leia rescued Luke while Kueller's fleet of *Victory*-class Star Destroyers and TIE fighters did battle with the New Republic forces Mon Mothma sent to help.

Skywalker and Organa Solo were left to face Kueller. He should not have been a match for either of them, but powered by his rage and with Skywalker still wounded, Kueller got the better of them. Skywalker almost surrendered to death, but then a local creature called a thernbee stumbled onto the scene. The beast had just devoured several cages containing ysalamiri—Force-dampening reptiles native to the planet Myrkr—and their ability had not yet faded. Kueller's dark side strength failed him, and Leia felled the darksider with a quick blaster shot. Justice finally came to Almania.

Kueller: Male Human, Jedi Guardian 9; Init +1; Defense 19 (+8 class, +1 Dex); Spd 10m; VP/WP 70/14; Atk +10/+5 melee (3d8+1/19–20, lightsaber) or +10/+5 ranged; SV Fort +8, Ref +7, Will +4; SZ M; FP 4; DSP 15; Rep 15; Str 13, Dex 13, Con 14, Int 12, Wis 11, Cha 14. Challenge Code: E.

Equipment: Lightsaber, ceremonial Hendanyn death mask, body armor, remote detonator.

Skills: Computer Use +6, Demolitions +7, Intimidate +14, Read/Write Basic, Speak Basic.

Force Skills: Battlemind +11, Enhance Ability +10, Force Push +7, Heal Self +8, Move Object +9, See Force +6.

Feats: Armor Proficiency (heavy), Armor Proficiency (light), Armor Proficiency (medium), Exotic Weapon Proficiency (lightsaber), Force-Sensitive, Weapon Group Proficiency (blaster pistols), Weapon Group Proficiency (simple weapons)

Force Feats: Alter, Control, Rage, Sense.

Brakiss

Of the many students who came to Luke Skywalker's new Jedi academy, a handful were actually spies sent by the Empire (or other interested parties), eventually weeded out by Master Skywalker. The handsome young student Brakiss, on the other hand, possessed real Force potential, and though he had already taken his first few steps toward the dark side, Luke Skywalker thought he could still be saved. Skywalker was wrong, and Brakiss fled the academy.

Brakiss was an emotional wreck until he was discovered by Kueller, another former student of the academy who had also turned to the dark side. Kueller and Brakiss worked together, with Brakiss operating Kueller's droid factories on Telti. After Kueller's death on Almania, Brakiss departed and drifted through the galaxy for a while, finally coming to the attention of the Second Imperium. This group was under the leadership of Emperor Palpatine, who somehow managed to survive yet again after his defeat on Onderon. Having always been a loyal Imperial subject, Brakiss swore loyalty to the Second Imperium immediately, and the Emperor commanded him to begin work on an academy equal to Skywalker's—but devoted to the dark side.

Within a few years, the Shadow Academy was ready. Housed in a torus-shaped space station ringed with deadly weapons emplacements and crowned by magnificent towers, Brakiss's academy was protected from discovery by a powerful cloaking device and equipped with a serviceable hyperdrive. It could move wherever it needed to and remain undetected, even in heavily traveled space. (For a time, it even lay in stationary orbit over Coruscant.) The station was also rigged to explode, with a remote detonator under the Emperor's control. Should any of Brakiss's students become too powerful—or should Brakiss displease the Emperor—the Shadow Academy would be blown to oblivion. Brakiss understood his tenuous position and resolved not to disappoint his Emperor.

Through the influence of the Second Imperium, students loyal to the Empire began to arrive for training. Those without true power in the Force were indoctrinated into the academy's corps of stormtroopers. Aiding Brakiss in both training and recruitment was the Dathomiri Force witch Tamith Kai, a member of the Nightsister Clan that also swore allegiance to the Second Imperium. Tamith Kai was able to use threats, violence, and pure cruelty to teach the students about the dark side, while Brakiss employed the somewhat subtler method of gaining their trust through the Force, and encouraging them to explore the dark side themselves. Between the two of them, they effectively managed a surprising number of students.

The Shadow Academy came to the attention of Luke Skywalker and the New Republic when Brakiss had Tamith Kai abduct the children of Han Solo and Princess Leia, Jacen and Jaina Solo, as well as their fellow student, a Wookiee named Lowbacca. Brakiss's intention was to bring the Jedi students to the Shadow Academy and train them in the ways of the dark side, enticing them with equipment and training Skywalker denied them (specifically light-sabers, and the skill to use them) or coercing them with brutality. The students were tempted, but were rescued by Luke Skywalker and another student, Tenel Ka, before the Shadow Academy's evil could corrupt them as well.

Brakiss learned his lesson from the experience: the Shadow Academy should concentrate its efforts on turning students who already had nothing to lose. Jacen and Jaina Solo had powerful reasons to resist the dark side—and their parents had the might of the New Republic to bring to their aid—but less privileged individuals could prove easier to sway. He was proved correct when Tamith Kai abducted a young Coruscant street urchin named Zekk who, while a friend of the Solo children, had none of their advantages. Zekk was turned far more easily, and even led assaults that put him into direct conflict with his former friends, though he refused to harm them.

After one such mission during which the Jedi students thwarted Brakiss's plans, the Emperor grew impatient and declared that Brakiss must wipe out Luke Skywalker's new Jedi academy and end the interference of the Jedi once and for all. The Emperor himself came to the Shadow Academy to oversee the operation, remaining hidden in his isolation chambers throughout, protected by his crimson-clad Royal Guard. The assault was a disaster, with Tamith Kai's hovering battle platform being destroyed and Luke Skywalker himself defeating Brakiss in combat. Barely managing to escape, Brakiss fled back to the orbiting Shadow Academy, demanding to see the Emperor. After cutting his way through the Royal Guard, Brakiss was stunned to

discover that the "Emperor" was nothing more than a holographic projection. Brakiss had been duped, and he died with the Shadow Academy when the remaining Royal Guard set off the explosives that were planted aboard the station.

Brakiss: Male Human, Noble 1/Jedi Councilor 8; Init +1; Defense 18 (+7 class, +1 Dex); Spd 10m; VP/WP 52/12; Atk +8/+3 melee* (3d8+1/19–20, lightsaber) or +7/+2 ranged; SQ Bonus class skill (Move Silently), call in a favor, Jedi Knight, healing; SV Fort +7, Ref +6, Will +9; SZ M; FP 3; DSP 6; Rep 5; Str 12, Dex 13, Con 12, Int 13, Wis 13, Cha 16. Challenge Code: E.

Equipment: Lightsaber*, resplendent silver robes, training station (Shadow Academy).

*Brakiss has constructed his own lightsaber.

Skills: Bluff +9, Computer Use +5, Craft (light-saber) +11, Diplomacy +7, Gather Information +7, Intimidate +11, Knowledge (Jedi lore) +5, Move Silently +5, Read/Write Basic, Search +5, Sense Motive +7, Speak Basic, Speak Paecian.

Force Skills: Affect Mind +9, Empathy +9, Force Defense +7, Friendship +18, Heal Self +7, Move Object +7.

Feats: Force-Sensitive, Sharp-Eyed, Skill Emphasis (Friendship), Weapon Group Proficiency (blaster pistols), Weapon Group Proficiency (simple weapons).

Force Feats: Alter, Control, Deflect Blasters, Force Lightning, Sense.

Tamith Kai

After the death of their leader Gethzerion, the Nightsisters of Dathomir were all but gone. Most of their dark clan was killed when Luke Skywalker destroyed Gethzerion's transport. The few survivors surrendered to the Force witches, to seek redemption. But not all of them found that redemption, and after a few years they were driven into exile again. Some of these formed a new clan of Nightsisters, drawing on Gethzerion's *Book of Shadows* to guide their endeavor. To ensure their success this time, they threw away several hundred years of tradition and embraced more modern thinking, not only allying themselves with representatives of the former Empire, but actually affording men equal status in their organization and training them in the ways of the Nightsisters.

One of these new Nightsisters was a woman named Tamith Kai, a raven-haired, violet-eyed beauty with a pale complexion and wine-colored lips. Among the Nightsisters, Tamith Kai was the most sophisticated, having worked offplanet with Brakiss, the headmaster of the Second Imperium's Shadow Academy. She found that she preferred life away from the primitive wilds of Dathomir. She volunteered to serve as Brakiss's permanent liaison and quickly became his assistant instructor. When students showed promise with the combative aspect of the dark side—or just needed discipline—Brakiss turned them over to Tamith Kai.

As a hardened warrior, Tamith Kai also led expeditions to abduct—or rather, "recruit"—new students for the Shadow Academy. She was responsible for capturing Jacen and Jaina Solo and the Wookiee Jedi student Lowbacca and delivering them to Brakiss's cloaked space station, and later, when they escaped, for locating and delivering new students from Coruscant. Tamith Kai's methods were brutal but effective; she was quite skilled at drawing out the anger in her students, teaching them to make use of their rage to become better warriors.

Tamith Kai met her end when the Shadow Academy attacked Luke Skywalker's new Jedi academy on Yavin 4. Commanding the ground forces from a floating battle platform, she was killed when the Dathomiri-Hapan Jedi apprentice, Tenel Ka, sabotaged the platform, sending it crashing into the river outside the Great Temple of Yavin 4.

Tamith Kai: Female Human, Force Adept 3/Dark Force Witch 5; Init +2; Defense 20 (+8 class, +2 Dex); Spd 10m; VP/WP 55/15; Atk +7 melee (1d6+2, punch) or +7 ranged (3d6, blaster pistol); SQ Force flight (10m), inspire fear –2, spider walk; SV Fort +7, Ref +7, Will +8; SZ M; FP 4; DSP 8; Rep 6; Str 14, Dex 14, Con 15, Int 10, Wis 12, Cha 12. Challenge Code: E.

Equipment: Blaster pistol, whip.

Skills: Climb +7, Handle Animal +7, Intimidate +7, Jump +5, Knowledge (Dathomir) +4, Read/Write Basic, Ride +10, Speak Basic, Speak Paecian, Survival +7, Swim +4.

Force Skills: Battlemind +10, Enhance Ability +8, Enhance Senses +5, Fear +5, Force Grip +7, Force Push +6, Move Object +10.

Feats: Athletic, Heroic Surge, Martial Arts, Force-Sensitive, Weapon Group Proficiency (blaster pistols), Weapon Group Proficiency (primitive weapons), Weapon Group Proficiency (simple weapons).

Force Feats: Alter, Control, Rage, Sense, Summon Storm.

Zekk

Zekk was one of the most promising students at Brakiss's Shadow Academy, a Force-strong youth from the canyons of Coruscant. Orphaned on the planet Ennth, Zekk sought a better life by stowing away on a transport to the capital world of the New Republic, where he eked out an existence as a street urchin. He was eventually taken in by a world-weary freighter pilot named Peckhum and made the acquaintance of Jacen and Jaina Solo, their brother Anakin, and their fellow Jedi students Lowbacca and Tenel Ka.

Throughout their time together on Coruscant, none of them—not even Zekk himself—realized his Force potential. He encountered Tamith Kai, Brakiss's Nightsister instructor, who kidnapped Zekk and brought him to the Shadow Academy. At first resistant to what he took for imprisonment, he changed his mind when Brakiss showed him how Zekk could wield the Force just like Jacen and Jaina—and how they thought so little of him that they hadn't bothered testing him. But at the Shadow Academy, Brakiss told him, Zekk could not only receive training in the Force, but through the dark side he could quickly outstrip his friends—who actually refused the training Brakiss offered them.

Zekk agreed, and together they found even more recruits from among the various youth gangs from the depths of Coruscant. Eventually, Zekk had to face Jacen and Jaina. He first clashed with them on Kashyyyk, the Wookiee homeworld, where he led a Shadow Academy raid on the Wookiee computer center. Zekk dueled with Jaina, but fled rather than deliberately injure her.

They battled again when the Shadow Academy attacked Luke Skywalker's Jedi academy on Yavin 4, and this time Zekk reconsidered his choices and turned away from the dark side. Granted leniency because of the extenuating circumstances of Brakiss's brainwashing techniques, Zekk nonetheless refused training at Skywalker's academy, preferring to have nothing further to do with the Force. He departed, eventually to become a bounty hunter.

Zekk: Male Human, Scout 2/Jedi Guardian 3; Init +2; Defense 19 (+7 class, +2 Dex); Spd 10m; VP/WP 35/13; Atk +5 melee (2d8+1/19–20, lightsaber) or +6 ranged; SQ Trailblazing; SV Fort +6, Ref +7, Will +4; SZ M; FP 2; DSP 4; Rep 5; Str 12, Dex 14, Con 13, Int 11, Wis 10, Cha 11. Challenge Code: C.

Equipment: Lightsaber.

Skills: Climb +6, Computer Use +2, Hide +5, Jump +5, Knowledge (Coruscant) +5, Move Silently +5, Repair +3, Read/Write Basic, Search +5, Speak Basic, Survival +8.

Force Skills: Enhance Ability +6, Heal Self +6, Move Object +5.

Feats: Dodge, Exotic Weapon Proficiency (lightsaber), Force-Sensitive, Mobility, Skill Emphasis (Survival), Weapon Group Proficiency (blaster pistols), Weapon Group Proficiency (blaster rifles), Weapon Group Proficiency (simple weapons).

Force Feats: Alter, Control.

Following his resurrection on the planet Byss ten years after the Battle of Yavin, Emperor Palpatine began work on a series of books he called *The Dark Side Compendium*. Though he intended the work to span several hundred volumes, he completed only three manuscripts before he was vanquished once and for all by Luke Skywalker, Han Solo, and Leia Organa Solo. The three books he completed were *The Book of Anger*, *The Weakness of Inferiors*, and *The Creation of Monsters*. Through these books, he hoped to pass on his knowledge of the dark side to future generations of darksiders—perhaps even future Sith acolytes.

Studying each volume requires 96 hours of reading time, over the course of a minimum of two weeks. Reading all three volumes allows the reader to gain a +2 dark side bonus on Knowledge (Sith lore) checks for every Dark Side Point he takes, to a maximum of a +6 dark side bonus and 3 Dark Side Points.

The Book of Anger

Palpatine knew from his own experience with Sith teachings that the best way to unlock the dark side potential in a Force-wielding student was through the student's rage. *The Book of Anger* outlined this proposal in an intriguing and perhaps even logical fashion, asserting that by exploring one's anger, one could ultimately learn to conquer it, thus taming the power of the dark side—instead of being tamed by it.

The Emperor wrote: "Many claim to have found serenity, and through serenity to have overcome anger. Such arrogance is astounding. These fools have never faced their anger, and thus have no idea whether they have truly overcome it or not. True calm is only achieved through testing the limits of one's anger and passing through unscathed. The capacity for this ability lies within everyone, though most fear to test their own strength, and are thus considered at best weaklings, and at worst irresponsible."

While sophisticated readers may find the Emperor's goading diatribes on the subject of anger transparent, less experienced individuals may find themselves agreeing with his conclusions. Characters who read *The Book of Anger* must attempt a Will save (DC 15) to avoid the enticing trap laid for them by the Emperor. Those who succeed see the book for what it is. Those who fail immediately gain 2 Dark Side Points, and if they turn to the dark side as a result of gaining these Dark Side Points, they automatically improve the Rage feat (if they possess it). The temporary gain connected with the feat improves to +4 vitality points per level (instead of +2).

The Weakness of Inferiors

In addition to attempting to lure the unwary with his views on using strong emotions, the Emperor sought to indoctrinate future darksiders with his own vision of the "natural order"—the superiority of the gifted, the trained, and the powerful. In typical fashion, he called this discussion *The Weakness of Inferiors*, a book devoted entirely to another insidious perspective on how "those of great strength" must guide "those of low capability" through life, by whatever means necessary.

The Emperor wrote: "Inferiors continually endanger their own lives and the lives of others through poor decisions, reckless behavior, and simple inability to engineer the reality of their ambitious dreams. They are like children, crying in frustration because they do not comprehend their own limitations. These weaklings need structure—to be shown their place in the existing social structure. It is left to the wise and powerful to provide that structure in order for civilization to survive and thrive in the galaxy. Those who cannot—or will not—accept that peace and order are far more important than their own selfish desires must be removed from society before they can inflict any lasting damage."

This sort of thinking laid the foundation for the Empire, and the Emperor hoped to lay the groundwork for future empires, modeled on his own. *The Weakness of Inferiors* suggests that by reading the book, the reader has somehow been made custodian of galactic civilization, and that by applying the Emperor's teachings the reader can bring peace and order to the galaxy. Most sentient beings would agree that peace and order are necessary—but they might not recognize the arrogance of imposing their own vision of "peace and order" on others.

Those who read *The Weakness of Inferiors* become particularly prone to draconian reasoning. Whenever a character uses the Affect Mind skill, he must make a Will save (DC 15). If the save fails, the character unconsciously forces his desires on the subject and gains 1 Dark Side Point. The character can overcome these thoughts of "inferiors" and "structure" by spending a month meditating on the will of the Force, after which he no longer needs to make the Will save when using Affect Mind.

The Creation of Monsters

Emperor Palpatine perished before he could complete this volume on the ancient art of Sith alchemy, but it is complete enough for most purposes. *The Creation of Monsters* provides not only detailed schematics for Sith alchemical apparati (see Chapter Four), but guidelines and advice on how to avoid the pitfalls of tinkering with the physical compositions of living, independent creatures. Reading *The Creation of Monsters* allows the character to gain the Skill Emphasis (Alchemy) feat for no cost, at any time that Alchemy becomes a class skill for that character.

The Emperor wrote: "Conquer the temptation to create specimens that are superior in every way. The danger of such monstrosities being turned against you is too great. Instead, focus on instituting controlling weaknesses into each and every beast you construct. Make it strong where you are weak, but weak where you are strong. It must have a fatal flaw that you—and only you—know how to exploit. And always, without fail, be prepared to destroy your most valued creation . . . or be prepared to be destroyed by it."

Note that while the Emperor was specifically speaking of alchemical monstrosities, his advice could easily apply to the instruction of Force-users in the ways of the dark side. Certainly the Emperor knew exactly how to take advantage of the vulnerabilities of his few students, and it was only his overconfidence that sealed his fate at Endor, and later at Onderon. ⁙

Chapter Six: Creatures and Archetypes

Overview

A Jedi's strength flows from the Force. A Jedi seeks not to alter the life around her, but to achieve harmony with, and draw strength from, all things.

The Sith also draw strength—frightening strength—from the Force's dark side. Their anger and hatred, to say nothing of their need to inspire fear, drives many to twist the world around them. Sith alchemists create unspeakable monsters by bending the genetic makeup of gentle humanoids, grow horned warbeasts from simple pack animals, and command winged nightmares that prey on the enemy's fallen dead. Even the residue of the dark side causes unnatural mutations in any population that endures enough exposure. The tombs of Sith Lords invariably crawl with wicked predators and mutated sentries created by the taint of evil.

The physical toll on an individual Force-user steeped in the dark side can also be great—if the darksider lives long enough to feel its sinister effects. In days past, darksiders killed each other in self-consuming conflicts, leaving many unaware of the price the dark side asks of its followers. Sheer will and the Force can lengthen a darksider's lifespan, giving disciples of darkness more time to prepare for their lives after death.

Indeed, the central world of the Sith Empire, Korriban, became a huge necropolis even as the Sith entered a golden age. When their civilization died out, Korriban became a dead planet, imbued with the dark side and populated by the spirits of countless Sith Lords. The dead, who let their rage and cruelty rule them in life, continued on after death out of sheer spite. Many are obsessed with finding a way to return to the physical plane. More than one dead Sith ghost has recruited a head-strong Jedi in an attempt to gain ultimate control over a powerful servant. Others simply possess whatever corpse is handy.

This chapter offers examples of some of the more fearsome dark monsters faced by the Jedi over the past five thousand years. Peaceful creatures have been mutated into brutal killing machines. Once-familiar alien species have been twisted beyond recognition. Spirits of the dead have returned to their places of burial to control the living. Shambling monstrosities and insane spirits now guard their evil tombs. Witness the monsters of the dark side.

The Physical World: Dark Creatures

Battle Hydra

Five thousand years before the Rebellion established a secret base on Yavin 4, Naga Sadow built temples there to focus the power of the dark side. Around the Massassi temples, the aura of the dark side mutated living creatures in the moon's lush jungle environment. When the tainted Jedi Exar Kun later commanded the Massassi to expand the temples, he altered many of these beasts even further as a test of his newfound Sith abilities.

The battle hydra is an example of Exar Kun's alchemical mastery and Naga Sadow's dark legacy. While no two are identical, each fits the same general description: a large, dragonlike reptile with broad, leathery wings over 2 meters across and a trailing, hook-tipped tail. Most battle hydras have a pair of heads mounted on sinewy necks. (Variations on this theme are common: Luke Skywalker's Jedi academy students reported encounters with a three-headed variety with no forelegs.) The monster also wields a long, leathery tail like a whip, sinking its poisonous tip into foes and prey alike. Four powerful legs tipped in hooked claws easily rip flesh from the hydra's victims. Battle hydras usually only attack with their claws after landing and beginning to feed.

In the four thousand years since Exar Kun's spirit was entombed in the very temples he fortified, the battle hydras regressed into typical predator behavior. A small population survived by lurking in mountain caves and emerging only to hunt. Despite their fearsome appearance, the creatures are actually quite shy and generally hunt alone, only attacking in numbers when commanded.

Battle hydras were forgotten for millennia until the early days of Skywalker's Jedi academy. Exar Kun's dark shade summoned mutated hydras to attack the comatose body of Luke Skywalker. Though they very nearly destroyed the Jedi Master, Skywalker was able to act through his nephew Jacen Solo and fight the monsters off with his lightsaber. Exar Kun called up another swarm of the creatures to kill Skywalker, but these were destroyed by Rogue Squadron pilot Corran Horn in a borrowed Z-95 Headhunter.

Since that time, Skywalker's students have only occasionally encountered battle hydras. Without Exar Kun's control, the beasts either flee on contact with sentients or, in rare cases, attack out of defensive instinct when surprised. Now that Exar Kun's spirit has been destroyed, the creatures may die out or even revert to their natural forms.

Whether hunting in the jungles of Yavin 4 or attacking a Jedi Master, the battle hydra's first attack usually comes from above. It dives down on its prey and snaps with multiple jaws. After this initial attack staggers its prey, the beast circles, whipping with its poisonous tail as a ranged attack (with a maximum range of 4 meters). When attacking in groups, hydras use their wings to keep out of striking distance, swooping down and hitting their foe with long envenomed tails until it falls helpless. In the wild, this only happens when the hydras are defending a nest against a larger opponent. Once the prey has been incapacitated (either through poison or the dive attack), the battle hydra carries off its prize (if the opponent is Large or smaller) or lands on the fallen body, clawing and biting until it has eaten its fill.

Exar Kun's Sith alchemy forever altered these creatures' physiology, giving them many unusual traits. For example, Kun introduced ancient Sith armor alloys into their basic physiology at the molecular level, reducing damage against attacks—even lightsaber attacks. They are also especially susceptible to manipulation through the Force. A trained dark side Force-sensitive may use the Affect Mind skill to command battle hydras in combat.

The creature presented here is the two-headed, four-legged variety of battle hydra. GMs may wish to add a head or two and drop the claw attack to represent further natural mutations.

Battle Hydra: Airborne predator 8; Init +9; Defense 20 (+4 natural, +7 Dex, –1 size); Spd 6m, fly 20m (average); VP/WP 38/17; Atk +10 melee (2d6+3, 2 bites), +5 melee (2d4+3, 2 claws) or +14 ranged (2d4 plus poison, stinging tail whip); SQ Damage reduction 7, low-light vision, poison, stinging tail whip, weak-minded; SV Fort +8, Ref +13, Will +2; SZ L; Rep 0; Str 17, Dex 24, Con 14, Int 2, Wis 10, Cha 13. Challenge Code: E.

Skills: Intimidate +12, Listen +9, Spot +10.

Feats: Alertness, Flyby Attack, Toughness.

Special Qualities: Poison—Exar Kun combined the natural venom from many different creatures when he mutated his original hydras. When the battle hydra hits with its stinging tail whip, a hooklike stinger injects acidic poison into the victim. This foul toxin is capable of destroying most of the victim's nervous system from the inside out within a matter of minutes. This poison requires a Fortitude save in the round after the attack hits and a second save 10 rounds later; otherwise, it conforms to the paralytic poison described in the *Star Wars Roleplaying Game,* Chapter 12: Gamemastering *Star Wars.*

Stinging Tail Whip—Although the battle hydra's name is derived from its most notable feature—multiple heads—its envenomed tail is certainly its most dangerous trait. The battle hydra can strike an opponent within 4 meters as a ranged attack, dealing both normal and poison damage. Note that since this is a ranged attack, the battle hydra needs to be at least 2 meters away from its victim.

Dxun Tomb Beast

The Onderon system has long been a focal point of dark side energy, ever since the Sith Lord Freedon Nadd built an empire for himself on that world thousands of years before the Battle of Endor. The system has four moons. The most notable one is Dxun, also known as the demon moon. It has a life-supporting atmosphere and a savage, brutal ecology of vicious predators and toxic flora. The geophysical stresses placed on the moon caused life to evolve hardy and mean.

Republic astrophysicists have reasoned that Dxun actually gained much of its original atmosphere (and plant and animal life) from the surface of Onderon itself. Once a year, Dxun orbits perilously close to the surface of Onderon—so close, in fact, that the atmospheres of the moon and the planet mix for a short time every summer. The same gravitational stresses pulling on Dxun from the three other moons then pull the two apart after their brief "kiss." After the first such event, flying creatures and airborne plant seeds from Onderon became trapped on Dxun when the two bodies separated.

As life fought tooth, claw, and stinger to survive on Dxun, natural selection soon saw the development of truly monstrous creatures. Many of the creatures that retained their capacity for flight then returned to Onderon the following year—to an ecosystem filled with comparatively weak animals and primitive tribes completely unable to handle them. Eventually, the so-called Beast Riders of Onderon tamed these Dxun predators, which came to be known as Dxun warbeasts.

Not all life left Dxun for Onderon, however. Monstrous killers continued to clash and evolve, becoming leaner, faster, and more effective. Gravity continued to twist and ravage Dxun, yanking mountain ranges from the depths of lakebeds.

Jedi Master Arca Jeth decided to inter the remains of Sith Lord Freedon Nadd on Dxun, where the world itself would prove an extremely effective deterrent to would-be Sith historians. Arca knew that these remains would become a focal point of power for Nadd's ghostly manifestation, as they were strong in the dark side. He had the tomb built from nearly indestructible Mandalorian iron to withstand the geophysical upheavals of the world and set it in a mountainous area dominated by territorial predators. The power of Nadd's dark essence twisted the dangerous hunters of Dxun even further. One variety in particular took to Nadd's crypt as a nesting ground, protecting the locus of evil from intruders. When Exar Kun finally fought his way into Nadd's resting place, he slew one of these Dxun tomb beasts. Fearsome as the tomb beast was, it fell quickly before Kun's rage.

The reptilian tomb beast, though smaller than the winged horrors ridden by the Beast Riders, makes up for its size and lack of flight with pure ferocity. The powerfully muscled animal's head is encased in thick bone and rests on a thick, almost nonexistent neck. A jagged, bony spike juts out from the lower jaw like a horn. The Dxun tomb beast uses the spike to gore and slash an opponent in combat. When hunting, the beast dives upon prey from the cliffs above, impaling its victim with the jaw spike.

Bacteria and microbes become septic on the tomb beast's jaw spike. The infected spike can poison the blood of any victim strong enough to survive the monster's gore attack. Should this poison attack prove insufficient to bring down its prey, the tomb beast's forelegs end in four long hooked climbing claws, each of which can cut a man in half with one swipe. These strong claws allow the tomb beast to scramble up the side of a sheer rock cliff face faster than it charges over open ground.

Tomb beasts are fiercely territorial and surprisingly intelligent. Mated pairs viciously attack any intruders who approach their nests. This territorial behavior also applies to their young—although the parents mate for life, they drive their offspring out of their territory soon after the adolescents make their first kill. Though Exar Kun destroyed the dark spirit of Freedon Nadd long ago, the tomb beasts continue to thrive and evolve in the hellish mountain terrain of Dxun.

Dxun Tomb Beast: Mountain predator 5; Init +7; Defense 18 (+7 natural, +3 Dex, -2 size); Spd 10m, climb 12m; VP/WP 51/40; Atk +14 melee (2d6+11 plus poison, gore) or +9 melee (2d8+11, claws) or +6 ranged; SQ Low-light vision, poison; SV Fort +9, Ref +7, Will +2; SZ H; Rep 1; Str 32, Dex 16, Con 20, Int 5, Wis 12, Cha 10. Challenge Code: D.

Skills: Climb +21, Hide +7, Jump +17, Spot +5, Survival (mountain)+5.

Feats: Improved Initiative, Power Attack.

Special Qualities: Poison—Rotting bits of flesh and gore produce a toxic buildup around the tomb beast's lower jaw spike. This buildup acts as an effective bacterial poison, which conforms to the contact poison description on page 219 of the *Star Wars Roleplaying Game*.

TE

Hssiss (Dark Side Dragon)

In the 25,000 years that the Jedi have protected the Republic, an endless number of worlds have seen the deaths of their dark side foes, ranging from malignant sorcerers to the Dark Lords of the Sith. The death of a powerful darksider leaves an aura of evil at the scene of his demise. Just as this spiritual taint taxes those who draw on the light side, it is powerful enough to turn the most innocuous animal into a vicious monstrosity after prolonged exposure.

One such localized area of dark energy was the planet Stenness. Four millennia before Palpatine's New Order, Jedi Master Thon arrived on Stenness and drove what he called a "great darkness" from the surface of the world. He forced this dark energy into geothermal lakes that harbored savage crocodilian predators known as hssiss. Unfortunately, the blight of evil on the land changed the reptiles into something different—something fouler.

Thon continued to train apprentices while corruption festered below the planet's surface. One such student, Nomi Sunrider, used rudimentary Jedi Battle Meditation to protect her daughter from an attack by a pair of hssiss. Around that same time, Jedi historians claim that a Hutt crime lord named Great Bogga transported several hssiss off Stenness. He began to market the offspring as protectors and pets to his colleagues and the occasional dark side adept (Great Bogga even kept one of the creatures as a personal bodyguard). By the time of Palpatine's ascension to the Chancellorship, the hssiss had become prized exotic animals among enemies of the Jedi. Most know them by the more poetic name "dark side dragon."

Despite their mutation by the dark side, the hssiss appear at first glance to be ordinary, if fierce, predatory reptiles. The creature's green, scaly hide covers a 3-meter body built low to the ground. Its long tail adds another meter or so to its body length. Prominent, horned eye crests rise over its bony skull, running into two rows of spikes down the creature's back. In the steam lakes of Stenness, hssiss usually hunt in pairs, creeping up on their prey from the nearby waters and grasping it in powerful jaws. The unlucky victim is held firmly in place by prominent canine teeth up to 10 centimeters long, while powerful claws gouge flesh from the victim's body.

Hssiss: Semiaquatic predator 3; Init +6; Defense 16 (+5 natural, +2 Dex, −1 size); Spd 12m, swim 18m; VP/WP 31/20; Atk +8 melee (2d6+6, bite) or +3 melee (2d4 +6, 2 claws) or +4 ranged; SQ Amphibious, dark side presence, improved grab; SV Fort +8, Ref +5, Will +2; SZ L; Rep 2; Str 22, Dex 14, Con 20, Int 2, Wis 12, Cha 11. Challenge Code: C.

Skills: Hide +8, Listen +5, Spot +7, Survival (aquatic) +3, Swim +10.

Feats: Improved Initiative, Power Attack.

Special Qualities: Improved Grab—Opponents may not move past a creature that is using improved grab. The hssiss can only use its improved grab on opponents at least one size category smaller than itself. If the hssiss hits with its bite attack, it deals normal damage and attempts to start a grapple as a free action (see Grapple on page 148 of the *Star Wars Roleplaying Game*). The hssiss then draws the held opponent toward it (that is, into the 2-meter-by-2-meter "space" around it).

After grappling, the hssiss may attempt a normal hold, or it may attempt to hold its opponent in its mighty jaws. To use the latter option, the hssiss makes an opposed grapple check with a −20 penalty. If this attempt succeeds, the creature grabs and holds its opponent without being grappled in return. Thus, the hssiss does not lose its Dexterity bonus to Defense while grappling, as it would with a normal hold. It suffers a −20 penalty on further opposed grapple checks, but may still use its claws against other opponents while maintaining the hold. It may also move, possibly dragging or carrying the held opponent along.

Regardless of the type of hold used, each successful grapple check the hssiss makes against a held opponent deals normal bite damage. A successful hold does not deal any additional damage, however.

Massassi

After a great schism drove a group of renegade Jedi to the other side of the galaxy, the fallen warriors ended up on the homeworld of a species called the Sith. These predatory, primitive people looked upon the dark ones from the sky as gods, a belief their new "deities" were happy to accept. Over many centuries, the Dark Jedi interbred with the Sith, building the wealthy and decadent Sith Empire.

The original Sith species upheld a crude caste system based on its many subspecies. The warrior caste, known as the Massassi, became the foot soldiers of the Sith Empire. When the Dark Lord of the Sith led his forces into space, Massassi crews piloted their massive battleships. On the ground, Massassi troops hurled themselves at their enemies with selfless fury. Like all "pure" Sith, the Massassi have crimson hides, glowing yellow eyes, and fierce, predatory profiles. Otherwise, they appear as fairly typical humanoids.

In combat, the Massassi prefer to wield simple martial weapons and the traditional Sith lanvarok, a deadly ranged weapon (see Chapter Four: Dark Side Equipment). A Massassi's battle armor primarily consists of a shield made from alchemically hardened metal alloys. The shield is strapped to the warrior's chest, providing a modicum of defense while offering virtually no restriction on movement. (It does, however, confer a −1 armor check penalty.) Massassi warriors are not particularly intelligent, but they are cunning. They blindly, even gladly, follow orders, even if it means they will die.

Scholars believe the Massassi became extinct long before the Rise of the Empire. It is possible, however, that scattered survivors still live on remote worlds once touched by the Sith of old, devolved into little more than predatory animals.

Massassi Warrior: Male or female Sith Thug 2; Init +6; Defense 16 (+4 armor, +2 Dex); Spd 10m; VP/WP −/12; Atk +6 melee (1d8+4, polearm) or +6 melee (1d8+4, sword) or +4 ranged (3d4, Sith lanvarok); SQ Low-light vision, warrior culture; SV Fort +4, Ref, +2, Will +0; SZ M; DSP 8; Rep 1; Str 18, Dex 14, Con 12, Int 8, Wis 8, Cha 6; Challenge Code: A.

Equipment: Massassi battle armor, polearm, sword, cloak.

Skills: Intimidate +2, Listen +2, Speak Sith, Spot +3.

THE SITH: SECT OR SPECIES?

The word "Sith" has changed in meaning over the millennia. What was once a proud, violent warrior species interbred with humanoid Dark Jedi, spawning an entire dark side culture many thousands of years ago. After the Sith Empire was destroyed through internal battles and the forces of the Old Republic, "Sith" came to mean a specific sect using dark side teachings to lure away unwary Jedi. In fact, the true Sith species is believed to have died out (or, like the Massassi warriors that accompanied Naga Sadow to Yavin 4, devolved into a more savage species). By the time Darth Vader is made Dark Lord of the Sith, the original species but a distant memory. In game terms, this simply means that although a Massassi, for example, is described as a "Sith thug," this refers to the Massassi's species, not necessarily knowledge of the dark arts of the Sith Force-user.

The "old" Massassi race described here is an example of the pure Sith bloodline. "Pure Sith" Massassi were originally bred to follow orders blindly and live for the glory of battle. However, both the original Massassi and their primitive, mutated descendants on Yavin 4 are long gone by the time of Palpatine and Skywalker. It is possible that they could have survived on a forgotten outpost world, but unless your campaign is set in the Tales of the Jedi era, Massassi will still be somewhat out of place.

LB

Feats: Exotic Weapon Proficiency (Sith lanvarok), Improved Initiative, Weapon Group Proficiency (simple weapons).

Special Qualities: Warrior Culture—Massassi are trained from birth to be ruthless, efficient soldiers for the glory of the Sith empire. This violent upbringing gives Massassi a +2 species bonus on Intimidate, Listen and Spot checks.

Primitive Massassi

When the renegade Sith Lord Naga Sadow failed in his bid to rule the Sith Empire, he fled to the fourth moon of a yellow-orange gas giant called Yavin. There, his Massassi crew helped build stone temples to focus the energies of the dark side (conveniently hiding Sadow's Sith battleship). For decades, Sadow practiced his Sith alchemy undisturbed. He created monstrous creatures, such as the gargantuan Sith wyrm, and twisted his Massassi into primitive, bestial guardians for his dark spirit. Sadow intended to return to the physical realm after death and continue indulging his lust for power. The Massassi warriors were left to adapt as best they could to life on Yavin 4, devolving even further into a primitive tribal society devoted to the protection of the temples and their

sinister occupant. In reverent tribute, shamanistic dark side priests manipulated the residual energies of Sadow's temples. Prophecies told of one who would come and release the Massassi people from their centuries of bondage and isolation on the jungle moon.

A thousand years after Sadow's arrival, the Jedi Exar Kun—still trying to convince himself that he was simply searching for ways to combat the dark side, not embrace it—arrived on the jungle moon seeking the secrets of the ancient Sith Lords. He was immediately attacked by the primitive Massassi, who took him to their Temple of Fire as a blood sacrifice to a creature they treated as a dark god—Naga Sadow's Sith wyrm.

Neither Exar Kun nor the Massassi realized that this was just another of Freedon Nadd's tests for Exar Kun, a means to force him to embrace the dark side. When Kun destroyed the creature with an ancient Sith amulet, he won the approval of Nadd, the full strength of the dark side, and the worship of the Massassi.

Kun set the Massassi to work, expanding the remaining temples. The Sith disciple also continued the fiendish work of the alchemist Naga Sadow. Using Sadow's ancient apparatus, he began to further mutate the Massassi into armored

NIGHT BEAST: KALGRATH, THE LAST MASSASSI

One lone Massassi warrior survived Exar Kun's suicidal stand against the might of the Jedi: a hulking brute named Kalgrath. Even as the entire population of Massassi on Yavin 4 poured into the Temple of Fire, Kun led Kalgrath into a series of isolation chambers Naga Sadow had built beneath the temple. There, Exar Kun altered the already mutated Massassi warrior even further. The Sith Lord caused Kalgrath's tough hide to harden until he could block most conventional energy weapons, altered the Massassi's hue from crimson to deep green (to better camouflage himself in the catacombs and jungles of Yavin 4), and rendered Kalgrath mute. In short, Kun turned the cunning, crafty warrior into a wily, intelligent, nigh-indestructible beast with ferocious destructive power. Kun then used the alchemy of the Sith to entomb Kalgrath in one of Sadow's isolation chambers as the Dark Lord's final physical defense against intruders.

Four thousand years later, Imperial forces launched another retaliatory attack against the rebels who had been using the Yavin moon as a base. The rebel forces survived, but a TIE fighter crashed into a section of the Massassi temple. It is not known whether this crash awoke Kalgrath, or simply disturbed Exar Kun's spirit (who then summoned Kalgrath to do his bidding). The end result was the same—a nigh-indestructible, 3-meter tall green monstrosity stormed into the hidden Rebel base. Kalgrath did not know the Massassi had all been killed in Kun's mad bid for supernatural power. He expected to find his people, but instead, he found humans infesting the temples like insects.

Luke Skywalker, hero of Yavin, had a final showdown with Kalgrath. The future Jedi Master showed his budding wisdom by refusing (some might say failing) to kill the monster. Instead, he and R2-D2 lured this "night beast" onto an unmanned supply ship headed toward the area of space that had once been the Sith empire. Only years later did Skywalker learn the true fate of the Massassi, but by then it was far too late to locate Kalgrath. It remains unknown whether the one-of-a-kind creature found his way to the fallen Sith Empire. Tionne, a renown Jedi researcher, believes the creature may have ended up on a deserted world called Ziost, but has little more than rumor and reports of "lurking shadows" to back up her hypothesis.

Kalgrath: Unique Massassi night beast, armored predator 9; Init +4; Defense 20 (+7 natural, +4 Dex, –1 size); Spd 12m; VP/WP 139/32; Atk +18 melee (2d6+9, bite) or +13 melee (2d4+9, 2 claws) or +13 ranged; SQ Damage reduction 10, darkvision, natural armor; SV Fort +17, Ref +10, Will +4; SZ L; Rep 1; Str 28, Dex 18, Con 32, Int 5, Wis 12, Cha 11; Challenge Code: E.

Skills: Intimidate +7, Listen +7, Spot +11, Survival +10.

Feats: Alertness, Power Attack, Track.

Special Qualities: Natural armor—Because Exar Kun intended for Kalgrath to face the Jedi, he used ancient alchemical techniques to temper Kalgrath's hide into frighteningly effective natural armor. Kalgrath gains a +7 species bonus to Defense and damage reduction 10.

monsters bred for pure violence. Even though the Massassi who had first discovered him had dismantled Exar Kun's own ship, they helped the new Sith Lord find and reactivate Naga Sadow's entombed Sith battleship.

Once freed from exile, Exar Kun went on a rampage with his Massassi warriors, leading them into battle against the Jedi througout the galaxy. Kun's Massassi even walked the surface of the Jedi center of learning, Ossuss, when Kun triggered a cosmological disaster (and the destruction of the Jedi library) in a bid to acquire ancient Sith artifacts.

Ultimately, Kun fulfilled the Massassi prophecy— from a certain point of view—when the primitive Massassi all gave their lives for their new master. Cornered by the combined might of the entire Jedi battle fleet, Kun ordered every Massassi on Yavin 4 (except one; see the sidebar on Kalgrath) into the Temple of Fire. There, where he first won their loyalty by slaying the wyrm, Kun used Sadow's ancient techniques and the life energy of every Massassi to leave his body and become one with the dark side. In the end, the Massassi died exactly as they lived, in absolute and unquestioning service to evil.

The primitive Massassi presented here is one of the tribe's many hunter-warriors. Primitive Massassi priests conform more or less to the generic dark side adept template presented later in this chapter (with a few simple modifications).

Primitive Massassi Warrior: Male or female mutated Sith Thug 4; Init +10; Defense 17 (+6 Dex, +1 class); Spd 10m; VP/WP –/18; Atk +10 melee (2d8+5, Massassi lanvarok) or +9 melee (1d8+6, spiked club) or +11 ranged (3d4, Massassi lanvarok); SQ Low-light vision, primitive, hunter culture; SV Fort +8, Ref, +7, Will +1; SZ M; DSP 10; Rep 0; Str 20, Dex 22, Con 18, Int 6, Wis 10, Cha 6; Challenge Code: B.

Equipment: Massassi lanvarok, primitive hunting garb.

Skills: Listen +4, Spot +4, Speak Massassi, Survival +8.

Feats: Exotic Weapon Proficiency (Massassi lanvarok), Improved Initiative, Skill Emphasis (Survival), Track, Weapon Focus (Massassi lanvarok), Weapon Group Proficiency (simple weapons).

Special Qualities: Hunter Culture—Primitive Massassi are trained from birth to be efficient providers for the good of the tribe. This predatory upbringing gives primitive Massassi a +2 species bonus on Listen, Spot, and Survival checks. Primitive Massassi receive the Track feat for free.

Primitive—This trait conforms to the "primitive penalty" given to the Ewoks on page 30 of the *Star Wars Roleplaying Game*.

Orbalisk

Lord Kaan's aborted assault on the Republic left one incompletely trained Sith Lord alive: Darth Bane. To save the Sith from extinction, Bane instituted his most important legacy: the rule of two. After that day, the Sith would consist of a master and an apprentice, "no more, no less." Since Bane's own master had been killed at Ruusan, he journeyed to Dxun, the legendary demon moon of Onderon, to find what knowledge he could at the tomb of Freedon Nadd. Despite his best efforts, Exar Kun did not have sufficient time to strip Freedon Nadd's tomb of all the Sith artifacts and mysteries it contained.

As Bane entered the Onderon system, the spirit of his former master, Lord Qordis, appeared to the Sith warrior. The dead man taunted Bane and accused him of cowardice, despite Bane's claim that he acted for the survival of the Sith. Not satisfied with this answer, Qordis used the dark side to knock Bane's ship out of the sky. Darth Bane barely survived the impact by using all the Sith power at his command. Goaded on by Lord Qordis's ghost and that of the mad Sith Lord Kaan, the evil genius who had detonated the suicidal "thought bomb" on Ruusan, Bane hacked his way through the poisonous foliage and razor-backed predators guarding the crypt—and approached his destiny.

Darth Bane found the tomb of Freedon Nadd much as Kun had left it. However, since Kun had destroyed Nadd's spirit on Yavin 4, the entity no longer lurked in its crypt. Bane quickly spotted an ancient Sith holocron that had eluded Kun's hasty search. As soon as he set foot inside the tomb, he realized he had been tricked. With a wet slurp, two mollusklike creatures dropped from the ceiling onto his body. Bane felt his entire body twist with the most potent pain he'd felt in his life. Trying desperately to remove the parasites, Bane slashed at one with his lightsaber, but the blow bounced off the creature's hard shell. The pain of the poison the creature injected was so great that Bane tried to slice off his own flesh, hoping the creature would come off with it. Instead, the wound healed before Bane's very eyes.

The ghostly Dark Lords demanded that Bane ignore the pain from the "orbalisks" (as they called them) and take the Sith holocron. Bane lost himself

in the device and learned what the creatures were— and why Qordis and Kaan had tricked him into becoming their host. These hard-shelled parasites injected their host with deadly venom. As a Sith warrior instinctively fights back with the power of the dark side, the creatures welcome that energy and feed off it. Furthermore, the venom they inject into their host—provided he survives—grants the victim enhanced strength, vitality, and accelerated healing, as well as an armored covering that is especially resistant to lightsabers. The orbalisks had lived and died over thousands of generations infused with the dark side residue of Freedon Nadd, and continued to crave that energy.

As the orbalisks bred and hardened quickly, Bane continually fought back against their venom with the strength of the Force. Within a couple of weeks, Bane was almost completely covered head to toe in nearly indestructible bioarmor. The exoskeleton surrounding him consisted of well-fed parasites that thrived on the dark side of the Force. Each day, Bane could feel his strength increase as the orbalisks reproduced and grew strong from his dark side presence. After it dawned on Bane that these parasites were going to grow over his face if he wasn't careful, he placed a helmet frame over his head. (For more information, see the Orbalisk Armor entry in Chapter Four).

In the wilds of Dxun, orbalisks are kept in check by specialized predators and an incredibly unforgiving environment. Many of Dxun's beasts have developed immunities and even antidotes to resist the parasites. When unable to attach to a living animal, the orbalisks crawl slowly over trees and other forms of plant life, drawing what little sustenance they can. They cannot reproduce or harden their outer shells while sustaining themselves on plants. Like most species that evolved on the moon of Onderon, they have no other natural checks on their reproduction. A single orbalisk would be harmless to anyone but its host, but if a few mated pairs were ever removed from Dxun and escaped into, say, the Coruscant sewage system, the consequences would be dire.

Orbalisk: Force-sensitive parasite 2; Init −4; Defense 16 (+2 natural, +8 size, −4 Dex); Spd 10cm, burrow 4cm; VP/WP 30/7; Atk +6 melee (special, bite) or +6 ranged; SQ Force-Sensitive, parasitic grip, poison; SV Fort +11, Ref −4, Will −1; SZ Fine; Rep 1; Str 3, Dex 2, Con 28, Int 2, Wis 9, Cha 4. Challenge Code: B (mated pair D).

 Skills: Hide +15, See Force +2, Survival +1.

 Feats: Force-Sensitive, Sense.

 Special Qualities: Parasitic Grip—An orbalisk that successfully hits with its bite attack does no damage, but automatically attaches itself to the flesh of its host and begins injecting venom into the host's bloodstream. A host can remove an attached orbalisk with an opposed Strength check or by killing it. Generally, the latter method often proves easier, since the parasite attaches so firmly that pulling it off would cause a substantial amount of the host to come off with the parasite. In game terms, the orbalisk's Strength increases to an effective score of 30 (that is, a Strength modifier of +10) when opposing any Strength checks specifically made to remove it from its host. If anyone successfully pulls the orbalisk free, the host immediately takes 1d4 wound damage. Any attempt to cut the orbalisk free by removing the flesh it's attached to invariably fails because of the healing properties the creature provides (see Orbalisk Armor, Chapter Four).

Poison—Orbalisks inject their venom into the host immediately after they hit with a bite attack. Once attached, they pump out another dose once per day. Note that the dark side helps fend off the poison—in fact, a character with 36 or more Dark Side Points no longer needs to save against the venom at all.

Every time orbalisk venom is injected into the bloodstream of the host, the victim must immediately make a Fortitude save (DC 18) and a second Fortitude save 6 rounds later. The poison has the following statistics:

Poison	Type	Initial Damage	Secondary Damage
Orbalisk venom	Injury DC 18*	1d6 Con	2d6 Con

*The victim gains a +1 dark side bonus on this save for every 2 Dark Side Points he has.

Sith Hound

Evil and frighteningly intelligent curs spawned from the depths of an otherworldly hell guard the tombs of the Sith necropolis world of Korriban. In reward for their faithful service, the beasts were taken to sites infused with the dark side, where they mutated into relentless and indefatigable Sith hounds. Exar Kun was especially fond of the creatures and personally brought them to the Massassi temples of Yavin 4.

The ancient Sith Lords alchemically altered the already brutal canines of their world, adding horns, increasing their size, and doubling their brain mass. Some have hypothesized that if Sith hounds had the physical capability and the inclination, they could even speak sentient languages. Sith hounds are unswervingly loyal to darksiders, to whom their senses are especially attuned. They were left on Korriban because the ancient Dark Lords of the Sith wanted trustworthy guardians to protect their remains. A Sith hound's most notable

feature is the remarkable intelligence evident behind its yellow eyes.

Sith hounds are one of the most unpredictable "animal" enemies in the galaxy. Sometimes they attack as soon as they feel threatened. More often they sit patiently, waiting for an opening in their opponent's defenses. This is especially true if they believe a foe does not realize their true nature. Packs of Sith hounds can execute complicated hunting and attack maneuvers, guided by their enhanced intelligence and canine ancestry. Never underestimate them.

Sith Hound: Predator 5; Init +7; Defense 13 (+3 Dex); Spd 10m; VP/WP 27/12; Atk +7 melee (1d8+2, bite) or +2 melee (1d6, claws) or +8 ranged; SQ Darkvision 20m; SV Fort +5, Ref +7, Will +2; SZ M; Rep 3; Str 14, Dex 16, Con 12, Int 9, Wis 12, Cha 12. Challenge Code: C.
  Skills: Listen +8, Spot +9, Survival +6.
  Feats: Improved Initiative, Track.

Sith Mutants

The most powerful Sith Lords possess a talent for the dark alchemy of the Sith. The Emperor, like Naga Sadow and Exar Kun long before him, became a master of manipulating the genetic building blocks of living creatures through the dark side. Over the millennia, many creatures have been broken, twisted, and rebuilt by this evil power.

Massassi Abomination

Although the Massassi pledged their loyalty to Exar Kun after he defeated the Sith wyrm, the Dark Jedi was still not satisfied. Filled with bitterness and spite, he swore to himself that he would make an example out of the warriors who had put him through his ordeal in the Temple of Fire. Furthermore, he realized that Naga Sadow had not gone far enough when he altered the Massassi. While they made excellent forest warriors, they were not prepared for the high-powered ordnance they would have to face when fighting the forces of the Republic. Exar Kun rejoiced when he discovered the giant alchemical machine that had belonged to Naga Sadow. At last, he had the means to shape his Massassi servants as he needed them, and he knew just the Massassi on whom he could experiment: Zythmnr, the priest who had ordered Kun to be sacrificed.

The Sith disciple first altered Zythmnr physically, fusing the old priest's skin with metallic bioarmor and enhancing the Massassi's skeletal structure and musculature accordingly. Vicious claws became razored gauntlets, thick hide became hardened plating, and Zythmnr's head was encased in a shelled helmet. The process was excruciating for the Massassi. He not only survived, but also continued to worship Kun, willfully insisting the experiments continue.

Exar Kun was more than happy to comply. He took his next step: infusing his new warrior with the dark side using some of his own physical makeup as a template. When Zythmnr readily took to the treatment—and even showed potential with Force skills—Kun chose several more "volunteers" to continue his work. Before long, he had several dozen living weapons that exuded the raw power and energy of the dark side. Upon feeling their power firsthand, the Jedi called them "abominations." Kun would take many of these bestial servants on his quests for Sith knowledge. In a few cases, he even left a handful of his favorite warriors behind to terrorize any that might oppose him. While the Jedi believed that all of the Massassi abominations died with their people, there may yet be descendants of this hideous species stranded on some remote, forgotten world.

Note: The processes by which the abominations and the Night Beast, Kalgrath, were created are similar, but not the same. The two should not be considered interchangeable.

Massassi Abomination: Male or female mutated Sith Thug 4/Dark Side Marauder 2; Init +5; Defense 24 (+3 natural, +5 Dex, +6 class); Spd 10m; VP/WP 25/20; Atk +14/+9 melee (2d8+7, Massassi lanvarok) or +13/+8 melee (2d6+7, heavy sword) or +11/+6 ranged (3d4, Massassi lanvarok); SQ Abominable presence, low-light vision, primitive; SV Fort +12, Ref +9, Will +1; SZ M; DSP 12; Rep 0; Str 24, Dex 20, Con 20, Int 10, Wis 10, Cha 8; Challenge Code: C.

Equipment: Heavy sword, Massassi lanvarok, warrior garb.

Skills: Battlemind +13, Climb +14, Intimidate +7 (against non-Force-sensitives), Intimidate +5 (against Force-sensitives), Jump +12, Speak Massassi.

Feats: Alter, Armor Proficiency (light), Control, Exotic Weapon Proficiency (Massassi lanvarok), Force-Sensitive, Power Attack, Rage, Weapon Focus (Massassi lanvarok), Weapon Group Proficiency (simple weapons).

Special Qualities: Abominable Presence—Massassi abominations exude the dark side of the Force, which grips Force-users and non-Force-users alike with fear. Massassi abominations gain +6 to Intimidate checks against non-Force-sensitives, and +4 to Intimidate checks against Force-sensitives without dark side points.

Primitive—This trait conforms to the "primitive penalty" given to the Ewoks on page 30 of the *Star Wars Roleplaying Game*.

Silooth

A huge armored, beetlelike creature mutated to the size of a bantha, the silooth was first utilized by the Sith Empire in the Battle of Kalsunor, long before the Golden Age of the Sith. Altered by Sith alchemy and mutation techniques, the normally docile creatures (which don't normally grow any larger than a womp rat) grew in size and ferocity. Then they were deposited on the planet Kalsunor, a world that resisted conquest by the Sith for a long time. The great creatures wreaked havoc on the planet, getting through defenses and causing chaos and destruction. Then the Sith warriors swarmed in to finish the battle.

The silooth is covered with segmented chitin plates that function as natural armor. Its eight legs have razor-sharp claws, and powerful mandibles clack noisily when it begins to rampage. If it grabs a victim in these mandibles, the silooth can deliver a deadly crush attack.

The mutated creature, imbued with the dark side of the Force, is filled with anger and ferocity. It attacks anything that comes near it, refusing to stop until whatever disturbed it is dead or totally destroyed. It refuses to flee or break off an attack once it has begun. Only death—either its own or the death of its victim—can halt a silooth's attack.

The great creatures have excellent low-light vision, but they can't see beyond 10 meters of their position. Once the silooth detects another life form, it moves toward the prey and begins a furious attack. It has the ability to make a ranged attack as it closes with its prey. This is accomplished by spewing acid from its maw. The acid spray can reach as far as 10 meters from the creature (to the limit of its vision).

After the Battle of Kalsunor, a vast army of silooths were left behind on that conquered world, and they continue to prey upon whatever life forms they encounter. Legends claim that larger, more powerful, and more rage-filled silooths exist in the deep canyons of the planet, but such claims have never been substantiated. Certain Sith holocrons hold the secret of silooth mutation, and it isn't uncommon to find one or two of these creatures in the service of a Sith Lord throughout the days of the Sith Empire. However, the Battle of Kalsunor is the only documented occurrence of mass production of these creatures. Perhaps their ferocity was too great even for the ancient Sith Lords, who had trouble controlling the beasts after the frenzied battle had ended.

Silooth: Mutated predator 10; Init +11; Defense 19 (+4 natural, +7 Dex, –2 size); Spd 16 m; VP/WP 95/40; Atk +18 melee (1d8+9, claw) or +15 ranged (3d10, acid spray); SQ Acid spray, low-light vision, crush; SV Fort +12, Ref +14, Will +5; SZ H; Rep 0; Str 28, Dex 24, Con 20, Int 4, Wis 14, Cha 12. Challenge Code: G.

   Skills: Hide +14, Listen +10, Move Silently +14, Spot +10.

   Feats: Improved Initiative, Power Attack, Weapon Focus (claw).

   Special Qualities: Acid Spray—The silooth possesses two internal sacs filled with inert liquid. When threatened or enraged, the silooth flexes muscles that squeeze the liquids into a third sac, where they mix to become a powerful acid. This third sac then contracts, spewing the acid at the creature's intended target. The acid is "fired" from the creature's maw. In the round in which it spews acid, the silooth cannot make a claw attack. The acid deals 3d10 damage to a hit target. The weapon threatens critical hits on a 20 and has a range of 10 meters—it cannot reach targets beyond that distance. It takes 4 rounds to refill the sacs, which means that the silooth can only spew acid once every 5 rounds (spew acid, refill for 4 rounds, spew again on the 5th round).

Crush—The silooth can crush an opponent it holds in its mandibles (see Grapple on page 148 of the *Star Wars Roleplaying Game*); the opponent must be Large or smaller (though anything that's Tiny or smaller slips through the mandibles, regardless of what the silooth tries to do). First, the silooth must grab its victim with a successful melee touch attack. Immediately after grabbing its victim, it must make an opposed grapple check to hold its victim. On a later turn, the silooth may attempt an opposed grapple check against its held victim. If it succeeds on this check, it crushes its victim for 2d8+8 points of damage; on a failed roll, the victim remains held.

If the victim survives the crush, he or she can attempt to escape the hold as per the rules for grappling.

Chrysalide Rancor ("Chrysalis Beast")

Over tens of thousands of years of space travel, the enormous reptilian beasts called rancors have evolved into a variety of subspecies on separate worlds. But not even the witches of Dathomir would recognize the Emperor Reborn's variant on that theme, the chrysalide or "chrysalis beast." As a living testimony to the Emperor's evil genius, chrysalide rancors grow to full size inside enormous alchemical cocoons.

The Emperor first used chrysalis beasts with deadly effectiveness against an Alliance strike team that had nearly reached his inner sanctum on Byss. The monsters proved especially useful against the Alliance's Viper Automaton droids, which were designed to counter powerful Imperial blaster weapons—not enraged behemoths.

Driven by the Emperor's evil, a chrysalide rancor attacks anything it can see—except another chrysalide rancor. It almost always goes after the largest target available.

Chrysalide Rancor: Mutated predator 12; Init +1; Defense 23 (+16 natural, –4 size, +1 Dex); Spd 30m; VP/WP 174/120; Atk +22 melee (2d8+14, 2 claws) or +17 melee (2d6+14, bite) or +9 ranged; SQ Damage reduction 8, low-light vision, rend, terrifying presence; SV Fort +18, Ref +9, Will +3; SZ G; Rep 5; Str 38, Dex 12, Con 30, Int 4, Wis 8, Cha 15. Challenge Code: H.

   Skills: Climb +25, Intimidate +14, Spot +10.
   Feats: Power Attack, Skill Emphasis (Intimidate).
   Special Qualities: Rend—If a chrysalide hits with both claw attacks, it latches onto the opponent's body and tears its flesh. This attack automatically deals 2d6+9 wound damage.

   Terrifying Presence—The chrysalide rancor has an extremely fierce, intimidating presence. It is capable of freezing opponents in fear. When the creature first attacks, it can make an Intimidate check as a free action to attempt to awe its opponent. The DC for this check is 15 + the level of the opponent. If the check is successful, the opponent must make a Will save (DC 15). If the opponent fails this Will save, he may take only a move action or an attack action on his next turn. If the opponent fails his save by 10 or more, he *cowers*. (A cowering character loses his Dex bonus and may not take an action on his next turn. Foes gain a +2 bonus to hit cowering opponents; see page 218 of the *Star Wars Roleplaying Game*.) The opponent continues to cower until he makes a Will save (DC 10), which he may attempt once per turn. A chrysalide rancor may make only one free Intimidate check in a given encounter.

Sith War Droid

The ancient Sith fashioned cruel battle droids designed to both brutalize and demoralize their enemies. The schematics for these ancient technological terrors can be found in most Sith holocrons, and many different varieties exist.

Some Jedi scholars believe that the Sith created war droids for one simple reason: They didn't trust living troops to always act in the interest of their superiors. With droids, the potential for betrayal is erased. Such constructs allow a relatively small number of Sith to inflict heavy casualties on the opposing side before they even wade into battle. Many have orbital delivery systems that allow them to make a "hard landing" by plummeting through a planet's atmosphere. After the specially designed cargo pod absorbs the brunt of the fall, the droid is immediately ready to enter the fray. (A modern version of the same deployment device is used by Imperial Probe Droids in the Rebellion era.)

Most war droids have powerful energy weapons that can lay down a steady stream of blaster fire. Many also have some kind of vibro weapon attached to at least one limb. An army of skeletal war droids dropped onto the planet Deneba ultimately slew the Jedi Master Arca Jeth, driving his apprentice Ulic Qel-Droma to the dark side.

Sith War Droid: Walking military droid; Thug 4; Init +9; Defense 19 (+4 armor, +5 Dex); Spd 10m; VP/WP —/12; Atk +6 melee (2d10+2, arm-mounted vibro-ax) or +10 ranged (3d10, blaster rifle); SV Fort +5, Ref +6, Will +1; SZ M; Rep 1; Str 14, Dex 20, Con 12, Int 6, Wis 10, Cha 8. Challenge Code: B.

Equipment: Armor, arm-mounted vibro-ax, arm-mounted blaster rifle.

Skills: Intimidate +6.

Feats: Improved Initiative, Weapon Focus (blaster rifle).

Sith Wyrm

When Exar Kun journeyed to Yavin 4 to delve into Sith secrets, the primitive Massassi guarding temples on the moon's surface decided to test him. Unable to use the light side of the Force, but unpracticed with the dark side, Exar Kun fell to the hunter-warriors and was taken to their Temple of Fire. There, a Massassi shaman named Zythmnr offered Kun to a creature they thought of as a god: a Sith wyrm. The monster was an absolutely enormous reptile/insect hybrid Naga Sadow had created centuries earlier. The Sith Wyrm prepared to devour Exar Kun.

Unknown to either the Massassi or Exar Kun, the spirit of Freedon Nadd was engineering this conflict to turn Exar Kun to the dark side. Freedon Nadd knew that Kun could only defeat the wyrm by taking up an ancient Sith amulet and focusing the energy of the dark side in concentrated blasts. The wyrm soon fell to Kun, who used his newfound power to destroy the spirit of Freedon Nadd as well. By then, however, Exar Kun was so fully enslaved by the dark side that it dominated his destiny forever.

The Sith wyrm was once a larval space slug that had attached itself to the hull of Naga Sadow's battleship en route to Yavin. Sadow, failing to tame the creature and seeing little other use for it, chose to mutate it into a colossal monster capable of swallowing a Jedi in one gulp. It is unknown whether Sadow was able to encourage the slug to reproduce asexually; if so, many more such beasts may exist deep underground on Yavin 4. By the time of the Rebellion, most scholars believe that the wyrm of legend was the only one to surface in thousands of years. Let us hope they were correct.

Sith Wyrm: Mutated subterranean carnivorous vermin 14; Init +0; Defense 12 (+10 natural, –8 size); Spd 16m, burrow 40m; VP/WP 326/304; Atk +26 melee (4d8+17, bite) or +5 ranged; SQ Darkvision 20m, swallow whole, track; SV Fort +25, Ref +11, Will +3; SZ C; Rep 4; Str 44, Dex 10, Con 38, Int 1, Wis 8, Cha 10. Challenge Code: I.

Skills: Listen +14, Hide +7, Spot +9, Survival –1

Special Qualities: Swallow Whole—After a successful grapple check, the Sith wyrm can swallow opponents it holds (see Grapple on page 148 of the *Star Wars Roleplaying Game*). The opponent can be up to Gargantuan in size. First, the Sith wyrm must make a successful melee touch attack to grab its victim. Immediately afterward, it must make an opposed grapple check to hold its victim. On a later turn, it may attempt an opposed grapple check against its held opponent. If the wyrm succeeds on its check, it swallows its victim whole; on a failed roll, the opponent remains held.

If the victim survives the attack and ends up in the Sith wyrm's stomach, he or she suffers 3d6 points of acid damage each round. If the swallowed character can deal 48 points of wound damage to the inside of the Sith wyrm (which has a Defense of 12), he or she breaks free.

The Supernatural: Dark Spirits

Dark Side Spirit

Ever since a faction of Dark Jedi left the Republic to found the Sith Empire countless millennia ago, the disciples of the dark side have been capable of affecting events long after their physical death. Dark Lord of the Sith Marka Ragnos, for example, appeared to two Sith Lords battling for his throne—Ludo Kressh and Naga Sadow—and warned them to fight the right battles lest the Sith Empire fall. Since Emperor Palpatine's death, Luke Skywalker and the students of his Jedi academy have repeatedly encountered the manipulative spirit of the Sith Lord Exar Kun. Kun himself, of course, was once a Jedi who fell under the sway of the spirit of Freedon Nadd. Both Kun and the corrupted Jedi Ulic Qel-Droma were made Sith Lords by the thousand-year-old spirit of Marka Ragnos, who ruled as Dark Lord of the Sith before Sadow or Kressh. The Emperor also continued in spirit form for a while, although he found his way back in a new body more than once. Even if a hero destroys a Sith Lord's body, his nemesis may seek revenge as a dark side spirit.

Many ghostly manifestations exist within the dark side, from Luke Skywalker's illusionary dueling opponent in the Dagobah cave to powerful avatars capable of utterly annihilating a Jedi Knight in a flash. The specific type of dark side spirit described here is essentially a noncorporeal version of the original being, an avatar of will expressed through dark side energy. Normally, powerful spirits of this type are deceased Sith Lords, although at least one—Exar Kun—voluntarily entered a state of living death. (Kun used his alchemical apparatus to transform himself into a dark side spirit when he saw a Jedi battle fleet preparing to attack the temples of Yavin 4.)

Each dark side spirit has a focal point of power that anchors it in the physical world. For example, the interred Sith Lords of Korriban use their burial sarcophagi to hold their spirits for millennia after death. Freedon Nadd clung to his tomb for countless centuries, waiting for the right opportunity to turn his successor to the dark side. Exar Kun—who didn't technically die so much as merge with the dark side and retain his identity—resisted the dissolution of his spirit by drawing on the remarkable focusing energies of the Massassi temples on Yavin 4.

GMs don't need to exercise such drastic measures. To create a dark side spirit, first select or create a character to use as the basis for the noncorporeal entity and apply the following template. Keep in mind that this template is intended for adversaries and nonheroic characters; player characters can only become dark side spirits by failing an attempt at Sith Sorcery (see Possession, below). Generic dark side spirits based on different Force-using classes can be found later in this chapter.

Vitality Points: A dark side spirit loses any Constitution bonus to its vitality points, but converts its die for rolling vitality points to a d12. Reroll the dark side spirit's vitality points using a d12 rather than the die for the class (or classes) it had in life. Assume that the dark side spirit has a full 12 vitality points at 1st level.

Wound Points: A dark side spirit is a nonphysical entity. Consequently, it has no Constitution score. Its wound points are instead equal to its Charisma score; it is a being sustained by its strength of personality rather than its physical composition.

Speed: The dark side spirit retains the speed and modes of movement it had in life. Becoming a nonphysical entity does not give the individual the ability to fly, for example, if it did not already have that ability. Dark side spirits are not hindered by terrain, though, and can pass as easily through solid objects as they can through thin air. The dark side spirit also gains the ability to travel by force of will (see below).

Defense: As a nonphysical entity, a dark side spirit is immune to physical attacks. Even to other nonphysical entities, a dark side spirit is immaterial. Any attack that relies on the dark side spirit's Defense (Move Object, for example) automatically fails.

Damage: The dark side spirit can make no physical attacks against a physical eneity, nor can it be harmed by physical attacks. However, it can use Force skills to successfully attack a physical entity.

Fortitude Saves: Because the dark side spirit has no Constitution score, it is immune to any power or skill that requires a Constitution check or Fortitude save. However, when the spirit is reduced to zero wounds (see the "Destroying a Dark Side Spirit" sidebar), it does not get a final Fortitude saving throw—the dark side spirit is automatically destroyed.

Skills and Force Skills: Skills and Force skills normally modified by Constitution are modified by Charisma instead. Because the dark side spirit still adheres to the dark side template, it retains its +4 bonus on dark side Force powers and –8 penalty on light side Force powers.

Force Powers: Force powers with physical effects (Alchemy, Force Grip, Force Push, Heal Another,

DESTROYING A DARK SIDE SPIRIT

Because so little can affect a dark side spirit, destroying one is often a monumental task. Though a dark side spirit should be a looming threat, it should not be impossible to destroy its influence once and for all. The Gamemaster need not decide that any one way is the correct way to destroy the spirit, though; the GM should always try to make getting rid of the dark side spirit a task that is within the heroes' means—though not necessarily obviously so. Some examples of destroying a dark side spirit are given below.

Destroying the Spirit's Source of Power: Dark side spirits are often connected to a particular dark side location, drawing their strength from their ancient crypt or the temple they once inhabited. Destroying the location—literally reducing it to its component pieces, with no hope of reconstruction—could sever the spirit's link to the physical world, banishing it forever. At the very least, the spirit should be weakened enough that a sufficiently powerful use of the Force—say, Affect Mind—could drive it off permanently.

Fighting Darkness with Light: Those strong in the light side of the Force can call upon it to overpower a dark side spirit. By expending a Force Point specifically to destroy the malevolent ghost, the Force-user deals 1d4 points of wound damage to the dark side spirit. Of course, the spirit can easily flee a single opponent who uses this method to destroy it, but if confronted with multiple light side adversaries, it could be permanently destroyed.

Similarly, the Force adept's ability to imbue a weapon with the power of the Force enables the Force adept to wield that weapon against a dark side spirit. The weapon's physical damage does not apply, but the bonus applied by imbuing the weapon with the

Force does (dealing 1d4 or 2d4 points of damage to the dark side spirit, depending on the level of the Force adept).

Light Side Powers: Another option would be to invent a Force skill that directs light side energy much the same way the Fear and Force Grip skills direct dark side energy. Because of its limited applications, however, the GM might want to make the skill usable untrained, so that players don't spend skill points to buy ranks in a skill that they may only use once.

Sith Amulet: The dark side is the energy of evil and destruction. For this reason, many dark side spirits are especially vulnerable to power similar to their own. A Force-user willing to tap into the energies of the dark side can destroy a dark spirit with an energy blast from a Sith amulet. (Exar Kun used this very tactic when he caused the "second death" of Freedon Nadd.) The spirit makes a Will save using the amulet wearer's Dark Side Point total as a DC. If the Will save succeeds once, any further attempts to destroy the spirit with that same amulet automatically fail.

Immediately after using an amulet in this manner, increase the user's Dark Side Point total to half his or her Wisdom score (if that total is currently less than half). If the user is already in the grip of the dark side, he or she earns 2 Dark Side Points instead of the usual 1. The amulet's wearer takes these points even if the target spirit makes its Will save and the attempt fails. These new Dark Side Points do not apply to the DC for the spirit's Will save.

Zero Wounds: When the dark side spirit's wound points are reduced to zero, the spirit is automatically destroyed; it does not get a Fortitude save.

Move Object, Force Lightning, and Force Whirlwind) are ineffective when used by or against a dark side spirit. The damage dealt—or vitality, wound, or ability points restored—is reduced to zero.

A dark side spirit cannot use Force powers based on Constitution (Battlemind, Enhance Ability, Force Defense, Force Stealth, Heal Self, and Rage) or Force powers that cause the dark side spirit to make a Fortitude save (Dissipate Energy). Similarly, a dark side spirit is not affected by Force powers that cause it to make a Fortitude save (Drain Force and Hatred).

Gamemasters should use these rules as guidelines for other Force powers that are not listed here.

Force Points: Same as the base character. A dark side spirit can spend and acquire Force Points as normal.

Dark Side Points: Same as the base character. A dark side spirit can acquire Dark Side Points as normal, but it cannot sacrifice Force points to reduce its Dark Side Points, nor reduce its Dark Side Points by performing dramatic acts of heroism. A dark side spirit is lost to the dark side for eternity.

Special Attacks: A dark side spirit retains all the special attacks of the person it was in life, although those attacks relying on physical contact are no longer effective against physical or even other nonphysical creatures. In most cases, this limits the dark side spirit to using Force skills and feats that affect a target's mind, and little else. The dark side spirit also gains a manifestation ability—it can possess the bodies of the living. See below for explanations of these latter abilities.

Manifestation: As nonphysical creatures, dark side spirits cannot affect or be affected by anything physical. When they manifest, they become audible and visible, but remain nonphysical. However, a manifested spirit can still use Force powers, as described above. Manifesting initially is considered a move action. Continuing to remain audible and visible costs the dark side spirit 1 vitality point per minute. A dark side spirit is visible and audible to other nonphysical creatures whether it manifests or not.

Possession: When dark side practitioners open themselves to the power of the dark side through the use of Sith Sorcery, they run the risk of becoming possessed by the dark side spirits they call upon. At the end of the minute during which the benefit of Sith Sorcery applies, the character using the feat must immediately attempt a Will saving throw (DC 10 + the bonus gained). Failure means that a dark side spirit has possessed the character. In some cases, this will be a specific spirit, but if the GM does not have a dark side spirit ready, he can use one of the pregenerated dark side spirits described later in this chapter.

Dark side spirits can also attempt to possess physical bodies at will. Attempting to possess a physical body is a full-round action. The target of the attempt may make a Will save (DC 5 + the dark side spirit's Charisma modifier) to prevent the possession attempt. Failure to possess the target body prevents the dark side spirit from ever attempting to possess that body again.

If the target fails its Will save, however, the dark side spirit occupies its physical form. The dark side spirit retains its Intelligence, Wisdom, Charisma, level, class, base attack bonus, base save bonuses, and mental abilities (such as skills and certain feats). The body retains its Strength, Dexterity, Constitution, vitality points, wound points, and natural abilities (such as species abilities and physical feats like Ambidexterity). As a move action, the dark side spirit can exit the body. If the body is slain while it is possessed, the dark side spirit is forced out but is otherwise unharmed.

While the dark side spirit occupies the possessed body, the body's original occupant is rendered nonphysical—becoming, in effect, another dark side spirit. This new dark side spirit can attempt to repossess its former body or can target a different body.

Special Qualities: A dark side spirit has all the special qualities of the base character and those described below.

Force Travel: A dark side spirit is able to use the Force to travel more or less instantaneously to any point in the galaxy, though there must be dark side energy there to act as a "beacon." The dark side spirit must already be familiar with the destination; he cannot simply "blind jump" to a destination by targeting an artifact he has heard of, for example. To use this ability, the dark side spirit attempts a Will save:

Distance	Will Save DC
Same city	0
Same continent	5
Same planet	10
Same system	15
Same sector	20
Same region	25
Same galaxy	30

This Will save is modified by the power of the dark side at the target destination:

AW

Dark Side Power Level	Save Modifier	Example
Nonexistent	Not possible	Anything not touched by the dark side
Dim	−5	A person with Dark Side Points equal to half his or her Wisdom score or less
Faint	+0	A person with Dark Side Points greater than half his or her Wisdom score
Moderate	+2	A person completely turned to the dark side; a weak dark side artifact
Strong	+5	A place touched by the dark side; a dark side artifact
Overwhelming	+8	A place infused with the dark side; a powerful dark side artifact

Saves: Same as the base character.

Abilities: Same as the base character, except that the dark side spirit has no Constitution score, and its Charisma score increases by +4. Because a dark side spirit has no Constitution, it is immune to any effect that requires a Fortitude save unless the effect works on nonphysical targets. It is also immune to ability damage and ability drain, and always fails Constitution checks.

Skills: Dark side spirits receive a +8 species bonus on Hide, Listen, Search, and Spot checks. Otherwise, the skills are the same as those of the base character.

Feats: Same as the base character

Equipment: Although the dark side spirit appears armed and garbed more or less as it did in life, wearing spirit forms of the same materials, its actual equipment does not become nonphysical and resides with its body.

Guardian Spirit

Thousands of years ago, the planet Korriban was the seat of power for the Dark Lords of the Sith Empire. Centuries before Palpatine's reign, it stood as a necropolis the size of a planet, the antithesis of the thriving heart of the Republic, Coruscant.

Like many cultures, the Sith buried slaves, courtiers, and priests with their honored dead. Unlike many such belief systems, however, the ancient Sith had firsthand knowledge that the dark side would keep the souls of those crypt keepers trapped with their dead masters. Driven by hatred of those who entombed them and the madness that is existence in the dark side, the relatively weak spirits of thousands of lesser Sith act as protectors for the remains of their superiors. Unable to exert enough strength to possess the living, these guardian spirits animate the fleshless corpses of various tomb robbers and space pirates that have unintentionally made Korriban their final resting place. A guardian spirit looks for all the world like a walking skeleton.

Millennia of madness in the dark side drive the possessing spirit insane. Therefore, they will not, and cannot, behave as sentient beings. They attack without mercy until they are physically destroyed. Even then, the guardian spirit may jump to another skeleton and rise again. Whatever they may once have been, these guardians now exist only as mindless walking dead, hulking, shambling *things* that must be destroyed to remove the taint of evil.

Guardian Spirit: Dark side walking dead, Thug 5; Init –2; Defense 11 (+3 armor, –2 Dex); Spd 6m; VP/WP –/12; Atk +7 melee (1d6+2, club) or +7 melee (1d8+2, sword) or +7 (1d10+2, heavy waraxe) or +3 ranged; SQ Body swap, walking dead; SV Fort +3, Ref –1, Will –1; SZ M; DSP 8; Rep 1; Str 14, Dex 6, Con 8, Int 1, Wis 6, Cha 2. Challenge Code: A.

Skills: Listen +4, Spot +4.

Feats: Alertness, Toughness.

Special Qualities: Walking Dead—Guardian spirits are little more than shuffling bags of bones animated and filled with malicious intent by the dark side. They are immune to disease, the effects of cold, and the vacuum of space. The spirit energy that drives them is no longer sentient or self-aware, so it is not as susceptible to Force mental abilities—indeed, they simply continue to obey the last command they received in life by protecting the necropolis from intruders. Since more of their guardian spirit's body is missing than present, they become harder to hit with certain types of primitive weapons. If a weapon that deals piercing or slashing damage hits a guardian spirit, the damage is cut in half (rounded down).

Body Swap—If a guardian spirit is destroyed and another corpse (no matter how fresh) is within 10 meters, the spirit attempts to possess the other body. (In the case of more than one corpse, choose randomly.) The spirit makes a Will save against DC 10. If the save succeeds, the ghostly energy moves into this new body. This possession by the dark side literally melts the flesh off the corpse. The new guardian spirit immediately takes on the characteristics of the original guardian spirit (no matter what the body was in life). This attempt is automatic in response to the destruction of the guardian spirit. If no body is nearby or the Will save fails, the dark side energy dissipates and the spirit is truly destroyed.

GM Archetypes

These generic archetypes represent typical opponents heroes might face—or allies they may fight alongside—in a dark side campaign. Gamemasters can use these archetypes to detail minor characters in a campaign, provide the basis for recurring GM characters, or quickly create a series of unexpected encounters. GMs should feel free to add histories and personalities to these templates, especially information on how, if ever, they discovered and turned to the dark side.

None of the opponents represented here feature species bonuses of any sort (except for a Human's extra skill points or feats, as noted in some of the statistic blocks). Such modifications need to be made by the GM if she decides to adapt these generic opponents into specific characters. Otherwise, the differences will most likely be minor. A Human dark side marauder and a Gungan dark side marauder will probably be indistinguishable to players.

Note on Feats: Many of the archetype statistic blocks "build" from left to right—that is, the character in the middle column is a higher-level version of the character in the left column, and the character in the right column is a higher-level version of the character in the middle column. In such cases, the "Feats" entry in the middle and right statistic blocks does not duplicate all the feats for each character; instead, the words "see left" indicate that a higher-level characters has all the feats that a lower-level character has. The higher-level character usually also has one or more feats that the lower-level character does not have, indicated by the word "plus" preceding the newly gained feat or feats.

Dark Jedi

As long as the Jedi have protected the Republic, there have been those who walk the line between light and darkness. A Jedi who strays from this path inevitably becomes a creature of the dark side. Corrupt Jedi guardians become lost to their anger and hatred, betraying the light side by using direct physical aggression, but the persuasive, philosophical methods of the Jedi consular offer a different path. The tainted consular becomes a master manipulator, using petty prejudice, paranoia, and fear as his primary weapons. Despite this focus on controlling others, the manipulator remains perfectly capable with his lightsaber—even if it's rarely activated.

In the thousands of years leading up to the Rise of the Empire, the sheer number of Jedi in the galaxy suggests that Dark Jedi are far more common at that time than in any other era. Some may have been influenced by Sith teachings, some may have suffered tragedies that opened them up to the dark side, and others may have given in to greed and the lust for power. By the time of the Rebellion, nearly all Jedi are extinct, except those few who went into hiding or joined Palpatine. In this time period, it's exceedingly unlikely that a Dark Jedi who has survived doesn't work for the Empire.

In the period immediately following Grand Admiral Thrawn's death, the Emperor Reborn imbued a number of Force-sensitives with raw dark side power. Although he called these acolytes and disciples "Dark Jedi," it is unlikely they ever received true Jedi training. By the time of the Yuuzhan Vong invasion, Luke Skywalker's Jedi academy has built a new generation of Jedi Knights, many of whom go too far in their pursuit of forbidden knowledge or vengeful justice.

Dark Jedi follow the same general era restrictions as the Dark Jedi guardian on page 263 of the *Star*

Generic Dark Jedi, male or female, any species

	Jedi Consular 4	Jedi Consular 8	Jedi Consular 12
Initiative:	+1	+1	+1
Defense:	15 (+4 class, +1 Dex)	17 (+6 class, +1 Dex)	19 (+8 class, +1 Dex)
Speed:	10m (or by species)	10m (or by species)	10m (or by species)
VP/WP:	24/10	39/10	62/10
Attacks:	Lightsaber +2 melee	Lightsaber +5/+0 melee	Lightsaber +8/+3 melee
	Blaster pistol +4 ranged	Blaster pistol +7/+2 ranged	Blaster pistol +10/+5 ranged
Damage:	Lightsaber 2d8–1	Lightsaber 3d8–1	Lightsaber 4d8–1
	Blaster pistol 3d6	Blaster pistol 3d6	Blaster pistol 3d6
Special Qualities:	—	Healing	Healing
Saves:	F +4, R +3, W +6	F +6, R +5, W +8	F +8, R +7, W +10
Size:	(by species)	(by species)	(by species)
Challenge Code:	B	C	D
Force Points:	2	4	6
Dark Side Points:	10	16	24
Reputation:	4	8	12
Abilities:	Str 8, Dex 12, Con 10, Int 15, Wis 14, Cha 14	Str 8, Dex 12, Con 10, Int 15, Wis 15, Cha 14	Str 8, Dex 13, Con 10, Int 15, Wis 15, Cha 14
Skills:	Bluff +9, Computer Use +5, Diplomacy +11, Gather Information +6, Intimidate +11, Knowledge (Jedi lore) +6, Sense Motive +6	Bluff +15, Computer Use +5, Diplomacy +11, Gather Information +6, Intimidate +13, Knowledge (Jedi lore) +6, Sense Motive +6	Bluff +19, Computer Use +5, Diplomacy +15, Gather Information +6, Intimidate +15, Knowledge (Jedi lore) +6, Sense Motive +6
Force Skills:	Affect Mind +12, Empathy +5, Fear +10, See Force +5, Telepathy +5	Affect Mind +16, Control Mind +17, Empathy +7, Fear +10, Illusion +9, See Force +7, Telepathy +7	Affect Mind +20, Control Mind +21, Empathy +7, Fear +14, Illusion +13, See Force +7, Telepathy +14
Feats:	Exotic Weapon Proficiency (lightsaber), Force-Sensitive, Skill Emphasis (Affect Mind), Weapon Group Proficiency (blaster pistols), Weapon Group Proficiency (simple weapons)	see left, plus Persuasive	see left, plus Skill Emphasis (Telepathy)
Force Feats:	Alter, Control, Force Mind, Sense	Alter, Control, Force Mind, Knight Mind, Sense	Alter, Burst of Speed, Control, Force Mind, Knight Mind, Sense
Equipment:	Lightsaber, blaster pistol, protocol droid	Lightsaber, blaster pistol, protocol droid	Lightsaber, blaster pistol, protocol droid

Wars Roleplaying Game. Only 8th- and 12th-level Dark Jedi are present in the Rebellion era. The 4th- and 8th-level manipulator is more appropriate for The New Jedi Order. During the Rise of the Empire era, all levels are appropriate.

Dark Side Adept

The evil shaman who corrupts the tribe for her own vicious ends, the wandering mystic enamored of forbidden knowledge, the brutal advisor to a weak-willed tyrant—no matter what her background, the dark side adept gains power through the exploitation of inferiors. Many hail from worlds completely removed from either Sith or Jedi tradition; instead, they often call upon the dark side of the Force as evil magic. Driven by greed, ambition, or even wicked curiosity, the dark side adept rarely stays long on her homeworld.

Like the normal Force adept class, the dark side adept can be found in any era, tucked away on a forgotten colony or an undiscovered world. During the Old Republic, the Jedi crushed most of these

Generic Dark Side Adept, male or female, any species

	Force Adept 4	Force Adept 6/ Dark Side Devotee 2	Force Adept 6/ Dark Side Devotee 6
Initiative:	+0	+0	+0
Defense:	14 (+4 class)	19 (+9 class)	20 (+10 class)
Speed:	10m (or by species)	10m (or by species)	10m (or by species)
VP/WP:	26/13	52/14	78/14
Attacks:	Spear +2 melee Blaster pistol +3 ranged	Spear +4 melee Blaster pistol +5 ranged	Spear +7 melee Blaster pistol +8 ranged
Damage:	Spear 1d8−1 Blaster pistol 3d6	Spear 1d8+1d4−1 Blaster pistol 3d6	Spear 1d8+2d4−1 Blaster pistol 3d6
Special Qualities:	—	Force weapon (+1d4), dark side talisman (+2)	Force weapon (+2d4)
Saves:	F +3, R +2, W +8	F +7, R +5, W +12	F +8, R +6, W +15
Size:	(by species)	(by species)	(by species)
Challenge Code:	B	C	D
Force Points:	2	4	6
Dark Side Points:	4	12	20
Reputation:	4	8	12
Abilities:	Str 9, Dex 11, Con 13, Int 14, Wis 15, Cha 14	Str 9, Dex 11, Con 14, Int 14, Wis 15, Cha 14	Str 9, Dex 11, Con 14, Int 14, Wis 16, Cha 14
Skills:	Intimidate +4, Sense Motive +9, Survival +5	Intimidate +6, Sense Motive +11, Survival +7	Intimidate +8, Sense Motive +12, Survival +8
Force Skills:	Affect Mind +9, Alchemy +6, Fear +9, Force Defense +8,, Force Grip +5, Move Object +9, See Force +9	Affect Mind +13, Alchemy +10, Fear +11, Force Defense +13, Force Grip +10, Heal Self +8, Move Object +13, See Force +11	Affect Mind +17, Alchemy +14, Farseeing +7,, Fear +18, Force Defense +17, Force Grip +13, Heal Self +11, Move Object +17, See Force +15
Feats:	Force-Sensitive, Iron Will, Weapon Group Proficiency (blaster pistols), Weapon Group Proficiency (primitive weapons), Weapon Group Proficiency (simple weapons)	see left, plus Skill Emphasis (Force Grip)	see left, plus Skill Emphasis (Fear)
Force Feats:	Alter, Control, Force Mind, Sense	Alter, Control, Force Mind, Prolong Force, Sense	Alter, Control, Force Lightning, Force Mastery, Force Mind, Prolong Force, Sense
Equipment:	Spear, blaster pistol, dark side talisman, robes	Spear, blaster pistol, dark side talisman, robes	Spear, blaster pistol, dark side talisman, robes

darksiders as soon as they discovered them. Therefore, dark side adepts encountered during the Rise of the Empire era might be the last survivors of their sect, seeking vengeance against the Republic. During the Rebellion era, Palpatine was usually content with wiping out the Jedi. The Emperor left other dark Force-users alone while he focused on more important goals: quelling the Rebellion and turning young Skywalker. During The New Jedi Order, dark side adepts are even more common, since there aren't nearly as many Jedi to hunt down their kind.

The low-level dark side adept is one that's probably still dominating the weak-minded on whatever primitive world she calls home. The mid-level adept has gone in search of greater secrets in the galaxy. The higher-level dark side adept has gained more than a few followers and could one day rule over a distant world or far-flung system.

Dark Side Avatar

Masters of the dark side often move beyond mere physical violence in their studies, relying on brutal servants and killers to enforce their desires. To that end, a dark master may train an elite warrior in the ways of evil, transforming her into a living extension of the master's cruel will. Soon the master learns he has trained the warrior too well—a mistake he only regrets for a short time before the killer turns on him. This is just one example of a dark side avatar—a warrior touched by the dark side, used as the master sees fit to carve terror and violence into his world.

Dark side avatars exist in all eras of the *Star Wars Roleplaying Game*, although they're likely to be far from the Core Worlds during Palpatine's reign in the Rebellion era. The lower-level avatar is likely to be encountered serving a dark master or leading a gang of dark side thugs. The 8th-level avatar could be a pirate raider or hired killer in the "civilized" galaxy, or the cruel chieftain of warrior bandits on the master's homeworld. The 12th-level dark side avatar may lead an army against the forces of light, dominating an entire sector as a warlord or training other darksiders in combat and strategy techniques.

Generic Dark Side Avatar, male or female, any species

	Soldier 3/Force Adept 1	Soldier 4/Force Adept 1/ Dark Side Marauder 3	Soldier 4/Force Adept 1/ Dark Side Marauder 7
Initiative:	+1	+1	+1
Defense:	19 (+8 armor, +1 Dex)	19 (+8 armor, +1 Dex)	20 (+9 class, +1 Dex)
Speed:	10m (or by species)	10m (or by species)	10m (or by species)
VP/WP:	42/18	80/18	118/19
Attacks:	Vibro-ax +6 melee	Vibro-ax +11/+6 melee	Vibro-ax +16/+11/+6 melee
	Blaster rifle +4 ranged	Blaster rifle +8/+3 ranged	Blaster rifle +12/+7/+2 ranged
Damage:	Vibro-ax 2d10+3	Vibro-ax 2d10+4	Vibro-ax 2d10+4
	Blaster rifle 3d8	Blaster rifle 3d8	Blaster rifle 3d8
Special Qualities:	—	—	—
Saves:	F +8, R +3, W +3	F +12, R +6, W +4	F +14, R +8, W +7
Size:	(by species)	(by species)	(by species)
Challenge Code:	C	D	E
Force Points:	2	4	6
Dark Side Points:	5	15	25
Reputation:	5	10	15
Abilities:	Str 17, Dex 12, Con 18, Int 10, Wis 10, Cha 12	Str 18, Dex 12, Con 18, Int 10, Wis 10, Cha 12	Str 18, Dex 12, Con 19, Int 10, Wis 10, Cha 12
Skills:	Climb +6, Demolitions +6, Intimidate +7, Pilot +7, Survival +3	Climb +7, Demolitions +6, Intimidate +9, Pilot +9, Survival +3	Climb +7, Demolitions +6, Intimidate +12, Pilot +10, Survival +4
Force Skills:	Enhance Ability +10	Battlemind +13, Enhance Ability +13	Battlemind +16, Enhance Ability +13, Force Grip +8
Feats:	Armor Proficiency (heavy), Armor Proficiency (light), Armor Proficiency (medium), Force-Sensitive, Power Attack, Weapon Group Proficiency (blaster pistol), Weapon Group Proficiency (blaster rifles), Weapon Group Proficiency (heavy weapons), Weapon Group Proficiency (primitive weapons), Weapon Group Proficiency (simple weapons), Weapon Group Proficiency (vibro weapons)	see left, plus Cleave, Great Cleave, Heroic Surge	see left, plus Blind-Fight, Endurance, Iron Will, Weapon Focus (vibro-ax)
Force Feats:	Alter, Control	Alter, Control, Rage	Alter, Control, Rage, Sense
Equipment:	Vibro-ax, blaster rifle, armored spacesuit	Vibro-ax, blaster rifle, armored spacesuit	Vibro-ax, blaster rifle, armored spacesuit

Dark Side Spirit

The sorcery of the dark side derives power from hate, rage, and fear. Many darksiders who become one with the Force abandon their physical forms, becoming ghostly incarnations of pure malice. Most of these spirits are lost forever in the madness of the dark side. Others find ways to attach their essence to objects and locations strong in dark power. The long-dead Sith Lord Exar Kun and the dark shades of the Necropolis on Korriban are among the most infamous examples of dark side spirits.

The dark side spirit's obsession with life after death may be rooted in the essential paradox of the dark side: The more successful the darksider, the more quickly that darksider's body decays. The dark spirit continues the quest for power after the body is no more. (Dark side spirits have a number of other unique properties; these are defined in more detail earlier in this chapter.) The ability to become a dark side spirit is not unique to the Sith; powerful dark side devotees and other Force-sensitives also have the will to defy death.

In the Golden Age of the Sith, dark side spirits such as the ghost of Sith Lord Marka Ragnos regularly

Various Generic Dark Side Spirits

	Dark Side Adept Spirit Force Adept 6/Dark Side Devotee 6	Dark Jedi Spirit Jedi Consular 12	Sith Lord Spirit Force Adept 2/Soldier 3/ Sith Warrior 3/Sith Lord 4
Initiative:	+0	+1	+1
Defense:	20 (+10 class)	19 (+8 class, +1 Dex)	24 (+11 class, +1 Dex, +2 Sith Sword Defense)
Speed:	10m (or by species)	10m (or by species)	10m (or by species)
VP/WP:	78/14	78/14	94/14
Attacks:	by weapon +7 melee by weapon +8 ranged	by weapon +8/+3 melee by weapon +10/+5 ranged	by weapon +13/+8/+3 melee by weapon +12/+7/+2 ranged
Damage:	by weapon	by weapon	by weapon
Special Qualities:	Force weapon (+2d4), dark side talisman (+2)		Enemy bonus +1
Saves:	F +8*, R +6, W +15	F +8*, R +7, W +10	F +15*, R +9, W +13
Size:	(by species)	(by species)	(by species)
Challenge Code:	D	D	F
Force Points:	8	6	6
Dark Side Points:	20	24	20
Reputation:	12	12	15
Abilities:	Str 9, Dex 11, Con —, Int 14, Wis 16, Cha 14	Str 8, Dex 13, Con —, Int 15, Wis 15, Cha 14	Str 15, Dex 13, Con —, Int 14, Wis 14, Cha 14
Skills:	Intimidate +8, Sense Motive +12, Survival +8	Bluff +19, Computer Use +5, Diplomacy +15, Gather Information +6, Intimidate +15, Knowledge (Jedi lore) +6, Sense Motive +6	Bluff +8, Craft (dark armor) +8, Diplomacy +12, Intimidate +10, Knowledge (Sith lore) +10, Pilot +5, Read/Write Sith, Survival +8
Force Skills:	Affect Mind +17, Farseeing +7, Fear +22, Force Defense +17, Force Grip +21, Heal Self +11, Move Object +17, See Force +15	Affect Mind +20, Control Mind +21, Empathy +7, Fear +14, Illusion +13, See Force +7, Telepathy +14	Affect Mind +7, Alchemy +8, Battlemind +9, Force Defense +12, Force Grip +11, Heal Self +9, Move Object +10, See Force +7
Feats:	Force-Sensitive, Iron Will, Skill Emphasis (Fear), Skill Emphasis (Force Grip), Weapon Group Proficiency (blaster pistols), Weapon Group Proficiency (primitive weapons), Weapon Group Proficiency (simple weapons)	Exotic Weapon Proficiency (lightsaber), Force-Sensitive, Persuasive, Skill Emphasis (Affect Mind), Skill Emphasis (Telepathy), Weapon Group Proficiency (blaster pistols), Weapon Group Proficiency (simple weapons)	Armor Proficiency (heavy), Armor Proficiency (light), Armor Proficiency (medium), Exotic Weapon Proficiency (Sith sword), Force-Sensitive, Starship Operation (capital ships), Weapon Focus (Sith sword), Weapon Group Proficiency (blaster pistols), Weapon Group Proficiency (blaster rifles), Weapon Group Proficiency (heavy weapons), Weapon Group Proficiency (primitive weapons), Weapon Group Proficiency simple weapons), Weapon Group Proficiency (vibro weapons)
Force Feats:	Alter, Control, Force Lightning, Force Mastery, Force Mind, Prolong Force, Sense	Alter, Burst of Speed, Control, Deflect Blasters, Force Mind, Knight Mind, Sense	Alter, Control, Hatred, Sith Sorcery, Sith Sword Defense
Equipment:	Dark robes	Jedi robes	Sith armor

See Fortitude Saves on page 122 and Possession on page 123.

advised and threatened their successors. During the Rebellion era, the dark side spirit of Exar Kun was in a state of suspended consciousness while the Empire nearly destroyed Yavin 4, but was soon awakened by the arrival of Luke Skywalker's Jedi academy. It would not be surprising to find others like Exar Kun scattered throughout the galaxy, especially in the area of space that was once the Sith Empire. It's safe to assume that such virtually immortal evil creatures exist in The New Jedi Order era, although so far none have played a major role in the conflict with the Yuuzhan Vong.

Each dark side spirit presented here is a high-level Force-user that clings to a ghostly existence for his

or her own vile purpose, whether dark side adept, Dark Jedi, or Sith Lord. Gamemasters can create lower-level dark side spirits by referring to the dark side spirit entry earlier in this chapter and combing it with a generic Force-user template.

Emperor's Hand

As one of Palpatine's personal assassins, an Emperor's Hand follows the Emperor's will with fierce devotion. Such an individual may be found working undercover in a crime lord's gang, insinuating himself into the life of a target, or simply hunting his quarry with cold efficiency from afar. The Emperor has many Hands, all

Generic Emperor's Hand, male or female, Human (extra skills and feats included)

	Scoundrel 6/ Emperor's Hand 2	Scoundrel 6/ Emperor's Hand 6	Scoundrel 6/ Emperor's Hand 10
Initiative:	+7	+8	+8
Defense:	22 (+9 class, +3 Dex)	24 (+10 class, +4 Dex)	26 (+12 class, +4 Dex)
Speed:	10m	10m	10m
VP/WP:	48/12	70/12	92/13
Attacks:	Vibroblade +6 melee Blaster +8 ranged	Lightsaber +9/+4 melee Blaster +11/+6 ranged	Lightsaber +11/+6 melee Blaster +13/+18 ranged
Damage:	Vibroblade 2d6+1 Blaster pistol 3d6 Hold-out blaster 3d4	Lightsaber 2d8+1 Blaster pistol 3d6 Hold-out blaster 3d4	Lightsaber 2d8+1 Blaster pistol 3d6 Hold-out blaster 3d4
Special Qualities:	Illicit barter, better lucky than good, sneak attack +2d6, resource access, authority, target bonus (+1)	plus sneak attack +3d6, target bonus (+3)	plus sneak attack +4d6, target bonus (+5), deadly strike
Saves:	F +3, R +11, W +3	F +5, R +14, W +5	F +6, R +16, W +6
Size:	Medium	Medium	Medium
Challenge Code:	D	E	F
Force Points:	3	4	6
Dark Side Points:	4	6	8
Reputation:	4	6	8
Abilities:	Str 12, Dex 17, Con 12, Int 14, Wis 12, Cha 12	Str 12, Dex 18, Con 12, Int 14, Wis 12, Cha 12	Str 12, Dex 18, Con 13, Int 14, Wis 12, Cha 12
Skills:	Astrogate +6, Bluff +11, Computer Use +6, Demolitions +6, Diplomacy +3, Disable Device +9, Disguise +9, Gather Information +8, Hide +13, Intimidate +11, Jump +3, Listen +5, Move Silently +11, Pilot +10, Sleight of Hand +9, Spot +8, Survival +5, Tumble +7	Astrogate +6, Bluff +11, Computer Use +6, Demolitions +7, Diplomacy +3, Disable Device +11, Disguise +9, Gather Information +8, Hide +16, Intimidate +11, Jump +3, Listen +5, Move Silently +14, Pilot +11, Sleight of Hand +10, Spot +8, Survival +5, Tumble +8	Astrogate +6, Bluff +15, Computer Use +6, Demolitions +7, Diplomacy +3, Disable Device +14, Disguise +11, Gather Information +11, Hide +20, Intimidate +11, Jump +3, Listen +6, Move Silently +18, Pilot +11, Search +7, Sleight of Hand +10, Spot +11, Survival +5, Tumble +8
Force Skills:	Affect Mind +9, Enhance Ability +6	Affect Mind +9, Enhance Ability +6, Enhance Senses +9, Force Defense +6, Force Stealth +6, Heal Self +6, Move Object +7, See Force +6	Affect Mind +9, Enhance Ability +6, Enhance Senses +9, Force Defense +9, Force Stealth +6, Heal Self +6, Move Object +7, See Force +6
Feats:	Alertness, Force-Sensitive, Improved Initiative, Point Blank Shot, Skill Emphasis (Bluff), Weapon Group Proficiency (blaster pistols), Weapon Group Proficiency (blaster rifles), Weapon Group Proficiency (simple weapons), Weapon Group Proficiency (vibro weapons)	see left, plus Exotic Weapon Proficiency (lightsaber), Precise Shot	see left, plus Track
Force Feats:	Alter	Alter, Control, Sense	Alter, Control, Sense
Equipment:	Vibroblade, blaster pistol, hold-out blaster	Lightsaber, blaster pistol, hold-out blaster	Lightsaber, blaster pistol, hold-out blaster

operating independently and with virtually no knowledge that others like them exist. All are trained in the Force, and some eventually fall to the dark side. Strangely, Palpatine finds that a more balanced approach to the Force results in more trustworthy undercover operators.

The 8th-level character is probably lurking undercover awaiting her first execution order. The 12th-level Hand has been at the Emperor's side for some time and operates much more independently. The 16th-level character is a cold, deadly killer—working independently, but still able to ruthlessly carry out orders for her master. Such a character might even vie with Imperial warlords for control of the galaxy in the wake of Palpatine's death, and has no doubt long since fallen to the dark side.

Tainted Jedi

Not all who leave the Jedi path do so to pursue evil. Tainted Jedi may discover that their temperament is not in line with Jedi teachings, or they may simply become disillusioned with the Force after witnessing

Generic Tainted Jedi, male or female, any species

	Jedi Guardian 4	Jedi Guardian 5/Scoundrel 3	Jedi Guardian 6/Scoundrel 6
Initiative:	+2	+3	+3
Defense:	18 (+6 class, +2 Dex)	22 (+9 class, +3 Dex)	24 (+11 class, +3 Dex)
Speed:	10m (or by species)	10m (or by species)	10m (or by species)
VP/WP:	35/14	62/14	82/14
Attacks:	Lightsaber +5 melee	Lightsaber +8/+3 melee	Lightsaber +11/+6 melee
	Heavy blaster pistol +6 ranged	Heavy blaster pistol +10/+5 ranged	Heavy blaster pistol +13/+8 ranged
Damage:	Lightsaber 2d8+1	Lightsaber 3d8+1	Lightsaber 3d8+1
	Heavy blaster pistol 3d8	Heavy blaster pistol 3d8	Heavy blaster pistol 3d8
Special Qualities:	—	Illicit barter, better lucky than good	plus sneak attack +2d6
Saves:	F +6, R +6, W +3	F +7, R +10, W +5	F +9, R +13, W +7
Size:	(by species)	(by species)	(by species)
Challenge Code:	B	C	D
Force Points:	2	3	4
Dark Side Points:	7	8	9
Reputation:	4	6	8
Abilities:	Str 12, Dex 15, Con 14, Int 10, Wis 13, Cha 8	Str 12, Dex 16, Con 14, Int 10, Wis 13, Cha 8	Str 12, Dex 16, Con 14, Int 10, Wis 14, Cha 8
Skills:	Computer Use +4, Jump +3, Pilot +5, Tumble +7	Astrogate +2, Bluff +2, Computer Use +4, Gather Information +3, Hide +9, Jump +3, Move Silently +9, Pilot +13, Tumble +8	Astrogate +5, Bluff +7, Computer Use +8, Diplomacy +1, Gather Information +7, Hide +11, Intimidate +1, Jump +3, Move Silently +11, Pilot +21, Tumble +8
Force Skills:	Battlemind +8, Enhance Ability +9	Battlemind +8, Enhance Ability +9	Battlemind +8, Enhance Ability +12
Feats:	Exotic Weapon Proficiency (lightsaber), Force-Sensitive, Starship Operation (space transports), Weapon Group Proficiency (blaster pistols), Weapon Group Proficiency (simple weapons)	see left	see left, plus Skill Emphasis (Pilot), Point Blank Shot, Starship Dodge
Force Feats:	Alter, Burst of Speed, Control, Sense	Alter, Burst of Speed, Control, Deflect Blasters, Sense	Alter, Burst of Speed, Control, Deflect Blasters, Sense
Equipment:	Lightsaber, heavy blaster pistol, light freighter	Lightsaber, heavy blaster pistol, light freighter, astromech droid	Lightsaber, heavy blaster pistol, light freighter, astromech droid

too many acts of cruelty or personal tragedy. Such an individual treads close to the edge of the dark side. He could easily be coaxed back toward the light side—or just as easily fall into darkness once and for all.

With the number of Force-sensitives in the galaxy before the Jedi Purge, heroes are more likely to encounter tainted Jedi during the Rise of the Empire than in any other era. Tainted Jedi encountered in the Rebellion era are old enough to remember those dark times. Most are hiding in their new lives, but troubled by disturbing visions. During the time of The New Jedi Order, some of Skywalker's students fail to complete their training and leave the Jedi path. Their numbers are few, but their power is undeniable.

The low-level tainted Jedi may still believe in the Jedi way, teetering on the edge of corruption. Without help and study, however, he will lose his way. The mid-level tainted Jedi has left the path entirely, giving up his training to satisfy more tangible or material desires.

The 12th-level character could be the leader of a pirate gang, an expensive hired killer, or even the ruler of a personal fiefdom somewhere in the galaxy.

Imperial Inquisitor

Less than a Sith—and much more than a bounty hunter—the Imperial inquisitor seeks out, tracks down, and captures Jedi at the Emperor's bidding. If a captured Jedi will not turn to the dark side and join Palpatine's New Order, he must die.

Imperial inquisitors are known for their ruthless determination. A lone inquisitor can easily divert a fleet and destroy half a world just to find one Jedi trainee. He may torture a village full of innocents to draw a Jedi ambasssador into a trap, or crush the windpipe of a Jedi Padawan simply to fill the youth's master with rage—and the power of the dark side. This ability to freely indulge one's will comes with a price. Palpatine and his closest advisors—including Vader

Generic Imperial Inquisitor, male or female, Human (extra skills and feats included)

	Jedi Consular 6/ Imperial Inquisitor 2	Jedi Consular 6/ Imperial Inquisitor 4	Jedi Consular 6/ Imperial Inquisitor 6
Initiative:	+0	+0	+0
Defense:	19 (+9 class)	20 (+10 class)	21 (+11 class)
Speed:	10m	10m	10m
VP/WP:	60/14	75/14	90/14
Attacks:	Lightsaber +6 melee Blaster pistol +5 ranged	Lightsaber +8/+3 melee Blaster pistol +7/+2 ranged	Lightsaber +11/+6 melee Blaster pistol +9/+4 ranged
Damage:	Lightsaber 3d8+1 Blaster pistol 3d6	Lightsaber 4d8+1 Blaster pistol 3d6	Lightsaber 4d8+1 Blaster pistol 3d6
Special Qualities:	Resource access	Authority	Favored enemy (Jedi guardian) High Inquisitor
Saves:	F +8, R +5, W +10	F +9, R +5, W +11	F +10, R +6, W +12
Size:	Medium	Medium	Medium
Challenge Code:	D	E	F
Force Points:	4	5	6
Dark Side Points:	8	12	18
Reputation:	6	12	18
Abilities:	Str 12, Dex 10, Con 14, Int 15, Wis 13, Cha 17	Str 12, Dex 10, Con 14, Int 15, Wis 13, Cha 17	Str 12, Dex 10, Con 14, Int 15, Wis 13, Cha 18
Skills:	Bluff +11, Computer Use +6, Diplomacy +5, Gather Information +13, Intimidate +15, Knowledge (Jedi lore) +10, Sense Motive +11	Bluff +13, Computer Use +6, Diplomacy +5, Gather Information +16, Intimidate +17, Knowledge (Jedi lore) +11, Sense Motive +11	Bluff +15, Computer Use +6, Diplomacy +5, Gather Information +17, Intimidate +18, Knowledge (Jedi lore) +12, Sense Motive +11
Force Skills:	Affect Mind +11, Drain Knowledge +6, Fear +7, Force Defense +8, Move Object +10, See Force +9, Telepathy +9	Affect Mind +13, Drain Knowledge +6, Fear +7, Force Defense +13, Move Object +11, See Force +11, Telepathy +9	Affect Mind +14, Drain Knowledge +6, Fear +7, Force Defense +16, Force Grip +8, Move Object +14, See Force +11, Telepathy +9
Feats:	Exotic Weapon Proficiency (lightsaber), Force-Sensitive, Iron Will, Track, Weapon Group Proficiency (blaster pistols), Weapon Group Proficiency (simple weapons)	see left, plus Persuasive	see left, plus Weapon Focus (lightsaber)
Force Feats:	Alter, Burst of Speed, Control, Force Whirlwind, Sense	Alter, Burst of Speed, Control, Force Whirlwind, Sense	Alter, Burst of Speed, Control, Force Whirlwind, Rage, Sense
Equipment:	Lightsaber, blaster pistol, encrypted comlink, personal transport (Lambda shuttle)	Lightsaber, blaster pistol, encrypted comlink, personal transport (Imperial Customs light cruiser)	Lightsaber, blaster pistol, encrypted comlink, personal transport (Imperial Victory Star Destroyer)

himself—keep inquisitors under constant scrutiny. Not surprisingly, many inquisitors learn to keep their personal motives and machinations from creeping to the surface. Most simply pursue their work with relish.

The lower-level inquisitor is likely a novice initiate, operating with one or two fellow inquisitors. The mid-level inquisitor has already turned many Jedi to the dark side, and thirsts to hunt down even more. A 12th-level inquisitor is capable of commanding a fleet of ships or legion of troops in her efforts to destroy the Jedi. When she captures an enemy, however, she still prefers to attend to her captive personally—usually with torture.

Jedi Knight

Ever since the first schism between darkness and light split the Jedi many thousands of years ago, Jedi Knights have been forced to destroy followers of evil. Unlike inquisitors, a Jedi seeks to bring dark-siders back to the light side, if possible. Darksiders usually refuse the offer.

With two notable exceptions, Jedi Knights typi-cally don't appear in the Rebellion era, because all Jedi alive are in hiding—or at least on the run. During the New Jedi Order, many of Luke Skywalker's

Generic Jedi Knight, male or female, any species

	Jedi Guardian 6	Jedi Guardian 10	Jedi Guardian 14
Initiative:	+1	+1	+1
Defense:	18 (+7 class, +1 Dex)	20 (+9 class, +1 Dex)	22 (+11 class, +1 Dex)
Speed:	10m (or by species)	10m (or by species)	10m (or by species)
VP/WP:	46/10	78/10	110/10
Attacks:	Lightsaber +5/+0 melee by weapon +7/+2 ranged	Lightsaber +9/+4 melee by weapon +11/+6 ranged	Lightsaber +13/+8/+3 melee by weapon +15/+10/+5 ranged
Damage:	Lightsaber 3d8–1	Lightsaber 4d8–1	Lightsaber 4d8–1
Special Qualities:	–	–	–
Saves:	F +5, R +6, W +7	F +7, R +8, W +10	F +9, R +10, W +11
Size:	(by species)	(by species)	(by species)
Challenge Code:	C	D	E
Force Points:	4	6	8
Dark Side Points:	0	1	2
Reputation:	10	12	15
Abilities:	Str 8, Dex 13, Con 10, Int 13, Wis 15, Cha 15	Str 8, Dex 13, Con 10, Int 13, Wis 16, Cha 15	Str 8, Dex 13, Con 10, Int 13, Wis 16, Cha 16
Skills:	Gather Information +9	Gather Information +11	Gather Information +11
Force Skills:	Affect Mind +6, Battlemind +9, Farseeing +4, Force Defense +9, Move Object +5, See Force +11	Affect Mind +6, Battlemind +13, Farseeing +9, Force Defense +13, Move Object +5, See Force +16	Affect Mind +11, Battlemind +15, Farseeing +11, Force Defense +17, Move Object +11, See Force +18
Feats:	Exotic Weapon Proficiency (lightsaber), Force-Sensitive, Iron Will, Skill Emphasis (Gather Information), Weapon Group Proficiency (blaster pistols), Weapon Group Proficiency (simple weapons)	see left	see left
Force Feats:	Alter, Control, Lightsaber Defense, Sense	Alter, Control, Deflect Blasters, Knight Defense, Lightsaber Defense, Sense	Alter, Control, Deflect Blasters, Force Whirlwind, Knight Defense, Lightsaber Defense, Master Defense, Sense
Equipment:	Lightsaber, datapad, comlink, personal transport	Lightsaber, datapad, comlink, personal transport	Lightsaber, datapad, comlink, personal transport

students are driven to seek out and rid the galaxy of evil. According to some, the Knights may go a bit too far in their efforts, however well-intentioned those efforts may be. Of course, in both the Rise of the Empire and New Jedi Order eras, these templates make for fine opponents in a dark side campaign.

Nightsister

On the primitive world of Dathomir, Gethzerion began her life as a daughter of the Singing Mountain Clan. After learning the secrets of what she called "Shadow Magic," she formed a sect of dark side Force adepts known as the Nightsisters. The light side Force-users of that world, the witches of Dathomir, wanted nothing to do with Gethzerion for the most part. However, a few of them were curious enough to join her and study her teachings. Gethzerion and her Nightsisters formed their own clan, opposing the lawful efforts of their light side rivals.

Throughout this conflict, Emperor Palpatine ensured that Dathomir remained a primitive, rancor-infested world where he could trap all known Force witches, light and dark. Luke Skywalker later rediscovered the clan, but when Gethzerion and her followers attempted to escape into the greater galaxy, Luke was forced to destroy their starship.

While Palpatine kept the Nightsisters on Dathomir, they grew strong. If not for the loss of so many of their number, they may have become a true threat in the greater galaxy. Still, the Nightsisters are survivors. After a shift in their belief system, many eventually found their way off Dathomir. A group of such exiles helped the Dark Jedi Brakiss watch over his Shadow Academy.

False Prophet of the Dark Side

Not actually a dark side pupil—or even a Force-user—the dark side prophet plays on the fear and ignorance of others for personal gain. Often, he has gained access to a small amount of dark side knowledge—just enough to pass himself off as a mystic or magician. Some even fancy themselves archeologists of a sort, although others might call them opportunistic

Generic Dark Force Witch, male or female, Human (extra skills and feats included)

	Force Adept 2/ Dark Force Witch 2	Force Adept 2/ Dark Force Witch 4	Force Adept 2/ Dark Force Witch 6
Initiative:	+1	+1	+1
Defense:	18 (+7 class, +1 Dex)	18 (+7 class, +1 Dex)	19 (+8 class, +1 Dex)
Speed:	10m (or by species)	10m (or by species)	10m (or by species)
VP/WP:	26/13	37/13	48/13
Attacks:	Spear +2 melee by weapon +3 ranged	Spear +4 melee by weapon +5 ranged	Spear +5 melee by weapon +6 ranged
Damage:	Spear 1d8	Spear 1d8	Spear 1d8
Special Qualities:	Inspire fear (−1), spider walk	Inspire fear (−1), spider walk	Inspire fear (−1), spider walk, enshroud
Saves:	F +5, R +5, W +8	F +6, R +5, W +9	F +7, R +6, W +10
Size:	Medium	Medium	Medium
Challenge Code:	A	B	C
Force Points:	2	3	4
Dark Side Points:	6	8	10
Reputation:	2	4	6
Abilities:	Str 10, Dex 13, Con 13, Int 13, Wis 15, Cha 14	Str 10, Dex 13, Con 13, Int 13, Wis 15, Cha 14	Str 10, Dex 13, Con 13, Int 13, Wis 16, Cha 14
Skills:	Climb +2, Craft (clothing) +5, Craft (rope) +3, Handle Animal +10, Intimidate +4, Jump +2, Ride +8, Survival +9, Swim +4	Climb +2, Craft (clothing) +5, Craft (rope) +4, Handle Animal +11, Intimidate +6, Jump +2, Ride +11, Survival +9, Swim +4	Climb +2, Craft (clothing) +5, Craft (rope) +4, Handle Animal +12, Intimidate +8, Jump +2, Ride +12, Survival +10, Swim +4
Force Skills:	Affect Mind +5, Enhance Senses +7, Force Grip +3, Force Push +3, Move Object +8, See Force +6	Affect Mind +7, Enhance Senses +9, Force Grip +4, Force Push +4, Move Object +10, See Force +8	Affect Mind +8, Enhance Senses +11, Force Grip +6, Force Push +6, Force Stealth +3, Move Object +12, See Force +10
Feats:	Athletic, Animal Affinity, Force-Sensitive, Martial Artist, Weapon Group Proficiency (blaster pistols), Weapon Group Proficiency (primitive weapons), Weapon Group Proficiency (simple weapons)	see left	see left
Force Feats:	Alter, Sense	Alter, Control, Force Whirlwind, Sense, Summon Storm	Alter, Control, Force Whirlwind, Sense
Equipment:	Spear, rancor mount, oiled lizard-skin tunic, dark robe	Spear, rancor mount, oiled lizard-skin tunic, dark robe, "maleling" slave	Spear, rancor mount, oiled lizard-skin tunic, dark robe, "maleling" slaves

Generic False Dark Side Prophet, male or female, Human (extra skills and feats included)

	Noble 2/Scoundrel 2	Noble 4/Scoundrel 4	Noble 8/Scoundrel 4
Initiative:	+0	+0	+0
Defense:	17 (+7 class)	18 (+8 class)	19 (+9 class)
Speed:	10m (or by species)	10m (or by species)	10m (or by species)
VP/WP:	16/11	28/11	40/11
Attacks:	Unarmed +1 melee Blaster pistol +2 ranged	Unarmed +5/+0 melee Blaster pistol +6/+1 ranged	Unarmed +8/+3 melee Blaster pistol +9/+4 ranged
Damage:	Blaster pistol 3d6	Blaster pistol 3d6	Blaster pistol 3d6
Special Qualities:	Call in a favor (1), inspire confidence (+1), illicit barter, better lucky than good	Call in a favor (2), Command (+2)	Call in a favor (4), inspire confidence (+2), command (+4)
Saves:	F +0, R +5, W +5	F +2, R +6, W +7	F +3, R +8, W +9
Size:	Medium	Medium	Medium
Challenge Code:	A	B	B
Force Points:	1	2	4
Dark Side Points:	2	4	6
Reputation:	10	15	20
Abilities:	Str 9, Dex 11, Con 11, Int 13, Wis 14, Cha 15	Str 9, Dex 11, Con 11, Int 13, Wis 14, Cha 16	Str 9, Dex 11, Con 11, Int 13, Wis 15, Cha 16
Skills:	Bluff +11, Computer Use +5, Diplomacy +13, Entertain (acting) +6, Gather Information +11, Intimidate +13, Listen +9, Search +8, Sense Motive +11, Spot +7	Bluff +16, Computer Use +5, Diplomacy +18, Entertain (acting) +11, Gather Information +19, Intimidate +18, Listen +13, Search +10, Sense Motive +15, Spot +9	Bluff +20, Computer Use +9, Diplomacy +25, Entertain (acting) +11, Gather Information +23, Intimidate +22, Listen +13, Search +14, Sense Motive +22, Spot +13
Force Skills:	—	—	—
Feats:	Persuasive, Sharp-Eyed, Trustworthy, Weapon Group Proficiency (blaster pistols), Weapon Group Proficiency (simple weapons)	see left, plus Skill Emphasis (Bluff), Skill Emphasis (Gather Information)	see left, plus Skill Emphasis (Diplomacy), Skill Emphasis (Sense Motive)
Force Feats:	—	—	—
Equipment:	Blaster pistol, dark robes	Blaster pistol, dark robes	Blaster pistol, dark robes

"tomb robbers." While such individuals are not true Sith or darksiders, they can often be useful pawns for Force-users fully steeped in dark side lore.

False dark side prophets exist after the Battle of Endor. The 4th-level prophet may simply be a con artist who has seen just enough entertainment holos to pass himself off as a dark wizard, while the 8th-level prophet has probably gained a significant amount of political or economic power on the Mid Rim or Outer Rim. The 12th-level dark side prophet may even have convinced himself that he actually does commune with the Force. Such a character may be in charge of an entire world or sector. He might just as easily be a wanderer who takes advantage of the mistaken beliefs of his disciples.

See Chapter Five for descriptions of the true Prophets of the Dark Side.

Shadow Academy Student

One of Luke Skywalker's early failures at his Jedi academy was a consular-in-training named Brakiss. The young student's descent into darkness would have repercussions well into the era of the Yuuzhan Vong invasion. Brakiss, with the help of a group of exiled Dathomiri Nightsisters, began training an entirely new sect of Force-users—a culture that drew on dark side abilities similar to those of the Nightsisters, but also instructed males.

This "Shadow Academy" was based in a mobile, hyperdrive-capable battlestation with a cloaking device. Brakiss could take his school, and his

students, wherever he pleased for training and stay one step ahead of Skywalker (although he gained some perverse satisfaction at staying just outside the Jedi Master's reach). The focus of the Shadow Academy student is on Jedi training, supervised at first by Brakiss, then his lieutenants.

The members of the Shadow Academy plagued the Solo children through much of their teenage training as Jedi on Yavin 4. Since the Academy does not begin until well after the Battle of Endor, Shadow Academy students do not appear until late in the Rebellion era. Once established, however, the Academy—and more important, those trained there—will be a threat for generations.

The 1st-level Shadow Academy student is not yet in thrall to the dark side, but has begun to feel his anger bubbling to the surface. The second-level student mirrors the skills of a Jedi Padawan, although the character himself has begun to fall to the dark path. The 4th-level student is ready to explore the galaxy, no doubt destined to become lost forever to darkness without Jedi intervention.

Sith Apprentice

Rich, bored youths fascinated with evil trinkets, jaded scholars drawn to the teachings of the Sith, dedicated followers of Naga Sadow, even Emperor Palpatine—all were once Sith apprentices. The Sith apprentice has usually impressed her master with an impressive act of loyalty or cruelty. The apprentice receives training in the language, lore, and Force techniques of the Sith.

Generic Shadow Academy Student, male or female, any species

	Jedi Guardian 1	Jedi Guardian 2	Jedi Guardian 4
Initiative:	+1	+1	+1
Defense:	15 (+4 class, +1 Dex)	16 (+5 class, +1 Dex)	17 (+6 class, +1 Dex)
Speed:	10m (or by species)	10m (or by species)	10m (or by species)
VP/WP:	11/13	18/13	35/13
Attacks:	Lightsaber +1 melee by weapon +2 ranged	Lightsaber +2 melee by weapon +3 ranged	Lightsaber +5 melee by weapon +5 ranged
Damage:	Lightsaber 2d8	Lightsaber 2d8	Lightsaber 2d8+1
Special Qualities:	—	—	—
Saves:	F +3, R +3, W +0	F +4, R +4, W +1	F +5, R +5, W +1
Size:	(by species)	(by species)	(by species)
Challenge Code:	A	A	A
Force Points:	1	1	2
Dark Side Points:	2	4	6
Reputation:	0	1	2
Abilities:	Str 11, Dex 12, Con 13, Int 10, Wis 8, Cha 12	Str 11, Dex 12, Con 13, Int 10, Wis 8, Cha 12	Str 12, Dex 12, Con 13, Int 10, Wis 8, Cha 12
Skills:	Computer Use +2, Intimidate +5, Knowledge (Jedi lore) +2	Computer Use +3, Intimidate +6, Knowledge (Jedi lore) +2	Computer Use +3, Intimidate +8, Knowledge (Jedi lore) +2, Move Object +3
Force Skills:	Battlemind +5, Enhance Ability +5	Battlemind +6, Enhance Ability +6	Battlemind +8, Enhance Ability +7
Feats:	Force-Sensitive, Quickness, Weapon Group Proficiency (blaster pistols), Weapon Group Proficiency (simple weapons)	see left, plus Exotic Weapon Proficiency (lightsaber)	see left
Force Feats:	Control	Control	Alter, Control, Rage, Sense
Equipment:	Lightsaber	Lightsaber	Lightsaber

This training mirrors the ways of the Jedi in many cases, including lightsaber training and mastery of specific Force powers. This is not surprising, since the original Sith sect descended from Dark Jedi who broke from the Jedi Order tens of thousands of years ago.

Heroes are more likely to encounter a Sith apprentice during the days of the Old Republic than at any other time. (During later eras, the "rule of two" precludes finding any apprentices other than Darth Maul or Anakin Skywalker.) During the time of the New Jedi Order, it's conceivable that ancient Sith lore could be uncovered by curious Force-sensitives.

The lower- or mid-level Sith Apprentice is a being strong in the Force, but unlikely to leave her master's side for long. The higher-level Sith apprentice has begun to study more and more on her own, and may well be plotting her master's demise.

Sith Minion

Before he ever coined the term "Emperor's Hand," Palpatine had another living weapon at his disposal—his minion Darth Maul. A Sith minion carries out the orders of his Sith Master or dies trying. A minion who lives long enough may become a Sith Lord in his own right. A Sith minion who fails usually finds a way to take his enemies with him, grasping at victory until his violent, bitter end.

As is the case with virtually all Sith, Sith minions were far more common during the Golden Age of the Sith Empire than any other era (particularly before Darth Bane instituted the "rule of two"). Except for Maul and Vader, the chances of encountering a Sith minion are not good in the Rebellion and New Jedi Order eras.

Generic Sith Apprentice, male or female, any species

	Force Adept 2	Force Adept 4	Force Adept 4/Sith Acolyte 2
Initiative:	+0	+0	+0
Defense:	14 (+4 class)	14 (+4 class)	17 (+7 class)
Speed:	10m (or by species)	10m (or by species)	10m (or by species)
VP/WP:	15/12	25/12	35/12
Attacks:	by weapon +0 melee Blaster pistol +1 ranged	by weapon +2 melee Blaster pistol +3 ranged	by weapon +3 melee Blaster pistol +4 ranged
Damage:	Blaster pistol 3d6	Blaster pistol 3d6	Blaster pistol 3d6
Special Qualities:	—	—	—
Saves:	F +3, R +2, W +5	F +3, R +2, W +6	F +6, R +4, W +9
Size:	(by species)	(by species)	(by species)
Challenge Code:	A	A	B
Force Points:	1	2	3
Dark Side Points:	3	6	12
Reputation:	0	2	4
Abilities:	Str 9, Dex 10, Con 12, Int 13, Wis 13, Cha 12	Str 9, Dex 10, Con 12, Int 13, Wis 14, Cha 12	Str 9, Dex 10, Con 12, Int 13, Wis 14, Cha 12
Skills:	Knowledge (Sith lore) +6, Read/Write Sith	Knowledge (Sith lore) +8, Read/Write Sith	Bluff +5, Intimidate +3, Knowledge (Sith lore) +8, Read/Write Sith
Force Skills:	Affect Mind +6, Farseeing +6, Force Grip +6, Illusion +5, Move Object +6, See Force +6	Affect Mind +8, Farseeing +12, Force Grip +8, Illusion +7, Move Object +8, See Force +9	Affect Mind +9, Alchemy +5, Farseeing +12, Force Grip +8, Illusion +9, Move Object +9, See Force +9
Feats:	Force-Sensitive, Iron Will, Weapon Group Proficiency (blaster pistols), Weapon Group Proficiency (primitive weapons), Weapon Group Proficiency (simple weapons)	see left, plus Skill Emphasis (Farseeing)	see left, plus Exotic Weapon Proficiency (Sith sword)
Force Feats:	Alter, Sense	Alter, Control, Sense	Alter, Control, Dissipate Energy, Sense, Sith Sorcery
Equipment:	Blaster pistol, dark robes	Blaster pistol, dark robes	Blaster pistol, dark robes

The low-level Sith minion is a Force-strong fighter, just beginning to realize his abilities. The mid-level minion has become a cunning warrior adept with his chosen weapon. The 12th-level character is a brutal enforcer for his Sith Master, and has been given access to more powerful Sith technology.

Sith Lord

Over five millennia ago, the mighty Sith Empire thrived on the far side of the galaxy. Sith Lords were plentiful and powerful. Although the Republic believed that the Sith were nothing but legends from a simpler time, the Sith had prospered and built an empire led by one—and only one—Dark Lord of the Sith. This formal title was usually given to a Sith Lord by the spirit of his predecessor.

As conflict within and without tore the Sith Empire apart, many declared themselves Dark Lords.

Centuries of treachery and betrayal destroyed all of the Dark Lords but one. Only Darth Bane, the savior of the Sith, remained. Over the thousand years leading up to the Battle of Naboo, the Sith studied and trained in secret. They left many of their traditions behind in exchange for power. Both Darth Sidious and his apprentice, Darth Maul, were Dark Lords of the Sith, for example. The title was also given to another of Palpatine's students, Darth Vader.

Because no known Sith Lords survive into the Rise of the Empire era (with the exceptions of Darth Sidious, Darth Maul, and eventually Darth Vader), heroes ought to encounter them only in the centuries and millennia preceding Palpatine's ascension to power. The 12th-level Sith Lord may control a world or even a government, while the 14th-level Sith Lord is probably well along in his plan to control the galaxy.

Generic Sith Minion, male or female, any species

	Soldier 3/Force Adept 1	Soldier 4/Force Adept 1/ Sith Warrior 3	Soldier 4/Force Adept 1/ Sith Warrior 7
Initiative:	+1	+1	+2
Defense:	15 (+4 class, +1 Dex)	18 (+7 class, +1 Dex)	23 (+9 class, +2 Dex, +2 Sith Sword Defense)
Speed:	10m (or by species)	10m (or by species)	10m (or by species)
VP/WP:	32/15	56/16	80/16
Attacks:	Vibroblade +6 melee Blaster pistol +4 ranged	Sith sword +10/+5 melee Sith lanvarok or blaster pistol +8/+3 ranged	Sith sword +14/+9/+4 melee Sith lanvarok or blaster pistol +13/+8/+3 ranged
Damage:	Vibroblade 2d6+3 Blaster pistol 3d6	Sith sword 2d6+3 Sith lanvarok 3d4 Blaster pistol 3d6	Sith sword 2d6+3 Sith lanvarok 3d4 Blaster pistol 3d6
Special Qualities:	—	Enemy bonus +2	Enemy bonus +2, uncanny dodge (retains Dex bonus, cannot be flanked)
Saves:	F +6, R +3, W +3	F +11, R +8, W +5	F +13, R +11, W +7
Size:	(by species)	(by species)	(by species)
Challenge Code:	B	C	D
Force Points:	2	4	6
Dark Side Points:	6	8	12
Reputation:	2	4	8
Abilities:	Str 16, Dex 13, Con 15, Int 10, Wis 11, Cha 12	Str 16, Dex 13, Con 16, Int 10, Wis 11, Cha 12	Str 16, Dex 14, Con 16, Int 10, Wis 11, Cha 12
Skills:	Intimidate +7, Knowledge (Sith lore) +4, Read/Write Sith, Survival +4	Intimidate +7, Knowledge (Sith lore) +4, Pilot +5, Read/Write Sith, Survival +4	Intimidate +7, Knowledge (Sith lore) +4, Pilot +5, Read/Write Sith, Survival +4
Force Skills:	Battlemind +5, Force Grip +4, Move Object +5	Battlemind +11, Enhance Ability +8, Force Grip +5, Move Object +6	Battlemind +13, Enhance Ability +11, Force Defense +9, Force Grip +6, Move Object +6, See Force +4
Feats:	Armor Proficiency (heavy), Armor Proficiency (light), Armor Proficiency (medium), Exotic Weapon Proficiency (Sith sword), Force-Sensitive, Weapon Group Proficiency (blaster pistols), Weapon Group Proficiency (blaster rifles), Weapon Group Proficiency (heavy weapons), Weapon Group Proficiency (simple weapons), Weapon Group Proficiency (vibro weapons)	see left, plus Exotic Weapon Proficiency (Sith lanvarok), Heroic Surge, Lightning Reflexes	see left, plus Cleave, Power Attack
			Weapon Group Proficiency (primitive weapons),
Force Feats:	Alter, Control	Alter, Control, Sense	Alter, Control, Rage, Sense, Sith Sword Defense
Equipment:	Vibro blade, blaster pistol	Sith sword, blaster pistol, Sith lanvarok	Sith sword, blaster pistol, Sith lanvarok

Generic Sith Lord, male or female, Sith

	Force Adept 2/Soldier 3 Sith Warrior 3/Sith Lord 2	Force Adept 2/Soldier 3 Sith Warrior 3/Sith Lord 4	Force Adept 2/Soldier 3 Sith Warrior 3/Sith Lord 6
Initiative:	+1	+1	+1
Defense:	21 (+10 class, +1 Dex)	24 (+11 class, +1 Dex, +2 Sith Sword Defense)	27 (+12 class, +1 Dex, +2 Sith Sword Defense, +2 Sith Sword Expert Defense)
Speed:	10 m (or by species)	10 m (or by species)	10 m (or by species)
VP/WP:	78/15	94/16	109/16
Attacks:	Unarmed +11/+6 melee Sith sword +12/+7 melee by weapon +10/+5 ranged	Unarmed +13/+8/+3 melee Sith sword +14/+9/+4 melee by weapon +12/+7/+2 ranged	Unarmed +15/+10/+5 melee Sith sword +16/+11/+6 melee by weapon +14/+9/+4 ranged
Damage:	Sith sword 2d6+2	Sith sword 2d6+2	Sith sword 2d6+2
Special Qualities:	Enemy bonus +1, resource access	—	Minions
Saves:	F +13, R +8, W +12	F +15, R +9, W +13	F +16, R +10, W +14
Size:	(by species)	(by species)	(by species)
Challenge Code:	D	E	F
Force Points:	5	6	7
Dark Side Points:	15	20	25
Reputation:	12	15	18
Abilities:	Str 15, Dex 13, Con 15, Int 14, Wis 14, Cha 14	Str 15, Dex 13, Con 16, Int 14, Wis 14, Cha 14	Str 15, Dex 13, Con 16, Int 14, Wis 14, Cha 14
Skills:	Bluff +8, Craft (dark armor) +8, Diplomacy +8, Knowledge (Sith lore) +10, Intimidate +10, Pilot +5, Read/Write Sith, Survival +8	Bluff +8, Craft (dark armor) +8, Diplomacy +12, Knowledge (Sith lore) +10, Intimidate +10, Pilot +5, Read/Write Sith, Survival +8	Bluff +10, Craft (dark armor) +8, Diplomacy +12, Knowledge (Sith lore) +10, Intimidate +13, Pilot +5, Read/Write Sith, Survival +8
Force Skills:	Affect Mind +7, Battlemind +9, Force Defense +8, Force Grip +11, Heal Self +8, Move Object +10, See Force +5	Affect Mind +7, Alchemy +8, Battlemind +10, Force Defense +13, Force Grip +11, Heal Self +9, Move Object +10, See Force +7	Affect Mind +7, Alchemy +14, Battlemind +13, Force Defense +15, Force Grip +11, Heal Self +9, Move Object +10, See Force +7
Feats:	Armor Proficiency (heavy), Armor Proficiency (light), Armor Proficiency (medium), Exotic Weapon Proficiency (Sith sword), Force-Sensitive, Iron Will, Starship Operation (capital ships), Weapon Focus (Sith sword), Weapon Group Proficiency (blaster pistols), Weapon Group Proficiency (blaster rifles), Weapon Group Proficiency (heavy weapons), Weapon Group Proficiency (primitive weapons), Weapon Group Proficiency (simple weapons), Weapon Group Proficiency (vibro weapons)	see left	see left, plus Expert Defense
Force Feats:	Alter, Control, Rage, Sense	Alter, Control, Hatred, Rage, Sense, Sith Sorcery	Alter, Control, Hatred, Rage, Sense, Sith Sorcery, Sith Sword Defense
Equipment:	Sith sword, dark armor (+2 Str), personal transport (shuttle)	Sith sword, dark armor (DR 5), personal transport (Sith Infiltrator)	Sith sword, dark armor (DR 10), personal transport (Sith battleship)

Chapter Seven: Dark Side Campaigns

How you use the dark side in your campaign depends on what era your adventures are set in and whether your players are running dark side characters. We've provided you with a lot of options throughout the first six chapters. Now we'll try to bring it together with some solid advice and suggestions for setting up an ongoing dark side campaign.

Pick an Era, Any Era

In your home campaign, you can pretty much do whatever you want with the *Star Wars* mythology. If you want to play close to the ongoing story of the Expanded Universe, however, you're going to have a harder time working some of the material in this book into your campaign. Let's take a look at the established eras and discuss how to play the dark side in any particular era.

Note that in this chapter, we're using dark side to refer to evil Force-users—not evil characters in general. You can establish evil campaigns in any era without much of a problem. When you add in tainted or dark Force-users, it gets a little trickier to remain faithful to *Star Wars* history as depicted in the films and Expanded Universe material.

The Old Republic

Pick a time from as far back as 25,000 years before the Galactic Civil War to as recent as 1,000 years before the rise of the Empire, and you've got a period that's perfect for fully utilizing the material in this book. This vast period of time encompasses the Golden Age of the Sith, the Sith Wars, and the final battle between the forces of light and dark that resulted in the near-extinction of the Sith. Because this time frame works so well as a place to set dark side campaigns, we're devoting an expanded section of this chapter to playing in a part of this era: the time around the Great Hyperspace War, when the Sith Empire first reveals itself to the unsuspecting Republic.

The Rise of the Empire

In the time when Darth Sidious secretly sets events in motion that eventually transform the crumbling Republic into an Empire, dark side characters have a few options. Of course, no Sith prestige classes are available, since there can be only two Sith, and the two are already accounted for in the films. However, characters can easily become tainted or dark, since plenty of opportunities abound for doing evil. Some characters

might even wind up helping the Sith Lords, although they probably won't ever learn the true identity of their dark masters.

Just as Sidious and Maul manipulate the Trade Federation and the Senate from the shadows, so too can they make use of the player characters. Hiring the heroes to perform actions that further his own dark plans is just the sort of thing that Sidious is famous for. If the actions look like they might help the Republic, at least on the surface, then good heroes might inadvertently slide toward the dark side by accomplishing Sidious's goals.

While Sith prestige classes might be banned in this and later eras, some of the other dark side prestige classes make fine awards for characters willing to walk the corrupt path during the rise of the Empire. Dark side devotees, dark side marauders, and dark Force witches can be used, provided the character meets the requirements for the prestige class.

In this troubled era, the beleaguered Jedi Knights are too few to adequately patrol and police the entire Republic. There are plenty of places for dark-siders to hide and operate from, both inside the Republic and within the lawless regions of space that surround it. Many senators, planetary governments, and various individuals in the trade guilds and bureaucracies have become corrupt, allowing the dark side even more room to play. Evil Force-users can flourish in this paranoid environment, seeking to increase their own power or influence the actions of others for their own gain.

Who can say if the dark side instigated the various problems that weakened the Republic, or if the corrupt portions of the Force simply took advantage of the developing situation? Either way, dark side characters literally have a galaxy full of people, places, and things to manipulate, convert, or destroy in their personal campaigns for power and glory. There are those more powerful and influential to serve, and those less powerful to exploit or crush as the dark spirit moves them. It's a great time to be tainted or dark.

The Rebellion Era

The time of the Galactic Civil War provides ample opportunity for characters to explore their darker tendencies. While most of the galaxy's citizens don't realize it, the Emperor has a host of darksiders helping him maintain his New Order. Even fewer of those citizens are aware of the Emperor's own dark side aptitude. In this tumultuous period of tyranny and

rebellion, under the careful and watchful eye of the Emperor and his servants, the dark side flourishes.

The restriction against Sith prestige classes remains in effect for campaigns trying to stick to the established timeline, though other prestige classes become available that never existed in prior eras. (But see the sidebar "Playing with History" for a different point of view.)

While dark side devotees, dark side marauders, and dark Force witches remain viable dark side prestige classes for the Rebellion era, the Empire provides additional options as well. In this era, Emperor's Hands and Imperial inquisitors may be selected by those tainted or dark characters who meet the requirements.

The Empire creates a perfect backdrop upon which to set a dark side campaign. It is the ultimate expression of the dark side unleashed, and its iron grip on the galaxy allows dark side characters plenty of room to operate. A darksider can work for the Empire or for one of the "neutral" groups such as a crime lord or mercenary band. He or she can infiltrate the Rebellion and work to undermine the freedom effort from within. Plenty of tension can be created as a low-level darksider works his way up the ranks, eventually having to prove his worth to the Empire or winding up on a

destruction list. You see, Vader and the Emperor jealously guard their positions, only allowing certain darksiders to operate without restrictions. These darksiders must be considered loyal to the cause of the New Order, willing to take orders from those of higher position, and not so ambitious as to pose any obvious threat to the Emperor's rule. Those who don't meet these requirements are usually eliminated.

While there are few active Jedi to oppose them, the darksiders must still contend with a public that has been trained to distrust Force-users. The Empire's propaganda machine has reduced belief in the Force to "a hokey religion," and many people have come to believe that the troubles that plagued the Republic were the result of the Jedi. Force-users, even those in the employ of the Empire, must be careful to keep the full extent of their abilities secret from the general population. Only in the hidden chambers of Imperial High Command is the Force still embraced as a means to power—and then only from the perspective of the dark side. The Rebellion has taken up the chant "May the Force be with you," but it will take a number of years for the belief and commitment behind those words to match what it was in the days of the Old Republic.

The New Jedi Order Era

Twenty-five years after the Battle of Yavin, the galaxy faces a new and deadly threat from beyond the borders of known space. As invaders push into New Republic space, other dangers plague the galaxy and allow the dark side to take root and once again extend its shadowy tendrils from one

PLAYING WITH HISTORY

The thing about roleplaying game campaigns is that every adventure you play builds upon the history of your particular version of the campaign world. At some point, a hero is going to perform an action or succeed at a task that causes the campaign to deviate from established history. In a *Star Wars* campaign, even if you try to remain faithful to the events in the movies and novels and comics, eventually something will happen during play that causes your campaign to branch off from the "true" path of the established story.

That's okay. That's what roleplaying games are all about. If you just wanted to re-create the events of the movies, you'd just play one of the many computer games that do that so well. The ability to tell your own story, to wander outside the borders of a film or novel or computer game scenario, is the major advantage of a tabletop roleplaying game.

You can take this concept a step further and decide to totally break with the continuity of the films and the Expanded Universe if you so desire. In that case, you might decide to allow your player characters to vie for a spot as a Sith Lord, regardless of the era your campaign is set in.

Maybe in your Rise of the Empire campaign, Sidious has overturned the rule of two and is working to reestablish the Golden Age of the Sith. Or maybe you'll want to allow Sidious to select a hero as his next apprentice after Darth Maul dies. In a Rebellion era campaign, the Emperor might have an army of Sith acolytes in the wings, waiting to unleash a new Sith Empire upon the galaxy. Or maybe Darth Vader has secretly been training his own apprentices for many years, waiting for a chance to overthrow the Emperor and establish himself as the most powerful being in the galaxy. In a later era, such as The New Republic or The New Jedi Order, you can alter history to allow a new Sith cult to arise. Your dark heroes might even be the catalysts for such an event, working to bring about a Sith rebirth after the deaths of the Emperor and Darth Vader.

Of course, our products and the Expanded Universe in general follow the established *Star Wars* history and timeline, so deviating from that timeline leaves you on your own. Still, if you're up to the challenge and you don't mind forging your own trail, then you can build exactly the type of *Star Wars* campaign you and your players want to play. And you can do so using exactly the elements you want to include, whether or not they fit the established sequence of events.

star system to another. The Jedi, about a hundred strong and led by Luke Skywalker, face division in their ranks as a growing number of members want to break away from the current leadership. The New Republic government, meanwhile, has turned a wary eye toward the actions of a few rash Jedi, thereby sparking the old fears and hatreds of the Empire's anti-Jedi rhetoric from earlier years.

The restriction against Sith prestige classes remains in effect throughout this era (though see the sidebar "Playing with History" for a different point of view), but the other dark side prestige classes remain viable options for characters who meet the requirements. Dark side devotees, dark side marauders, dark Force witches, Emperor's Hands, and Imperial inquisitors can all exist in this time frame.

There are more Jedi available in this era to oppose darksiders, but at the same time there are also more Jedi around to be tempted by the dark side. Even if you don't go for a full-fledged dark side campaign, the possibilities for putting your Jedi heroes through the early stages of corruption are endless in the time of The New Jedi Order. In addition, the New Republic begins to see some of the same problems that plagued the latter years of the Old Republic. The petty squabbles of old, the species-centered viewpoints, even the propensity for corruption have begun to seep back into the fabric of leadership. This time of invasion comes at a dangerous stage for the new government, challenging the Republic to overcome its flaws or get swept away by the Yuuzhan Vong. That makes it a fertile arena for great roleplaying adventures and for dark side campaigns specifically.

The threat the Yuuzhan Vong pose to the galaxy and their early victories make it understandable that some of the Jedi would become impatient with Luke Skywalker's apparent lack of direction for the Jedi in these galactic events. This impatience, however, can lead to frustration and fear—both clear paths to the dark side. Some Jedi might also feel anger and hatred toward the Yuuzhan Vong, especially if their worlds or loved ones have been endangered. Against this volatile backdrop, the dark side finds more and more converts—either willing darksiders or those who let circumstances slide them along the corrupt path.

Dark Side Sites

Some areas, like some beings, are strong in the dark side. They resonate with corrupt energy. These places emanate evil and darkness, creating cold spots in the Force that disturb those who are sensitive to the energy that binds the galaxy together. For those who draw upon the dark side, these spots

serve as wells of power that can sometimes be tapped for greater effect.

Dark side sites can be created in a number of ways. When acts of great evil or violence take place at a location and are accompanied by the manipulation of the Force, a dark side site can come into being. If a powerful darksider operates in a specific place for a long period of time, or if that darksider meets a violent end at a specific location, that place can also become imbued with the dark side.

Such a site feels cold and dark even on the brightest, warmest days. It radiates evil, casting shadows the way a glowrod casts light. While these dark side sites are few and far between, when one comes into existence it lingers, haunting the galaxy for many years.

While the dark side sometimes permeates extremely large areas, in general a dark side site will be relatively small. A tiny cave, a ruined temple, an ancient battlefield, a crypt of some long dead Sith Lord—these are the typical dark side sites that might be encountered. Sometimes an entire moon or planet might radiate with the dark side, as in the cases of Dxun and Korriban, but such sites are rare. In a few cases, a dark side spirit (see Chapter Six) might also haunt a dark side site.

Dark Side Sites and Non-Force-Sensitives

Those without a strong connection to the Force find dark side sites to be creepy. As long as they remain in the area, non-Force-sensitive beings feel uneasy, nervous. They can't identify the source of their discomfort, but they probably won't want to remain in such an area any longer than necessary.

If a non-Force-sensitive character tries to use a Force Point within the bounds of a dark side site, nothing happens. The Force Point doesn't get used up, and no bonus gets applied to the character's d20 rolls for the round. The character is, in effect, cut off from utilizing the Force due to the constant but barely perceptible uneasiness that hangs like a cloud over him or her.

Once the character leaves the influence of the dark side site, he or she can once again utilize Force Points as normal.

Dark Side Sites and Force-Sensitives

Characters with a connection to the Force (those who have selected the Force-Sensitive feat) can feel the ever-present evil that permeates a dark side site. Characters who have levels in a Force-user class might experience challenges, tests, temptation, or even visions while within the influence of a dark side site. Staying focused, calling on the light side of the Force, even keeping one's own fear in check proves difficult inside the dark emanations of such a location. For this reason, characters sometimes have a harder time concentrating, using skills, defending themselves, or making attacks while bathed in the aura of a dark side site.

When a Force-sensitive character enters a dark side site, that character must make a Will saving throw. The DC for the save depends on whether the character has any Force-user classes and on the power of the dark side site. Dark side sites are rated as minor sites, major sites, and extreme sites.

A minor site could be the crypt of a Sith Lord or a hidden vault of Sith artifacts. A major site might take the form of a cave where a powerful darksider died in combat, the tomb of a Sith Master, or ancient ruins that once housed Sith alchemy machines. An extreme site could include a well of power on the demon moon of Dxun, the private sanctuary of a powerful Sith Lord, or the killing fields of Ruusan where great numbers of both Sith and Jedi fell in apocalyptic conflict.

If the Force-sensitive character fails the save, the following penalties are applied to the character for the next hour:

- ⊖ Force Points can't be used to call upon the light side of the Force (a character can use a Force Point to call upon the dark side, however);
- ⊖ -4, -6, or -8 penalty on skill checks and attacks (depending on the rating of the site);
- ⊖ -2, -4, or -6 penalty to Defense (depending on the rating of the site).

Every hour that the character remains within the influence of the dark side site, he or she must make another saving throw.

Table 7-1: Dark Side Site Saving Throws

Site Power	Force-Sensitive	Force-User
Minor	15	10
Major	25	20
Extreme	35	30

A tainted or dark character isn't affected by the aura of a dark side site; no saving throw is required for characters with these templates. In addition, a dark character can draw upon the energy of a dark side site for an additional boost of power. The dark character receives a +2, +4, or +6 dark side bonus, depending on the rating of the site, to all Force-based skill checks while inside the aura of the dark side site and for 24 hours after leaving the site. Drawing on the site for this kind of power gains the dark character a Dark Side Point.

Dark Side Site Examples

The following examples of dark side sites can be used in your campaign, or can serve as models for designing your own sites. Remember that dark side sites should not be common. Even in the days of the Sith Empire, the circumstances and power needed to create a dark side site didn't come together very often.

Minor Site: Lake Krul

During the time period that culminated in the Battle of Ruusan, a particularly evil dark side marauder named Kaox Krul roamed the galaxy. One of the strongest warriors to serve Sith Lord Kaan and the Brotherhood of Darkness, Krul died in one of the skirmishes that led up to the battle between the forces of light and darkness. On a small, uninhabited world in the Mid Rim, Krul met a Jedi Knight and her Padawan learner in fierce combat. The Jedi crash-landed on the planet after a wild battle and chase through the star system. Krul followed them to the surface and hunted the Jedi for two days before finally cornering them on the shore of a beautiful lake.

Beside the quiet lake, under the glow of two small moons, the dark side marauder and the Jedi engaged in a life-or-death dance of violence. The Padawan fell first, brought down by Krul's flashing lightsaber. The Jedi Knight, grief-stricken by the death of her student, doubled her efforts. The clash between marauder and knight lasted until the first bright rays of dawn broke over the horizon. Jedi and marauder seemed to be too evenly matched. Tired, bruised, battered, and cut, the two continued to fight as the daytime sky filled with the dark clouds of a gathering storm. Rain began to splatter around the combatants, and as the fight went on, both marauder and Jedi began to give in to their anger and hatred of one another.

They both called upon the dark side.

With invigorating dark side power coursing through both of them, the struggle became even more devastating. Thunder boomed around them with each punch and kick and lightsaber parry. Lightning danced over the surface of the lake and lanced into the ground around the warriors. The Jedi slashed. The marauder dodged and whirled. Thunder pealed. Lightsaber blades cracked and sparkled and bounced off each other again and again. And the sky opened wide and unleashed a deluge of stinging rain.

Krul, hoping to buy a moment of rest, wrapped himself in the Force and hovered over the center of the lake. The Jedi Knight, refusing to let the marauder escape, followed suit. They hurled their

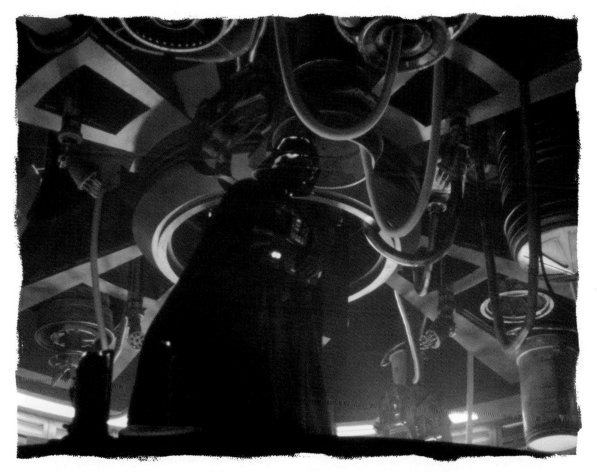

anger at each other through the Force as they met in the air above the churning waters of the lake. The storm intensified, as if spurred on by the combatants' fierce emotions. Krul's lightsaber struck high, the Jedi's weapon thrust low, and a wave of lightning washed over the two of them as each killing blow landed. Wrapped in the dark side of the Force, filled with anger and hatred, marauder and Jedi died in that moment, their ravaged bodies falling into the roiling water and sinking below the windswept waves.

In that moment, the lake changed. The trees and grass and bushes around it became twisted and dark. The surface of the water, once clear and bright, became muddy and dank and took on a sickly appearance. And so a dark side site was born.

Using Lake Krul in Your Campaign

Lake Krul can be placed on any uninhabited or sparsely inhabited planet in the Mid Rim of the galaxy. The lake, about one kilometer in circumference and surrounded by dark, twisted vegetation, appears to be constantly shrouded in shadows. A dank wind constantly blows through the small forest, making the shadows dance and giving the place an unnatural kind of movement. As soon as anyone steps within the ring of twisted trees,

which circles the lake for about half a kilometer in all directions, the effects of the dark side site can be felt.

The lake itself has a stagnant, dead look to it. The muddy, debris-strewn surface looks more like a swamp than a lake. Nothing natural lives within the lake or the forest, though occasionally a dark side mutant of some sort might be spotted. Legends claim that on stormy nights visitors might hear the hum and crack of lightsabers as two spectral beings battle over the center of the lake. Others claim that you might meet the dark side spirit of Kaox Krul, dripping with the vile waters of the lake and still appearing to be wrapped in dark padded battle armor. A hole burned through his gut shows where the death blow hit him.

This site makes a great meeting place for a dark-sider and his band of thugs or pirates. It can also serve as a place of historical interest to a Jedi looking for information on the Sith or the ancient Jedi. Indeed, if the rumors are true, dark padded battle armor and a pair of lightsabers might be found somewhere within the dark depths of the tepid lake.

Major Site: The Cave on Dagobah

On the planet Dagobah, a dark side site of great power and significance hides deep within an endless

swamp. The site is a cave that stretches beneath the roots of a massive gnarltree. Legends associate the creation of this dark side site with the Dark Jedi of Bpfassh who once terrorized the systems of the Sluis sector. Regardless of its origin, the cave pulsed with the power of the dark side of the Force.

Master Yoda used this cave as a test for Luke Skywalker during the young man's Jedi training. Just the sight of the place made Luke tremble. "There's something not right here," Luke tells Yoda. "I feel cold, death."

Yoda agrees. "That place . . . is strong with the dark side of the Force," he explains to his student. "A domain of evil it is. In you must go."

When Luke asks what's inside the cave, Yoda answers, "Only what you take with you."

The dangers of the dark side cave on Dagobah aren't physical in nature. Instead, the cave plays on the fears and desires of those who come within the range of its influence, seeking to tempt or frighten them with strange visions and dire predictions. The interior of the underground cave is wet and slimy. It is dark and quiet. Here, amid the dangling roots and deep shadows, the dark side generates illusions to play upon the doubts and fears of those who enter the cave.

Using a Dark Side Cave in Your Campaign

Since Dagobah isn't a planet that gets a lot of visitors, you might want to use the cave as a model for another site on a location more in keeping with the needs of your campaign. A dark side cave tests those who enter, attempting to lure them or frighten them into embracing the dark side. Under careful, controlled conditions (as when Yoda watched over Luke Skywalker), the cave can serve as a test of the character's resolve and moral fiber. Luke, for example, failed the test of the cave by relying on his weapons instead of his Jedi training. The test pulled from Luke his greatest fear— Darth Vader. He was also shown a vision of a possible future, seeing his own face within Darth Vader's helmet.

When a Force-sensitive character enters a dark side cave, his or her fears and desires provide the basis for the test to come. The dark side draws either from the character's fear or desire, manifesting an appropriate illusion. When confronted by this extremely realistic illusion, the character must make a Will saving throw (DC 15 + the number of Dark Side Points the character has). If the save fails, the character gains a Dark Side Point. If the save succeeds, the character overcomes the dark side and gains a Force Point (or reduces the number of Dark Side Points he or she has by one).

Extreme Site: The Demon Moon of Dxun

It orbits the world of Onderon, giving rise to the most terrible legends—and even more terrible truths. The moon Dxun, called the demon moon, houses all kinds of monstrous creatures. A dense jungle covers the moon, but the place is far from pleasant. It rains almost constantly throughout the endless jungle, and a thick, seminoxious fog clings to the horizon like the obscuring webs of some giant spider. Frequent quakes rock the demon moon, and volcanoes regularly spew molten lava and clouds of hot gas.

This environment, combined with pockets of dark side power, has created some of the toughest, most brutal life forms in the galaxy. Even the plants developed potent natural defenses in order to survive. Some became poisonous. Others grew wicked barbs. Many became carnivorous, hunting and killing prey as efficiently as predators from the animal kingdom.

In the ancient past, a planetoid entered Onderon's orbit and increased the number of the world's moons to four. The new celestial body altered the orbital paths of all the moons. Dxun's new path allowed its atmosphere to brush against Onderon's for a few weeks during the planet's summer season. Over the millennia, this periodic meeting has had two notable effects. First, the atmosphere of Onderon has become slightly noxious, while Dxun's atmosphere has become slightly more tolerable. Second, Dxun's largest flying predators have been able to migrate from the moon to the planet during these periods to find more plentiful food on Onderon.

As civilization developed on Onderon, the humans gathered in one huge walled city to defend themselves against the predators from the demon moon. It was in this city, called Iziz, that the darksider Freedon Nadd would eventually rise to power.

While the demon moon was hellish and its inhabitants were savage, the place was not inherently evil. Not originally. When Jedi Master Arca Jeth decided to inter the remains of the evil Sith Lord Freedon Nadd and his descendants, King Ommin and Queen Amanoa, on the demon moon, things changed. Of course, the plan was that the natural dangers inherent in the ecology would serve as a natural defense for the Sith tomb.

Nadd's tomb was built from Mandalorian iron, a nearly indestructible alloy that repels lightsaber energy. This not only prevented interlopers from invading Nadd's resting place (and stealing the Sith artifacts also interred there), but protected the tomb from the massive tidal shifts that racked Dxun. Arca did not foresee the consequences of his actions, however. The evil residue of Nadd's dead body (as well as the dark side auras of numerous

Sith artifacts) began to twist and alter the very life of Dxun itself. The orbalisk, a deadly, predatory parasite, became capable of feeding on dark side energy. Plants that grew around the tomb changed, becoming even more deadly. Many different types of predators inhabited the area surrounding the tomb, changing into creatures of the darkness. Seekers of dark knowledge—including Exar Kun, instigator of the Sith War, and Darth Bane, savior of the Sith—faced such monsters as they fought to enter the wellspring of Sith knowledge contained in the Mandalorian iron vault.

By the time of Darth Bane, the entire demon moon became a dark side site. The dense jungle is considered to be a minor dark side site. There are also a few major sites scattered throughout the jungle and at least two major sites: Freedon Nadd's tomb and the well of darkness.

The iron tomb that houses the remains of three powerful darksiders has contained a wealth of Sith artifacts over the centuries, and some of those items probably remain locked away well into The New Jedi Order era. This extreme site radiates with the presence of a dark side master and his descendants. Although Exar Kun destroyed Freedon Nadd's spirit, the dark lord's presence can still be felt, even if he can no longer manifest and influence the actions of any visitors who may come to pay their respects—or loot his final resting place.

The well of darkness is a great pit located within a cave filled with orbalisks. For some reason that may never be known, the dark side power that seeped out of Freedon Nadd's tomb seems to have pooled in the fissure that looks like an open wound in Dxun's rocky flesh. Those who enter the cave claim to hear the whispered voices of long-dead Sith Lords calling to them from deep within the well. Too soft and indistinct to hear clearly, the voices nevertheless fill visitors with fear and dark images of unnameable horrors. It is believed that if a visitor can overcome his fear and absorb the horrors projected at him, he can learn dark side secrets lost to the depths of time. Of course, those who fail to embrace the specters of the well are often lost to madness.

Using the Demon Moon in Your Campaign

From Exar Kun to Darth Bane, Dxun has been a sort of pilgrimage for those attempting to master the dark side of the Force. Dark side secrets and Sith artifacts—or at least the promise of such—have drawn would-be darksiders from across the galaxy. Few were able to survive in the harsh environment, and most of those who made it to one of the dark side sites found only death or madness waiting for them.

You can use Dxun as a testing ground for a dark side character, especially one with a master. A character exploring the dark side on his own might want to travel to the demon moon to uncover a secret or two to help him gain power and prestige. The lure of Sith artifacts will probably be too great for a dark side hopeful to resist. Freedon Nadd's tomb is not without guardians, however, and if a character survives the various dangers of the demon moon, he'll still have to contend with tomb beasts and other horrors. It should be extremely difficult for a character to break into the tomb and survive a visit to its dark interior. Of course, success should grant the character an artifact or two, such as a Sith amulet or a Sith holocron.

The well of darkness presents an entirely different challenge—and an extremely tempting reward. The cave surrounding the well houses a huge colony of orbalisks, which present a challenge in and of itself (see Chapter Six for details on these creatures). In addition, the well spins three separate illusions to test the intruder. Each illusion is more potent, more horrific than the previous one. The illusions threaten to shatter the mind of the recipient while promising great power. Barely perceptible voices rise out of the well, caressing the intruder with the cold touch of the dark side and filling his mind with images of evil.

The first illusion tests the resolve of the character, trying to determine whether the intruder is worthy of the dark side. A vision of terrible violence and evil, delivered upon someone or something the intruder holds dear, seems incredibly real and frightening. The cave fades away and the character suddenly finds himself in a place he knows well, watching the terrible drama unfold but unable to participate in any way. The character must make a Will save (DC 15 minus the number of Dark Side Points the character possesses). If the save succeeds, the character gains a Dark Side Point, resists giving in to the madness-inducing illusion, and can proceed onto the next test. If the save fails, the character suffers a bout of madness that results in 1d6+1 points of damage to the character's Wisdom score. The Wisdom returns normally, at a rate of 1 point per day. (If the character's Wisdom score drops to 0, the character falls into a deep, nightmare-plagued sleep.)

The second illusion draws the character deeper into the darkness, this time playing upon the character's dreams and hidden desires. The character sees himself as the focus of this illusion, the recipient of everything he always wanted—power, influence, wealth, prestige, love. Only one thing stands in the character's way, either a cherished friend, respected mentor, or loved one. To reach the dream, the character must destroy the thing in his path. Then the character must make a Will save

(DC 25 minus the number of Dark Side Points the character possesses). If the save succeeds, the character gains a Dark Side Point, can proceed onto the next test, and gains a +2 dark side bonus on one of the following: any single Force-based skill check, melee attack roll, or ranged attack roll. If the save fails, the character suffers from madness that deals 1d8+2 points of damage to the character's Wisdom score. All but 1 point of this damage returns normally, at a rate of 1 point per day. The last point, however, is a permanent Wisdom drain from this illusion.

The final illusion deals with anger and aggression. The character is worked into a rage by images that he just hates with every fiber of his being. This uncontrolled anger opens the character to the full force of the dark side. This requires a Will save (DC 35 minus the number of Dark Side Points the character possesses). If the save succeeds, the character gains a number of Dark Side Points needed to achieve the dark template (if the character is already dark, he or she gains 2 Dark Side Points), gains a Force Point, and learns a dark side secret. This can be access to a new skill or feat (which will still need to be selected in the usual manner), the details on building a piece of Sith equipment, or some similar bit of arcane knowledge. If the save fails, the character loses 2 points of Wisdom permanently and suffers enough additional Wisdom damage to be reduced to 0 points of Wisdom. All but 2 points of this damage returns at a rate of 1 point per day. The final 2 points are permanently drained by the effects of the illusion.

The Sith Campaign

Five thousand years before the Galactic Civil War, the Republic was younger and the galaxy was both smaller and larger than in later generations. Smaller, because the Republic covered less territory and less of the galaxy had been explored and settled. Larger, because hyperspace routes were less accurate, and more care had to be taken to make sure a vessel arrived at its desired destination safely. The Frontier, Wild Space, and the Unknown Regions were larger, wilder, and less civilized than what we know of the Rise of the Empire, Rebellion, New Republic, and The New Jedi Order eras.

A campaign in this period can be set within the Sith Empire, or it can deal with life in the Republic, or it can explore the conflict that arises when the two civilizations meet. Whichever way you approach it, this era provides one of the best backdrops to set a dark side campaign against. There are more dark-siders and actual Sith running around in this time frame than in any other, and since fewer stories have

thus far been told in this era, you have a lot more latitude when it comes to making your adventures match what we know of *Star Wars* history.

Hyperspace Travel in Earlier Eras

Table 11–5: Hyperspace Travel Time, found in the *Star Wars Roleplaying Game,* shows travel times as they exist from the time of the Rise of the Empire and moving forward. If you set your campaign in the time of the Sith War or earlier, you need to make some adjustments to the table.

Most hyperspace routes in the Core, the Colonies, and the Inner Rim have been charted even as far back as the time of the Sith Empire. Travel within these regions remains unchanged from the times listed on the table.

Travel in the Expansion Region and beyond must be adjusted, since few space lanes are developed in the galactic frontier until after the Sith War. Double the time listed for traveling to the Expansion Region, the Mid Rim, the Outer Rim, Wild Space, and the Unknown Regions. If you determine that a particular location has been charted out, you can use the time listed in the table as is.

Also, hyperdrives faster than ×1 aren't developed until sometime after the Sith War, and even hyperdrives with a ×1 multiplier are exceedingly rare the farther back in time you set your campaign.

Life 5,000 Years before the Battle of Yavin

This era makes a great campaign setting because it has all the elements you need to generate exciting adventures. Large portions of the galaxy remain unexplored, waiting to be discovered. The Sith Empire still exists, growing in power and darkness, ready to invade the Republic. The Jedi Order is strong and Jedi Knights are numerous, prepared to protect the Republic from any and all threats. And the greatest threat, war, looms on the horizon.

Five thousand years before the galaxy exploded in civil war, the Old Republic expands by leaps and bounds. Thanks to the efforts of the Jedi Knights, dedicated scouts, and brave explorers, a significant portion of the galaxy has been charted, settled, and tamed. There are still places and species to discover, however, and the uncharted frontier looks huge on every astrogation chart.

This is a time of rugged frontiers. Pioneers try to establish homes on harsh new colony worlds, battling both nature and natives in some cases. The Republic funds many of these efforts in order to continue its expansion program.

Some alien species are being encountered for the first time. Some of these meetings go well, and friendships and alliances are forged. Others go

150

poorly, leading to small-scale wars on a number of distant fronts.

In addition, not every star system or star system collective wants to become subsumed into the expanding Republic. The galactic government fights a number of ongoing battles to unify scattered systems and keep the union strong. Some nonaligned sectors will never join the Republic, such as the stars of Hutt Space, and will remain neutral until they are eventually conquered by the Empire many millennia later. Others will join the Republic because of the threat of force, the need for security, or the economic benefit inherent in the galactic government.

The galaxy breaks down into a few major segments. The Republic, with its combination of politicians, diplomats, security personnel, colonists, and ordinary citizens, fills much of known space as the galactic government continues to expand. The capital of the Republic, Coruscant, remains the heart of the galactic union. A cosmopolitan world, it has begun to resemble the massive cityscape it will one day become, but there are still expanses of undeveloped land in evidence during this period.

The Jedi Order, guardians of the Republic, continue to explore the mysteries of the Force, train new students, and offer aid to the galactic government as needed. While the Jedi Council exists in a rudimentary form, the Order has yet to become as regimented as it will be by the last days of the Republic, before the Empire dawns.

The neutrals actually fall into two camps: those who are nominally considered to be citizens of the Republic and those who aren't. Privateers, smugglers, contract mercenaries, cargo haulers, couriers, crime lords, independent scouts and explorers, and hyperspace mappers might work for the Republic on occasion or operate under a Republic charter. Some of these types might actively work against the Republic. Others don't pay much attention at all to politics beyond paying taxes and document fees when they absolutely have to.

Some neutrals operate in regions of space that the Republic hopes to bring into the galactic union. In these cases, neutrals either hope to join the Republic, or they work to keep their star systems free and independent. Those in the latter camp often find themselves opposed by Republic security forces or even Jedi Knights as the Republic works to consolidate known space.

Finally, there is the Sith Empire. At the start of this age, the Sith Empire has been cut off from Republic space for thousands of years. While the Sith Empire has grown powerful, and individual Sith Lords have unlocked untold secrets of the dark side, the evil government has reached a period

TIMELINE

The following five distinct periods make excellent settings for a dark side campaign.

Pre-5,000 Years before the Battle of Yavin
A dark side campaign set in this time frame focuses exclusively on the Sith Empire, many generations removed from the original Dark Jedi who were exiled from the Republic. This is the Golden Age of the Sith, when the power of the dark side held sway over a distant portion of the galaxy.

5,000 Years before the Battle of Yavin
The defining moment of this era is the Great Hyperspace War, when the Sith Empire once again comes into conflict with the Republic. This period provides three possible base campaigns: Heroes of the Sith Empire seeking to resolve the power struggle tearing apart the ancient civilization; Sith heroes working to defeat the Republic and spread the Sith domain; or Republic heroes (both Jedi and their allies) defending the Republic from the Sith invaders.

3,996 Years before the Battle of Yavin
This period includes the Sith War and the time leading up to it, when Jedi Knights sought to protect the Republic while various Sith traditions began to assert themselves around the galaxy. Weak-willed Jedi converted to Sith teachings, and a terrible conflict raged from the Empress Teta system to Ossus and Yavin and beyond. In this period, Jedi renounce their oaths and codes to take up the power of the dark side.

2,000+ Years before the Battle of Yavin
The cult of the Brotherhood of Darkness arose when a rogue Jedi Knight broke away from the teachings of the Jedi Council and founded a new order of the Sith. This new order grew in power for almost a thousand years, eventually deciding to go to war with the Republic.

Circa 1,000 Years before the Battle of Yavin
Sith Lord Kaan gathered twenty thousand followers and set out to establish a dictatorship of rule by the strong. After a series of titanic battles, this conflict came to a climax at the Battle of Ruusan.

of crisis. The Empire has been slowly starving for centuries, gripped by a fierce and terrible hunger for fresh land and new resources. There appear to be no new worlds to conquer, no new enemies to subjugate and exploit. Factions have arisen, and two powerful Sith Lords vie for control of the stagnating Empire. Naga Sadow and Ludo Kressh, rivals for the coveted title of Dark Lord of the Sith, gather supporters and prepare to launch a civil war that could very well destroy the Empire. Soon, hyperspace explorers from the Republic will inadvertently wander into Sith space. Then a new goal will suggest itself, offering a new hope to the floundering Empire. The Republic, unaware, unsuspecting, makes a tempting target. To expand the Sith Empire, the Sith Lords plan to launch a war of conquest against the Republic and revitalize the Sith's Golden Age.

Technology of the Age

Most of the technology that permeates the time of the Rise of the Empire and the Galactic Civil War exists even in this distant time frame. However, there are enough differences to make the worlds of this period seem alien and unique. Hyperdrives tend to come in multipliers of ×2 or greater, meaning that the average lightspeed flight takes longer even in the heart of civilized space. A few expensive and somewhat experimental hyperdrives with ×1 multipliers exist, but only the best military vessels or courier ships have them installed. Nothing faster exists in this time period, not even some new vessel type in an experimental stage.

Weapons require some modifications in this time frame. Slugthrowers, for example, are more common. Light armor and melee weapons see more use. Blasters of all types have their range increments cut in half, greatly reducing their range. The cost for blasters also goes up: Multiply the costs shown on Table 7–2 in the *Star Wars Roleplaying Game* by four. Blasters are just not as common as personal weapons in this era. They see more use as ship-mounted weapons, and the cost and technology required to construct them as pistols and rifles puts them out of the reach of the common character.

Lightsabers also look a bit different in this ancient age. The technology for placing the power cells inside the handle casing hasn't been invented. Instead, the grip of the lightsaber is connected by cable to a belt-worn power pack. This has three noticeable effects. First, the cable reduces the lightsaber's mobility, making the following feats off limits in this era: Master Defense and Throw Lightsaber. Second, the lightsaber's weight is greater than the weight listed on Table 7–2 in the *Star Wars Roleplaying Game*. The weight of a lightsaber, cable, and belt power pack is 3 kg. Third, the threat range for these ancient lightsabers is reduced from 19–20 to 20. Also note that in this era, double-bladed lightsabers don't exist. They aren't invented until the next age, the time of the Sith Wars.

Otherwise, most of the technological wonders of the *Star Wars* universe exist in some form in this long-ago period. Comlinks are bulkier, repulsorlifts a touch slower, medpacs a bit larger and somewhat more expensive (150 credits instead of 100 credits), and the Holonet doesn't yet connect all of the worlds of the Republic. Instead, most interstellar communications is handled by diplomatic courier ships that carry holocube messages from place to place, or by traveling to speak directly with the person you need to communicate with.

Classes in this Time Frame

The expanding frontier and the abundance of colony worlds make the fringer class fairly common among hero characters operating in the most distant portions of the Republic. Nobles exist in equal measure, both in the Republic and the Sith Empire. Scoundrels see lots of action throughout the galaxy of this time period, and are especially common for characters who rise out of the neutral portions of space. Characters of the scout class are abundant in this era, either as guides and explorers, or as the wild and reckless hyperspace mappers who risk their ships and their lives by randomly setting coordinates in their nav computers and seeing where their lightspeed jump takes them. Soldiers are in high demand: The Republic needs security forces to protect the newly settled frontier, and the Sith Empire requires troops to aid in their war of expansion.

Force-users can be found throughout the galaxy. Jedi consulars and guardians fill the ranks of the Republic's Jedi Order, while Force adepts exist in both Republic space and within the Sith Empire. Some Jedi, just as in any era, become tainted or dark as they seek to master the Force. To these corrupt Jedi, the Sith might provide the means and the ability to fully explore the dark side of the Force.

Characters from the Sith Empire start out as Force-sensitive characters of any non-Force-using class and multiclass into a dark side devotee or marauder as soon as they are able, or they begin play as a Force adept and accumulate dark side power as the Force moves them. While characters without the Force-Sensitive feat exist within the Sith Empire, they rarely achieve any ranks of distinction or power without the dark side to aid them. These characters tend to be commoners or professionals within the Sith Empire, rarely attaining any heroic classes as they struggle through this dark side-based society.

The Factions of the Age

Various groups—both official and illegal—help keep the wheels of government and commerce turning. Some of the most important of these factions are detailed below.

The Republic

From the capital of Republic City on Coruscant, the galactic government called the Republic oversees trade, expansion, and the common defense of its member worlds. The Republic is a union of star systems that covers most of known space. A number of star systems continue to resist joining the union, most notably the region known as Hutt Space, but in general the citizens of the galaxy are happy to be a part of the ever-growing Republic.

In this era, some star systems actually wage war against the Republic to maintain their freedom and neutrality. Some of these regions had legitimate reasons to remain separate, and for the most part the Republic left such systems alone. Others, however, were controlled by despots or crime lords who were intent on maintaining their level of power and influence despite the call for unity and equality. Encounters in these places led to small-scale battles as the Republic attempted to offer peace and prosperity to all who would join its cause.

The Republic maintains its own security force in this period and also helps support the defense systems of its member worlds. It has a deep and long-lived relationship with the Jedi Order, whose members consider themselves to be guardians of the Republic and all it stands for. Member worlds provide senators who help draft legislation and ratify treaties. The Republic Senate meets regularly on Coruscant, though at any given time approximately half of the senators are offworld attending to matters of state or reporting back to their constituents.

The Republic grants charters to various trade and commerce guilds, allowing them to operate within the confines of Republic space. Independent traders usually belong to one or more guilds, depending on the types of goods and services they deal in. In addition to its own survey teams, the Republic also contracts independent and corporate scouts to help map the galaxy and locate new worlds for colonization, resources, and trade.

Life can be very different, depending where you are in the Republic. The Core Worlds continue to serve as cosmopolitan centers of learning and commerce, while the ever-expanding frontier can be rugged, harsh, and more than a little rough around the edges. The Core remains safe, secure, and prosperous. The frontier, on the other hand, can be dangerous, with colonists constantly struggling to survive and make ends meet.

As with any large organization, the Republic has its share of corruption. However, the ideals that created the union still have many advocates, and the Republic is strong and expanding. The ineffectiveness and overt corruption of the Rise of the Empire era are still many millennia away at this point in time.

The Sith

This period begins with the Sith Empire still cut off from the Republic. In fact, neither the Republic nor the Sith believes that the other still exists—both have been reduced to the status of legends in the other's region of space. After a century of iron rule, Dark Lord Marka Ragnos has died, leaving a power vacuum that threatens to erupt in civil war. The Sith Empire has grown stagnant and is in need of new worlds to conquer and exploit.

Many powerful Sith seek to gain control of the Empire. The strongest of these are Ludo Kressh and Naga Sadow, who both command impressive bands of followers from among the Sith. As these two rivals attempt to win the Empire, a hyperspace mapping ship from the Republic accidentally stumbles into Sith space. The feuding Sith Lords have no interest in peaceful trade with the Republic, however. The conservative Kressh believes the intrusion to be the precursor of invasion, while the ambitious Sadow sees an opportunity for conquest and glory.

The Sith command vast armies of followers, including creatures they have mutated using Sith alchemy and magic. Only those Sith with the Force-Sensitive feat aspire to the upper echelons of Sith society. Those without a connection to the Force are considered almost worthless, good for common labor and bureaucratic jobs but little else. In addition, because of the influence of the dark side, Sith society is plagued by paranoia, greed, ambition, and power plays on a grand scale. It is literally a society dedicated to the survival of the fittest—and meanest, and most powerful.

If you live within the Sith Empire, you must be ready to give as good as you get—and you must have the power or potential power to back up any play you make. Otherwise you become the victim or slave of a more powerful adversary. Indeed, everyone gathers an impressive list of adversaries and allies while working their way up the ranks of power. Manipulation, machinations, and violence often go hand in hand as everyone seeks to claw their way to the top. It's a rancor-eat-rancor society, inspired by the dark side of the Force and steeped in a shadowy, ancient tradition.

Criminal Organizations

For as long as there has been trade and commerce, there have been criminal organizations. From smuggler chiefs to pirate captains, information brokers to mercenary warlords, there are those willing to trade in controlled substances, weapons, ships, and even lives to satisfy their own lust and greed. Some crime

AW

syndicates specialize in one area, while others diversify in the tradition of the largest corporations. Racketeering, thievery, blackmail, extortion, smuggling, spice and arms dealing, hijacking, and slavery—these activities and more bring a great deal of credits to the galaxy's underworld.

While some crime lords follow a code of conduct and might even be said to have some measure of honor, by and large they are dangerous, violent, unscrupulous characters who have only their own interests at heart. Dealing with crime lords or their subordinates can be extremely risky. More often than not, you're bound to come out on the losing end of any transaction.

Larger criminal organizations operate beyond the bounds of any single planet or star system. They maintain their own fleet of ships, their own private armies, and their own bureaucracy to keep the organization running and profitable. Smaller bands might consist of a handful of ships and limit their activities to a single world or star system. Independent smugglers and mercenaries often hire out to criminal organizations to supplement their income.

Some crime lords use the various small-scale battles being waged throughout the Republic as a means to increase profits. Selling arms and information to the warlord of a neutral planet that's trying to fend off the Republic can fill the coffers of any weapons dealer and is too good an opportunity to pass up. As the Sith Empire begins to invade the Republic, more than a few crime lords will seek to make deals and alliances with the Sith. Throughout history, after all, the dark side has been a good source of income for those willing to ignore the tug of conscience and morality.

Corporations

Interstellar corporations grow richer and more influential as the Republic expands. Some corporations specialize in one type of product, while others offer a wide variety of products for a larger base of consumers. Each corporation is a microcosm of the greater planetary and galactic governments to which it belongs, with a ruler (the CEO), a senate (the board of directors), an army of financial bureaucrats, a security force, and a small fleet of ships. Larger corporations usually have a central headquarters on one of the Core Worlds, with satellite offices throughout the regions of space they operate in.

Most corporations maintain their own survey and exploration teams, and those in need of new sources of natural resources even employ hyperspace mappers to find previously undiscovered (and therefore unclaimed) star systems. Some corporations

154

operate from a set of clearly defined ethics and try to make life in the galaxy better while still earning an acceptable profit. Other corporations are only in it for the credits, willing to cut corners and harm the environment if it means more profit for their shareholders.

Some corporations even sponsor colonies, setting up new settlements where colonists work for the company as they build new lives and homes on the frontier. When a corporation behaves ethically, such an arrangement benefits everyone—including the Republic. When a company doesn't, the result can be slave labor—or worse.

All corporations belong to one or more of the powerful trade guilds, depending on where they operate and what goods and services they produce. The guilds set standards, negotiate differences among members, and represent their members in the halls of government. A corporation has to be extremely large and powerful to operate without guild sanction, and even then most of the massive intergalactic conglomerates tend to support the guilds—at least to all outward appearances.

With the advent of the Great Hyperspace War, many corporations turn their peacetime factories to the war effort, supplying ships and arms for the Republic (and often for the many neutral groups operating in and around the Republic) to help fend off the invading Sith. Rumors that some corporations are seeking to make deals with the Sith have not been confirmed at this time.

Traders

From small, single-ship free traders to merchants and cargo haulers with large fleets at their disposal, the traders that operate within the Republic keep the galactic union connected. Because of the lack of real-time communications networks (the HoloNet is still a few thousand years away), traders act as couriers and mail carriers as their ships ply the hyperspace lanes. They even ferry passengers from planet to planet when they have room in their cargo holds. But the real job of the trader is to move goods from one part of space to another.

Some traders operate as part of a larger corporation and work exclusively for that entity. The vast majority of traders, however, are independent merchants who travel from port to port looking for a surplus in one place and a demand in another. How much they can carry, how fast they can move it, and how quickly they can find buyers sets the good traders apart from the mediocre ones.

Travel time limits most traders to one section of space. There, they can establish familiar routes and routines, make contacts, and find ways to keep their holds full and their ships turning a profit. They learn to understand the complicated flow of supply and

demand, allowing them to recognize patterns and react before the market changes.

All traders operate with the sanction of the various guilds and must register with the Republic's Port Authority System. Of course, a trader's ship usually has a spare identity responder code or two to fall back on when necessary, but most try to operate with official sanction. But when a tariff can't be paid or a captain doesn't want to be spotted in a particular port of call, switching to a different ship name and registry can save a trader a lot of grief and trouble—and usually a lot of money.

Traders often don't buy their ships outright. The registration is held by a bank or other sponsor, someone who provided the starting capital and whom the trader must make regular payments to until the loan is paid off. When a sponsor also happens to be a crime lord, a trader may be forced to make smuggling runs as part of his debt. The life of a trader isn't always easy, but it's usually not boring—and traders do get to travel around more of the galaxy than most of the other citizens of the Republic.

Jedi

Since the Republic was formed, the Jedi Knights have served as the guardians of this grand union. The Jedi Order isn't as formal and codified as it will be by the time of the Rise of the Empire. There are no established laws forcing families to identify Force-sensitive children among them, and the Jedi don't go out of their way to identify potential recruits. Instead, they trust to the Force to lead mentors and students to each other. Indeed, formal academies don't yet exist, so the bond between master and apprentice is stronger.

The practice of starting very young children on the Jedi path, as it will come to be established later in the Republic's history, would be considered wrong to the Jedi of this era. They prefer to select students who are in their teenage years, students who can commit to the Force and the Jedi Code of their own accord. These students are considered to be more dedicated, more likely to withstand the rigors of training and eventually becoming full-fledged Jedi Knights.

The Jedi mostly operate independently, traveling the galaxy to help where they may. Only in times of great crisis do more than a handful come together to deal with a situation. The return of the Sith will be one such situation.

The Jedi of this period help the Republic as diplomats and ambassadors, seeking peaceful solutions to whatever problems they come across. They specifically seek to help squelch the many small wars going on as the Republic attempts to unify the galaxy. While Jedi won't start a fight, they will draw lightsabers to defend themselves and the helpless, or to stop a brutal warlord from continuing hostilities.

Crime lords and corrupt officials often receive the attention of the Jedi. Anyone who breaks the laws of the Republic or attempts to harm society must eventually deal with the Jedi Knights. When a separatist movement erupts somewhere in the Republic or on its borders, a Jedi is usually called in to mediate the dispute. If time permits, the Jedi makes a recommendation to the Republic. If not, the Jedi may be put in a situation where he or she must proceed to save lives and property.

Finally, the Sith become an increasingly serious problem for the Jedi of this age. Ancient hatreds flare as the Great Hyperspace War engulfs the galaxy, and an ancient animosity pits the light side against the dark.

Running a Hyperspace Wars Campaign

First, determine what kind of campaign you want to run. If it's a traditional campaign of good against evil, your players should create characters from the Republic (a mix of normal characters and Jedi works best, though an all-Jedi group can exist in this period). If you want to try your hand at a dark side campaign, have each player create a hero from the Sith Empire (while a mix of normals and Force-users can work, it's probably best to let each player run a Force-using Sith character).

Start the campaign prior to the outbreak of the Great Hyperspace War, centered either in the Republic (usually somewhere on the frontier) or in the Sith Empire. Then, as events unfold, your heroes can be right in the thick of discovery, exploration, intrigue, and eventually all-out war.

For the Republic heroes, not every adversary needs to be a Sith. Crime lords, separatists, pirates, raiders, tainted and dark Jedi, and corporate goons make excellent opponents. Plus, there are worlds full of adventures based on exploring hyperspace and discovering new planets and star systems. Eventually the focus will turn to the Sith as the war heats up, but save those adventures and use them as sparingly as you can to keep such encounters with the dark side fresh and exhilarating.

For Sith heroes, save the Jedi for key adventures. Meanwhile, other Sith, vying for the same power and resources, serve as a constant threat, as do the followers of whatever Sith Lord currently opposes your faction. In Republic space, Sith heroes must deal with Republic agents of all types, corporate security forces, crime lords and their minions, pirates, raiders, and anyone else who considers them to be invaders. Eventually the focus will turn to the battle between light and dark as the war escalates, but save

battles with Jedi for important adventures and climatic scenes.

Adventure Hooks

Here are a few story nuggets for a dark side campaign that you can develop into complete adventures. Each of these is set in the time of the Great Hyperspace War.

Prove Your Loyalty

Start up your dark side campaign by letting the 1st-level Sith heroes demonstrate their loyalty and devotion to the dark side and the Sith Lord they call master. Whether your heroes pledge allegiance to Naga Sadow or Ludo Kressh or some other rival Sith Lord, they need to prove themselves before earning the complete trust and respect of their leader. To accomplish this, the Sith Lord sends them on a mission to a distant part of the Sith Empire.

On the planet Korriz, the Sith heroes must overtake the servants of Lord Garu before they reach the alchemy workshop of Tritos Nal. This ancient master of Sith magic has crafted a powerful Sith sword especially for Lord Garu. The Sith heroes are ordered to dispatch Garu's servants and "acquire" the weapon for their Patron.

The first challenge facing the heroes is finding and overcoming Lord Garu's servants. There is one 1st-level servant for each hero character in the party. The servants include one soldier, one scout, and the rest are Force adepts. As these darksiders follow orders of a similar nature to those of the heroes, they fight to the death. They aren't willing to return to their lord and master after having failed in their mission.

The second challenge involves convincing Tritos Nal that they deserve the specially crafted weapon. This could involve deceit, bribery, negotiation, or combat, though the old alchemist is probably too tough for the Sith heroes to take on in straight combat. He's a Force adept 6/dark side devotee 2; you can use the generic template for the dark side adept from Chapter Six.

In the end, if the Sith heroes accomplish their mission, they present their Patron with a powerful weapon. (Of course, the weapon is of no real consequence to their Patron. He simply coveted what his rival was receiving and was willing to test and perhaps lose a few weak servants in the process of stealing the sword.) The Patron awards the heroes accordingly and decides to trust them with more important missions moving forward. Unfortunately, the Sith heroes also wind up making a dangerous enemy in Lord Garu.

The Trouble with Rivals

By the time your Sith heroes have achieved 3rd level, they've probably started to gain the attention of rivals for power within the Sith Empire. This adventure pits the Sith heroes against rivals within their own faction—other characters seeking the favor and attention of their Sith Patron.

When the heroes are sent to collect tribute for the Patron from his subject worlds, the rivals follow. The rivals plan to either sabotage the efforts of the heroes or eliminate the heroes. Either way, they plan to reveal them as failures to the Patron and complete their mission to gain the Patron's favor.

The rivals are characters of the same level as the heroes. There are half as many rivals as there are heroes, though if the Sith heroes require a greater challenge, you can increase the number of rivals to a maximum of one per hero. Make sure there's a mix of combat types and Force-users among the rival group.

The subject world should be unique and visually interesting. A world where lava flows freely from great crevices, or wind and snow whip through frozen canyons of glacial ice, or crystalline formations glow across plains of perpetual darkness, makes a great backdrop for this type of adventure. The population of the world labors for the glory and profit of the heroes' Sith Patron, outwardly paying homage while inwardly cursing his (or her) name. In addition to the challenge posed by the rivals, some members of the subject population might decide to rebel against the Patron and his avatars. If the heroes must stomp out an uprising while also dealing with the rivals, then the action can get pretty intense. How they deal with both situations should really show their commitment to the dark side—or their lack thereof.

Capture the Invaders

Later in the campaign, when you're ready to introduce the Sith Empire to the Republic, use a variation of this adventure idea. One day a ship emerges from hyperspace somewhere within the Sith Empire. The ship contains two hyperspace mappers from the Republic looking for new worlds for the Republic to ally with or expand into. Like most hyperspace mappers, this pair of scouts is wild and more than a little reckless, willing to take great risks in order to see what lies beyond the next jump to light speed. When their ship randomly emerges from hyperspace, it collides with a small asteroid and suffers damage. It won't be able to make the return jump until the damage is repaired. Until then, it floats practically dead in space, with minimal sublight engines available for maneuvering.

In this adventure, the hyperspace mappers arrive in a section of space that borders an area controlled by the Sith heroes' Patron and his chief rival. The Sith Lord orders the heroes to capture the ship and its occupants—they must learn where these invaders

come from and what they want with the Sith Empire. "Do not let this vessel fall into the hands of another Sith Lord," the Patron cautions. "I have foreseen that that ship is important to my power base and to the very survival of the Sith Empire. Do not fail me."

The Patron isn't the only Sith Lord aware of the arrival of the unidentified ship. His rival, the Sith Lord Garu, also has an interest in the fate of this craft. While the Patron decides to keep a low profile and only sends the Sith heroes and their relatively small ship to investigate, Lord Garu sends a minor battle fleet to capture the vessel. Now the heroes must run a gauntlet of enemy ships to reach the hyperspace survey ship and the mappers it contains. Or, conversely, they can wait for Garu's minions to capture the vessel and then follow them to retrieve it at a time when stealth and cunning might be more advantageous to their success.

This could lead to the mappers becoming separated, one in Lord Garu's hands and the other in the hands of the Sith heroes' Patron. Of course, neither mapper wants to help the Sith. Once they figure out that there are no opportunities for expansion or trade here, they're going to want to rush back to Republic space and warn officials about what they've discovered. The Sith don't want this to happen. Indeed, both Garu and the Patron want to know everything about the mappers—who they are, where they come from, what they are doing in Sith space.

The hyperspace mappers are 3rd-level scouts. They're capable and extremely lucky. If they can't get their ship working again, they'll steal whatever they can find to try to get back home. The Sith heroes will have to chase them and hunt them down across a number of star systems as this pivotal adventure unfolds. In the end, however it turns out, the Sith Empire should become aware of the Republic. Whether or not one of the hyperspace mappers gets away to warn the Republic about the Sith Empire depends on the actions of the heroes.

This Weakness, This Republic

After discovering that the Republic exists, the Sith Empire begins to make excursions into that part of the galaxy. The method the Sith use depends on whether one of the hyperspace mappers escaped from Sith space.

If the mappers remain prisoners of the Sith Empire, then the Sith heroes are one of many secret excursion teams sent to gather information on the strengths and weaknesses of the Republic. They can approach this kind of mission any way they want, as long as they understand that they are to keep a low profile and protect the mystery of the Sith. If they reveal their true origins, they will endanger the Sith Empire and hurt the building war effort. What do the Sith want to know about? Intelligence concerning the state of the Republic, its resources and level of technology, as well as its level of readiness from a military perspective will help the Sith tacticians plan for war. Also, the Sith want to know if the legends concerning their ancient enemies, the Jedi, have a more solid basis in fact. Do the Jedi still exist? In what numbers? Will they stand against the Sith warriors and defend the Republic, as they did in the ancient past? As the Sith heroes go about gathering information, they might run into any number of obstacles, including Republic security forces, outlaws and pirates of all types, separatist warlords, and even wandering Jedi Knights.

If either or both of the mappers escaped from the Sith Empire and returned to the Republic, then events take on a more urgent process that resembles what occurred in the Tales of the Jedi comic books. In this situation, the Sith Empire (or at least a major part of it) decides that time is of the

GENERIC JEDI CHARACTERS

The pregenerated Jedi guardians and Jedi consulars that appear here are offered as samples of typical Jedi opponents that Sith heroes might face in a dark side campaign set in and around the Great Hyperspace War. Gamemasters can use them to flesh out adventures on the fly or as the basis for recurring characters. GMs are encouraged to add personalities and histories to these archetypal templates. ⁘

essence and a swift invasion of Republic space is called for. The Sith heroes become wrapped up in the quickly escalating war, handling commando or sabotage missions to weaken the Republic. War spreads rapidly, and the Sith heroes must fight with every dark side power at their command as they battle against Republic security forces and armies of Jedi Knights.

The war might last for several adventure arcs, or it might become the entire focus of your campaign, depending on the kind of stories and adventures you

Generic Jedi Guardians, male or female, Human (extra skills and feats included)

	Jedi Guardian 4	Jedi Guardian 8	Jedi Guardian 12
Initiative:	+2	+2	+2
Defense:	16 (+4 Class, +2 Dex)	20 (+8 Class, +2 Dex)	22 (+10 Class, +2 Dex)
Speed:	10m	10m	10m
VP/WP:	31/12	68/12	95/13
Attacks:	Unarmed +6 melee	Unarmed +11/+6 melee	Unarmed +15/+10/+5 melee
	Lightsaber +6 melee	Lightsaber +11/+6 melee	Lightsaber +15/+10/+5 melee
Damage:	Unarmed 1d3+2	Unarmed 1d3+3	Unarmed 1d3+3
	Lightsaber 2d8+2	Lightsaber 3d8+3	Lightsaber 4d8+3
Special Qualities:	–	Jedi Knight	Jedi Knight
Saves:	Fort +5, Ref +6, Will +4	Fort +7, Ref +8, Will +6	Fort +9, Ref +10, Will +8
Size:	Medium	Medium	Medium
Challenge Code:	D	E	F
Force Points:	2	4	6
Dark Side Points:	0	3	4
Reputation:	4	6	8
Abilities:	Str 15, Dex 14, Con 12, Int 10, Wis 14, Cha 8	Str 16, Dex 14, Con 12, Int 10, Wis 14, Cha 8	Str 16, Dex 14, Con 13, Int 10, Wis 14, Cha 8
Skills:	Computer Use +4, Craft (lightsaber) +4, Intimidate +3, Read/ Write Basic, Speak Basic	Computer Use +4, Craft (lightsaber) +5, Intimidate +4, Jump +7, Read/ Write Basic, Speak Basic, Tumble +5	Computer Use +4, Craft (lightsaber) +7, Intimidate +5, Jump +7, Knowledge (Jedi lore) +4, Read/ Write Basic, Speak Basic, Tumble +6
Force Skills:	Battlemind +7, Enhance Ability +5, Force Defense +5, Force Push +4, See Force +6	Battlemind +8, Enhance Ability +5, Force Defense +6, Force Push +5, Heal Self +4, Move Object +4, See Force +7	Battlemind +11, Enhance Ability +7, Force Defense +7, Force Push +7, Heal Self +5, Move Object +6, See Force +8
Feats:	Force-Sensitive, Exotic Weapon Proficiency (lightsaber), Heroic Surge, Power Attack, Weapon Group Proficiency (blaster pistols), Weapon Group Proficiency (simple weapons)	see left	see left
Force Feats:	Alter, Control, Lightsaber Defense, Sense	Alter, Control, Lightsaber Defense, Sense	Alter, Burst of Speed, Control, Deflect Blasters, Knight Defense, Lightsaber Defense, Sense
Equipment:	Comlink, lightsaber, datapad	Comlink, lightsaber, datapad	Comlink, lightsaber, datapad

827EZA

and your players want to run. Using hatred and anger to fuel their efforts, the Sith consider the Republic to be weak and inferior in all ways, regardless of how the war progresses. If even one Sith remains, he (or she) will believe himself superior to whatever the Republic can throw his way.

Jedi Hunt

Eventually, you're going to want to have your Sith heroes tangle with a powerful Jedi Knight. That's where the true test of strength and ability will come into play, and the natural animosity between the two factions makes for good banter and drama. There are two approaches to this adventure hook.

The first sends the Sith heroes on the trail of a Jedi Knight. They have been ordered to hunt down a Jedi and capture him so that the Sith can determine the strengths and weaknesses of an enemy they haven't faced in thousands of years. The Sith heroes must enter Republic space, locate a Jedi, then find a way to set a trap and capture the Jedi without killing him or getting killed in the process.

The second approach puts a Jedi Knight on the trail of the Sith heroes as they explore and spy on Republic space. The Jedi senses their presence, or the Sith heroes slip up and reveal themselves in some way. Then it's light side against dark side in an epic game of katarn-and-nerf—with both sides taking on both roles as the adventure unfolds.

In the end, an epic clash takes place. Either use a Jedi Knight of a level that would provide an extreme challenge to the Sith heroes, or a pair of Jedi Knights of levels comparable to an extreme challenge. This clash should take place in a unique setting, on a strange planet or asteroid, where both sides can unleash their full powers without worrying about the amount of residual damage they may cause.

Generic Jedi Consulars, male or female, Human (extra skills and feats included)

	Jedi Consular 4	Jedi Consular 8	Jedi Consular 12
Initiative:	+1	+1	+1
Defense:	16 (+4 Class, +2 Dex)	18 (+6 Class, +2 Dex)	20 (+8 Class, +2 Dex)
Speed:	10m	10m	10m
VP/WP:	16/9	32/9	48/10
Attacks:	Unarmed +3 melee	Unarmed +6/+1 melee	Unarmed +9/+4 melee
	Lightsaber +3 melee	Lightsaber +7/+2 melee	Lightsaber +10/+5 melee
Damage:	Unarmed 1d3	Unarmed 1d3	Unarmed 1d3
	Lightsaber 2d8	Lightsaber 3d8	Lightsaber 4d8
Special Qualities:	None	Jedi Knight, Healing	Jedi Knight, Healing
Saves:	Fort +3, Ref +3, Will +6	Fort +5, Ref +5, Will +8	Fort +8, Ref +7, Will +10
Size:	Medium	Medium	Medium
Challenge Code:	D	E	F
Force Points:	2	4	6
Dark Side Points:	0	2	3
Reputation:	4	7	9
Abilities:	Str 10, Dex 12, Con 9, Int 14, Wis 15, Cha 13	Str 10, Dex 13, Con 9, Int 14, Wis 15, Cha 13	Str 10, Dex 13, Con 10, Int 14, Wis 15, Cha 13
Skills:	Bluff +6, Computer Use +7, Craft (lightsaber) +7, Diplomacy +10, Gather Information +8, Read/Write Basic, Sense Motive +7, Speak Basic	Bluff +9, Computer Use +8, Craft (lightsaber) +8, Diplomacy +11, Gather Information +9, Intimidation +6, Read/Write Basic, Sense Motive +8, Motive +8, Speak Basic, Treat Injury +7	Bluff +11, Computer Use +8, Craft (lightsaber) +8, Diplomacy +13, Gather Information +11, Intimidation +8, Knowledge (Jedi lore) +11, Read/Write Basic, Sense Motive +10, Speak Basic, Treat Injury +10
Force Skills:	Affect Mind +5, Empathy +7, Enhance Ability +3, Force Defense +3, Heal Another +6, See Force +7, Telepathy +7	Affect Mind +7, Empathy +7, Enhance Ability +4, Force Defense +4, Force Stealth +4, Friendship +5, Heal Another +6, Heal Self +3, See Force +8, Telepathy +7	Affect Mind +9, Empathy +8, Enhance Ability +5, Force Defense +6, Force Stealth +6, Friendship +6, Heal Another +7, Heal Self +5, See Force +9, Telepathy +8
Feats:	Force-Sensitive, Exotic Weapon Proficiency (lightsaber), Heroic Surge, Trustworthy, Weapon Group Proficiency (blaster pistols), Weapon Group Proficiency (simple weapons)	see left, plus Weapon Finesse (lightsaber)	see left
Force Feats:	Alter, Control, Force Mind, Sense	Alter, Control, Force Mind, Sense	Alter, Control, Force Mastery, Force Mind, Lightsaber Defense, Sense
Equipment:	Comlink, lightsaber, datapad	Comlink, lightsaber, datapad, medpac	Comlink, lightsaber, datapad, medpac

Index

Note: For topics mentioned on more than one page, a page number in *italic* type indicates the location of a main entry for that topic (if a main entry exists).

INDEX

159

Tell us what you think about the Star Wars® *The Dark Side Sourcebook*! Please answer the following questions and mail the card to us. You'll be entered in a random drawing for an **autographed copy** of the *Star Wars Starships of the Galaxy* accessory. Five winners will be chosen!

1. Compared to previous versions of the *Star Wars* sourcebooks (West End Games), how would you rate this most recent version?

Much better than previous versions □5 □4 □3 □2 □1 Much worse than previous versions □ Never played other versions

2. How will you use this book?
- □ I will use the new (d20) system as is.
- □ I will convert the new (d20) system to the previous (d6) system.
- □ I will use "custom rules" developed by me and/or my gaming group.
- □ I will use this book as a general *Star Wars* reference.

3. What kind of *Star Wars* products have you purchased in the past? (check all that apply)
- □ Toys
- □ Action figures
- □ Computer games
- □ Models
- □ Card games
- □ Collectable items
- □ Multimedia
- □ Other, please specify:
- □ Miniatures
- □ Magazines
- □ Novels

4. What is your preferred era of play?
- □ Republic
- □ Classic/Rebellion
- □ New Jedi Order/New Republic
- □ Other, please specify:

5. Where did you purchase this *Star Wars* sourcebook?
- □ Hobby/Game store
- □ Toy store
- □ Bookstore
- □ It was a gift
- □ Wizards of the Coast® website
- □ Other website, please specify:
- □ I don't know
- □ Other, please specify:

6. How much money do you spend on each of the following types of game products each month?

	$0	$1–10	$11–20	$21–40	$41 or more
Tabletop paper roleplaying games	□	□	□	□	□
Trading card games	□	□	□	□	□
Computer roleplaying games	□	□	□	□	□
Other electronic games	□	□	□	□	□
Board games	□	□	□	□	□
Miniatures games	□	□	□	□	□

7. How many hours do you spend per month playing each of the following types of games?

	0	1–5	6–10	11–20	21 or more
Tabletop paper roleplaying games	□	□	□	□	□
Trading card games	□	□	□	□	□
Computer roleplaying games	□	□	□	□	□
Other electronic games	□	□	□	□	□
Board games	□	□	□	□	□
Miniatures games	□	□	□	□	□

8. How long have you been playing any version of the *Star Wars Roleplaying Game*?
- □ Less than 6 months
- □ 6 months to 1 year
- □ 1–3 years
- □ 3–5 years
- □ 5–7 years
- □ More than 7 years

9. What other Wizards of the Coast *Star Wars Roleplaying Game* products have you bought?
- □ Star Wars Roleplaying Game
- □ Star Wars Character Record Sheets
- □ Star Wars Adventure Game
- □ Star Wars Secrets of Naboo Campaign Pack
- □ Star Wars Gamemaster Screen
- □ Star Wars miniatures
- □ Star Wars Living Force™ Campaign Guide
- □ Other, please specify:

10. What other paper-based roleplaying game systems do you play? (check all that apply)
- □ Alternity®
- □ GURPS
- □ Rifts
- □ Other, please specify:
- □ Star Wars
- □ Shadowrun
- □ Mage: The Ascension
- □ Vampire: The Masquerade
- □ Dungeons & Dragons®
- □ None

11. What was the **first** paper-based roleplaying game that you played? (please check one)
- □ Star Wars
- □ Alternity
- □ Rifts
- □ Shadowrun
- □ Star Trek
- □ GURPS
- □ Paranoia
- □ Other, please specify:
- □ Dungeons & Dragons
- □ Mage: The Ascension
- □ Vampire: The Masquerade

12. Do you play the *Star Wars* Customizable Card Game? □ Yes □ No

13. How often do you participate in the following activities?

	Frequently				Never
Game conventions	5	4	3	2	1
RPGA™ or RPG tournaments	5	4	3	2	1
Reading *Star Wars Gamer* magazine	5	4	3	2	1
RPG-related Internet activities	5	4	3	2	1
In-store RPG promotions or demos	5	4	3	2	1
RPG campaigns	5	4	3	2	1
Reading game-related novels	5	4	3	2	1
Reading *Star Wars Insider* magazine	5	4	3	2	1
Collecting *Star Wars* merchandise	5	4	3	2	1

14. What percent of the time, on average, do you play in each of the following roles in a typical month?
Gamemaster (GM) ____%
Player Character (PC) ____%
Total = 100%

15. Are you aware of the RPGA (Roleplaying Game Association)? □ Yes □ No
If yes, are you a member? □ Yes □ No
If no, are you interested in receiving more information? □ Yes □ No

16. Are you aware of the official *Star Wars* Fan Club? □ Yes □ No
If yes, are you a member? □ Yes □ No
If no, are you interested in receiving more information? □ Yes □ No

17. Do you read any of the following novel series? (check all that apply)
- □ Star Wars
- □ Alternity®
- □ Other, please specify:
- □ Star Trek
- □ Shadowrun
- □ Dark●Matter™
- □ Forgotten Realms®

18. What types of fiction do you read regularly? (check all that apply)
- □ Fantasy
- □ Mystery
- □ Romance
- □ Horror
- □ Historical
- □ Science fiction
- □ Classical literature
- □ Action/Adventure
- □ Other, please specify:

19. What is your gender? □ Male □ Female
20. What is your birth date? ____/____/____ Month Day Year

Full Name:
Address:
City/Town: State/Province:
Country: ZIP/Postal Code:
Phone: Email:
□ Please check here if you would like to be contacted or receive promotional offers.

BUSINESS REPLY MAIL
FIRST-CLASS MAIL   PERMIT NO. 609   RENTON, WA

POSTAGE WILL BE PAID BY ADDRESSEE

ATTN: CONSUMER RESPONSE
WIZARDS OF THE COAST
PO BOX 980
RENTON WA 98057-9960

**NO POSTAGE
NECESSARY
IF MAILED
IN THE
UNITED STATES**

Fold on dotted lines, tape shut, don't staple